Bernard Shaw and His Contemporaries

Series Editors
Nelson O'Ceallaigh Ritschel
Massachusetts Maritime Academy
Pocasset, MA, USA

Peter Gahan
Independent Scholar
Los Angeles, CA, USA

The series *Bernard Shaw and His Contemporaries* presents the best and most up-to-date research on Shaw and his contemporaries in a diverse range of cultural contexts. Volumes in the series will further the academic understanding of Bernard Shaw and those who worked with him, or in reaction against him, during his long career from the 1880s to 1950 as a leading writer in Britain and Ireland, and with a wide European and American following.

Shaw defined the modern literary theatre in the wake of Ibsen as a vehicle for social change, while authoring a dramatic canon to rival Shakespeare's. His careers as critic, essayist, playwright, journalist, lecturer, socialist, feminist, and pamphleteer, both helped to shape the modern world as well as pointed the way towards modernism. No one engaged with his contemporaries more than Shaw, whether as controversialist, or in his support of other, often younger writers. In many respects, therefore, the series as it develops will offer a survey of the rise of the modern at the beginning of the twentieth century and the subsequent varied cultural movements covered by the term modernism that arose in the wake of World War 1.

More information about this series at
http://www.palgrave.com/gp/series/14785

Audrey McNamara
Nelson O'Ceallaigh Ritschel
Editors

Bernard Shaw and the Making of Modern Ireland

palgrave
macmillan

Editors
Audrey McNamara
School of English, Drama and Film
University College Dublin
Dublin, Ireland

Nelson O'Ceallaigh Ritschel
Massachusetts Maritime Academy
Pocasset, MA, USA

Bernard Shaw and His Contemporaries
ISBN 978-3-030-42115-1   ISBN 978-3-030-42113-7   (eBook)
https://doi.org/10.1007/978-3-030-42113-7

This Palgrave Macmillan imprint is published by the registered company Springer Nature Switzerland AG.
The registered company address is: Gewerbestrasse 11, 6330 Cham, Switzerland

*For Ian
and
Carolina*

FOREWORD

When government buildings in Dublin were bombed, Shaw observed (with what seemed more like relief than concern) that "I am an Irishman without a birth certificate". He had good reasons not to over-invest in the notion of filiation, which used to seem the crucial point of a birth certificate. Thousands of such certificates were destroyed in the hostilities—and a remarkable number, it has recently emerged, were saved. But Shaw never believed in patrilineage. The more surrogate parents, the better, as far as he was concerned—because this blessed state left him free to invent himself and appoint alternatives at will. In his ideal world, each post office might contain a "paternity register", with self-descriptions by every male who had fathered a child: if any child were discontented with the biological father, that child could scan the register and choose an alternative. Or father himself, which is what Michael Holroyd said Shaw did in creating George Bernard Shaw (GBS) as "the self-invented child of his own writings".

This would become a major element in the story of Irish modernism. Wilde joked that his parents seemed to have lost him: "I don't actually know who I am by birth", says Jack Worthing in *The Importance of Being Earnest*: "I was ... well I was found". Yeats wrote many tales of foundlings, so many that he may at moments have fancied himself to be one. Synge's Christy Mahon decides, having killed his father, to self-authenticate: "Is it me?" And Joyce's Stephen Dedalus becomes "himself his own father, made not begotten".

One could see this Oedipal denial of fathers as a denial, also, of a hateful Irish past, filled with compromise, oppression and humiliation. That was certainly how Shaw viewed what he called "the slack-jawed blackguard-ism" of his father's Dublin. Yet he, like the other writers just mentioned, espoused an Irish future, exhilarating to precisely the extent that it could still be made. Central to their notions of self-invention was the ancient myth of androgyny: that manly women and womanly men could somehow incarnate a future free of the horrific results of binary thinking—empire, hypernationalism, machismo. Through the 1890s, both Shaw and Wilde depicted forceful women and retiring men, paving the way for those moments of high modernism when Joyce gave voice to Molly Bloom, Yeats to Crazy Jane and, of course, Shaw to Joan of Arc. It was as if each author found in such figures images of self-election and self-determination. In some ways, it is Shaw's Joan who best captures the meaning of libera-tion. Listening to inner voices, she by-passes the world of priests and preachers and bishops, and insists on a mysticism which derives only from herself. Shaw's anti-clericalism was rooted in a very Protestant idea: that all religious professions—whether puritan clergymen denouncing social activists, or Catholic priests inveighing against trade unionists—were con-spiracies against the laity. And, of course, he extended the critique to all professionals (doctors, lawyers etc.) whose jargon was but a form of self-love, designed to prevent people from thinking for themselves.

There are certain dangers in claiming Shaw or Wilde as key figures in Irish literary tradition, as there are in making such claims for Yeats, Joyce or Synge. They all belong in the end to the wider world. But there are dangers also in denying the influence of that Irish context which enabled them to achieve articulation—and, indeed, to take Ireland as a test-case of the modern. The Irish element in Yeats, Joyce and Synge has always been taken for granted, if only because of the recurrence in their work of the national setting—but in the case of Shaw and Wilde this was not always so clearly seen. As a student over forty years ago I never knowingly set out to prove that those two great comic dramatists were Irish. I simply assumed it—on the basis of so many techniques and themes shared not just with each other but with later Irish authors. Later, as a lecturer, I was repeat-edly astonished to find that many of their greatest admirers and advocates had no understanding of this background. It is hard to believe that the first-ever international conference on Shaw in Ireland occurred as late as 2012 (but following three Shaw Summer Schools hosted by Dublin Institute of Technology, Kevin Street during the 1990s under Eibhear Walshe, and the Dublin Shaw Society that flourished during the second half of the twentieth century): but that says as much about Irish as about foreign blindness to the kind of analyses which enrich this volume. Shaw's overt influence on O'Casey and Behan has been long documented and well acknowledged by both succeeding playwrights, but it is fascinating to read here of the inspiration which he provided for Kate O'Brien and Elizabeth Bowen, not to mention the possibility that he also opened many themes and techniques for Brian Friel. When the late great Donal McCann joked that the latter was "a good man fallen among academics", he was not only referring (most unfairly) to the Field Day movement but literally tracing a revolutionary lineage back to GBS.

The Shaw who emerges in this volume is as alert to an English as to a Protestant substratum in Irish nationalism. Again and again, he told his readers in London papers that the Irish, in resisting invaders, were simply doing what any true-born English persons would do, should their country be occupied. This was a view already propounded at some length by John Henry Newman, whose strictures on the logic of Irish nationalism were designed to be overheard in England. By an analogous logic, Shaw's education of his English readers on many themes was also designed to be overheard in Ireland. He was critical of narrow nationalism but also of the imperialism into which it could so easily morph. And his linked exposés of the injuries of class touched off allergic reactions in both countries, perhaps more often in England than in Ireland (although William Martin Murphy is shown here to have responded with brazen effrontery to the challenge posed by Shaw to philistine capitalists).

From his vantage point in London and Ayot St Lawrence, Shaw saw clearly that the Irish Question was also an English Question—something as true in the age of Brexit as it was when first he made the observation. As a socialist radical, he intuited the ways in which Irish answers to certain questions were prophetic of ones still to be offered in England: the expropriation of the landed, gentry, for instance, or the delinking of church and state. As a colony, Ireland was also a laboratory, a forcing-ground of the modern; and Shaw realized that England had some catching-up to do. Even before formulating a defence of Roger Casement in 1916, he had wisely advised the London authorities to treat the captured rebel leaders as prisoners of war, rather than to shoot them as if they were no better than common deserters on the Western Front. He had written *O'Flaherty, V. C.* in 1915 in order to demonstrate just how inflected were the views of those Irishmen fighting in the British army—and he instinctively understood that the 1916 rebel leaders were themselves huge admirers of English literary traditions.

Had he been listened to, events might have taken a happier turn. It is arguable that, in his advocacy of Irish independence, he did more for that cause than many of the insurrectionary leaders. His analysis was much like that of Synge—that Ireland would gain less from bombing campaigns than from the spread of socialist ideas among the English. After all, both men reasoned, the interests of the English working class and of Irish separatists were overlapping, and they required only the removal of a parasitic landlord class. If androgyny might replace the polarized, unequal relationships between men and women in a sexist culture, then the overthrow of imperial orders might reduce the appeal of nationalisms, making way for a truly international order.

Yet Shaw could understand the appeal of nationalism in Irish circumstances, and his attitude to Michael Collins, as revealed in these pages, was respectful. In all likelihood, he would have endorsed James Connolly's idea that once Ireland was repossessed by its own people, the empire would soon be gone. Of course, as a gradualist (or "stages theory" man), he would not have agreed with Connolly's method, summed up in the rebel's phrase that "a pin in the hand of a child could pierce the heart of a giant".

Even after the cessation of the Anglo-Irish war, Shaw went out of his way to assure prospective English visitors that they could tour Ireland in total safety. He had, after all, shown in *John Bull's Other Island* that while the Irish and English might oppose one another in theory, in the everyday life of individuals, they invariably became fast friends. He was right in his guess that those English brave enough to visit Ireland so soon after the War of Independence would be warmly applauded and embraced. He himself wrote much of Saint Joan in county Kerry in the summer of 1923 as the country emerged from the atrocious experience of war and civil war.

For Shaw the role of women was a central test of any society, and he followed the playwright Henrik Ibsen in that belief. President Michael D. Higgins brilliantly evokes the recurrence of the feminist theme through so many works of the Irish revival by referring to "five Noras"—Ibsen's, Shaw's, Synge's, O'Casey's and Joyce's. One could find a very different meaning in each experience and a sense of liberatory intent in their various ways of coping with difficult situations, but it is also true that each of the male authors depicts the women as not fully free agents. Those who "choose freedom" and walk away from the prison house of domesticity may be as finally constrained as those who decide to conduct their rebellions within the system, whether in silence, madness or sheer counter-statement. As Marx had so sadly observed, people do make and remake the world, but never in circumstances of their own choosing.

President Higgins, in commenting on a philistine capitalism which agitated against an art gallery for Dubliners, makes a crucial link between democracy and pleasure—the practice of the former should ensure the right to the latter. This was a point on which Yeats and Shaw—for all their other differences—concurred. Each of them saw a play as a way of challenging the preconceptions of an audience while also affording deep aesthetic pleasure. They collaborated closely in their earlier years in stage productions, and this reminds us of oft-neglected facts. The social radicalism of the younger Yeats has often been under-estimated, as has the formal modernist audacity of the mature Shaw (his use of theatre as opera anticipates Tom Murphy, for instance, just as the choric antiphonies between falsetto Irish voices and Broadbent's basso profondo prefigure Friel's in Translations). Both Shaw and Yeats had much the same view of the English language as Frantz Fanon would take of French: that it should be treated as a captured weapon, seized from an imperial enemy and liberated from its darker historic meanings.

Reading through these pages, one is struck by that versatility of mind which permitted Shaw to know so many different human types at a level of true intimacy, whether the leaders of the literary movement at Coole or the political inventors of modern Ireland at Kilteragh. He had a tremendous sympathy for women who had lost their men in some tragedy or other of the national struggle—his letter to a sister of Michael Collins just days after his assassination is moving in its rallying of her spirits, and the energy which he invested in advising and supporting Hanna Sheehy Skeffington is a true act of solidarity. Tony Roche captures Shaw's affinity for radical, marginal women very well in his chapter here. Perhaps that affinity was rooted in Shaw's insistence that women were in almost every respect just like men and should be treated so. Nor is this a simple matter of one radical dissident empathizing with another. What recurs through all of Shaw's career, despite the common complaint that he was a cool rationalist, is a sense of emotional and ethical engagement with the unlucky, the misjudged, the outcast. His politics were hardly those of Parnell but he steadfastly defended him, and likewise in his solidarity with Oscar Wilde. Casement would be just a single figure in a long line of Irishmen facing English courts who found in him one of their most formidable apologists and advocates—and that advocacy was ultimately rooted in feeling and compassion. It is high time to retire Yeats's nightmare in which he was haunted by Shaw in the image of a mechanical sewing machine: first-hand acquaintance with GBS at the dinner table revealed to William Butler Yeats a very different man.

The chapter gathered here ask us to consider Shaw in entirely new ways. His engagement with the forces of religion is a rich topic indeed, and it may well be that, after the foolish attempt by Catholic prelates to prevent the children of striking Trade Unionists from procuring helpful accommodation with sympathetic families in England, he ran out of patience with it. Yet Joan of Orleans somehow manages to reincarnate elements of that mysticism which animated Peter Keegan in a 1904 play. Equally interesting is the question of how someone generally considered anti-war could produce what seems like a recruiting play in *O'Flaherty, V. C.* ... and then proceed in the play to dismantle the pretensions of both imperialist and nationalist. Shaw was keenly aware that among the many Irish who enlisted in the British army during World War I were many who had been Parnellites and others who felt that England would reward their contribution with some form of Home Rule. Yet he was also the man who joked when asked by curious English people about the meaning of the words "Sinn Féin", that "I tell them it is the Irish for John Bull".

He must have been astounded, as were many others, when Sinn Féin won an unprecedented number of seats on an anti-conscription policy in 1918. At last the ideas of Francis Sheehy Skeffington seemed to prevail. And Shaw might have hoped, as the First Dáil of 1919 called for a radical redistribution of land and a reimagination of community, that the hopes voiced in various of his essays might now be fulfilled. Sadly, it was the rather dire warnings issued in *John Bull's Other Island* which would be confirmed over time.

Horace Plunkett is reported in this volume as attending Shaw's lecture on "Equality" at the Abbey Theatre in 1918. What an amazing occasion that must have been—a reminder of the immense role played by the national theatre in an occupied land. In the lecture, Shaw in effect said, "it's the economy, stupid", and renewed the call made in *John Bull's Other Island* for a debate about land use rather than land ownership. Plunkett, as a leader of the co-operative movement, heartily agreed: yet, like many admirers of Shaw's play, he found the writer stronger on diagnosis than on prescription. But there is always embedded in every description an implied set of solutions. It was not just Marx but Flaubert who said that nothing could be more radically transformative than an account of things as they are. Shaw has proved a striking prophet, not only on the matter of Ireland but also on the pains felt by England as the most deeply penetrated colony of all. That he could issue such prophecies in plays of verbal wit and formal audacity is something to lift every human heart. Nelson O'Ceallaigh Ritschel and Audrey McNamara have, yet again, done him proud and left us all in their debt.

Clontarf, Dublin   Declan Kiberd
29 November 2018

Acknowledgements

We wish to thank Peter Gahan, friend, eminent Shaw scholar and series editor of *Bernard Shaw and His Contemporaries*. Peter's excellent advice throughout the process of organizing and editing of this anthology has been supreme and much appreciated. We also wish to thank our editors at Palgrave Macmillan, Eileen Srebernik and Jack Heeney. Their support and commitment to the project has been steadfast, professional and extremely constructive.

We also wish to thank the scholars who have contributed work to this anthology (listed in the order in which their contributions appear): Declan Kiberd; President of Ireland Michael D. Higgins; Anthony Roche; David Clare; Elizabeth Mannion; Aisling Smith; Susanne Colleary; Aileen R. Ruane; Peter Gahan and Gustavo A. Rodríguez Martín. All have been generous, patient and supportive through the entire process.

Special thanks also go to Declan Kiberd, who has been a stalwart scholar of Irish literature for decades, in addition to exemplifying, by impressive example, the process of encouraging new scholarly voices to extend the discussion of Irish literature and drama, and who has known for decades that Bernard Shaw has been and remains an integral part of that literary canon. We are extremely grateful for the Foreword to this study.

Anthony Roche, the leading scholar and light, also for decades, of Irish drama is to be thanked further, and much further than our words here can express. His inspiration over the years has led many of us to delve further into Irish drama, and his enthusiasm and support is always present—his assistance on a few occasions with this anthology has been exceedingly appreciated.

President of Ireland Michael D. Higgins also receives our great thanks. His commitment to Ireland's literary voices, his generosity to us both, his friendship that is deeply cherished and his support since the first year of his presidency, 2012, are eternally appreciated. His inspirational presidency, embodying the best of Shavian attributes and directions, has opened Ireland to a celebratory inclusiveness and an understanding that are now embedded within the Irish identity. Knowing that Ireland's literary heritage is never far from its international and multinational role at home and abroad awakens in us all social responsibility that Shaw so well understood and practised. Helen Carney and Claire Power, stalwart leaders on President Higgins's staff, are also thanked for their support and assistance, as always.

Another special thank you goes to Gerardine Meaney, who during her time as Director of Humanities in University College Dublin (UCD), facilitated and supported the first Irish International Shaw conference in UCD, Dublin, in 2012. Her generosity in sharing her wealth of advice and experience contributed to the success of the conference and laid the seed for this anthology. In thanking Gerardine, we cannot but acknowledge the hard work and invaluable contribution to the conference of the administrative manager of the Humanities, Valerie Norton.

Elisabeth Mannion is further thanked. She responded immediately to the call for papers and has remained a friend through Irish literary scholarship. Similarly, David Clare is further thanked for his expert and concise advice along the way, supplying key suggestions on possible contributors. A great friend and scholar, David is much appreciated. Susanne Colleary, for her continued support, friendship and sound advice during this process and all things Shaw, is also much appreciated. Gustavo A. Rodríguez Martín, friend and scholar, who has furthered the Shavian cause in Spain, is warmly thanked.

Officers of the International Shaw Society (ISS) are also to be thanked, not just for their commitment to the continuation of Shaw Studies, but also for their strong support of Palgrave Macmillan's *Bernard Shaw and His Contemporaries* series and the University Press of Florida's earlier Shaw Series, edited by Richard Dietrich. Current ISS President Bob Gaines is greatly thanked, as are former presidents Richard Dietrich (the ISS's founder), Leonard Conolly and Michael O'Hara—as well as additional ISS officers (former and present), such as Ellen Dolgin and Jennifer Buckley. Dick Dietrich has been a keen supporter of Shaw Studies for decades, and without him, it is difficult to imagine the ISS emerging when it did. Many thanks are to owed Dick.

Great thanks are extended to the Society of Authors, on behalf of the Bernard Shaw Estate, for permission to quote from Shaw's work.

We also wish to thank scholars and friends who have played key roles in our respective journeys through Shaw and Irish Studies: the late Don B. Wilmeth, Stephen Watt, Gary Richardson, Spencer Golub, L. Perry Curtis, David Krause, Nicholas Grene, Brad Kent, Julie Sparks, Al (Charles) Carpenter, Martin Meisel, Stanley Weintraub, Louis Crompton, Charles Berst, Sue Morgan, Bernard Dukore, Sally Peters, Susanne Colleary, Zeljka Doljanin, Eamonn Jordan, Gerardine Meaney, Ian Walsh, Colette Yeates, Eva Urban-Deveraux and Kasia Lech.

On personal levels, Nelson wishes to thank partner and wife, Carolina Ritschel, for her support and love. Audrey wishes to give special thanks and love to her son Ian, her mother Laura, her late sister Denise and brothers Patrick, Brian, David and Noel—and their families.

Praise for *Bernard Shaw and the Making of Modern Ireland*

"The complexities of G. B. Shaw's distinctive relationship and encounters with the country of his birth gives rise to this unique volume of essays. How Ireland manifests in dramaturgical practices, economic reflections, and in the political activism of G. B. Shaw is sometimes obvious, but more often than not less so. Distinguished, distinctive and original, these essays exemplify the sorts of telling engagements that Shaw's radical and inflammatory works and ideas incite. For example, consideration is given to connections between Shaw and other Irish writers, including Elizabeth Bowen and Kate O'Brien, and Shaw's relationship with trade union activism to Shaw's engagements with an international media and his fascination with the gentry houses associated with Horace Plunkett and Lady Augusta Gregory. Indeed, these essays suggest not only the significance and vitality of Shaw's provocative literary, cultural, economic and political contributions, but that his uncanny and prescient insights are now even more deserving of consideration of the world in which we now find ourselves."

—Eamonn Jordan, Associate Professor of Drama Studies,
University College Dublin

"By considering Shaw's writings and actions in regards to the debates and movement towards Irish independence this rich volume of essays discovers in his work surprising connections to other Irish writers such as Kate O'Brien, Elizabeth Bowen and Sean O'Casey, reveals how his activism and friendships in Ireland shaped his subsequent work, and explores his staging of the complex interplay between the national and international in his dramas. These fascinating essays open up new areas and modes of enquiry for Shaw scholarship but will also be of great interest to students of Irish studies, modernism and theatre studies."

—Dr Ian R. Walsh, Lecturer in Drama and Theatre Studies, *NUI Galway*

CONTENTS

NOTES ON CONTRIBUTORS

David Clare is Lecturer in Drama and Theatre Studies at Mary Immaculate College, University of Limerick. He previously held two Irish Research Council (IRC)-funded postdoctoral fellowships at National University of Ireland, Galway. Clare's books include the monograph *Bernard Shaw's Irish Outlook* (Palgrave Macmillan, 2016) and the edited collection *The Gate Theatre, Dublin: Inspiration and Craft* (2018). His essays on Irish and Irish Diasporic writers have appeared in numerous journals and edited collections, and he is the curator of the IRC-funded www.ClassicIrishPlays.com database.

Susanne Colleary is teaching fellow at Trinity College Dublin and a lecturer/theatre practitioner at Sligo Institute of Technology. She has published two books, *The Comic 'i'* (2015) and *The Comic Everywoman* (2019), in addition to being widely published on Irish theatre, drama and comedy. Recent theatre works include *Marian and Joseph: A Revolutionary Love Story* (Sligo and Samuel Beckett, Dublin, (2016), written and directed by Susanne. *Here We Are at The Risk of Our Lives* (Dublin, 2016) was created with artist Sue Morris. Susanne's most recent play *Murmur* is an absurdist comedy, written for women, which will be produced in 2020. She is co-editing *Tell Me Who I Am* (Trinity Education Papers 2020), which deals with the political and the social in young people's theatre work, and is an essayist and reviewer for the *Arena Arts Show* on RTE Radio One.

Peter Gahan is co-editor of Palgrave Macmillan's book series *Bernard Shaw and His Contemporaries*, serves on the editorial board of *SHAW: The*

Journal of Bernard Shaw Studies, edited *Shaw and the Irish Literary Tradition* (2010), and is author of *Shaw Shadows: Rereading the Texts of Bernard Shaw* (2004) and *Bernard Shaw and Beatrice Webb on Poverty and Equality in the Modern World, 1905–1914* (2017).

President of Ireland Michael D. Higgins is currently serving his second term, having been first elected in 2011 and re-elected in 2018. President Higgins has forged a career as an academic (Political Science and Sociology), poet and political representative on many levels. He was a member of Dáil Éireann for 25 years and member of Seanad Éireann for 9 years. He was Ireland's first Cabinet Minister for Arts, Culture and the Gaeltacht (1993–1997) and has campaigned for decades for human rights and the promotion of peace, as well as advocating for climate sustainability—in Ireland and across the world. In 2016, he published *When Ideas Matter: Speeches for an Ethical Republic*, which followed four collections of poetry and political science studies, such as *Renewing the Republic* (2012). His ties to literary Ireland are numerous. In 2012, he opened the George Bernard Shaw: Back in Town Conference, University College Dublin (in conjunction with the International Shaw Society). He is married to Sabina Coyne Higgins, who was a founding member, along with Deirdre O'Connell, of the Focus Theatre in Dublin.

Declan Kiberd is Keough Professor of Irish Studies at the University of Notre Dame. He was for many years Professor of Anglo-Irish Literature and Drama at University College Dublin. He was recently elected a member of American Academy of Arts and Sciences—and has long been a member of the Royal Irish Academy. He has been Director of the Yeats International Summer School and President of the Shaw Society. Among his many books which cover Shaw are *Men and Feminism in Modern Literature* (1985), *Inventing Ireland* (1995) and *Irish Classics* (2000). He served for six years as a director of the Abbey Theatre in Dublin.

Elizabeth Mannion holds a PhD from Trinity College, Dublin. Beth's teaching and research focus on theatre and an interdisciplinary range of Irish Studies, from revivalist drama to contemporary crime fiction. She is the author of *The Urban Plays of the Early Abbey Theatre*, editor of *The Contemporary Irish Detective Novel* (Palgrave Macmillan), and co-editor of the forthcoming *Guilt Rules All: Irish Mystery, Detective, and Crime*

Fiction (Syracuse University Press). She teaches at Baruch College (City University of New York) and is currently completing a monograph on the theatre of Wallace Shawn.

Audrey McNamara holds a PhD in Drama from University College Dublin and lectures there. Her monograph *Bernard Shaw: From Womanhood to Nationhood—The Irish Shaw* is forthcoming. Publications include essays on the work of Bernard Shaw, Conor McPherson, Enda Walsh and Benjamin Black. She wrote the programme note for the Abbey Theatre's production of *Pygmalion* (2014) and was a plenary speaker for the National Theatre of London's production of *Man and Superman*. She was guest co-editor with Nelson O'Ceallaigh Ritschel for *Shaw 36.1: Shaw and Money* (2016) and *Shaw and Modern Ireland* (Palgrave, 2017), and guest co-editor of *The Eugene O'Neill Review Spring 2018 Edition*.

Nelson O'Ceallaigh Ritschel is the author of five monographs, including the most recent titles, *Bernard Shaw, W. T. Stead, and the New Journalism* (Palgrave Macmillan, 2017) and *Shaw, Synge, Connolly, and Socialist Provocation* (2011). He is the co-editor of Palgrave Macmillan's *Bernard Shaw and His Contemporaries* series and a member of the Editorial Board of *SHAW: The Journal of Bernard Shaw Studies*, and has co-guest edited special editions of *SHAW* (Spring 2016) and *The Eugene O'Neill Review* (Spring 2018). In 2017 he was interviewed for the sixty-minute programme *The Point* on National Public Radio in the United States, titled "George Bernard Shaw and the Freedom of the Press". He is a professor of Humanities at Massachusetts Maritime. He has completed a new monograph on Bernard Shaw, Sean O'Casey, and James Connolly.

Anthony Roche is Professor Emeritus in the School of English, Drama and Film at University College Dublin and the author of numerous books and articles on Irish drama and theatre. Recent publications on Shaw include: "Bernard Shaw and 'Hibernian Drama'", in *Oscar Wilde in Context*, eds. Kerry Powell and Peter Raby (2013); "The Abbey Theatre", in *George Bernard Shaw in Context*, ed. Brad Kent (2015); a chapter titled "Bernard Shaw: The Absent Presence", in Anthony Roche, *The Irish Dramatic Revival* (2015); and "Bernard Shaw: Crusading New Journalist and Anti-poverty Pioneer", in *Irish Studies Review* 26/1 (2018).

Gustavo A. Rodríguez Martín holds a PhD in English Philology from the Universidad de Extremadura (Spain), where he lectures on Modern Literature, Phonetics, and ESL (English as a Second Language). He is the editor of the Continuing Checklist of Shaviana, the annual annotated bibliography published in the *SHAW Journal*, and the author of the bibliographical essay on Shaw for *The Year Work's in English Studies*. His research mainly focuses on the intersection between linguistics and literary stylistics. He is currently working on an edited volume in this series, provisionally titled *Bernard Shaw and the Spanish-Speaking World*.

Aileen R. Ruane is a doctoral candidate in Études littéraires at Université Laval. She holds an MA in French Studies from the University of Illinois at Urbana-Champaign. Her doctoral thesis analyses Québécois translations of Irish theatre via the concept of performativity, specifically in the works of Bernard Shaw, W.B. Yeats, Martin McDonagh, and Mark O'Rowe. She will soon begin work on a Fonds de Recherche du Québec—Société et Culture postdoctoral fellowship project at Concordia University, tentatively titled "Féminité performative et féminismes performants: les théâtres québécois et irlandais et leurs traductions aux XXe et XXIe siècles."

Aisling Smith obtained her PhD in Drama, Theatre, and Performance studies from National University of Ireland, Galway in 2019 and is both an early-career research practitioner and a freelance theatre director. In completing her PhD project "Re-directing George Bernard Shaw: Exploring the Staging of Shaw's Play-Texts for Contemporary Audiences through Practice as Research", Aisling produced experimental stage productions of Shaw's *O'Flaherty V.C.*, *Pygmalion*, and the *Millionairess*. Aisling also holds a BA in English and Classical Studies from University College Dublin and an MA in Text and Performance from The Royal Academy of Dramatic Art and Birkbeck University of London.

CHAPTER 1

Introduction

Audrey McNamara and Nelson O'Ceallaigh Ritschel

On 26 November 1926, a letter was composed in Paris and mailed to George Bernard Shaw on the occasion of Shaw's recent Nobel Prize. The brief letter, merely one sentence, offered "felicitations to you on the honour you have received and to express my satisfaction that the award of the Nobel prize for literature has gone once more to a distinguished fellow townsman" (Joyce, *Joyce Letters, III*, 146). The letter was from James Joyce, which Shaw scholar Dan Laurence maintained was the only congratulatory Nobel Prize letter Shaw kept (Ellman, "Notes", *Joyce Letters, III*, 146).[1] It was a significant acknowledgement from arguably Ireland's most important modernist fiction writer to a contemporary, if older, modernizing Irish dramatist who had done much to pave the road to

Progress is impossible without change, and those who cannot change their minds cannot change anything (*Shaw, Bernard.* Everybody's Political What's What. *New York: Dodd Mead, 1945. p. 330*)

A. McNamara (✉)
School of English, Drama and Film, University College Dublin, Dublin, Ireland

N. O'Ceallaigh Ritschel (✉)
Massachusetts Maritime Academy, Pocasset, MA, USA
e-mail: nritschel@maritime.edu

© The Author(s) 2020
A. McNamara, N. O'Ceallaigh Ritschel (eds.), *Bernard Shaw and the Making of Modern Ireland*, Bernard Shaw and His Contemporaries, https://doi.org/10.1007/978-3-030-42113-7_1

1

modernism. It is a matter for debate as to the extent that Joyce recognized Shaw as an Irish or Dublin author from their perspective internationalisms but the recognition was posited. Arguably, Joyce had maintained an occasional eye on Shaw for some time, from turning to Grant Richards with his *Dubliners* manuscript so soon after the publisher had released a separate volume of Shaw's *Mrs Warren's Profession* in 1902.[2] As the play was blocked by the Lord Chamberlain's Office from professional performance in England, which persisted from the 1890s into the 1920s, on the grounds of immorality, Joyce most likely saw Richards as a possible publisher for *Dubliners*, which too challenged the sham guise of social morality—and, of course, Richards eventually published the book in 1914 after Joyce's fallout with the Dublin publisher Maunsel. And as Joyce thematically undermined militarism within his literature, Shaw too had done the same, from his 1894 play *Arms and the Man* through to his 1914 master journalistic response to the early months of the Great War, *Common Sense About the War*—a work that Shaw made clear in its early pages that in writing it, "I shall retain my Irish capacity for criticizing England with something of the detachment of a foreigner" (16–17). But while Joyce and Shaw hailed from Dublin and wrote mostly in exile, only one would consistently be viewed as an Irish writer and always be included within the arena of Irish Studies. Yet, this grievous error with regard to Shaw has been challenged repeatedly, and now with more and more critical voices.

In his superb study *The Irish Dramatic Revival 1899–1939* (2015), Anthony Roche begins his Shaw chapter, titled "Shaw and the Revival: The Absent Presence", by writing that in his "two magisterial literary studies, *Inventing Ireland* (1995) and *Irish Classics* (2000), Declan Kiberd has persuasively made clear the case for George Bernard Shaw to be considered an Irish writer" (79). Roche followed this by lamenting that studies of the Irish Dramatic Revival failed to seriously consider Shaw as part of that revival or to consider Shaw's lasting imprint on Ireland. Indeed, as inspirational as the above two Kiberd books have proven to be for scholars who have considered Irish drama and literature since, Shaw has for most remained an outsider, perhaps flippantly brushed aside due to his long residence in England—despite the fact that, as Nicholas Grene noted in his 1992 essay "Shaw in the Irish Theatre: An Unacknowledged Presence", such a fate did not greet other Irish writers who chose to live in self-exile, such as Sean O'Casey and Joyce. Nonetheless, despite the fact that the three major critics of Irish drama since the early 1990s, Grene, Kiberd, and Roche, have not ignored him, Shaw remained outside the realms of Irish Studies until, arguably, 2010.

Victor Merriman considered Shaw's presence or lack of presence, not in Dublin during the Irish Dramatic Revival, but within Irish Studies itself in his 2010 essay "Bernard Shaw in Contemporary Irish Studies: 'Passé and Contemptible'?" After considering Shaw within, or without Irish Studies at the time, Merriman concludes:

> The whole point about modernity, which Shaw asserts time and again, and recent events dramatize [international downturns in world economies], is that, while it is the impetus for national movements and national consciousness, it is a transnational economic and cultural system. It knows no boundaries, and recentering Shaw's work, and his sharp, utopian, critical stance in Irish Studies, may enable its practitioners precisely to go beyond the kind of inherited disciplinary boundaries summarized by Fintan O'Toole: "From the 1890s, until recently, the principal subject of Irish writing had been 'Ireland.' … Thus … *John Bull's Other Island* is an Irish play because it deals with the matter of Ireland. But *Pygmalion*, because its settings and characters are English, isn't. Never mind that what it deals with—class, language, sexuality—things which are central to the experience of Irish people as they are to anyone else." ["Review of *I Know My Own Heart*, by Emma Donoghue," in *Critical Moments*, ed. O'Hanlon and Furay, 118]. Applied to current debates around Irish Studies, Shaw's strategy of establishing and then disrupting dialectical consciousness using all available forms—from drama to policy analysis and journalism—may enable a rethinking of problems and possibilities arising within that field. If it does, it may well enable insights struggled for in Irish Studies, in their turn, to inspire critique—and human progress—not only in Ireland but in other parts of a troubled, shrinking world. p. 231

There is much in these words, from Merriman and O'Toole, regarding the necessity of including, forcibly even, Shaw within Irish Studies. Interestingly, and arguably, Merriman's essay appeared in a volume that launched a new initiative to reconnect Shaw to Irish Studies.

Merriman's essay was included in a special-themed volume of *SHAW: The Annual of Bernard Shaw Studies* titled *Shaw and the Irish Literary Tradition*, edited by Dublin-born Shaw scholar Peter Gahan, author six years earlier of the imminently insightful *Shaw Shadows: Rereading the Texts of Bernard Shaw*.[3] The ambitious volume included stalwarts of Shaw Studies, such as Stanley Weintraub, Martin Meisel, and Christopher Innes, mixed with important Irish Studies scholars such as Eibhear Walshe, James Moran, Brad Kent, Heinz Kosok, Victor Merriman, Terry Phillips, scholars of international focuses such as Kimberly Bohman-Kalaja, and one of the co-editors of this anthology, Nelson O'Ceallaigh Ritschel. The volume represented important steps for both Shaw Studies and Irish Studies, recentering, to use Merriman's term, Shaw into the Irish equation and that equation into Shaw Studies, commencing a new exploration of Kiberd's argument that Shaw *is* of the Irish literary tradition.

In the year following *Shaw and the Irish Literary Tradition*, O'Ceallaigh Ritschel's *Shaw, Synge, Connolly, and Socialist Provocation* (2011) was published, revealing, as Richard Dietrich noted in his Foreword to the book, "how often things Shaw said, wrote, and did *really mattered* to the Irish in Ireland who had revolution on their minds and were responded to in ways that directly affected the outcome of events, most particularly in the works and deeds of two of Ireland's major cultural leaders of the twentieth century, John Millington Synge and James Connolly" (xii). The book used as a springboard Kiberd's statement in *Irish Classics* that Shaw's influence in Ireland was significant: "His plays were much admired not just by intellectuals but by trade unionists" (345). Following this book, in 2012, was the International Shaw Society's conference at University College Dublin, organized by the co-editor of this anthology, Audrey McNamara. The conference, which was opened by Michael D. Higgins, President of Ireland (whose opening speech from the conference is included in this anthology), featured a keynote address by Grene, as well as plenary lectures by Gahan, Roche, and O'Ceallaigh Ritschel. A major convergence of purpose was underway, as the conference facilitated platforms that assisted the next noted contribution to the agenda of "recentering" Shaw within the Irish literary tradition and Irish Studies: David Clare's 2016 *Bernard Shaw's Irish Outlook*. Clare's book drew on both Kiberd and O'Toole, along with Dietrich's call in the above-mentioned Foreword, a work that establishes Shaw, "like Joyce and Yeats, ... wrote *always* as an Irishman" (xi). Clare's book demonstrates just that; that even in plays set outside of Ireland, Shaw's thoughts and consciousness are never far from Ireland: it is a seminal work indeed. This not only echoed Merriman's quoted excerpt from O'Toole, but also through Kiberd's balanced argument in *Irish Classics* that a play such as *Arms and the Man* (1894) set in 1880s Bulgaria reflects an Irish sense through its character Bluntschli, the Swiss mercenary, who, as the outsider on many levels, is "set down" within a culture not his natural own, much like Shaw himself being an Irishman "set down" in London, beginning in 1876 (345). Yet the impact of McNamara's conference did not end with Clare's book. These exciting directions in research related to "Shaw and Ireland" include

O'Toole's 2017 *Judging Shaw*, that seemingly prompted the Irish television documentary *My Astonishing Self* in the same year—collectively elevating Shaw's presence in Ireland.

The 2012 Dublin Shaw conference also led, directly or indirectly, to the next books by Gahan and O'Ceallaigh Ritschel, *Bernard Shaw and Beatrice Webb on Poverty and Equality in the Modern World, 1905–1914* and *Bernard Shaw, W. T. Stead, and the New Journalism: Whitechapel, Parnell, Titanic, and the Great War*, respectively. While focusing on Shaw's international concerns beyond, and outside of Ireland, the two books, in their own ways, echo Merriman's view that the Irish Shaw can still change the dynamics of Irish Studies by focusing on the international and Irish implications of Shaw's work, particularly as these monographs focus on Shaw's crusading political work outside his plays. In a similar vein, Roche's plenary lecture in the 2012 conference fed what would become his Shaw chapter in *The Irish Dramatic Revival 1899–1939*. In addition, one might also say that the formation of Palgrave Macmillan's *Bernard Shaw and His Contemporaries* series grew from conversations between Gahan and O'Ceallaigh Ritschel concerning the 2012 conference in the three years following it. Given such stimulation generated by considering Shaw within his native city, it seems that the conference itself should be the starting point to present representations of new and emerging scholarship on Shaw and Ireland, specifically setting President Higgins's seminal speech that opened the conference as the starting point. The President's speech represents a significant recognition of Shaw's contributions to the making of modern Ireland and the international stage. Concentrating on Shaw's public persona, President Higgins traces Shaw's social and political engagement, as an Irishman, within an international community and opens the debate for Shaw's ongoing influence on and relevance in modern Ireland. It heralds the platform from which new "Shaw and Ireland" directions are taking off, as seen in the work of long-established, recently established, and important emerging voices within "Shaw and Ireland" scholarship.

This unique collection explores the many facets of Shaw's work in the opening decades of the twentieth century and demonstrates how influential a figure he was in the ongoing debate and movement towards Irish independence. This collection also highlights the international vision Shaw had for a modernizing Ireland. The first essay following President Higgins's speech, "The Rush of Air, The Windows Opened on Extravagance and Storm of Ideas: Kate O'Brien's *The Last Summer* and

Bernard Shaw's *Man and Superman*", by Anthony Roche, demonstrates how Kate O'Brien's work is strongly influenced by the work of Bernard Shaw. He argues that "a revolution of consciousness [was] initiated within Kate O'Brien by what she saw and heard on stage" when she attended Shaw's *Man and Superman* performed in the Abbey in 1917. In the essay, Roche also convincingly turns the notion of a fractious relationship between Shaw and the Abbey on its head. David Clare's "Shavian Echoes in the Work of Elizabeth Bowen" argues that Bowen endorsed Shavian ideals with regard to notions of Irish and English identity. He discusses how these notions are represented within a literary context that spills over from the stage and are overtly present in both Bowen's literary journalism and her novels. Through an exploration of a selection of Shaw plays and writings by Bowen he creates an indelible thread of influence. He concludes by noting that this Shavian influence can be detected and connected to the work of many other Irish writers.

Elizabeth Mannion examines how the rally to support the workers of the Irish Transport and General Workers' Union (ITGWU), held in the Albert Hall in 1913, was instrumental in the change in the way Shaw created his religious characters. She argues that he turned them from a source of amusement to a source of disdain. She claims that "when it came to the Kiddies Scheme and religious officials standing in the way of tenement children receiving relief, the stakes were rather too high to keep the jokes flowing, and the Church behavior beyond the range of humor". Also looking at the role of the ITGWU, in the second and third decades of the twentieth century, Nelson O'Ceallaigh Ritschel explores events, stemming from what can be described as an Irish socialist revolution in his essay, "Bernard Shaw and Sean O'Casey: Remembering James Connolly". Using the trio as a triangulation of personalities, he explores the different perspectives at play during this very chaotic and important period in Irish history.

In "The Economics of Identity: *John Bull's Other Island* and the Creation of Modern Ireland", Aileen Ruane uses a post-colonial method to interrogate how Shaw fosters an economic agenda "using his stereotypes … as a fundamental marker of identity". Examining how the land question is dealt with within the play and how deeply rooted this question was in the Irish psyche, she argues that Shaw "was firmly on the side of modernization, but asks that audience to question its roots and the ideology that inspires it". Further exploring the Irish psyche, Susanne Colleary's "*O Flaherty V.C.*: Satire as a Shavian Agenda" takes account of the patriot, the nationalist, and the materiality of family life during WWI in Ireland. In particular, Colleary highlights how the female characters, Mrs. O'Flaherty and Tessie, "represent comic and at times ironic stereotypes in critiquing Irish small-mindedness", which is responsible for the stunting of economic and social progress. Through this interrogation, Colleary "highlights the chasm between Mother Ireland and the harsh poverty of daily life that permeated these 'flesh and blood' women's lives".

The critique of Shaw's female characters continues in Audrey McNamara's "Shaw, Women and the Dramatizing of Modern Ireland". Concentrating on three plays, McNamara investigates how Shaw writes against the mythologized Yeatsian ideal of Kathleen Ni Houlihan by addressing the main female character's roles in *John Bull's Other Island*, *Pygmalion*, and *Heartbreak House*. McNamara argues that these characters are valuable in connecting Ireland to the international vision Shaw had for Ireland. Reinforcing Shaw's international outlook for Ireland, Aisling Smith in "WWI, Common Sense and *O'Flaherty V.C.*: Shaw Provides a Modernist Outlook for Ireland" argues that this call for "a new nationalist outlook" reverberates through to modern times. She maintains that "the themes of class, national patriotism, and identity explored within it by Shaw, as he advocated for cultural change, have proved prevailing issues; which not only influenced the founding of modern Ireland, but continue to be direct concerns of contemporary society", continuing on themes of identity and bearing in mind that theatre is an "active force".

Delving deeply into Shaw's Irish connections, "Bernard Shaw in Two Great Irish Houses: Kilteragh and Coole" by Peter Gahan traces and explores Shaw's friendship with the hosts of these two houses, Horace Plunkett and Lady Augusta Gregory. Gahan's Joycean style of writing concentrates on what he terms as "the revolutionary period that led to Irish independence" stretching from 1910 to 1922. This enlightening chapter reinforces the engagement Shaw had with Irish affairs from the east to the west coast of Ireland, connecting him in a physical as well as an intellectual sense. Following the theme of Shaw's public persona, introduced in President Higgins's speech, the final essay by Gustavo Rodrígues Martín "Shaw's Ireland (and the Irish Shaw) in the International Press (1914-1925)" brings the volume full circle. Rodrigues Martin explores how Shaw, through his widely commented on public persona, was an international influence "as a supporter of Irish political independence". He interrogates Shaw's roles as playwright and activist and maintains that Shaw's success as a playwright ensured widespread media attention and "played a major role in highlighting the visibility of the political situation in Ireland".

Of course, the future potential for scholarship on Shaw and Ireland, which itself stems from Shaw's internationalism and nationalism, is wide open, and the scholarship represented in this anthology is just that, representative of what has and will stem from 2012. Naturally then, the essays in this anthology are not meant to be the end all of Shaw and Irish considerations, but indicative of the growing possibilities that will lead to further scholarship, in further directions on Shaw and Ireland as Shaw strove towards the making of a modern Ireland.

NOTES

1. Shaw, who had declined to purchase a subscription to the first book publication of *Ulysses* in 1922, returned the compliment to Joyce for his congratulatory note in 1926 by writing in 1939 to the editor of *Picture* Post, to correct an erroneous article published in the magazine that claimed Shaw was "disgusted by the unsqueamish realism of *Ulysses*, and burnt" his copy. Shaw wrote: "The story is untrue ... having passed between seven and eight thousand single days in Dublin I missed neither the realism of the book nor its poetry. I did not burn it; and I was not disgusted. If Mr. Joyce should ever desire a testimonial as the author of a literary masterpiece from me, it shall be given will all possible emphasis and with sincere enthusiasm" (quoted in Ellman, "Notes", *Joyce Letters, III*, 444–445).

2. Grant Richards had published Shaw's *Pleasant Plays* and *Unpleasant Plays* during the 1890s. *Mrs Warren's Profession* was included in *Unpleasant Plays*. In fact, it was usually the practice with publications of Shaw's plays prior to 1914 to publish more than one play per book, which was occasionally broken as in the 1902 publication of *Mrs Warren's Profession*. Another example of this was the 1912 paper edition of *John Bull's Other Island*, known as the Home Rule edition to coincide with the 1912 Home Rule Bill. The play had first been published with *Major Barbara* and *How He Lied to Her Husband* in 1907.

3. In 2015 *SHAW: The Annual of Bernard Shaw Studies* became the bi-annual *SHAW: The Journal of Bernard Shaw Studies*. Essentially, the publication went from an annual book volume to a bi-annual journal with special themed editions in the spring, followed by general themed editions in the fall.

REFERENCES

Ellmann, Richard. 1966. Notes. In *James Joyce, Volume III*. New York: The Viking Press.

Joyce, James. 1966. *James Joyce, Volume III*. New York: The Viking Press.

Shaw, George Bernard. 2006. In *Common Sense About the War. What Shaw Really Wrote About the War*, ed. J.L. Wisesenthal and Daniel O'Leary, 16–84. Gainesville: University Press of Florida.

CHAPTER 2

Speech at the First International Shaw Conference, Dublin

National Gallery of Ireland, 29 May 2012

President of Ireland Michael D. Higgins

Tá áthas an domhain orm an chéad Chomhdháil Idirnáisiúnta Shaw in Éirinn a oscailt agus tá súil agam go mbainfidh na rannpháirtithe tait-neamh agus tairbhe as an bplé seo ar shaol, ar shaothar agus ar ré suntasach George Bernard Shaw.

[It gives me great pleasure to open the first International Shaw Conference in Ireland and I wish the participants a fruitful time as they discuss the life, work, times and significance of George Bernard Shaw.]

I thank Audrey McNamara for her invitation and I wish to pay tribute to the assistance she has received from Professor Meaney and the Humanities Institute University College Dublin (UCD), the International Shaw Society, the School of English, Drama and Film, and many others on both sides of the Atlantic, not least Professor Nelson O'Ceallaigh Ritschel and Peter Gahan.

M. D. Higgins (✉)
Dublin, Ireland
e-mail: Claire.Power@president.ie

© The Author(s) 2020
A. McNamara, N. O'Ceallaigh Ritschel (eds.), *Bernard Shaw and the Making of Modern Ireland*, Bernard Shaw and His Contemporaries, https://doi.org/10.1007/978-3-030-42113-7_2

11

Indeed, I would like to take the opportunity to pay tribute again, having already done so at the London School of Economics and Politics, to what I consider a marvellous work of scholarship, Dr. O'Ceallaigh Ritschel's *Shaw, Synge, Connolly and Socialist Provocation*, which is such a significant contribution to the understanding of the literary, historical and biographical themes of the early decades of the twentieth century, their intersection and Shaw's role in the immense social and political changes that were taking place.

Nicholas Grene argued in his essay "Shaw and the Irish Theatre – An Unacknowledged Presence" that it was a peculiar phenomenon that Shaw, as one of Ireland's most popular and most frequently performed dramatists, should so long have remained the "invisible man" of Irish theatre. "Relegated" may be a more appropriate word than invisible.

While the recent sell-out production in 2011 of *Pygmalion* in the Abbey Theatre directed by Annabel Comyn is testament to the enduring attraction of Shaw's work, bearing in mind that, although Shaw was perhaps the most performed playwright throughout the history of the Abbey, this recent production was the first time that *Pygmalion* had been staged by the Abbey Theatre. It had, of course, been staged by the Gate Theatre in 2004. The story of the rise of Eliza Doolittle from lowly but respectable occupation through the class system to wealth and adulation has perhaps a resonance for a twenty-first-century audience that has been forced back on its fantasies by recent events.

I have a particular interest in Shaw as a public man—that phrase a public man includes a number of identities—presentation of the Self—as moralist, as essayist, as dramatist, as Fabian lecturer, as advocate, as ironist.

George Bernard Shaw had little time for sentimental evasion even at the height of his success in the theatre, he took time to write to the papers about the excessive romanticizing that surrounded the sinking of the Titanic. It was Shaw who reminded the world that the romanticizing only obscured the real facts from the public when the facts were needed. Shaw asked, "What is the use of all those ghastly, blasphemous, inhuman, braggartly lying?" Even in 1912, at the height of his success in theatre he did not shy away from expressing his civic responsibility and views that he believed were his vocation as he saw it, to invite the public to address facts, no matter how unpopular. He did not trim his message on such issues as the slums of Dublin or in exposing the philistinism of an uninformed commerce.

And that responsibility to world citizenship fed Shaw's plays and life's work. Yet I believe that Shaw's rationalism, delivered through the gradualism of the Fabians, required such a suspension of passion as would separate him from John Millington Synge, when it came to the politics of freedom, be it on national independence or gender issues.

That Shaw was very interested in the human story and championed the rights of all who were underprivileged both socially and economically is obvious from the range of his work.

A prolific dramatist, he wrote over 50 plays; those like *Widower's Houses*, which deals with slum landlordism; *Major Barbara* on capitalism; *Candida* and *Getting Married*, which deal with gender relationships; *Saint Joan*, which is referred to by some critics as one of his greatest dramatic works, but for my purposes, as we are in the years of so many centenary celebrations, his great Irish play *John Bull's Other Island* has particular relevance for those later generations of scholars seeking to recover the context and the political movements of the early twentieth century.

The honour that Shaw's plays and public life brought to Ireland went far beyond his 1904 play. He was part of the dialogue in Dublin and London with William Butler Yeats, Lady Augusta Gregory, John Millington Synge and Dublin socialists such as Frederick Ryan, the trade union organizer William O'Brien, Francis Sheehy-Skeffington, James Larkin and James Connolly.

He shared with them an admiration for Ibsen and an appreciation of Ibsen's universal themes, but Shaw's circumstances were different from some of those such as Synge. The difference in life circumstances could not be greater. It was reflected in the gradualism of the one and the passion of the other. Yet those who differed on tactics could come together on a principle—as in 1913, for example, when Shaw shared a platform in London with James Connolly, A. E. George Russell in a rally in support of Larkin and locked out Dublin workers. This testifies to Shaw's commitment, politics and his role as a public intellectual.

Shaw, of course, also wrote in the immediate aftermath of 1916 to the London press in an attempt to prevent or suspend the executions of the rebel leaders, including Connolly. He also ran a huge correspondence with contacts in the establishment in his efforts to save Roger Casement.

George Bernard Shaw remains one of Ireland's, and particularly Dublin's, most illustrious sons. Having emigrated from Dublin in 1876 to London, where he established himself as a music and theatre critic, he was to carve out a space as a public intellectual engaging with the social issues and, indeed, the confrontations in the discourse of the times. A Fabian socialist he was one of the four founders of the London School of Economics with Sydney and Beatrice Webb and a regular lecturer on Fabian themes.

Bhí saol poiblí ag George Bernard Shaw mar mhorálaí, mar dhrámadóir agus mar raconteur. Ba dhuine mór le rá é ag an am agus b'shin an chúis go bhfuair sé léirmheas dímholta ó fhoinsí mar The Irish Independent nó Arthur Griffith.

[George Bernard Shaw had a public life as a moralist, dramatist and raconteur. He was a celebrity of his time, and this would be the regular basis for the most virulent criticism of him from such sources as *The Irish Independent* or Arthur Griffith.]

The Irish Independent caricatured Shaw's form of presentation at his lectures and mocked his humour. That humour with its belief of subverting the middle classes' notions of themselves, their "respectability" and its repressions was seized on as a means to dislodge his arguments delivered at his lectures. For William Martin Murphy it was a short distance from this to referring to Shaw's presentations as "anti-Catholic".

The debate as to whether the public in general might benefit from public provision in the arts, as they had in the provision of public parks, the National Gallery debate is a good example William Martin Murphy had written in the Irish Independent that the project was one promoted by "dilettantes" and as he put it in an editorial in relation to the National Gallery proposal:

There is no popular demand and one which will never be of the smallest use to the common people of the city.

George Russell (A. E.) was pithy in his castigation of such opponents as Murphy. He referred to them as "the meanest, the most uncultured, the most materialistic and carping crowd what ever made a citizen ashamed of his fellow countrymen".

The Gallery of course went on even in its earliest years to receive extraordinarily generous donations and bequests.

Being as we now are at the beginning of a series of centenary celebrations of significant events in the second decade of the twentieth century that includes the Home Rule Acts, the founding of the Ulster Volunteers, the Irish Volunteers, the founding of the Labour Party in 1912, the 1914 World War, the Rising of 1916 and much more, we are challenged as to what we should remember, what we should revise, what we should emphasize and how we should execute this challenge.

Recovering the plural and tolerant discourse necessary for an ethical contemplation on all of these events of which Shaw was a part is a valuable part of the necessary act of remembering. We must do so in an ethical, flexible, pluralist and even forgiving way.

We are well capable of such an ethical exercise I believe and it will be, I hope our choice, rather than any evasive blandness which would be neither authentic nor valuable.

The launch of Dr. O'Ceallaigh Ritschel's book *Shaw, Synge, Connolly and Socialist Provocation* is well placed at the centre of your deliberations, engaging as it does, both the promise and the contradictions of those two early decades that preceded Independence.

Preparing for the opening of your Conference constituted its own provocation for myself.

I was set to thinking, for example, of the extraordinary influence of writers at the end of the nineteenth and the beginning of the twentieth century, Ibsen, and in particular his *Doll's House* on so many writers and politicians, and in so many different ways.

I was intrigued by an image that occurred to me of five Noras— the Noras of Ibsen, Synge, Shaw, O'Casey and the living Nora of James Joyce.

Through these characters so much can be understood, not only of the writer's intention, but of the enduring value of the moral principles involved. Ibsen's Nora, after all, leaves and rejects any sentimental forgiveness. Shaw's Nora—was her decision representative of a sophisticated calculated rationalism or is it a defeat?

It is so appropriate that your conference has a paper that deals with the "Woman Question".

Dr. O'Ceallaigh Ritschel has, of course, dealt with the contrasting treatment of the Nora question, and to the contrasting treatments of its enslavement and its dilemma of loveless bondage. In the contrasting strategies of John Millington Synge's Nora of *In the Shadow of the Glen* and Shaw's Nora of *John Bull's Other Island*: in the former a confrontation of bourgeois morality with a celebration of life, sexuality, freedom and language itself results in the choice of the freedoms; in the latter Shaw's rationalism asserts itself with its necessary concession to reformism, his choosing to subvert the audience with a subtle irony that is, perhaps at times, lost.

Synge's Nora is prophetic perhaps in valuing words, a stranger with a fine piece of talk over the propertied relations that would be recounted in later rural Ireland or the anthropology of Nancy Scheper Hughes—the uncomfortable silences of loveless unions cemented by property, respectability and duty.

Shaw's belief in Fabian gradualist change, however, I repeat, did not exclude him from those issues that combined both radical and reformist socialists—such as the Lockout of 1913 or the provision of a Gallery for the Arts in Dublin.

Your conference is timely and emphasizes the importance of us never forgetting the centrality of the literature debate in the events that led up to 1916 and Independence.

The differences between Shaw, Synge and O'Casey as they responded to the context and policy of their times, are of first order importance, not only to literary scholarship but to students of history and political theory, and above all to our citizens now and in the future.

The line that was crossed by some writers of course, who sought to make literature an instrument of emancipation is worthy of debate as is the later extreme alternative response that separates literature from life, and that ends up, with at best, an evasion. The freedom of the writer's imagination will always be in tension with the curve of historical change but it is never determined. When the balance works, literary brilliance can be both emancipatory of past and present, but above all, an invitation to the life of the spirit in a world waiting to be born, and makes of literature a celebratory emancipation.

Your conference will, I hope, spark an enduring debate. There are so many good questions. The Ibsen influence is but one theme in the literary heritage, nevertheless an important one.

Writing in Shaw's time was often in the flux of life and change. One can only imagine the atmosphere that prevailed in the public debate on the response to the Lockout of 1913, the executions of 1916, or indeed the debate about the public and art. These debates must be regarded, when all the excesses of revisionism gone wrong have been taken into account, to have been about in their time, about the promise of democracy and the public world.

As I finish I am anxious to recognize and remind us all again as how we come to be in this beautiful setting [National Gallery of Ireland]. The legacy of the residual, George Bernard Shaw estate or the Hugh Lane estate is of such benefit to generation after generation of Irish people, but it was made possible only by the debate being won and such words as those I quoted from the editorial of a leading Irish newspaper of 22nd January 1913 in relation to the proposal for a National Art Gallery being defeated.

The forces that decide democratic rights of workers and the rights of the public to the liberating power and pleasure of art were from the same stable. The people of Dublin were not only to be denied trade union rights but to be locked away from the Arts and their liberating power as well. That the writers' views won out with the public is something for which we should be grateful. I regret the fact that I will not be able to be present for what promises to be a series of papers that engages with such rich themes. I look forward, however, to perhaps reading them in the near future.

Tá áthas an domhain go bhfuil díospóireacht ar George Bernard Shaw ar siúl agus guím gach rath ar bhur gcomhdháil.

[I am so pleased George Bernard Shaw is being debated and I wish your conference success.]

CHAPTER 3

"The Rush of Air, the Windows Opened on Extravagance and Storm of Idea …": Kate O'Brien's *The Last of Summer* and Bernard Shaw's *Man and Superman*

Anthony Roche

Despite her wide reading in both Irish and European literature, Irish novelist Kate O'Brien (1897–1974) is slow to make any explicit literary references in the course of her texts. At some point in each of her novels, a famous author and the title of one of their literary works break through to the surface of her prose. Such a citation is a significant event in the book, especially if the author is Irish. In O'Brien's 1938 novel, *Pray for the Wanderer*, there is a late breaking quotation from James Joyce's *Ulysses*: "He returns after a life of absence to that spot of earth where he was born".[1] The theme of exile is relevant to the situation of the novel's protagonist, Matt Costello, who has returned to the family home in Mellick (O'Brien's fictional version of her home place, Limerick) from his

A. Roche (✉)
University College Dublin, Dublin, Ireland
e-mail: anthony.roche@ucd.ie

© The Author(s) 2020
A. McNamara, N. O'Ceallaigh Ritschel (eds.), *Bernard Shaw and the Making of Modern Ireland*, Bernard Shaw and His Contemporaries, https://doi.org/10.1007/978-3-030-42113-7_3

life as a successful novelist in London (Costello's novels are banned in 1930s Ireland, as two of O'Brien's were to be). The connection with Joyce is not surprising: both Catholic graduates of University College Dublin (UCD), Kate O'Brien and James Joyce as contemporary Irish novelists championed individual liberty and challenged the political and cultural *status quo* in Ireland. The key literary reference in O'Brien's 1943 novel *The Last of Summer* is a good deal more unexpected and one I wish to pursue in this chapter.

The novel is set in Ireland in the ten days preceding the outbreak of World War II (WWII) in August/September 1939. Events are precipitated by the arrival of a glamorous French theatre and film actress, Angèle Maury, at the Catholic Big House family of the Kernahans near Mellick. Though none of the characters has ever seen her before, this was the home of Angèle's Irish father Tom Kernahan before he emigrated to France in the years before World War I. The two young men of the house, Martin and Tom Kernahan, both fall in love with her and make their intentions known in the course of *The Last of Summer*. Martin, the more flamboyant and rhetorical of the two, is the first to make his move. He does so during the lengthy day out taken by the younger Kernahans, Martin, Tom and their sister Jo, accompanied by their various suitors and the exotic newcomer. Part of their day-long itinerary brings them to the Cliffs of Moher, a stunning series of cliffs on the western seaboard of County Clare that range for five miles and rise 700 feet into the air before a sheer plunge into the turbulent Atlantic Ocean below. Martin draws Angèle away from the others towards what the novel describes as "the edge of the terrible headland"[2] because he wants her to look over the edge—a suitably romantic gesture in a singularly sublime setting. Though reluctant, Angèle allows herself to be drawn to the cliff's edge and looks over. At which point Martin declares his intentions in a lengthy speech describing the profound impact on him of a first viewing of Shaw's *Man and Superman*:

> "When I was a very raw new student in U.C.D.," he said, "only a day or two up, I think, I strolled into the Abbey Theatre one night by myself, and *Man and Superman* was on. I'd never before seen a play by a living playwright, and I'd never seen naturalistic acting. It just knocked me sideways. It was, I suppose, an absurd experience, excessive and out of proportion every way – but I wasn't eighteen yet, and I was a country lout."
>
> "What made you think of it now?"

"Well, somewhere at the end, when he [Jack Tanner] is caught and all thetalk's no good, he says to her [Ann Whitefield], 'If we two stood on the edge of a precipice now I'd hold you tight and jump.' Words to that effect. Of course the preceding fireworks support the case – but the panic is on general principles – intellectual – and most men could claim a share in it sometime." (68–9)

Martin Kernahan's memory is more precise and accurate than he gives it credit for. He has Jack Tanner's lines from the close of Shaw's *Man and Superman* almost exactly: "If we two stood now on the edge of a precipice, I would hold you tight and jump".[3]

Unfortunately, the dates do not add up between Martin's claim in the novel to have seen *Man and Superman* at the Abbey Theatre and the dates when Shaw's play was actually performed there. Nicholas Grene and Deirdre McFeely's invaluable "Shaw Productions in Ireland, 1900–2009" lists three productions of *Man and Superman* at the Abbey Theatre during this period: in 1917, 1925 and 1927.[4] Very precise ages are given by Kate O'Brien for all of the major characters in *The Last of Summer*, a novel much concerned with both private and public histories. When Angèle meets the formidable mother, Hannah Kernahan, the latter lists the ages of her three grown-up children: "Tom is my elder son, […] he is twenty-seven, and Martin is my second son; he is close on twenty-five. There is also Jo, my daughter, who will be twenty-two this month" (12). Since the novel is very precisely historicised in September 1939, this enables the reader to establish birth dates for all three of the Kernahan siblings. Martin, the second, would accordingly have been born in late 1914. Students usually went to University College Dublin at the age of seventeen and took a degree lasting three years. (Kate O'Brien, unusually, was nineteen when she went there.) Martin Kernahan's period as a student at UCD would therefore have covered the years 1932 through 1935. During that time, according to Grene and McFeely's chronology, no production of Shaw's *Man and Superman* was staged at the Abbey.

The same was not, however, the case for Kate O'Brien, who attended University College Dublin from the historically groundbreaking year of the Easter Rising, 1916, through 1919. She took a B.A. in Arts and Classics, which included the study of English. In an account of her time at UCD published in 1955, O'Brien wrote of it as follows: "I came up [from Limerick] to a Dublin still smoking from Easter Week. The first European War was on, and all general conditions were sad and miserable. We were a hungry, untidy, dirty lot – we of 1916-1919. But did we enjoy ourselves? Did we read, did we think, did we loaf, did we argue?"[5] In her 1963 largely autobiographical prose work, *My Ireland*, a full twenty years after the publication of *The Last of Summer*, Kate O'Brien gives an account of her first year in Dublin and the intellectual blossoming it enabled in words that strongly echo those of Martin Kernahan in the novel. Shaw is central to both. The passage centres on her attendance at a performance of *Man and Superman* at the Abbey. This was the first occasion on which the theatre had produced the play. O'Brien gives the date of her visit as November 1916; Grene and McFeely date the production as February 1917.[6] Lennox Robinson's history of the theatre confirms Grene and McFeely's date (26 February 1917) as the accurate one.[7] O'Brien's moving the occasion a full three months earlier would locate the date of her transformative experience and the Abbey's first production of Shaw's play in the revolutionary year of 1916. This account of her first visit to the Abbey Theatre amplifies Martin Kernahan's even as it reveals the latter to be one of the most autobiographical passages in any of Kate O'Brien's fiction:

> The first performance I saw in the Abbey was not typical of that theatre, for it was *Man and Superman*. The occasion was not only my first attendance at the Abbey; it was my first hearing of a play by Bernard Shaw; and to heap up the heavy charge of experience, Jack Tanner was played by an enchanting fair-haired young actor called Fred O'Donovan. I went into the theatre that Saturday afternoon a nervous, green convent-school creature, just up from Limerick, and I suppose that I came out looking much the same. But in fact I came out afraid to breathe; I felt as if I had been filled within by some very brittle, burning kind of light. I was astonished; and I was to remain enclosed in that condition for nights and days. Shaw's propositions, rapid, mad, uncatchable, rang about my brain – like icicles clashing. I thought that I would never sleep again, never be able to sit still, or hear what people said, or eat my supper. [...] No ethic, no specific emotion had captured me. Simply it was the rush of air, the windows opened on extravagance and storm of idea; the laughing, the insolence, the glorious speed, and above all the realisation that one did not have to agree with one word said. Gide's counsel: "*Jette mon livre, Nathanael ...*" – was in essence Shaw's advice to me at that first encounter long ago. I have never forgotten the shock of it, or the tingling refreshment.[8]

This is the language of epiphany, of ecstasy, akin to a religious conversion, and was certainly a "Road to Damascus" moment in the emerging independent woman and writer that was Kate O'Brien in her years at UCD. It speaks to how central the writing of Bernard Shaw was to that experience and reveals how, as Paige Reynolds so aptly puts it, O'Brien was from her earliest years drawn to "Irish theatre, not fiction or poetry" in her engagements with Irish modernism.[9] It is worth remarking that O'Brien's earliest success as a writer was with a play, *Distinguished Villa*, in 1926 and that, even when she turned to prose fiction with her first novel *Without MyCloak* in 1931,"the lessons learned as a dramatist by Kate O'Brien found their way into her writing of prose narrative".[10] I wrote that about O'Brien's 1934 *The Ante-Room*, which examined how Ibsen's theatre informed the novel. In the 1943 *Pray for the Wanderer*, Bernard Shaw is the pervasive dramatic presence, *Man and Superman* the key dramatic text.

Needless to say, there were no texts by Bernard Shaw on the reading lists of the study of English at University College Dublin between 1916 and 1919. The twentieth century and its literature were resolutely shunned. The heavy emphasis was on nineteenth century English Literature (especially the Romantic poets) and reached a climax in the prose writings of Cardinal Henry Newman, the displaced Englishman who founded the Catholic University in Dublin in 1850, the predecessor to University College Dublin. O'Brien's teachers were mostly aged Jesuits going through the motions for the hundredth time. An exception was the young poet Austin Clarke, who was clearly inspirational, the only one from whom "I could get light, and direction".[11] O'Brien's sense of herself as a writer received a rare and early confirmation when Clarke, "that rapidly muttering, fresh-minded and always-in-flight young lecturer", read out one of her English essays in class and said that in it he found "the outward sign of inward grace".[12] It was in their own discussions among themselves that the brighter UCD students discussed the most exciting contemporary literature: "first readings of Joyce",[13] former UCD undergraduate, now in his early thirties and living on the Continent. Joyce had just published *Dubliners* and, in the same year as O'Brien's arrival at UCD, *A Portrait of the Artist as a Young Man*.

But for O'Brien, on arrival in the city of Dublin, what she valued most of all was the theatre it offered. Confirmed in its importance for her by the random encounter with Shaw at the Abbey, she undertook her own private curriculum of drama in the Dublin theatres: "There was, of course, unceasing political and patriotic argument, as at that time was inevitable. There was also good theatre – Ibsen at Hardwicke Street, Shaw at the Abbey, Shakespeare and Sheridan and Gilbert and Sullivan at the Gaiety, for a shilling a time".[14] It is no accident that O'Brien's involvement in the "political and patriotic argument" of the time is followed by the two contemporary radical playwrights she most favoured: Henrik Ibsen at the Irish Theatre (IT) in Hardwicke Street and Bernard Shaw at the Abbey. Her regular attendance at the little-known (and sparsely attended) productions of the Irish Theatre shows how serious a theatregoer the young Kate O'Brien was. It was then the most radical theatre in Dublin. The Irish Theatre was founded by the playwright Edward Martyn, who had contributed the Ibsenite Irish play *The Heather Field* to the first programme of W.B. Yeats and Lady Gregory's Irish Literary Theatre in 1899. The young James Joyce was the first to decry the defection of the nascent Irish National Theatre from a commitment to modernist ideals to an increasingly exclusive emphasis on peasant drama in his excoriating pamphlet, *The Day of the Rabblement.*[15] In 1914 Martyn founded the Irish Theatre to promote the best of foreign drama, plays in the Irish language and contemporary Irish plays in urban settings with a European focus. He called on young revolutionaries who loved the theatre to run it: its other directors were Thomas MacDonagh, his brother John, and Joseph Mary Plunkett.[16] Oddly, as William J. Feeney notes in his pioneering study *Drama in Hardwicke Street*, the Irish Theatre only staged one play by Ibsen during its six-year history, "[a]lthough Martyn long had championed the cause of Ibsen".[17] That play was Ibsen's *An Enemy of the People*, a production of which opened at the Irish Theatre on 24 April 1917 directed by John MacDonagh. The one Ibsen play put on by the Irish Theatre was staged during the same year as Kate O'Brien's exposure to radical Irish theatre and that coincidence, along with Martyn's well-known Ibsen associations, may well have encouraged her to believe Ibsen productions were more frequent there. *An Enemy of the People* was rehearsed at Edward Martyn's South Leinster Street residence next door to the Kildare Street Club. When club members heard the IT actors rehearsing the play's town meeting scene next door, they assumed a real revolutionary meeting was in progress and called in the detectives, who arrived the next day to search Martyn's premises.[18]

The Irish Theatre was also the first theatre in Ireland to stage the plays of Anton Chekhov, with a production of *Uncle Vanya* in June 1915 which was directed by Thomas MacDonagh, featured his brother John in the title role, Máire nic Shiúbhlaigh as Sonya and Pádraig Pearse's brother Willie as the Professor. A year later, two of those young theatre makers were dead: Thomas MacDonagh and Willie Pearse, executed for their parts in the 1916 Rising. And two were interned: John MacDonagh and Máire Nic Shiúbhlaigh were in Wales in Frongoch. Released in December of 1916, John MacDonagh returned to Dublin and immediately set about a new production of *Uncle Vanya* which opened in February 1917 in memory of his brother and Willie Pearse, where he not only played the leading role but directed and in which Máire Nic Shiúbhlaigh once more took on the role of Sonya.[19] In these Irish Theatre productions, which Kate O'Brien regularly attended during her years at UCD, theatre and politics were inescapably intertwined. Thomas MacDonagh had been a lecturer in English at UCD before he taught a final tutorial on a Jane Austen novel and went off in April 1916 to fight in the Easter Rising. After his execution, there was an unexpected job vacancy at UCD, which was filled by Austin Clarke. Understandably discomfited by the circumstances under which he had come into the position, it should occasion no surprise that Kate O'Brien found the young lecturer "shy, unhappy, I suspect, in his first job".[20] This interacting of university life, the contemporary Dublin theatre and the revolutionary moment all create an important context and environment for Kate O'Brien's description of the important freedom she enjoyed with her immediate peers as a young student at University College Dublin: "We had to muddle through, find our way round for ourselves and to learn, by trial and error, and each one according to his tempera-ment, how to find what we sought as members of a university who were also citizens in a cold, living, extremely interesting, tragic and history-flooded town. [...] We were free to surmise as to what that life might be for each of us, as private individuals".[21]

Kate O'Brien, as she says, was free and encouraged to "muddle through [and] to find our way round for ourselves". to develop an ethos of personal liberty. It was in this spirit that she found her way to the Abbey Theatre for that fateful production of *Man and Superman*. O'Brien's experience that night initiated regular visits to the Abbey Theatre, "many mad dashes over O'Connell Bridge [...] to get into the back of the Abbey pit before curtain-up".[22] She only subsequently came to realise the theatrical potency of the accomplished naturalistic acting she was witnessing. The Abbey presented an ensemble where the more experienced players and "the young ones of the company worked together, in good plays and bad, in a unity of ease, precision and power which I, for one, being totally inexperienced, took to be what acting in general was, until later I learnt what acting in general is".[23] She singles out what were for her the three greatest acting performances delivered at the Abbey during this time: Sara Allgood as "an ignorant peasant woman in *Maurice Harte*"; "Paul Farrell's playing of the priest [the defrocked mystic, Peter Keegan] in *John Bull's Other Island*": "Nor can I suppose that on the night I rapturously enjoyed a performance of Caesar in *Androcles and the Lion* I recognised an actor of genius in F.J. McCormick".[24] It is quite striking that two of the three plays at the Abbey which O'Brien singles out for praise are by Bernard Shaw (*Maurice Harte* was written by T.C. Murray and was much closer to traditional Abbey fare than any of Shaw's).

There is a central paradox in the two statements about Bernard Shaw and the Abbey so far quoted by Kate O'Brien. On the one hand, in her account of her three years at UCD, she said she went to the Abbey for Shaw, that he was the playwright of choice at that venue and the one she most associated with it. And yet she also says at the beginning of her account of that first visit that the play she chanced upon, Shaw's *Man and Superman*, was "not typical of that theatre". The association of Shaw with the Abbey has very rarely been made. Critics have tended to focus on what they present as an adversarial relationship between the two. An excessive and overdetermining emphasis is given to the fact that the Irish play Shaw submitted to Yeats and Gregory in 1904, *John Bull's Other Island*, was rejected. Various objections were lodged by Yeats and the Abbey: its length was inordinate, the Irish players could not manage the play's two English characters (Tim Haffigan and his butler, Hodson); the production demands of the play were beyond the theatre's resources, etc. Shaw was convinced the Abbey refused *John Bull* because its spirit was inimical to that of the new National Theatre: "[it was] uncongenial to the whole spirit of the neo-Gaelic movement, which is bent on creating a new Ireland after its own ideal, whereas my play is a very uncompromising presentment of the real old Ireland".[25] Accordingly, nothing by Shaw was staged at the Abbey Theatre for the first five years of its existence. This did not mean there was no Shaw in Dublin. Annual visits of Shaw programmes from London played at the more capacious and populist venues.[26] In November 1907, the Barker-Vedrenne Company was presenting a production of *John Bull's Other Island* to a packed Theatre Royal while meagre audiences attended the latest offerings from Yeats and Gregory at the Abbey; the irony was not lost on them.[27] Yeats and Gregory had been seeking to present a Shaw play at the Abbey for some time when in 1909 the perfect opportunity presented itself. Shaw's *The Shewing-Up of Blanco Posnet* was refused performance in England by the Lord Chamberlain's reader and was instead premiered at the Abbey in September 1909, despite the objections of Dublin Castle. Yeats and Gregory were quick to defend their decision and to argue against those who contended "that it is not a befitting thing for us to set upon our stage the work of an Irishman, who is also the most famous of living dramatists".[28] This statement did not lead, however, to any increase or see any more productions of Shaw plays on the Abbey stage in the years that followed. The exception was *Blanco Posnet*, which Abbey audiences loved and which received regular revivals. Inveterate theatregoer and Abbey Theatre architect Joseph Holloway's diary records the reaction of the opening night audience to Shaw's play: "The drama was followed with intense interest right up to the end, and heartily applauded. [...] The babble of voices express[ed] wonder at the Censor's verdict on the play",[29] as the audience sought in vain for blasphemies as they enjoyed a melodramatic romp through the Wild West. Had Kate O'Brien ventured into the Abbey any earlier than late 1916 she would not have encountered a Shaw play, unless a revival of *Blanco Posnet*, which would scarcely have engendered a "conversion" experience. Then, in 1916, as far as Shaw and the Abbey were concerned, all changed, changed utterly (and my echoing of Yeats's iconic poem about the Rising, "Easter 1916", is deliberate). In that year, the Abbey decided to stage an ambitious season of Shaw plays. This followed on the failure to stage Shaw's one-act play, *O'Flaherty V.C.*, the year before. Written specifically for the Abbey, and set in a dramatic equivalent of Lady Gregory's Coole Park estate, where the Shaws had stayed some months earlier, *O'Flaherty V.C.* takes as its subject the conscription of troops for the Front. This was an incendiary subject in the Ireland of the time, where conscription of Irish troops to serve in the English army was being stoutly resisted. Once more there followed objections to staging a Shaw play at the Abbey, this time from the military authorities. Lady Gregory was in the U.S. shepherding an Abbey tour. Yeats was on his own and he capitulated; *O'Flaherty V.C.* was never to be staged at the Abbey.[30]

In 1916 Gregory was back in Dublin and determined to put an end to the absence of Shaw from the Abbey stage. She wrote to the playwright suggesting a season of his plays be staged there. In characteristically ironic and perverse mode, Shaw replied that it had much better be and he would much prefer to see a season of Ibsen plays at the Abbey. In the end Lady Gregory prevailed and a strong programme of Shaw plays was put in place for the 1916–1917 season. She had clearly long nurtured such an ambition, but what precipitated it on this occasion was the abrupt departure of St. John Ervine as manager and his replacement by J. Augustus Keogh. Ervine, an admirable playwright whose *Mixed Marriage* in 1911 was a prescient examination of sectarian conflict in Belfast, proved a disaster as manager and stirred up the players against him with his strict authoritarian line and financial waywardness. The revolutionary period of Easter 1916 was also the least propitious time to have a Northern Ireland Protestant of Unionist sympathies as manager of Ireland's National Theatre. Yeats's letter of dismissal balances praise for Ervine's playwriting skills with a blunt account of how the resident acting company at the Abbey was being decimated by resignations: "I should not have complained if it was only [Arthur] Sinclair and his group, but I find that others among the players [word illegible] had trouble and *who* with that trouble will not work under you".[31] Ervine was dismissed as manager and replaced by J. Augustus Keogh, the person who was going to do most to establish Bernard Shaw as the house playwright at the Abbey. Keogh was Dublin-born but had mostly pursued a theatrical career in London. At the time of his appointment, he was stage manager of the Royalty Theatre in London but resigned in order to take up his new position in the city of his birth. Keogh inherited a vacuum, since so many of the players had fled Ervine's management that the company had to be rebuilt virtually from scratch. Lady Gregory adverts to this in her letter to Shaw of 12 August 1916: "I set out the day before yesterday from Burren to Dublin. [...] I went up to see how we were to begin rebuilding, Ervine having scattered our Company and spent our money. We are free of him now, and have taken on J. Augustus Keogh as Manager".[32] The name would have been known to Shaw, since Keogh, according to Robert Hogan and Richard Burnham, "was a bright, bumptious, energetic, and ambitious young man who had considerable stage experience, [and] who was fascinated by the work of Shaw".[33] Keogh's first proposal as manager was for the Abbey at last to stage its own production of *John Bull's Other Island*. This would be the first occasion on which the play Shaw had written for Ireland's National Theatre would be performed there, and was clearly going to prove a significant theatrical occasion. Before that, however, there were more immediate gaps to be filled in the theatre's schedule. Keogh did so with two productions of Shaw plays by his own company: *Widowers' Houses*, which opened on the 7th of August, and *Candida* two weeks later. In her letter of 12 August, Lady Gregory reported to Shaw on how his very first play had gone over with a Dublin audience: "He is putting on this week as his own speculation (we are not paying him yet) Widowers' Houses. I thought the performance very good and very well produced. [...] Keogh was excellent as Lickcheese. There was a good audience and it went extremely well, every point taken up, and great applause on the slum question".[34] The latter should come as no surprise, since Dublin at the time had the worst slums in Europe and plays at the Abbey addressing urgent social problems were virtually non-existent at the time. The Shaw plays would help bring about a change, and a play on just these conditions entitled *Blight* was staged there in 1917.[35] *Blight* was co-authored by Oliver St. John Gogarty, who as a practising doctor knew all about conditions in Dublin's inner city. And of course the O'Casey plays would follow from the early 1920s on.

Lady Gregory attributes her "brainwave", the ambitious plan she now proceeds to lay out before Shaw, to the extremely positive reaction of the Dublin audience to *Widowers' Houses*: "So a brilliant thought struck me, to turn in Napoleon's way a defeat to a victory; and our peasant plays being for the moment knocked on the head, to do an autumn season of G.B.S. – our Irish Shakespeare – I hope for an annual festival of him! [...] I would like to put on John Bull (written for us and never acted by us); Devil's Disciple, which should appeal to the romantic side of our audience; Doctor's Dilemma, not my favourite but which I am inclined to think acts best of all [...]. And I should like much to put on Androcles, if we could borrow the lion [!] – it is so delightful, and religious discussion should be popular here".[36] Lady Gregory eventually had her wish. *John Bull* went on the following month, the other Shaw plays she mentions at various intervals over the next four years. She ended her letter with a compliment to the author, or what the Irish call *plámás* (flattery, sweet talk, cajolery): "Of course I don't know what you, the victim, will think of all this, but I don't think you would be displeased with the shows".[37] Shaw nevertheless proved resistant to the idea at first, proffering a season of Ibsen instead; his objections seemed to be that the Abbey was not technically up to the demands of his plays and that they would not find an audience there. Gregory was having none of this and eventually got him to agree to the two Keogh productions, while he was still suggesting Ibsen to follow. Shaw replied to her on 22 August 1916: "On the whole, if Widowers' Houses and Candida have any success, I should stick to their period, and boldly try Ibsen: I believe he might give the theatre a new lease of life. And it would be a labor of piety too: he is the greatest of educators; and Ireland needs him badly".[38] Everything that Shaw claims for Ibsen can and could be said about Shaw in an Irish context, especially at this moribund stage in the Abbey's career. As Yeats wrote to Joyce in early 1917 when rejecting the latter's Ibsenite play *Exiles*: "it is a type of work we have never played well. It is too far from the folk drama; and just at present we do not even play the folk drama very well".[39] Keogh now followed up on Gregory's approaches with his own proposal to Shaw, and reported back on 29 August: "Mr. Shaw is a little difficult about his plays, and I have decided the best thing to do is to open on the 25th of next month with John Bull ...If we do well with this play, in all probability we can have anything of Shaw's".[40] When *John Bull's Other Island* opened as planned for the first time at the Abbey on 25 September 1916, according to Robert Hogan and Richard Butnham's history, "the house was full and rocked to continuous laughter". Further, this production earned a place in Abbey history, playing to packed houses for two weeks and "apparently establish[ing] a new box office record for the theatre".[41] As J. Augustus Keogh had confidently and accurately predicted, there was no more withholding of his plays by Shaw and the Abbey could now produce anything they wished from the playwright's repertoire. There was one exception. He held back on Lady Gregory's desire to see *The Devil's Disciple* produced at the Abbey, explaining in a letter to her of 4 May 1917: "I have practically pledged myself not to allow The Devil's Disciple to be played during the war".[42] It was eventually produced there on 5 April 1920.

What followed in the next ten months was extraordinary and extremely rare at the Abbey or any other theatre. Between 7 August 1916 and 25 June 1917 nine plays by Bernard Shaw were produced at the Abbey Theatre. After the first three already mentioned came *Arms and the Man* on 16 October 1916; *Man and Superman* on 26 February 1917, produced for the first time ever at the Abbey but for only the second time in Dublin: this was the production seen by Kate O'Brien; *The Inca of Perusalem* on 12 March; *The Doctor's Dilemma* on 26 March; *You Never Can Tell* on 18 June; and *How He Lied to Her Husband* in a double bill with *Candida* on 25 June 1917. They were all directed by J. Augustus Keogh. Roughly one in every two plays produced at the Abbey during this time was by Bernard Shaw; Gregory's remark about him as "our Irish Shakespeare" comes to mind. Had Kate O'Brien wandered into the Abbey to any performance during this year, she would most likely have happened upon a Shaw play. Had she wandered in any earlier than late 1916, in fact at any time during the prior eleven years of the Irish National Theatre's existence, the last thing she would have encountered was a play by Shaw. Hence her claim that "the first performance I saw in the Abbey was not typical of that theatre", to which one needs to add in italics *up to that time*. My claim that from late 1916 on all changed utterly is not exaggerated. For this change, whereby Shaw now became a prominent part of the Abbey Theatre's repertoire, continued for over twenty years: a lifetime in theatrical terms. As with most Abbey Theatre managers, J. Augustus Keogh did not last long. Headstrong and overspending on the Shaw productions, he was replaced as manager by Fred O'Donovan in June 1917. Those who attribute the emphasis on Shaw in the Abbey's 1916–1917 repertoire exclusively to Keogh's interest and involvement claim that the interest in Shaw at the Abbey departed with him. This was certainly Keogh's own view, which he expressed to Shaw when he sought exclusive rights to Shaw's plays for touring in Ireland. Shaw reported and commented on this in his letter to Lady Gregory of 28 April 1917: "Keogh's trump card, which he has already thrown down boldly, is that when he leaves the Abbey Theatre there will be no more of my plays there as they do not 'meet with the approval of Mr. Yeats for production at the Abbey.'"[43] Shaw says that Keogh's request for rights will naturally include Dublin and that he "will ask me whether I seriously mean to impoverish myself and break his back by keeping them out of Dublin for the sake of a rival theatre which never performs them at all, and never did except as a stopgap in a desperate emergency". Shaw is clearly ventriloquising through Keogh here, playing devil's advocate by seeing if the Abbey Theatre's commitment to staging his plays will continue beyond the departure of J. Augustus Keogh as Manager. He puts it up to Gregory and Yeats in an uncompromising manner in the remainder of the same letter. The playwright will proceed to grant Keogh exclusive Irish rights to his plays unless the Abbey agrees to a certain guaranteed minimum of Shaw productions per annum: "Under these circumstances I should have to hold a pistol to the head of the Abbey Theatre by saying that it must either give me a minimum number of performances every year or else see my plays go to Keogh".[44] Gregory and Yeats obviously agreed, because the productions there continued. Gradually, they built up again, from two in 1918 through three in 1919 to an impressive five in 1920.

The renewed increase in the number of Shaw plays at the Abbey from 1920 onwards came from the involvement of playwright Lennox Robinson as director. Robinson had long chafed at the narrowness of the Abbey's repertoire and in 1919 founded the Dublin Drama League, which presented plays from outside Ireland and plays of the avant-garde. They were played on the two nights the Abbey was dark (Sundays and Mondays) and were able to draw on the Abbey acting company for their casts. In the following ten years, the Dublin Drama League presented a wide range of plays and playwrights from the classic global repertoire: Euripides, Ibsen, Strindberg, Chekhov, Andreyev, Pirandello, O'Neill, Glaspell and many others. Meanwhile, the Abbey continued in the main to present their more traditional and expected Irish theatrical fare. The playwright who did most to break down this theatrical apartheid was Bernard Shaw, since his plays were presented under both flags, of Irishness and internationalism, of the traditional and the avant-garde. The commitment of the mainstage Abbey Theatre to the plays of Bernard Shaw continued unabated throughout the 1920s, averaging an impressive four productions per year and rising to an extraordinary seven in the years 1925 and 1927. All were directed by Lennox Robinson. But at the same time the Dublin Drama League also presented a production of Shaw's *Heartbreak House* on 14 and 15 March 1926 and *Caesar and Cleopatra* on 29 and 30 May 1927 as representative of the European avant-garde.[45] Behind Robinson's lead one senses the unwavering support for the Shaw programme at the Abbey of Lady Gregory and even of W.B. Yeats, who was President of the Dublin Drama League (and whose plays were the only ones other than Shaw's to be presented in both categories and by both producing agencies). There were fewer productions of Shaw plays at the Abbey in 1930s; but that can at least partly be attributed to the arrival of the Gate Theatre in 1928, which largely took over from the Dublin Drama League to present international plays nightly rather than twice a week. The Abbey presented recognisably Irish plays; the Gate was devoted to the European avant-garde. Shaw's theatre again broke down that distinction; his plays were produced at both Dublin theatres. In 1930 the Gate produced the entire five-part *Back to Methuselah* across several nights; and *Heartbreak House* became a regular at the Gate Theatre in the 1930s: co-founder Hilton Edwards performed as well as directed in what became a bravura signature role as Captain Shotover.

What Lady Gregory said to Shaw about needing to recruit new actors who could play peasant work was not entirely true. Combined with Yeats's remark to Joyce about the Abbey not even doing folk drama well any more, it is clear in retrospect that the two directors seized the opportunity from 1916 onwards to move standard Abbey fare away from traditional rural drama towards plays which provided a greater range of acting opportunities, in particular the urban sophistication and social conscience of Shaw's dramas. A versatile and outstanding range of actors was recruited or promoted who in fact could play in both styles but excelled in the Shaw. Many of them were the actors who became known through their later work on O'Casey—Arthur Shields, Barry Fitzgerald, F.J. McCormick— but they came to this from seven years of continuous acting in Shaw. The year of Augustus Keogh was dominated by the theatrically dazzling double act of Fred O'Donovan and Maire O'Neill. O'Donovan had played the lead role in the 1909 Abbey premiere of *Blanco Posnet*, which was reviewed by Joyce for a Triestine newspaper. The night before *Blanco Posnet*, Fred O'Donovan had impressed Joyce as Christy Mahon in Synge's *Playboy of the Western World*.[46] In the words of Kate O'Brien, in 1917, Shaw's "Jack Tanner was played by an enchanting fairhaired young actor called Fred O'Donovan". Maire O'Neill was in reality Molly Allgood, younger sister of Sara (hence the change of name, to distinguish herself from her older, established actor sister). She had starred in early Abbey plays, notably as Pegeen Mike in *The Playboy*, a part specifically written for her by her fiancé, playwright J.M. Synge. O'Neill had departed the Dublin for the London stage in 1912 but had returned to the Abbey in 1916 coincidentally in time to work on the Shaw scripts. Keogh, who had worked with her in London, immediately cast the actress in his 1916 production of *Candida*; and she was to pair with O'Donovan throughout the next eleven months in the various Shaw productions. Naturally enough, then, it was Maire O'Neill who brought her renowned vivacity and facility with language (for Synge's is even trickier than Shaw's) to the part of Ann Whitefield opposite Fred O'Donovan's Jack Tanner. It was Fred O'Donovan who took over as Manager from Keogh in the summer of 1917. He lasted twenty months, but departed the Abbey in February 1919, "complaining of Yeats's 'interference' in rehearsals, and of his 'not getting more pay'".[47] Maire O'Neill was gone by the end of the season along with Keogh, to return to the London stage (her enhanced salary had been a problem throughout her year back at the Abbey). The emphasis on finding suitable actors to play Shaw at the Abbey continued, with the rapid ascent of Arthur Shields and his brother Barry Fitzgerald from the minor roles in which they had previously been appearing to leading role status. One has only to recall Barry Fitzgerald's sparkling performances in such John Ford movies as *How Green Was My Valley* (1942) and *The Quiet Man* (1952) to realise how fully he would have developed the comic potential and quirky characteristics of the Waiter in Shaw's *You Never Can Tell*, a role he played on several occasions at the Abbey. These might now be termed the "Shaw years", where it could legitimately be claimed as Kate O'Brien did that "one went to the Abbey for Shaw". The extraordinary group of actors recruited to play in them and the transformative impact of Shaw productions on the hitherto moribund Abbey did indeed give the theatre "a new lease of life", as Shaw had predicted for a season of Ibsen. It was Bernard Shaw in an Irish context who proved to be the "greatest of educators and Ireland needed him badly". The impact was immediate and profound. For evidence, one need look no further than the ecstatic response of a nineteen-year-old Kate O'Brien to what she witnessed that night.

The last section of my chapter will examine Kate O'Brien's *The Last of Summer*, and what that novel makes of the impact of Shaw's *Man and Superman* on the writer. The novel is set in Ireland and *Man and Superman* is not. But it is no accident that the quotation from Shaw should be spoken at the Cliffs of Moher. In front of the cliffs is the Atlantic Ocean, into whose depths Martin and Angèle gaze from a great height. Directly behind them stretches the Burren, one of the most extraordinary landscapes in Ireland or elsewhere. This is how Kate O'Brien describes it in *My Ireland*:

> [The Burren] is a rising and falling stretch of alkaline carboniferous limestone, and I suppose its area is about ten miles by ten. The land is ridged and shelved in plateau formation, much of the surface being naked stone, or lightly lichened; but in its valleys and slopes there is a sweet green herbage, on which small sheep and light cattle thrive. [...] It is a region by itself, the Burren; it is elevated and lonely, and looks to have been shaped and undulated into its present grace by winds and suns beyond imaginable time.[48]

O'Brien frames this description of the Burren's natural beauty through the lens of Bernard Shaw. She reminds her reader that Shaw stayed with Lady Gregory not only at Coole Park but "at her seaside house along this Burren strand",[49] where he played and talked with her little granddaughters. In her letter to Shaw of 12 August 1916 Gregory remarked to him that she had come straight to Dublin from the Burren and would "in an hour or two go back to Burren [from Coole Park], to the children".[50] Kate O'Brien goes on to speculate about what might have been discussed between Shaw and Gregory in that locale and on that occasion: "[as] a man of the theatre, he was surely interested if Lady Gregory told him when he was at Burren that it was only within a very short walk [...] – at Duras House, in 1898 – that that which was to be the Abbey Theatre was conceived and almost brought to birth, in a chance conversation, on a summer afternoon".[51] O'Brien frames her discussion of the Burren in *My Ireland* through referring to a less-well-known Shaw play, the 1921 *Back to Methuselah*, his visionary five-part speculation about the far future. The play is set in 3000 AD and O'Brien gives prominence to the fact that one of its settings is the Burren. (After *John Bull's Other Island*, Shaw's two Irish settings had strong associations with Lady Gregory: the Big House of *O'Flaherty V.C.*and the Burren of *Back to Methuselah*.) As the stage directions state: "*Burrin pier on the south shore of Galway Bay in Ireland, a region of stone-capped hills and granite fields*".[52] One can see why Shaw chose it as one of the settings for his futuristic fable. The Burren looks like the surface of the moon, stretches back thousands of years and will clearly look the same 1080 years in the future. An Elderly Gentleman dressed in an elaborate English Victorian outfit, who is visiting the area, is addressed by a woman, evidently from her dress a native of the place: "*A woman in a silk tunic and sandals, wearing little else except a cap withthe number 2 on it in gold*". The English gentleman finds it "extremely unusual and hardly decent".[53] The Woman asks why he has been sent to the Burren, in a line quoted by Kate O'Brien in *My Ireland*: "Have you been sent here to make your mind flexible?"[54] Shaw's text elaborates on O'Brien's précis: "Perhaps you do not know that you are on the west coast of Ireland, and that it is the practice among natives of the Eastern Island to spend some years here to acquire mental flexibility. The climate has that effect".[55] O'Brien stresses the timelessness of the location when she adds: "And [the Woman] stood between two old stone stumps as she spoke, and the clear water of the bay lapped over her feet. The stumps are there, and you and I can go and sit on them".[56] On their day out in *The Last of Summer*, the Kernahan family travel from their home near Limerick through the Burren to the Cliffs of Moher. In this timeless landscape, reaching back and forward at the same time, it should now appear less surprising and more apposite that Martin Kernahan produces a quote from Shaw's free thinker Jack Tanner at the dizzying summit of the Cliffs of Moher as an inducement to flexibility of mind on the part of the visitor, the young French woman who accompanies him.

It is important that Kate O'Brien first experienced *Man and Superman* as a piece of live theatre. For one thing, it emphasised the dramatic qualities of Shaw's plays and partly did so by depriving this one in particular of the weighty extra baggage with which the printed version was freighted. In addition to the lengthy preface which usually preceded Shaw's printed plays, there was also "The Revolutionist's Handbook", its authorship ascribed to Jack Tanner rather than Bernard Shaw. The text of *Man and Superman* published in 1903 contained all three; in the Dan H. Laurence *Collected Plays* Volume II of 1971, the entire text runs to 300 pages. Stripped of the Preface and the Handbook, the dramatic text still clocks in at 200 pages. From the very first production of the play at the Royal Court Theatre in 1905, the entirety of Act Three was excised and the whole play not given until 1915. The removal of this act is facilitated by its stand-alone nature, as a dream sequence in which Don Juan and the Devil engage in debate about Creative Evolution. Deprived of the "Don Juan in Hell" sequence, *Man and Superman* runs to 140 pages This is the short-ened (but still lengthy) version of the play that ran at the Abbey in 1917, played (as it must be) at what O'Brien described as "glorious speed". In this form, the overtly philosophical content is lessened and the romantic complications of the central characters foregrounded.

When *Man and Superman* is brought into comparison with *The Last of Summer*, what the two are seen most to share is a triangular relationship. This has already been sketched in relation to O'Brien's novel: the two brothers Martin and Tom Kernahan both actively woo their beautiful young French cousin, Angèle Maury. In the Shaw play, the beautiful young Ann Whitefield has just become an heiress on the death of her father and has two potential husbands: a romantically besotted young man, Octavius Robinson, whom Ann playfully addresses as "Ricky-Ticky-Tavy" or simply "Tavy"; and an older, more cynical man, Jack Tanner, whom her father's will has appointed as one of Ann's two guardians. What the two scenarios also share regarding their central relationships is a whiff of incest. For much of their courtship of Angèle, both of the Kernahan brothers blithely ignore the fact that the woman they are pursuing is their first cousin; but when Tom wins the day and Angèle accepts his marriage proposal, his first activity (prompted by his ultra-Catholic mother) is to seek out the church authorities for an exemption that will prove time-consuming and difficult to obtain. In *Man and Superman* the age difference between Ann Whitefield and Jack Tanner has led her to have romantic fantasies about him since she was a girl; but his quasi-paternal role complicates an adult love relationship. In both triangular relationships, there is on the surface the more obvious pairing: Octavius follows so blissfully in the wake of Ann that he is to all appearances her husband-to-be. In *The Last of Summer*, Martin is a much more flamboyant wooer than his quiet older brother; his drawing Angèle to the melodramatic heights of the cliff edge at Moher is played out in full view of the picnic party, including Tom. Both of the Kernahan men present Angèle with a sea shell at the end of the day out. Tom has won his with his marksmanship at the fair; Martin has purchased his and presents it to her with a florid speech. Tom moves her gold hair aside and holds the conch shell to her ear: "While she listened their eyes met, and paused in reflection"(79). From this moment on, a third of the way through *The Last of Summer*, Angèle (who has never been in love before and is still a virgin, as is he) has marked Tom for her own, as Martin rapidly realises. At the end of this long day, she reflects: "For once she knew that a true feeling dominated her; and that she was neither afraid of it nor ashamed" (105). What Tom offers her is a deeply rooted way of life, an alternative to the improvisational restless existence of an actress's life. She sees it as a rare and real opportunity to occupy the environment her father exiled himself from. Tom is frequently seen posed against scenes of Ireland's natural beauty; but he is rarely alone in those landscapes: his mother is usually by his side, as they whisper conspiratorially.

Jack Tanner all along denies that he has any romantic interest in Ann Whitefield and repeatedly states he has no intention of marrying her, even as some of the other characters (such as his chauffeur, Henry Straker) all along assume and gesture at the certainty that Jack and Ann will end up together. Jack is still loudly protesting against this outcome virtually to the last page, even as he realises that this is the outcome all of the other characters (and not just Ann) have determined for him: "I will not marry you. I will not marry you./ Oh, you will, you will" (728). Ann finds Tavy childish and tiresome as a suitor, and clearly has her heart set on Jack, however much he may seek to elude her designs. Both scenarios centre on an outing: the picnic party at the Cliffs of Moher in the novel and the sudden decision of Tanner and the others in the play to quit England and scoot across the Continent with one car vying to outdo the other in speed (Shaw's play embraces modernity and a new century by bringing a motor vehicle on stage and driving it off at the close of Act Two). The seating arrangements in the cars lead to a good deal of farcical high jinks in both, as the men and women manoeuvre around each other. Ann's younger sister Rhoda was to ride with Tanner until Ann strenuously objects to an innocent young woman being let into Jack's company for any length of time; she suggests that she would be a more suitable companion. Jack finally comes to admit his feelings for Ann but continues to hold out against marriage. He articulates his reasons all the way through about the sacrifice of independence that will be involved in such an outcome: "I [do] love you. The Life Force enchants me: I have the whole world in my arms when I clasp you. But I am fighting for my freedom, for my honor, for my self, one and indivisible" (729). A few lines later, he speaks the line quoted by Martin in *The Last of Summer*: "If we two stood now on the edge of a precipice, I would hold you tight and jump". Ann at first seeks to back off from the proposal—"Let me go: I cant bear it". But when Jack responds in kind, "Nor I. Let it kill us", she finally succumbs: "Yes: I dont care. I am at the end of my forces. I dont care. I think I am going to faint". At which point all of the other characters come back on stage, see how Jack and Ann are with each other and promote the more conventional romantic solution of marriage. Angèle Maury has declared to herself at the start of the novel, as she heads to encounter her father's Irish family for the first time, that she is seeking above all else to "learn to stand and debate with life" (2). What Paige Reynolds says of O'Brien's *Pray for the Wanderer* is no less true of *The Last of Summer* and *Man and Superman*: what "appears on one level to be a domestic drama, a romance depicting a fairly conventional love triangle" turns out upon further examination to be primarily concerned with a quest for what O'Brien terms "personal liberty".[57]

Reynolds goes on to note how the "narrative trajectory is interrupted, and almost dominated, by a series of long conversations and debates unfolding between" the protagonist and the novel's other characters.[58] Whether intentional or no, this account of O'Brien's distinctive narrative method is a very precise description of Bernard Shaw's dramatic practice, capturing how his plays proceed: by a series of long conversations and debates. The presence of drama in O'Brien's fiction is realised in *The Last of Summer* through the presentation of Angèle Maury. She is the one who brings the very different world of the theatre into the natural ambience of Waterpark House. When her aunt points to the discrepancy of her surname, Angèle responds that she has not just followed her mother into the profession of the theatre but has taken her name also: "Angèle Maury seems a better name for the stage" (10). (Her father would appear to have been work-shy; and Hannah has much to do to free the Big House from debt when her own Kernahan husband dies.) Angèle's aunt is neither convinced nor impressed: "Perhaps. Certainly *Kernahan* was never a stage name". Angèle has deliberately applied make-up as she prepares to meet them, a vivid red lipstick which draws a sneer from a passing child and the disapproval of her puritanical aunt. Naturally reticent when meeting a group of strangers, family members who have all along denied or been unaware of her existence until now, she presents herself to them self-consciously in what are described in theatrical terms: "She was used to movement, to change of scenes or of companions, but she had neither a forgetful nor an easily adapted temperament; she kept her thoughts a step or two behind immediate events, as a rule – a form of absent-mindedness which made her sometimes seem to miss her cue of casual reaction" (38). Angèle allows herself to feel romantic love for the first time, but there is danger in the openness it encourages, leaving her vulnerable to the machinations of a domineering mother determined to hold on to her son. She realises that Hannah is "her enemy" but then rallies her spirit with the following declaration of identity: "She felt afraid, and shivered a little inwardly. But her spirit rose nevertheless to the immediate issue and she reminded herself that she was not an actress for nothing" (192).

There is a similar theatrical self-consciousness to Ann Whitefield in *Man and Superman*. For most of the play, she performs a role: that of the good daughter entirely submissive to the wishes of her parents. Early on, she declares: "I feel that I am too young, too inexperienced, to decide. My father's wishes are sacred to me" (553). Beneath this self-abnegating mask Ann pursues her own path, especially in her desire to track and secure Jack Tanner. Jack discusses this role-playing propensity of Ann's with her mother: "She will do just what she likes herself whilst insisting on everybody else doing what the conventional code prescribes" (722). Jack has consistently described Ann as a boa constrictor, to which she responds playfully at one point by twirling her feather boa around his neck: "Doesnt it feel nice and soft, Jack?" (576). She presses the comparison on him further with an even more intimate gesture: "I suppose what you really meant by the boa constrictor was this [*she puts her arms round his neck*]" Her mother says that Jack (unlike Octavius) can stand up to her daughter— "you are able to take care of yourself. Youd serve her out" (722)—but it is equally clear that she can stand up to him.

I would like finally to consider the settings of both works and how they bring larger issues of national identity to bear on the personal relationships. Where certain of Kate O'Brien's novels take place on the Continent (notably in Spain), *The Last of Summer* is set in Ireland from beginning to end. But the novel takes place on the eve of World War II and the daily news sets the global context of the coming catastrophe before the characters. The source of this news is the radio: "An English voice – that of a B.B.C. announcer – filled the room; Martin lay in a dejected attitude in an armchair near the radio set [and said]: 'Berlin is saying that the new British proposals about Poland have come too late'" (185). In the print medium, Martin can find no copies of European newspapers locally, given the "almost non-existence, from the point of view of Drumaninch, of contemporary Europe" (175). His mother is shown conspicuously reading *The Irish Press*, a nationalist newspaper that was a propaganda outlet for Taoiseach [Prime Minister] Eamon de Valera and his Fianna Fail party throughout the 1930s.[59] It is widely known that de Valera will be following a deliberately neutral policy for Ireland in the coming war, as the older women keep reassuring themselves. Contemporary Europe is inescapably and directly brought into Drumaninch by the presence of Angèle Maury, who expresses concern throughout for the fate of family and friends back in Paris. The two younger Kernhans have both been pursuing postgraduate degrees there: Martin speaks to Angèle in French when he wants their conversation to be private. The rural Irish setting of the novel, therefore, is not as cut off as might at first appear from the rest of Europe. But Hannah Kernahan is deliberately running a policy of political and cultural isolationism in the little kingdom over which she presides. And rather than allowing for Angèle's hybrid identity, she insists on the young woman's otherness as the reason why her son Tom should not marry her: "she thought again of Angèle. Thought of her with a kind of pity – poor rootless, wandering waif; lonely, struggling actress, part of the dangerous, crude world outside Eire – to which presumably she would return" (148).

The other hybrid character in the novel, mentioned on the Cliffs of Moher, is Shaw, the Irish-born playwright who lived most of his life in England and set almost all of his plays there: an important author to cite in a novel set in Ireland in the late 1930s, where there is a narrowing of national identity in the face of war. Shaw productions dwindled to nothing after 1940 at the Abbey Theatre (though they continued at the Gate). This coincided with the death of Yeats and the arrival of Ernest Blythe as managing director (for almost three decades). Blythe, who insisted all of the Abbey actors know Irish, ushered in a period of profound theatrical conservatism and narrow-gauge nationalism at the Abbey, which no longer could find room for the plays of either Shaw or Shakespeare (neither was Irish enough). Kate O'Brien would have been aware of this development when she came to write *The Last of Summer* in 1942 and her invocation of Shaw on the Cliffs of Moher is a cry of protest at what the novel represents as a closing of the Irish mind. Angèle concludes that she might well stay and fight Hannah for Tom "if it weren't for the war, if it weren't for wanting to be at home for the war" (235). Tom will remain in neutral Ireland with his mother. The attitude Hannah expresses towards Europe is exactly the ideology of isolationism, a view of the rest of the world as distant and irrelevant, that Taoiseach Eamon de Valera had been developing since he came to power in 1932. Mother Ireland still holds her eldest son in thrall, and free from foreign influence.

The first half of *Man and Superman* is set in England. But where so many of Shaw's plays remain there this play cuts loose at the end of Act Two (by means of that open touring car) and heads for the Continent. Initially, the travellers make for Nice in the South of France but by a never fully explained accident end up in Spain's Sierra Nevada in Act Three and Granada in Act Four. The final act brings on a major character, Hector Malone. He is identified only as "The Irishman" at the start of the scene, before he is properly introduced. Ireland is thereby brought into Shaw's play towards the end as one of its broader frames of cultural, historical and geographical reference. Another is the United States. Both countries are represented by Hector Malone, an Irish American.[60] The removal of the English characters to a foreign location reveals the narrowness of some of their attitudes, an endemic Little Britonism. Tanner's chauffeur, Henry Straker, so advanced in his class attitudes to his employer, proves a good deal less so when speaking (down) to the Irish American newcomer, who corrects the pronunciation of his first name from Ector to Hector: "STRAKER [*with calm superiority*] Hector in your own country: thats what comes o livin in provincial places like Ireland and America. Over ere youre Ector" (699). (Straker is operating as if he were still in England.) We have already met the Irish American's son, also Hector Malone, at the start of *Man and Superman*. Young and very American Hector is involved in the second of the play's romantic plots. He is secretly married to Violet Robinson (Tavy's sister) for reasons that soon become clear. Hector Malone senior, if he knew of it, would cut off his son, not for marrying an English woman but for marrying one who hasn't a title. His one-man war against the English for their 800-year oppression of the Irish takes the form of wanting his son to capture a titled lady as his bride. As Hector tells Violet in Act One, his father "has a prejudice against the English middle class" (607). But Violet is holding out for the money, hence the concealment of their marriage. Both play and novel feature a blocking parental figure who stands in the way of their young son or daughter marrying the person of their choice. This standard romantic trope is complicated and deepened by the extreme Irishness of the parents in each case. (They are both single parents and so do not have to share that role or power with another.) Hannah Kernahan initially appears to welcome her son's engagement to his French cousin; but her Oedipal hostility has only been concealed and gradually emerges as something poisonous. Hector Malone's opposition is overt from the beginning but as Act Four proceeds he acquires a more flexible attitude. This is largely brought about by meeting his English daughter-in-law Violet and coming to admire her independence and strength of character (as with all of Shaw's heroines). Hector does not know that the two young people are already married, however, and when this becomes clear the son gets on his high horse and tears up his father's latest remittance, declaring a desire to embrace poverty. The older man replies with genuine concern: "Hector: you dont know what poverty is" (709). This statement, echoing Shaw's lifelong detestation of poverty, is historicised and deepened by an earlier exchange between Malone and Violet about the Irish Famine:

> MALONE. Me father died of starvation in Ireland in the black 47. Maybe youve heard of it.
> VIOLET. The Famine?
> MALONE [*with smouldering passion*] No, the starvation. When a country is full o food, and exporting it, there can be no famine. Me father was starved dead; and I was starved out to America in me mother's arms. English rule drove me and mine out of Ireland. Well, you can keep Ireland. Me and me like are coming back to buy England; and we'll buy the best of it. I want no middle class properties and no middle class women for Hector. (704)

But when his Hector proves adamant in proudly refusing his father's money, Malone's racial memory of poverty in an Irish historical context leads him to plead with Violet to reconcile father and son: "Youll try to bring him to his senses, Violet: I know you will" (711). Where one parent (Hannah Kernahan) hardens in mind, the other (Hector Malone) softens and grows more flexible. This important Irish dimension of *Man and Superman* would have had particular resonance for an Abbey audience in 1917.

When she writes about the Abbey Theatre in *My Ireland*, Kate O'Brien regrets that she never saw the normally effete Yeats (whom she and her fellow UCD students followed around St. Stephen's Green and mocked) roused to passionate and savage indignation at the riots over O'Casey's *The Plough and the Stars* in 1926: "I have always regretted that I never saw Yeats in an Abbey Theatre row".[61] Clearly, there was no public row at the Abbey that night in 1917 at Shaw's *Man and Superman*. The fireworks were all internal: a revolution of consciousness initiated within Kate O'Brien by what she saw and heard on stage. She deliberately contrasts the lack of external change one might perceive in her afterwards ("I suppose I came out looking much the same") as opposed to her inner illumination by "some very brittle, burning kind of light". Roy Foster has pointed out that, though the "Rising is often called a revolution of poets [...] playwrights and actors were far more prominent".[62] This was touched on earlier with the involvement of Thomas MacDonagh in the first Irish production of Chekhov's *Uncle Vanya* in June 1915 at the Irish Theatre, which O'Brien also attended. In addition to being a revolutionary, MacDonagh was a poet and playwright, a university lecturer, a feminist and a Catholic who married a Protestant. The more radical features of the Rising were erased or crudely simplified in the Ireland of the following decades. Those who bore the brunt of this conservatism were the women, especially in de Valera's Constitution of 1937, which confined them to the home.[63] For Irish women more than anyone else it remained an unfinished revolution. Kate O'Brien continued the fight for "personal liberty" in the novels she was to write across three decades. Her attending Shaw's *Man and Superman* at Dublin's Abbey Theatre in the same year as the Rising, and what it wrought in her, is an important part of that revolutionary historical moment.

NOTES

1. Kate O'Brien, *Pray for the Wanderer* (London, Toronto: William Heinemann, Ltd., 1938), 283.
2. Kate O'Brien, *The Last of Summer* (London: Virago Press, 1980), 67. All future references are to this edition and will be given parenthetically in the text.
3. Bernard Shaw, *Man and Superman*, in *Collected Plays and Their Prefaces: Vol. 2* of the Bodley Head Bernard Shaw (London: Max Reinhardt, 1971), 729. All future references are to this edition and will be given parenthetically in the text.

4. Nicholas Grene and Deirdre McFeely, 'Shaw Productions in Ireland, 1900–2009', in *Shaw and the Irish Literary Tradition*, ed. Peter Gahan, *SHAW: The Annual of Bernard Shaw Studies* 30 (2010), 238–59.
5. Kate O'Brien, "As To University Life", *University Review* 1:6 (1955), 6. O'Brien gives the year of her arrival at UCD as 1817, which is out regarding both century and year.
6. Kate O'Brien, *My Ireland* (London: B.T. Batsford Ltd., 1962), 117; "Shaw Productions in Ireland 1900–2009", 241.
7. Lennox Robinson, *Ireland's Abbey Theatre: A History 1899–1951* (London: Sidgwick and Jackson Ltd., 1951), 115.
8. Kate O'Brien, *My Ireland*, 117. Peter Gahan opens his Introduction to *Shaw and the Irish Literary Tradition* by citing this passage and discussing Kate O'Brien in relation to Bernard Shaw. See Peter Gahan, "Introduction", *SHAW: The Annual of Bernard Shaw Studies* 30, 1.
9. Paige Reynolds, "Spectacular Nostalgia: Modernism and Dramatic Form in Kate O'Brien's *Pray for the Wanderer*", Special Issue on Kate O'Brien, guest edited by Paige Reynolds, *Irish University Review* 48:1 (Spring/Summer 2018), 55.
10. Anthony Roche, "*The Ante-Room* as Drama", in *Ordinary People Dancing: Essays on Kate O'Brien*, edited by Eibhear Walshe (Cork: Cork University Press, 1993), 89. For the plays of Kate O'Brien, see James Moran, "Kate O'Brien in the Theatre", *Irish UniversityReview* (Spring/Summer 2018), 7–22.
11. Kate O'Brien, "U.C.D. as I Forget It", *University Review* 3:2 (1962), 10.
12. Ibid.,10.
13. Ibid.,7.
14. Kate O'Brien, "As to University Life", 6.
15. See James Joyce, *The Day of the Rabblement*, in *Occasional, Critical and Political Writing*, edited by Kevin Barry (Oxford and New York: Oxford University Press, 2000), pp. 50–2.
16. On the Irish Theatre, see William J. Feeney, *Drama in Hardwicke Street: A History of the Irish Theatre Company* (Cranbury, N.J., and London: Associated University Presses, 1984).
17. William J. Feeney, *Drama in Hardwicke Street: A History of the Irish Theatre Company* (London and Toronto: Associated University Presses, 1984), p. 163.
18. Ibid.,165.
19. See Anthony Roche, "Thomas MacDonagh's 1916: Protagonist and Playwright", *New Hibernia Review* 21:1 (Spring 2017), 18–40.
20. Kate O'Brien, "U.C.D. as I Forget It", 10.
21. Kate O'Brien, "As To University Life", 9.
22. Kate O'Brien, *My Ireland*, 117.

23. Ibid., 118.
24. Ibid., 118.
25. Bernard Shaw, "Preface for Politicians", *John Bull's Other Island*, in *Collected Plays and their Prefaces: Vol. 2*, 808.
26. In addition to regular professional Shaw productions from London starting in 1907, accomplished amateur companies under the direction of Anthony Evelyn Ashley and partner/wife Flora MacDonnell staged some noteworthy Shaw productions in Dublin. This started with a Shaw week in August 1907—the first ever such week in Dublin—performing *Arms and the Man*, *The Man of Destiny*, and *How He Lied to Her Husband* under the name of the Players' Club. Later, Ashley and MacDonnell staged *John Bull's Other Island* in October 1912 (with no company name), which coincided with the Home Rule Bill and the paper edition of the play in the same year, which was arranged to sell for six pennies. In 1913, Ashley and MacDonnell joined with Casimir Markievicz, forming the Dublin Repertory Theatre, to stage *The Devil's Disciple* in May, and revived their production of *John Bull's Other Island* in October. In November 1914, Ashley and MacDonnell staged *Mrs Warren's Profession* under the threat of censorship from Dublin Castle. All of the Ashley-MacDonnell-connected Shaw productions received much Dublin press coverage as all, except for *Mrs Warren's Profession*, were staged in week-long runs at the Gaiety Theatre. Judging from the coverage, these were successful Shaw productions and contributed to Shaw's presence in Dublin. See "Shaw and the Dublin Repertory Theatre" in *SHAW: The Journal of Bernard Shaw Studies, 35.2*, by Nelson O'Ceallaigh Ritschel, 2015.
27. See *The Collected Letters of W.B. Yeats: IV 1905–1907*, edited by John Kelly and Ronald Schuchard (Oxford: Oxford University Press, 2005), 632.
28. *The Arrow*, 25 August 1909 – "*The Shewing-Up of Blanco Posnet*: Statement by the Directors", in *The Collected Works of W.B. Yeats 8: The Irish Dramatic Movement*, edited by Mary Fitzgerald and Richard J. Finneran (New York and London: Scribner, 2003), 207–8.
29. *Joseph Holloway's Abbey Theatre: A Selection from his Unpublished Journal*, edited by Robert Hogan and Michael O'Neill (Carbondale and Edwardsville: Southern Illinois University Press, 1967), 130.
30. A visiting company (Jack Dwan's) presented a production of Shaw's *O'Flaherty V.C.* at the Abbey in 1927; it was the first occasion in all of those years on which Lady Gregory had to pay for her own seat. Two performances of the play were given by the Stage Society in London in late 1920. Arthur Sinclair and Sara Allgood played O'Flaherty and his mother; Shaw had written the parts specifically for them in 1915.
31. Letter from W.B. Yeats to St. John Ervine, 16 July 1916, cited in Robert Hogan and Richard Burnham, *The Art of the Amateur 1916–1920, The*

Modern Irish Drama: A Documentary History V (Dublin: The Dolmen Press; Atlantic Highlands, N.J.: Humanities Press Inc., 1984), 33.

32. Letter of Lady Gregory to Bernard Shaw, 12 August 1916, Nicholas Grene and Dan. H. Laurence (editors), *Shaw, Lady Gregory and the Abbey* (Gerrards Cross: Colin Smythe, 1993), 118.
33. Robert Hogan and Richard Burnham, *The Art of the Amateur 1916–1920*, 33.
34. *Shaw, Lady Gregory and the Abbey*, 118.
35. See Brad Kent "Missing Links: Bernard Shaw and the Discussion Play", in Nicholas Grene and Christopher Morash (editors), *The Oxford Handbook of Modern Irish Theatre* (Oxford: Oxford University Press, 2016), 147.
36. *Shaw, Lady Gregory and the Abbey*, 119.
37. Ibid.
38. Ibid., 122.
39. Cited in Richard Ellmann, *James Joyce: New and Revised Edition* (New York: Oxford University Press, 1982), 401.
40. Letter from J. Augustus Keogh to Lady Gregory, Robert Hogan and Richard Burnham, *The Art of the Amateur 1916–1920*, 34.
41. Ibid., 36.
42. Letter from Shaw to Lady Gregory, 4 May 1917, *Shaw, Lady Gregory and the Abbey*, 133.
43. Letter from Shaw to Lady Gregory, 28 April 1917, Shaw, Lady Gregory and the Abbey, 132.
44. Letter from Shaw to Lady Gregory, 28 April 1917, *Shaw, Lady Gregory and the Abbey*, 132.
45. See Brenna Katz Clarke and Harold Ferrar, *The Dublin Drama League 1919–1941* (Dublin: The Dolmen Press; Atlantic Highlands, N.J.: Humanities Press Inc., 1979), 31.
46. Joseph Holloway reported on this on the Tuesday, 24 August 1909 entry in his diary: "All the fuss that is being made over the production of Shaw's play tomorrow night drew a big house to-night to the re-opening of the Abbey with *The Playboy* and *The Rising of the Moon*… I had a chat with James Joyce who had been out of town for five years and had never been to the Abbey before. […] I again had a few words with him after Act 1 of *The Playboy*, which he said he liked in the acting. He thought [Fred] O'Donovan's Christy Mahon the true type intended by the author." *Joseph Holloway's Abbey Theatre*, 129. Joyce does not comment on O'Donovan's performance as Blanco Posnet in his coverage of Shaw's play. See James Joyce, "The Battle between Bernard Shaw and the Censor: 'The Shewing-Up of Blanco Posnet', *Occasional, Critical and Political Writing*, edited by Kevin Barry, translations from the Italian by Conor Deane (Oxford and New York: Oxford University Press, 2000), 152–4.

47. Hugh Hunt, *The Abbey: Ireland's National Theatre 1904–1978* (Dublin: Gill and Macmillan, 1979), 113. O'Donovan, who had directed the first full-length Irish film, *Knocknagow*, in 1916 wanted to return to working in film.
48. Kate O'Brien, *My Ireland*, 46.
49. Ibid.
50. Letter from Lady Gregory to Bernard Shaw, 12 August 1916, *Shaw, Lady Gregory and the Abbey*, 118.
51. Kate O'Brien, *My Ireland*, 47.
52. Bernard Shaw, *Back to Methuselah: A Metabiological Pentateuch, in Collected Plays and their Prefaces*: Volume 5 of the Bodley Head Bernard Shaw (London: Max Reinhardt, 1972) 491.
53. Ibid., 494.
54. Cited in Kate O'Brien, *My Ireland*, 45.
55. Bernard Shaw, *Back to Methuselah*, 496.
56. Kate O'Brien, *My Ireland*, 45.
57. Paige Reynolds, "Modernism and Dramatic Form in Kate O'Brien's *Pray for the Wanderer*", *Irish University Review* 48:1, 57.
58. Ibid.
59. See Ronan Fanning, *Eamon de Valera: A Will to Power* (London: Faber and Faber, 2015), 157: de Valera gained "complete of the control of the editorial content of the paper as well as over the appointment of all staff".
60. David Clare discusses Hector Malone Senior as an Irish Diasporic character in *Bernard Shaw's Irish Outlook* (Basingstoke, Hampshire: Palgrave Macmillan, 2016), 32.
61. Kate O'Brien, *My Ireland*, 116.
62. R. F. Foster, *Vivid Faces: The Revolutionary Generation in Ireland 1890–1923* (London: Penguin Books, 2015), 112.
63. As Diarmuid Ferriter points out, Kate O'Brien's autobiographical novel *Pray for the Wanderer* and its male protagonist were "scathing about de Valera and his Constitution". See Diarmuid Ferriter, *The Transformation of Ireland 1900–2000* (London: Profile Books, 2005), 370.

References

Clare, David. 2016. *Bernard Shaw's Irish Outlook*. New York: Palgrave Macmillan.
Clarke, Brenna Katz, and Harold Ferrar. 1979. *The Dublin Drama League 1919–1941*. Dublin/Atlantic Highlands: The Dolmen Press/Humanities Press Inc.
Ellmann, Richard. 1982. *James Joyce: New and Revised Edition*. New York: Oxford University Press.

Fanning, Ronan. 2015. *Eamon de Valera: A Will to Power*. London: Faber and Faber.

Feeney, William J. 1984. *Drama in Hardwicke Street: A History of the Irish Theatre Company*. Cranbury/London: Associated University Press.

Ferriter, Diarmuid. 2005. *The Transformation of Ireland 1900–2000*. London: Profile Books.

Foster, R.F. 2015. *Vivid Faces: The Revolutionary Generation in Ireland 1890–1923*. London: Penguin Books.

Gahan, Peter. 2010. Introduction. *Bernard Shaw and the Irish Literary Tradition. SHAW: The Annual of Bernard Shaw Studies* 30: 1–26. 1.

Grene, Nicholas, and Deirdre McFeely. 2010. Shaw Productions in Ireland, 1900–2009. *SHAW: The Annual of Bernard Shaw Studies* 30: 236–259.

Hogan, Robert, and Richard Burnham. 1984. *The Art of the Amateur 1916–1920, The Modern Irish Drama: A Documentary History V*. Dublin/Atlantic Highlands: The Dolmen Press/Humanities Press, Inc.

Holloway, Joseph. 1967. *Joseph Holloway's Irish Theatre: A Selection from His Unpublished Journal*. Ed. Robert Hogan and Michael O'Neill. Carbondale/Edwardsville: Southern Illinois University Press.

Hunt, Hugh. 1979. *The Abbey: Ireland's National Theatre 1904–1978*. Dublin: Gill and Macmillan.

Joyce, James. 2000a. *The Day of the Rabblement. Occasional, Critical and Political Writing*, 50–52. Ed. Kevin Barry. Oxford/New York: Oxford University Press.

———. 2000b. The Battle Between Bernard Shaw and the Censor: 'The Shewing-Up of Blanco Posnet'. *Occasional, Critical and Political Writing*, 152–154.

Kent, Brad. 2016. Missing Links: Bernard Shaw and the Discussion Play. In *The Oxford Handbook of Modern Irish Theatre*, ed. Nicholas Grene and Christopher Morash, 138–151., 147. Oxford: Oxford University Press.

Moran, James. 2018. Kate O'Brien in the Theatre. *Irish University Review* 48 (Spring/Summer): 7–22.

O'Brien, Kate. 1938. *Pray for the Wanderer*. London/Toronto: William Heinemann Ltd..

———. 1955. As To University Life. *University Review* 1 (6): 3–11. 6.

———. 1962. *My Ireland*, 241. London: B.T.Batsford Ltd.

———. 1963. U.C.D. as I Forget It. *University Review* 3 (2): 6–11. 7–10.

———. 1980. *The Last of Summer*. London: Virago Press.

Reynolds, Paige. 2018. Spectacular Nostalgia: Modernism and Dramatic Form in Kate O'Brien's *Pray for the Wanderer*. *Irish University Review* 48 (1 Spring/Summer): 54–68. 55.

Ritschel, NelsonO'Ceallaigh. 2015. Shaw and the Dublin Repertory Theatre. *SHAW: The Annual of Bernard Shaw Studies* 35 (2): 168–184.

Robinson, Lennox. 1951. *Ireland's Abbey Theatre: A History 1899–1951*, 115. London: Sidgwick and Jackson Ltd.

Roche, Anthony. 1993. *The Ante-Room* as Drama. *Ordinary People Dancing: Essays on Kate O'Brien*, 85–100. 89. Ed. Eibhear Walshe. Cork: Cork University Press.

———. 2017. Thomas MacDonagh's 1916: Protagonist and Playwright. *New Hibernia Review* 21 (1Spring): 18–40.

Shaw, Bernard. 1971a. *Man and Superman. Collected Plays and their Prefaces:* Volume 2 of the Bodley Head Bernard Shaw. Ed. Dan H. Laurence, 489–802. London: Max Reinhardt.

———. 1971b. Preface for Politicians. In *John Bull's Other Island. Collected Plays and their Prefaces:* Volume 2 of the Bodley Head Bernard Shaw, ed. Dan H. Laurence, 807–871. London: Max Reinhardt.

———. 1972. Part IV: Tragedy of an Elderly Gentleman. In *Back to Methuselah: A Metabiological Pentateuch. Collected Plays and Their Prefaces:* Volume 5 of the Bodley Head Bernard Shaw, ed. Dan H. Laurence, 491–563. London: Max Reinhardt.

Shaw, Bernard and Lady Gregory. 1983. *Shaw, Lady Gregory and the Abbey.* Ed. Nicholas Grene and Dan H. Laurence. Gerrards Cross: Colin Smythe.

Yeats, William Butler. 2003. *The Shewing-Up of Blanco Posnet:* Statement by the Directors. In *The Collected Works of W.B. Yeats 8: The Irish Dramatic Movement*, ed. Mary FitzGerald and Richard J. Finneran, 207–208. New York/London: Scribner.

———. 2005. *The Collected Letters of W.B. Yeats: IV 1905–1907.* Ed. John Kelly and Ronald Schuchard. Oxford: Oxford University Press.

CHAPTER 4

Shavian Echoes in the Work of Elizabeth Bowen

David Clare

When critics discuss Bernard Shaw's influence on twentieth-century Irish literature, they often concentrate on the Shavian elements found in the work of successful dramatists, including St. John Irvine, Seán O'Casey, Denis Johnston, Mary Manning, Teresa Deevy, Louis D'Alton, Brendan Behan, and Brian Friel. However, in recent years, critics have increasingly come to recognise that Shaw left a significant imprint on twentieth-century Irish *fiction* writers, as well. As Peter Gahan, Martha Fodaski Black, and other commentators have shown, James Joyce, Kate O'Brien, Frank O'Connor, Seán Ó Faoláin, and C.S. Lewis all owed a profound debt to Shaw.[1] Despite this new trend in the criticism, Shaw's influence on Elizabeth Bowen—one of Ireland's greatest novelists—has yet to be appropriately recognised. In this chapter, I will demonstrate that Shavian echoes can be heard in a number of Bowen's works. Bowen's interest in Shaw is evident from the fact that she openly refers to the playwright and

D. Clare (✉)
Mary Immaculate College, University of Limerick, Limerick, Ireland
e-mail: david.clare@mic.ul.ie

© The Author(s) 2020
A. McNamara, N. O'Ceallaigh Ritschel (eds.), *Bernard Shaw and the Making of Modern Ireland*, Bernard Shaw and His Contemporaries, https://doi.org/10.1007/978-3-030-42113-7_4

his work a number of times in her literary journalism.[2] However, it is also evident from her subtle allusions to his plays, prefaces, and essays throughout her oeuvre.

Critics could point to very obvious parallels between the work of Bernard Shaw and Elizabeth Bowen. For example, both writers frequently allude to Shakespeare and the King James Bible, and both openly admitted their debts to the novels of Charles Dickens.[3] Another obvious similarity is the frequent occurrence in their work of—in Frank O'Connor's words—"the *eternal triangle* of husband, wife and lover, or husband, wife and mistress."[4] In Shaw's case, his obsession with the *ménage á trois* has rightly been linked by critics (and by Shaw himself) to the *ménage* in his childhood home: the fact that his parents shared their Dublin residence with George John Vandaleur Lee, his mother's singing teacher (and possibly her lover). This, however, was not the only reason for Shaw's interest in the "eternal triangle." Like Bowen, Shaw was attracted to this character set-up due to his involvement in a chaste marriage. Shaw's marriage with Cork gentlewoman Charlotte Payne-Townshend was platonic, and this arguably led him to channel his sexual energies into emotional—and possibly physical—affairs with actresses.[5] Likewise, Elizabeth Bowen's relationship with her husband, Alan Cameron, was non-sexual, leading her to conduct affairs with Oxford academic Humphrey House, Cork writer Seán Ó Faoláin, Belgian-American lesbian poet May Sarton, and several others. (It is believed that Cameron was either incapable of sexual activity, due to a wound he received during the Great War, or—more likely—that he was gay; when House slept with Bowen in 1933, he was surprised to discover that she was still a virgin, despite having been married for ten years.)[6] Shaw and Bowen were both aware of the prevalence of the "eternal triangle" in their work.[7] While this is an interesting link between their oeuvres, it is not necessarily an instance of Shaw influencing Bowen. The mark that Shaw left on Bowen can be more definitively established by recognising and analysing the open references and the less obvious allusions to Shaw in her essays and fiction.

Bowen's 1946 essay "Ireland Makes Irish," first published in *Vogue*, is built around the idea that people who come to live in Ireland "for any length of time" take on Irish characteristics.[8] She adds:

> What has proved so winning, so holding [to visitors and invaders], is, I think, the manner of life here – life infused with a tempo and temperament bred of magic Irish light and the soft air.[9]

These ideas strongly echo those expressed by Shaw in his major Irish play, *John Bull's Other Island* (1904), in which he suggests that the Irish temperament is the product of the Irish climate, and that even people who come to live in Ireland for a short time become noticeably Irish.[10] In later Shaw works, such as the 1921 play *Tragedy of an Elderly Gentleman* (Part IV of the *Back to Methuselah* cycle) and the 1946 essay "Shaw Speaks to His Native City," he goes on to suggest that English people should be sent to Ireland for a spell, to help make their minds more "flexible."[11]

In Bowen's essay "Ireland Today," written—scholars believe—in 1952 or 1953, she once again links the Irish "temperament" to the Irish "climate."[12] She includes another Shavian observation in her analysis, as well, writing:

> The impulse to [emigrate from Ireland] … is not always mercenary; it may be ambitious – to do well in Ireland is to be reminded that probably, one could do better elsewhere. The clever, effective or restless person is likely to find his own small island claustrophobic.[13]

This strongly recalls Shaw's famous statements regarding the need for ambitious people to emigrate from Ireland. When discussing his own decision to leave Dublin for London in 1876, he frequently—like Bowen in this passage—linked it to a wider desire among highly motivated Irish people to leave the land of their birth. For example, in the autobiographical preface to the 1930 edition of his juvenile novel *Immaturity*, he writes:

> There was no Gaelic League in those days, nor any sense that Ireland had in herself the seed of culture. Every Irishman who felt that his business in life was on the higher planes of the cultural professions felt that he must have a metropolitan domicile and an international culture: that is, he felt that his first business was to get out of Ireland. I had the same feeling. For London, as London, or England as England, I cared nothing … But as the English language was my weapon, there was nothing for it but to go to London.[14]

The need for restless Irish people to emigrate is also associated with Shaw, because he built a whole play around the idea: *O'Flaherty, V.C.* (1917). In this play and its preface, Shaw tries to convince Irishmen to join the British Army during the Great War, but not by using conventional arguments. He appeals to every Irishman's love of "change and adventure," suggesting that O'Flaherty, in going to serve in France, has escaped the "discontent" that plagues many men who stay in Ireland—a discontent born of the "thwarted curiosity" and "deadly boredom" that maddens the ambitious Irishman and causes him to fall into an "ignorance and insularity [that] is a danger to himself and his neighbors."[15]

Bowen's 1941 essay "James Joyce," published in the Dublin journal *The Bell* (edited by Ó Faoláin), is one of the pieces of literary journalism in which she mentions a Shaw work directly. While discussing the role of humour in Joyce's fiction, she references the "cosmic devouring laughter," which is "most heard" in Ireland and which is potentially disturbing to people from other countries, especially the English. To support her point, she adds: "Remember, in *John Bull's Other Island*, how shocked the Englishman was when they all laughed when the poor pig died in the motor-crash."[16] Bowen has, of course, misremembered the play's plot. It is actually the Irish mystic (and friend to animals) Keegan who is disgusted by the townspeoples' laughter. That said, the Irish characters instinctively hide their laughter from the Englishman Broadbent. They do this, not simply because they want to keep him from realising that they are laughing at his poor driving skills; they also presumably believe that he might be shaken by their "cosmic devouring" levity.

While, in *John Bull's Other Island*, Shaw focusses more on the sinister side of Irish laughter (specifically, the degree to which it is infused with sneering and derision), Bowen saw it as simply a fact of life in Ireland, and—while certainly curious—not necessarily a cause for concern over the state of the nation's soul. A good example of her view of such laughter comes from *A World of Love*, Bowen's "underappreciated" novel from 1955, which is set in Co. Cork and at Shannon Airport.[17] In this work, one of the local Big House owners, the English Lady Latterly, wants to employ only severe and strict English retainers (indeed, her exacting standards mean that all of her Irish servants have already quit or given notice). By contrast, Antonia, the Irish Anglican owner of Montefort, another local Big House, employs an Irish Catholic servant named Kathie, who is full of mischief and fun. Kathie cheekily uses the satin that Jane, Antonia's niece, has thrown away in order to make a hat for herself, and (most importantly, for our discussion here) she explodes into convulsions of laughter when talking to Antonia about the unusual antics of Maud, Antonia's other niece. Bowen tells us that the laughter "convulsed" Kathie and that she actually "vomited laughter."[18] As an Irish woman, Antonia is relatively non-plussed at hearing such laughter from a servant, and is not even particularly put out when Kathie follows up the laughter with some arguably impertinent remarks. By contrast, Lillia—the English mother of Jane and Maud—distrusts Kathie and disparages her work, and one gets the sense that she would be just as negative about such lack of decorum from an Irish servant as her countrywoman Lady Latterly would be.

The inclusion of "cosmic devouring laughter" is not the only link between *A World of Love* and Shaw's work. During the scene at Lady Latterly's dinner party, the only two Irish guests, Terence and Jane, get into conversation, discussing (among other topics) Jane's deceased and dashing cousin, Guy. Terence and Jane gradually become isolated from the rest of the table as the English guests increasingly ignore them. As the party winds down, Bowen observes, "outside waited the stilly night."[19] This is an allusion to Thomas Moore, who, like Terence and Jane, was ultimately alone (that is, not fully accepted) in the English drawing-rooms where he sang songs like his own "Oft in the Stilly Night" (1816).[20] The song's lyric captures the social isolation experienced by Terence and Jane in the lines, "I feel like one, / Who treads alone / Some banquet-hall deserted, / Whose lights are fled,/ Whose garland's dead, / And all but he departed." The lyric's chorus, with its concluding lines "Sad memory brings the light / Of other days around me," alludes to the subject of Terence and Jane's conversation: that is, memories of times when the Irish Ascendancy (to which Terence and Jane both belong) and Jane's cousin Guy were still alive.[21] In keeping with the gothic ghostliness of Moore's song, Jane later thinks that she sees Guy's ghost appear in the empty seat across from her at Lady Latterly's table.

Bowen's sympathetic use of Moore here and her positive treatment of him in her history of Dublin's Shelbourne Hotel echo Shaw's respect for Moore and his best-known work, *Irish Melodies* (published in ten instalments between 1808 and 1834).[22] In a letter, Shaw calls Moore "a real poet," and, in the preface to *John Bull's Other Island*, he calls Moore's lyric, "The Minstrel Boy" (1813), "visionary."[23] The regard for Moore shared by Shaw and Bowen stands in stark contrast to the disrespect repeatedly aimed at the once celebrated "Bard of Erin" by W.B. Yeats and James Joyce throughout their careers.[24] For a long time, Yeats and Joyce strongly influenced Irish critical opinion of Moore; in recent years, however, critics have increasingly come to share Shaw and Bowen's appreciation for Moore's lyrics and for his brave work as a cultural ambassador for Ireland in England.[25]

The social isolation that overtakes Terence and Jane at Lady Latterly's party can arguably be traced back to a moment early on in their conversation when "Terence's eyes consulted Jane's" just before he "pinched [a] moth to death." Bowen continues: "Talk … stopped: everyone was aware of the old assassin wiping his fingers off on the sheeny napkin."[26] This episode paints Terence and Jane as conspirators, and their marginalised nationality is referenced in Bowen's use of the word "sheeny," recalling the pejorative term for a Jewish person. This scene can be liked to Bowen's sympathetic depiction of the Jewish character, Max, in her novel *The House in Paris* (1935)—a novel set in England, France, and Ireland in which Bowen highlights the condescending attitudes of the English characters to Jews like Max but also to the Irish character, Bill Bent. The English Mrs. Michaelis dismissively says of Max, "There is always that touch—Jewish perhaps—of womanishness about him."[27] As regards Bill, we are told that the Michaelis family are "amusing, though not unkind" about "this hysterical little man" who is married to their Aunt Violet. And we later learn that for the Michaelis family, "the idea of … Violet in Ireland [had always] made them uncomfortable; it seemed insecure and pointless, as though she had chosen to settle on a raft."[28] Bowen's linking of the Jews and the Irish in *A World of Love* and *The House in Paris* strongly recalls Shaw's groundbreaking tendency to do the same throughout his work. In *John Bull's Other Island*, Larry Doyle says: "We Irishmen were never made to be farmers; and we'll never do any good at it. We're like the Jews: the Almighty gave us brains, and bid us farm them and leave the clay and the worms alone."[29] In *Man and Superman* (1903), the Irishman Malone is a shareholder in the Jew Mendoza's firm of brigands, and, in *The Doctor's Dilemma* (1906), the Irishman Sir Patrick Cullen and the Jew Leo Schutzmacher are the only two doctors who are not taken in by Louis Dubedat's lies. In *You Never Can Tell* (1898), the Irish Disaporic character, Fergus Crampton (who is based on real-life Irish diplomat, Sir John Crampton), is compared by Valentine to "a Jew," and in *Tragedy of an Elderly Gentleman*, Shaw suggests that the world would be "a tame dull place" without "its Jews and its Irish."[30]

The Shavian influence on *The House in Paris* may also possibly extend to the scene on the boat, in which Karen Michaelis is returning to Britain after visiting Bill Bent and Aunt Violent at their home in Cobh, Co. Cork. The scene eventually turns into a comic two-hander between the English Karen, who plays the "straight person," and a lively, young, Roman Catholic, Cork woman, who plays the "comic" role and who Karen refers to internally as "Yellow Hat."[31] Karen's unrelenting stiffness and Yellow Hat's inappropriate forwardness in this scene bear a striking resemblance to the roles played by A and Z on the lounge deck of the Empress of Patagonia in Shaw's 1934 play *Village Wooing*. I have been unable to determine if Bowen attended the first English production of *Village Wooing* at Tunbridge Wells in May 1934 or the first London production at the Little Theatre in the Adelphi later that summer (starring Sybil Thorndike as Z and Arthur Wontner as A). However, even if she did not, she may well have read the play as she worked on *The House in Paris*. (*Village Wooing* was first published on 15 February 1934, a year and a half before Bowen's novel appeared on 26 August 1935.)

A World of Love and *The House in Paris* are not the only Bowen novels influenced by Bernard Shaw's work. As Douglas Mao has shown, *The Last September* (1929) and Shaw's *Heartbreak House*(1919) are just two of many Anglophone works that appeared between the world wars that depict "pre-catastrophic experience"—that is, that evoke life in the time period leading up to a cataclysmic event.[32] Mao sees this tendency among interwar writers as arising from their belief that "the Great War … [was a] false or incomplete apocalypse" and that a more "authentic apocalypse [was bound] to come" in the not-too-distant future.[33] In *The Last September*, the shattering event at the work's end is the destruction of Danielstown, a Cork Big House which is burned by rebels during the Irish War of Independence. In Shaw's play, it is the bombing during a world war of Heartbreak House, an estate in north Sussex. In an essay about her own north Cork Big House, entitled "Bowen's Court, 1958," Bowen discusses Shaw's analysis of European Big Houses in the preface to *Heartbreak House*.[34] Given Bowen's clear awareness of—and interest in— *Heartbreak House*, it seems likely that when writing her "pre-catastrophic" Big House novel *The Last September*, she was at least partially inspired by Shaw's "pre-catastrophic" Big House play. The most striking similarity between the two works is the unsuccessful attempts by the aristocratic characters to ignore the socio-political circumstances threatening their very existence. Bowen, in the novel, alludes to the tendency among the Irish Ascendancy to deliberately "not notice" political foment, while Shaw suggests through his play's repeated references to sleep—including, most obviously, the name Hushabye and Mangan's hypnotic sleep—that the British aristocracy are not awake to their impending doom.[35]

Another important link between Shaw's work and *The Last September* is one noted elsewhere by the present writer: that is, the influence that Shaw's characterisation of Tom Broadbent, the Stage Englishman in *John Bull's Other Island*, had on the characterisation of Gerald Lesworth, the main Stage English figure in Bowen's novel. As I have shown in my monograph *Bernard Shaw's Irish Outlook* (2016), over the past two-and-a-half centuries, there has been a tendency in Irish literature to depict English people as either "racist, officious hypocrites" or "sentimental, romantic duffers," and Shaw, in *John Bull's Other Island*, broke new ground by creating a Stage English character—Broadbent—who combines these two traditional Stage English types. As I also note during my analysis, Bowen followed in Shaw's footsteps by creating Gerald, a character who is similarly a combination of "racist, officious hypocrite" and "sentimental, romantic duffer."[36]

Gerald, however, was not the first Broadbent-influenced character created by Bowen. The unnamed Englishman at the centre of Bowen's 1926 short story "The Back Drawing-Room" is also a combination of the two traditional Stage English types. "The Back Drawing-Room" contains an Irish story within an English one. It starts at a party in England, at which intellectuals are debating various subjects in a pompous, knowing tone. Bowen, never happy herself in such atmospheres, scathingly and comically mocks the guests by commenting (as narrator) that before the story opened "the conversation … had veered dangerously near the comprehensible" until it was rescued by the entrance of the ever-vague and universally respected Mrs. Henneker. When the subject turns to spiritualism, it arouses the interest of a "little fair, plump man," who most of the gathered intellectuals regard disdainfully because he sits "modestly and unintelligently … looking propped up and a little dejected, like an umbrella that an absent-minded caller has brought into the drawing-room." When the subject turns to ghosts, he cannot resist sharing a "ghost story" that he experienced personally while visiting a cousin in Ireland.[37] His interruption of the intellectual discourse is quite abrupt and lowers the tone of the conversation, and there are many rude attempts by the guests to interrupt his story until its inherent suspense finally captivates those listening.

As this unnamed storyteller recounts his experiences in Ireland, Bowen ensures that his descriptions of his often comical misadventures betray not just his racist condescension towards the Irish but also his naively sentimental regard for the country. His racism and his preference for "English" correctness, efficiency, and propriety manifest themselves in his various criticisms of Ireland and the Irish. He disparages Irish roads and the botched attempt to repair them by the government, he laments the lack of central heating, and he notes the unfashionable thickness of Irish lace curtains. He is also worried, upon entering an Irish Big House uninvited, that "anybody seeing me might suddenly [shoot] me, in their impulsive, simple way."[38] (It is unclear if it is the aristocratic Irish Big House owners or the Irish servants who are the possessors, in his English eyes, of "impulsive, simple ways," though one strongly senses that this Englishman makes no distinction.)

His romantic, sentimentality manifests itself in his Broadbent-like reflections on the melancholy and "beauty" of the Irish landscape and on Irish "hospitality," as well as his appreciation of the "unconventionality" of the Irish.[39] That said, his Stage English hypocrisy is directly linked to the Irish "unconventionality" that he professes to admire but that, as an Englishman, he claims not to share: in the presumed vacuum of convention that is Ireland, he happily abandons his English propriety and boldly asserts his own personal agenda at all times while in Ireland—even at the risk of acting "unconventionally" himself. Like Broadbent not letting "the right side of [his] brain know what the left side doeth" (lest his previously articulated principles stop him from obtaining something he wants), Bowen's Stage Englishman drops his English propriety and not only enters the Big House uninvited; he also proceeds into a back drawing-room where a "tall and pretty" young woman is crying, despite the fact that he is aware that it is "quite an intimate room, where I believe only favoured visitors are usually admitted."[40]

The Stage Englishman's "duffer" nature is revealed through his frequent, Broadbent-like social faux pas, not only during the scenes at the English party, but also during the scene in the back drawing-room. He says to the crying young woman, with a Stage English fear of emotion, "My dear lady ... really, my dear lady!," brusquely encouraging her to pull herself together; it is certainly not the amorous (or simply socially successful) encounter he was presumably hoping for.[41] Then again, since this is one of Bowen's gothic short stories, there was never any chance of the Stage Englishman having a proper interaction with the young woman: when he gets back to his cousin's house, he finds out that the Big House he claims to have visited was actually burned down by rebels two years previously and that the young woman and her family are currently living in either Dublin or England.

Maud Ellmann, in her outstanding study *Elizabeth Bowen: The Shadow Across the Page* (2004), has rightly noted that Shaw's *Pygmalion* (1913) is an important influence on Bowen's last novel, *Eva Trout* (1968). Ellmann writes:

> In Shaw's version of the [Pygmalion] story, Henry Higgins uses elocution
> lessons to animate his Galatea, transforming a Cockney flower-seller into a
> passable imitation of a duchess. Similarly Iseult [the schoolteacher in *Eva
> Trout*] teaches speech to [the orphan] Eva, who is often described as a
> statue, in order to release her soul from its prison of stone.[42]

Eva, despite coming from a rich family, was educated erratically, and
Iseult's ultimately failed attempt to teach her how to speak articulately and
to think in an orderly way is not the only link between Shaw's most famous
play and Bowen's final novel. The mission to get Eva to behave in a way
worthy of her inherited wealth and in a way that will not limit her ability
to realise her ambitions in life is overseen not just by Iseult but also by her
legal guardian, Constantine—her deceased, homosexual father's former
lover. This set-up is clearly meant to mirror the triangle of Eliza Doolittle,
Henry Higgins (the teacher of language), and Colonel Pickering (the person bankrolling the "experiment"), especially since Constantine oversees
Eva's monetary affairs until her trust fund matures when she is twenty-
five.[43] Given that *Eva Trout* is a novel heavily concerned with queer sexuality,[44] Bowen's use of *Pygmalion* as an intertext may indicate that she shared
Fintan O'Toole's belief that the "confirmed bachelor" Higgins is a clos-
eted homosexual. (O'Toole cites Higgins's interest in "dressing Eliza"
and his private collection of Japanese kimonos.)[45]

As we have seen, Bowen's engagement with Shaw's work can be
detected in both her fiction and her journalism. And his influence on her
should come as little surprise. Between Shaw's winning of the Nobel Prize
for Literature in 1925 and his death in 1950, he was one of the most
famous people in the world, and, during the twentieth century, he was
"the most frequently performed dramatist after Shakespeare."[46] It is therefore only to be expected that an Irish writer like Bowen would have
explored his plays, prefaces, and essays and (consciously or unconsciously)
incorporated them into her own. As Graham Price has shown, Brian Friel
attempted to suppress his debt to Shaw (and Wilde) out of what Harold
Bloom calls "the anxiety of influence"—that is, the tendency among
authors to disown, disparage, or misinterpret writers they fear have had
too big an influence on their work.[47] Undoubtedly, this same anxiety has
kept many Irish writers from appropriately advertising their debt to Shaw.
I am convinced that further critical study will reveal that many more twentieth-century Irish writers were influenced by Shaw than has traditionally
been credited.

NOTES

1. For Black and Gahan's work linking Shaw and Joyce, see Martha Fodaski Black. *Shaw and Joyce: "The Last Word in Stolentelling."* Gainesville: UP of Florida, 1995; Peter Gahan *Shaw Shadows: Rereading the Texts of Bernard Shaw.* Gainesville: UP of Florida, 2004. 85–6, 260, 273; Peter Gahan. "Introduction. *Bernard Shaw and the Irish Literary Tradition.*" *SHAW: The Annual of Bernard Shaw Studies* 30 (2010): 1–26. 2–3. For Shaw's seismic impact on a young Kate O'Brien, see Eibhear Walshe. *Kate O'Brien: A Writing Life.* Dublin: Irish Academic Press, 2006. 23. For Frank O'Connor's keen interest in Shaw's work (especially *Saint Joan* and *Candida*), see Michael Steinman. *Frank O'Connor at Work.* Syracuse: Syracuse UP, 1990. 125–126; Frank O'Connor. *The Art of the Theatre.* Dublin: Maurice Fridberg, 1947. 34–36; Frank O'Connor. *Leinster, Munster and Connaught.* London: Robert Hale, 1950. 47–50; Frank O'Connor. *The Road to Stratford.* London: Methuen, 1948. 64. For a critic demonstrating that Shaw was a big influence on Seán Ó Faoláin's conception of himself as a public intellectual, see Brad Kent. "Bernard Shaw, Sean O'Faolain, and the Irish Public Intellectual," *Irish University Review* 47.2 (2017): 331–349. For important links between Shaw's work and C.S. Lewis's, see David Clare. *Bernard Shaw's Irish Outlook.* New York: Palgrave Macmillan, 2016. 60, 64–65, 110, 171; John Aquino. "Shaw and C.S. Lewis's *Space Trilogy,*" *Shaw Review* 18.1 (1975): 28–32.
2. For Bowen's reflections on Shaw and his work in her literary journalism, see Elizabeth Bowen. "Pictures and Conversation." *The Mulberry Tree: Writings of Elizabeth Bowen.* Ed. Hermione Lee. London: Virago, 1986. 265–98. 276; Elizabeth Bowen. "James Joyce." *Elizabeth Bowen's Selected Irish Writings.* Ed. Eibhear Walshe. Cork: Cork UP, 2011. 69–75. 71; Elizabeth Bowen. "Review of *James Joyce's Dublin*, by Patricia Hutchins." *Elizabeth Bowen's Selected Irish Writings.* Ed. Eibhear Walshe. Cork: Cork UP, 2011. 186–8. 187; Elizabeth Bowen. "Bowen's Court, 1958." *Elizabeth Bowen's Selected Irish Writings.* Ed. Eibhear Walshe. Cork: Cork UP, 2011. 188–97. 194; Elizabeth Bowen. "Review of *Ellen Terry and Bernard Shaw: A Correspondence* edited by Christopher St. John, *The River Line* by Charles Morgan, and *Parson Austen's Daughter* by Helen Ashton." *Tatler & Bystander* 193 (10 Aug. 1949): 236–237.
3. For Bowen pointing out her debt to Dickens, see Elizabeth Bowen. "Frankly Speaking: Interview, 1959." *Listening in: Broadcasts, Speeches, and Interviews.* Ed. Allan Hepburn. Edinburgh: Edinburgh UP, 2010. 323–343. 328. For Shaw admitting that he "lift[ed] characters bodily out of the pages of Charles Dickens," see Bernard Shaw. *Back to Methuselah.* London: Penguin, 1990. 8.

4. Frank O'Connor. *Mirror in the Roadway: A Study of the Modern Novel.* New York: Knopf, 1956. 206. Emphasis mine.

5. As Michael Holroyd has noted, "Charlotte had an apprehension of sexual intercourse", so the couple engaged in "careful sexual experience" during the first eighteen months of their marriage. (Michael Holroyd. *Bernard Shaw: The One-Volume Definitive Edition.* London: Vintage, 1998. 247.) However, in time, the relationship became an "affectionate" but "platonic" friendship, as well as a close working partnership. (Paul Kozelka. Foreword to *Four Plays by Bernard Shaw.* New York: Washington Square Press/Simon & Schuster, 1968. xi.) Indeed, throughout the marriage, Charlotte provided Shaw with steadfast, invaluable support—both practical (e.g. preparing his plays for the press) and emotional.

6. Maud Ellmann. *Elizabeth Bowen: The Shadow Across the Page.* Edinburgh: Edinburgh UP, 2004. 32.

7. Shaw plays that prominently feature love triangles include (among others) *Candida* (1894), *Arms and the Man* (1894), *The Man of Destiny* (1897), *The Philanderer* (1898), *John Bull's Other Island* (1904), *How He Lied to Her Husband* (1904), *The Doctor's Dilemma* (1906), *Heartbreak House* (1919), and—after a fashion—*Man and Superman* (1903). For love triangles (and other triangular structures) in Shaw's work, see Fredric Berg. "Structure and Philosophy in *Man and Superman* and *Major Barbara.*" *The Cambridge Companion to George Bernard Shaw.* Ed. Christopher Innes. Cambridge: Cambridge UP, 1998. 144–161. It should be noted that, in this study, the dates used for each Shaw play refer to either the first publication or the first production, whichever came first (and either of which might be some time after the script's composition). Shaw sometimes published his plays in book form or in periodicals before he was able to get them produced, especially early in his career.

Bowen works that prominently feature love triangles include (among others) "Requiescat" (1923), *Friends and Relations* (1931), *The House in Paris* (1935), "Summer Night" (1941), *The Heat of the Day* (1948), and—after a fashion—"A Love Story" (1941). For love triangles in the work of Bowen, see Ellmann, *Elizabeth Bowen: The Shadow Across the Page,* Chapter Three.

8. Elizabeth Bowen. "Ireland Makes Irish." *Elizabeth Bowen's Selected Irish Writings.* Ed. Eibhear Walshe. Cork: Cork UP, 2011. 126–131. 126.

9. Bowen, "Ireland Makes Irish," 126.

10. Bernard Shaw. *John Bull's Other Island.* London: Penguin, 1984. 11, 80–82.

11. Shaw, *Back to Methuselah,* 194; Bernard Shaw. "Shaw Speaks to His Native City (1946)." In *The Matter with Ireland.* Ed. Dan H. Laurence and David H. Greene. 2nd ed. Gainesville: UP of Florida, 2001. 334–8. 337. The

notion that the Irish have flexible minds is also present in Shaw's *O'Flaherty V.C.* (1917), in which Mrs. O'Flaherty "turns threateningly to her son with one of those sudden Irish changes of manner which amaze and scandalize less *flexible* nations." (Bernard Shaw. *Selected Short Plays*. New York: Penguin, 1987. 268. Emphasis mine.)

12. Elizabeth Bowen. "Ireland Today." *Listening in: Broadcasts, Speeches, and Interviews*. Ed. Allan Hepburn. Edinburgh: Edinburgh UP, 2010. 116–129. 117.

13. Bowen, "Ireland Today," 121.

14. As quoted in Bernard Shaw. *An Autobiography 1856–1898*. Ed. Stanley Weintraub. New York: Reinhardt, 1970. 75.

15. Shaw, *Selected Short Plays*, 256.

16. Bowen, "James Joyce," 71.

17. Neil Corcoran. *Elizabeth Bowen: The Enforced Return*. Oxford: Oxford UP, 2004. 62.

18. Elizabeth Bowen. *A World of Love*. London: Vintage, 1999. 123; 124.

19. Bowen, *A World of Love*, 67.

20. I am referring to the fact that Moore was repeatedly passed over for preferment and patronage by his powerful, English friends, which eventually resulted in his adopting an "avowedly self-determining position" with regard to his career and income. (Ronan Kelly. *Bard of Erin: The Life of Thomas Moore*. London: Penguin, 2008. 228.)

21. Thomas Moore. *The Poetical Works of Thomas Moore*. London: Longman, 1860. 148.

22. Elizabeth Bowen. *The Shelbourne Hotel*. New York: Knopf, 1951. 19, 79, 128.

23. Bernard Shaw. *Collected Letters, 1926–1950*. Ed. Dan H. Laurence. New York: Viking Penguin, 1988. 832; Shaw, *John Bull's Other Island*, 12.

24. For Yeats's negative feelings towards Moore, see Kelly, *Bard of Erin*, 198, 556–557. For a discussion of Joyce's various disrespectful remarks regarding Moore in his fiction, see Kelly, *Bard of Erin*, 556. It should be noted that Kelly detects a degree of playful "affection" beneath these memorable jibes.

25. For recent scholarship on Moore, see, for example, Francesca Benatti, Seán Ryder, and Justin Tonra, eds. *Thomas Moore: Texts, Contexts, Hypertext*. Oxford: Peter Lang, 2013.

26. Bowen, *A World of Love*, 67.

27. Elizabeth Bowen. *The House in Paris*. New York: Anchor, 2002. 124.

28. Bowen, *The House in Paris*, 74; 75.

29. Shaw, *John Bull's Other Island*, 120.

30. Bernard Shaw. *Plays Pleasant*. Harmondsworth: Penguin, 1949. 238; Shaw, *Back to Methuselah*, 206. Shaw also memorably links the Irish and

the Jews in his brilliant 1896 review of Dion Boucicault's *The Colleen Bawn* (1864). (See Bernard Shaw. "Dear Harp of my Country!" *The Portable Shaw*. Ed. Stanley Weintraub. New York: Penguin, 1986. 111–116. 114.)

For Sir John Crampton as a model for Fergus Crampton, see Clare, *Bernard Shaw's Irish Outlook*, 34–36.

31. Bowen, *The House in Paris*, 93.
32. Douglas Mao. "Our Last September: Climate Change in Modernist Time." *The Contemporaneity of Modernism: Literature, Media, Culture.* Eds. Michael D'Arcy and Mathias Nilges. New York and Abingdon: Routledge, 2016. 31–48. 34.
33. Mao, "Our Last September," 33. It should be noted that, although *Heartbreak House* was first published in 1919 and first performed in 1920, Shaw wrote the play between 1913 and 1919, with compelling evidence suggesting that it was effectively completed by late 1917. (See Stanley Weintraub and Anne Wright. Introduction to *Heartbreak House: A Facsimile of the Revised Typescript*. By Bernard Shaw. New York: Garland Publishing, 1981. xiv–xx.) As such, Shaw effectively wrote the play *during* the war—that is, before he could have known whether or not the conflict would prove to be an "incomplete apocalypse."
34. Bowen, "Bowen's Court, 1958," 194.
35. Elizabeth Bowen. *The Last September*. London: Vintage, 1998. 82. For *Heartbreak House* as—at least on some level—an Irish Big House play, see Audrey McNamara. "Longford Productions, Bernard Shaw, and the Irish Big House." *The Gate Theatre, Dublin: Inspiration and Craft*. Eds. David Clare, Des Lally, and Patrick Lonergan. Dublin: Carysfort Press/Oxford: Peter Lang, 2018. 181–192; David Clare. "Landlord-Tenant (Non) Relations in the Work of Bernard Shaw," *SHAW: The Journal of Bernard Shaw Studies* 36.1 (2016): 124–141. 133–136.
36. See Chapter Four of Clare, *Bernard Shaw's Irish Outlook*.
37. Elizabeth Bowen. "The Back Drawing-Room." *Collected Stories*. London: Vintage, 1999. 199–210. 200.
38. Bowen, "The Back Drawing-Room," 207.
39. Bowen, "The Back Drawing-Room," 204; 205; 205, 206.
40. Bowen, "The Back Drawing-Room," 207; 208.
41. Bowen, "The Back Drawing-Room," 208.
42. Ellmann, *Elizabeth Bowen: The Shadow Across the Page*, 216.
43. Bernard Shaw. *Pygmalion*. New York: Dover, 1994. 16.
44. In addition to the homosexual affair between Eva's father and Constantine, it is suggested that Eva is bisexual, since she falls in love with both women (Iseult and Elsinore) and men (Henry).

45. Fintan O'Toole. "Shaw Was an Anarchist: Where is all the Chaos?" *Irish Times* 14 May 2011. B9.
46. Meena Sodhi. *Shaw's* Candida: *A Critical Introduction*. New Delhi: Atlantic, 1999. 22.
47. Graham Price. "An Accurate Description of What Has Never Occurred: Brian Friel's *Faith Healer* and Wildean Intertextuality," *Irish University Review* 41.2 (Autumn/Winter 2011): 93–111. 94–95.

REFERENCES

Aquino, John. 1975. Shaw and C.S. Lewis's *Space Trilogy*. *Shaw Review* 18 (1): 28–32.

Benatti, Francesca, Seán Ryder, and Justin Tonra, eds. 2013. *Thomas Moore: Texts, Contexts, Hypertext*. Oxford: Peter Lang.

Berg, Frederic. 1998. Structure and Philosophy in *Man and Superman* and *Major Barbara*. In *The Cambridge Companion to George Bernard Shaw*, ed. Christopher Innes, 144–161. Cambridge: Cambridge University Press.

Bowen, Elizabeth. 1949. *Review of Ellen Terry and Bernard Shaw: A Correspondence* edited by Christopher St. John, *The River Line* by Charles Morgan, and *Parson Austen's Daughter* by Helen Ashton. *Tatler & Bystander* 193: 236–237.

———. 1951. *The Shelbourne Hotel*. New York: Knopf.

———. 1986. Pictures and Conversation. In *The Mulberry Tree: Writings of Elizabeth Bowen*, ed. Hermione Lee, 265–298. London: Virago.

———. 1998. *The Last September*. London: Vintage.

———. 1999a. The Back Drawing-Room. In *Collected Stories*, 199–210. London: Vintage.

———. 1999b. *A World of Love*. London: Vintage.

———. 2002. *The House in Paris*. New York: Anchor.

———. 2010a. Frankly Speaking: Interview, 1959. In *Listening in: Broadcasts, Speeches, and Interviews*, ed. Allan Hepburn, 323–343. Edinburgh: Edinburgh University Press.

———. 2010b. Ireland Today. In *Listening in: Broadcasts, Speeches, and Interviews*, ed. Allan Hepburn, 116–129. Edinburgh: Edinburgh University Press.

———. 2011a. Bowen's Court, 1958. In *Elizabeth Bowen's Selected Irish Writings*, ed. Eibhear Walshe, 188–197. Cork: Cork University Press.

———. 2011b. Ireland Makes Irish. In *Elizabeth Bowen's Selected Irish Writings*, ed. Eibhear Walshe, 126–131. Cork: Cork University Press.

———. 2011c. James Joyce. In *Elizabeth Bowen's Selected Irish Writings*, ed. Eibhear Walshe, 69–75. Cork: Cork University Press.

———. 2011d. Review of *James Joyce's Dublin*, by Patricia Hutchins. In *Elizabeth Bowen's Selected Irish Writings*, ed. Eibhear Walshe, 186–188. Cork: Cork University Press.

Clare, David. 2016a. Landlord-Tenant (Non)Relations in the Work of Bernard Shaw. *SHAW: The Journal of Bernard Shaw Studies* 36 (1): 124–141.

———. 2016b. *Bernard Shaw's Irish Outlook*. New York: Palgrave Macmillan.

Corcoran, Neil. 2004. *Elizabeth Bowen: The Enforced Return*. Oxford: Oxford University Press.

Ellmann, Maud. 2004. *Elizabeth Bowen: The Shadow Across the Page*. Edinburgh: Edinburgh University Press.

Fodaski Black, Martha. 1995. *Shaw and Joyce: "The Last Word in Stolentelling"*. Gainesville: University Press of Florida.

Gahan, Peter. 2004. *Shaw Shadows: Rereading the Texts of Bernard Shaw*. Gainesville: University Press of Florida.

———. 2010. Introduction. *Bernard Shaw and the Irish Literary Tradition*. *SHAW: The Annual of Bernard Shaw Studies* 30: 1–26. Print.

Holroyd, Michael. 1998. *Bernard Shaw: The One-Volume Definitive Edition*. London: Vintage.

Kelly, Ronan. 2008. *Bard of Erin: The Life of Thomas Moore*. London: Penguin.

Kent, Brad. 2017. Bernard Shaw, Sean O'Faolain, and the Irish Public Intellectual. *Irish University Review* 47 (2): 331–349.

Kozelka, Paul. 1968. *Foreword to Four Plays by Bernard Shaw*. New York: Washington Square Press/Simon & Schuster.

Mao, Douglas. 2016. Our Last September: Climate Change in Modernist Time. In *The Contemporaneity of Modernism: Literature, Media, Culture*, ed. Michael D'Arcy and Mathias Nilges, 31–48. New York/Abingdon: Routledge. Print.

McNamara, Audrey. 2018. Longford Productions, Bernard Shaw, and the Irish Big House. In *The Gate Theatre, Dublin: Inspiration and Craft*, ed. David Clare, Des Lally, and Patrick Lonergan, 181–192. Dublin: Carysfort Press/Oxford: Peter Lang.

Moore, Thomas. 1860. *The Poetical Works of Thomas Moore*. London: Longman.

O'Connor, Frank. 1947. *The Art of the Theatre*. Dublin: Maurice Fridberg.

———. 1948. *The Road to Stratford*. London: Methuen.

———. 1950. *Leinster, Munster and Connaught*. London: Robert Hale.

———. 1956. *Mirror in the Roadway: A Study of the Modern Novel*. New York: Knopf.

O'Toole, Fintan. 2011. Shaw Was an Anarchist: Where Is all the Chaos? *Irish Times* 14 May: B9.

Price, Graham. 2011. An Accurate Description of What Has Never Occurred: Brian Friel's *Faith Healer* and Wildean Intertextuality. *Irish University Review* 41 (2): 93–111.

Shaw, Bernard. 1949. *Plays Pleasant*. Harmondsworth: Penguin.

———. 1970. *An Autobiography 1856–1898*. Ed. Stanley Weintraub. New York: Reinhardt.

———. 1984. *John Bull's Other Island*. London: Penguin.

———. 1986. Dear Harp of my Country! In *The Portable Shaw*, ed. Stanley Weintraub, 111–116. New York: Penguin.

———. 1987. *Selected Short Plays*. New York: Penguin.

———. 1988. *Collected Letters, 1926–1950*. Ed. Dan H. Laurence. New York: Viking Penguin.

———. 1990. *Back to Methuselah*. London: Penguin.

———. 1994. *Pygmalion*. New York: Dover.

———. 2001. Shaw Speaks to His Native City (1946). In *The Matter with Ireland*, ed. Dan H. Laurence and David H. Greene, 2nd ed., 334–338. Gainesville: University Press of Florida.

Sodhi, Meena. 1999. *Shaw's Candida: A Critical Introduction*. New Delhi: Atlantic.

Steinman, Michael. 1990. *Frank O'Connor at Work*. Syracuse: Syracuse University Press.

Walshe, Eibhear. 2006. *Kate O'Brien: A Writing Life*. Dublin: Irish Academic Press.

Weintraub, Stanley, and AnneWright. 1981. Introduction to *Heartbreak House: A Facsimile of The Revised Typescript*. By Bernard Shaw. New York: Garland.

CHAPTER 5

"An Incorrigible Propensity for Preaching": Shaw and His Clergy

Elizabeth Mannion

On the evening of November 1, 1913, while Irish General Transport Workers' Union (IGTWU) leader James Larkin was incarcerated in Dublin's Mountjoy prison, a rally on behalf of the union was underway at the Royal Albert Hall in London. The Hall seated approximately 8000 people, and the *Observer* reported in the next day's paper that "practically every seat in the vast auditorium was occupied" in support of the rank-and-file and Larkin, who was in the early days of a seven-month sentence for seditious language.[1] The Irish workers had gone on strike August 26, following a concentrated effort by William Martin Murphy to prevent the IGTWU from making his Tramways Company a union shop. Murphy had demanded his employees not to join the IGTWU and turned out anyone who had either already joined or refused to agree not to do so in the future.[2] Other businesses signed on to Murphy's strategy for labour compliance, resulting in thousands of out-of-work Dubliners. But the workers were not without their supporters, and the crowd assembled that November night was eager to raise its voice in solidarity: all that was

E. Mannion (✉)
City University of New York, New York, NY, USA

© The Author(s) 2020
A. McNamara, N. O'Ceallaigh Ritschel (eds.), *Bernard Shaw and the Making of Modern Ireland*, Bernard Shaw and His Contemporaries, https://doi.org/10.1007/978-3-030-42113-7_5

needed was a little encouragement. It came in the forms of Dora Montefiore, George (AE) Russell, James Connolly, Delia Larkin, and expat Dubliner Bernard Shaw.

Shaw's relationship with Ireland was wrapped in "a binary opposition: a love of Ireland and a detestation of Dublin,"[3] evidence of which is most often found in his correspondence, but seen occasionally in his speeches and plays. It did not prevent him from supporting city activities and contributing to causes when moved to do so, and he was prone to embrace his born-and-bred Dubliner status when it might strengthen a point, as it did on this particular Saturday night. His opening pronouncement that he was present as "a Dublin man to apologise for the priests of Dublin"[4] was received enthusiastically. Shaw was alone neither in noting lacklustre church support for the workers, nor in noting outrage over the church's reaction to relief efforts organized by Dora Montefiore.

Montefiore, who was well known for her leadership in the Social Democratic Federation, became involved with Dublin labour only one month prior to joining that illustrious line-up on the Albert Hall stage. She recalled sharing the platform with Larkin at an October 10 meeting in London, when Larkin began

> to tell the English workers what straits the Dublin workers were in after seven weeks of slow starvation. As I listened to his appalling story, it flashed across my mind that here was a great opportunity for organized workers in England to prove their solidarity with the locked-out men in Dublin, by taking in to their homes some of the children who were suffering so severely from the effects of industrial strife. When Larkin had finished speaking I wrote out a slip of paper and passed it across to him, asking him if a plan like this ... could be arranged...and would it have his backing. He wrote a few words in the affirmative.[5]

This plan, which became known as the Kiddies Scheme, put Montefiore in direct conflict with the Catholic Church in Ireland and dragged Shaw into the Lockout. His involvement with this pivotal event in early twentieth-century Irish history also appears to mark a tipping point in the Shavian cleric. This figure, so multidimensional through plays written up to 1913, becomes less so thereafter. Shaw's correspondence does not allude to any conscious attitudinal shift, but the characterizations are remarkably altered, raising the question as to whether this is in any way a slow reaction to Kiddies Scheme events.

The church's reaction to the Kiddies Scheme was swift and decisive: "The Archbishop of Dublin, William Walsh, wrote to the commercial Dublin papers warning the suffering mothers to find other means to feed their starving children: 'I can only put it to them that they can be no longer held worthy of the name Catholic mothers if they so far forget that duty as to send away their little children to be cared for in a strange land, without security of any kind that those to whom the poor children are to be handed over are Catholics.'"[6] The Ancient Order of Hibernians, along with "some fanatical priests [were] given the official imprimatur of Archbishop Walsh, [and with this] a Roman Catholic phalange moved into action."[7] That phalange included and was exploited by Murphy, whose *Irish Independent* was among the Dublin papers that labelled Scheme supporters anti-Catholic. The *Independent* took its condemnation one step further though, reducing the Albert Hall meeting to nothing more than "a British anti-Catholic rally."[8]

The Church, having already challenged parents from the pulpit and through the press, sent clergy to the docks from where children were scheduled to depart:

> Over a period of several days, beginning on October 22, outraged priests and angry mobs recruited by the Ancient Order of Hibernians grabbed many of the children from the hands of the social workers washing them at the Tara Street baths; pulled others off boats at the North Wall of the Liffey or off trains at Kingsbridge station; attacked anyone attempting to leave Dublin with a child; and marched triumphantly along the quays singing "Faith of Our Fathers" after each day's successful "rescues." Although eighteen children made it to Liverpool, plans for getting three hundred more out of Dublin were abandoned.[9]

Montefiore and her young colleague, Lucille Rand, were charged with felonious kidnapping. The charges against both women were ultimately dismissed, with no jail time served. The 61-year-old Montefiore left Dublin in December, and never returned to Ireland. When she recalled the events, she reserved special mention for "the violence of the priests of Dublin, backed up by the fanaticism of the Ancient Order of Hibernians."[10]

George (AE) Russell loathed public speaking, but he was already invested significantly enough in the Lockout to move past any discomfort in addressing the crowd. Along with Horace Plunkett, AE had organized food donations from the Irish Agricultural Organization Society, and in early October, the *Irish Times* had published his "Open Letter to the Employers," in which he condemned "the aristocracy of industry" for their ignorance: "you do not seem to realize that your assumption that you are answerable to yourselves alone for your actions in the industries you control is one that becomes less and less tolerable in a world so crowded with necessitous life."[11] He also challenged their complicity in the deplorable tenement living conditions endured by so many of the workers. He echoed these issues at the rally, but only after voicing outrage at the "super-human beings…[who] assert it is better for children to be starved than to be moved from the Christian atmosphere of the Dublin slums."[12] He was quick to call out the politicians who refused to get involved, claiming they functioned in fear of disagreeing with the church. AE's comments drew fire in the Dublin press, where he was labelled anti-religious, a claim with which he was quick to take exception, most publicly in his "Appeal to Dublin Citizens" that appeared in the *Times* on November 13: "I am charged with being against religion; I…who has never written a single poem which did not try to express a spiritual mood…I have known, worked with, and loved many noble men, true priests of Christ, and they would not, I am sure, assert that the spirit which drives a mob to bludgeon and kick parents before the eyes of their children is the Spirit which is present at the elevation of the Host.[13] His indignation aside, AE had a point.

Shaw joined Russell in addressing the clerical role in the Lockout. But his tone was more measured than it appears the crowd desired. They hissed at his first mention of the priests, and Shaw quickly made clear that this was not the reaction he sought, indicating, as he had already in plays from *Mrs. Warren's Profession* (1893) to *Getting Married* (1908), that he did not paint them all with one brush. Shaw's clergy are as nuanced as his secular authority figures. His Albert Hall remarks actually indicate a disappointment in the priests, which could only be the case if he expected more of them than they delivered:

> [T]hose men, although they are pious and doing a good deal of good work, are very ignorant and simple men in the affairs of the country and especially industrial affairs. If by any means these words reach them, I hope they will be obliged to me for the apology I have made for them. There is something even more terrible than the horror of their individual action, and that is the terror of the great Church to which they belong being made the catspaw of a gentleman like Mr Murphy.[14]

Murphy's *Independent* reported Shaw's speech as an attack on priests with no mention of Shaw's condemnation of the "absurdity of the government's arrest of Larkin,"[15] an arrest that the publisher had endorsed. The *Irish Times* was also quick to chastise Shaw personally, dismissing him as an interloper at worst and a mouthy eccentric Londoner at best. But the Lockout was not the first Irish controversy to engage Shaw. That earlier event—concerning Home Rule Party leader Charles Stewart Parnell—also featured the playwright in a clerical debate that played out in the press, but, ironically, considering the criticism levelled at the Catholic Church in Ireland for their public commentary on the matter, Shaw did not tangle with them. Rather, his outrage was reserved for the Nonconformists.[16]

At the height of the 1890 debate surrounding Parnell's party leadership in the wake of the O'Shea divorce scandal, Shaw became publicly entangled with Methodist minister Hugh Price Hughes, Westbourne Park Baptist minister John Clifford, and City Temple pastor Joseph Parker. The opposition to Home Rule of these three leading Nonconformists led to their targeting Parnell and crossing swords with Shaw. Shaw was no doubt piqued by their tendency to deliver opinions through a "public persona [that] came to be characterized by a pugnacious defence of their own interests and righteousness."[17] A November 27, 1890 letter to the editor of *The Star*, in which Clifford echoed the Nonconformist rallying cry that the "immoral" Parnell must be released from the leadership of his party, compelled Shaw to assert that Clifford had "no right to speak of Mr. Parnell as 'convicted of immorality'; it is the law that has been convicted of immorality. If 'the conscience of the nation is aroused,' so much the better; but I doubt it."[18] It was the marriage laws to which Shaw took exception, not the "perfectly natural and right"[19] affections between Parnell and Kitty O'Shea.

Shaw was still fired up about marital decrees almost a decade later and could well have been referring to Parnell and O'Shea when, in the first published preface to *Getting Married*, he deemed marriage contracts "inhuman and unreasonable to the point of downright abomination" and the reason "bolder and more rebellious spirits form illicit unions."[20] In that same 1907 preface, he recalls a "conference of married men" organized by Hughes as confirmation that "respectable men all regarded the marriage ceremony as a rite...that placed their pleasures on exactly the same footing as their prayers."[21] It was not a compliment. Remnants of Shaw's sparring with the Nonconformists can be found as late as *Back to Methuselah* (written 1918–20), when the political leadership disregards any spiritual merits of Creative Evolution, instead considering it solely as an opportunity—bible and science! —to garner the Nonconformist vote for the Liberal Party. But the first traces of Shaw's animus against the Nonconformist priests are, in quick succession, the play script of *Mrs. Warren's Profession* (1893) and the preface of *Candida* (1894).[22]

The Nonconformist references in *Mrs. Warren's Profession* are non-linear, but rich. Prior to joining Westbourne Park Baptist Chapel, Clifford had been associated with Praed Street Chapel, and a Mr. Praed serves as foil to Shaw's first clerical character, Rev. Samuel Gardner of *Mrs. Warren's Profession*.[23] Gardner is "a pretentious, booming, noisy person, hopelessly asserting himself…without being able to command respect":[24] a description that seems drafted from between the lines of Shaw's November 27 letter to *The Star*, in which he targets Clifford and Hughes for self-righteous thoughtlessness and makes clear that his disrespect for their position is based on what he considers their lack of respect for the public good.[25] The sanctimonious Gardner is keen to avoid Mrs. Warren— "Kitty" to Praed—once he recognizes her as an indiscretion from his student days. The easy-going Praed is sensitive about discussing Kitty's profession with Vivie, but he never passes judgment on it. He also purposely withholds information to avoid conflict of any kind and maintains a certain wilful ignorance, assuming everything will work itself out: behaviours that reflect Parnell's position when his relationship with Katharine ("Kitty") O'Shea was first exposed in the press and Shaw's opinion that Parnell should "sit tight"[26] until the moralizing classes exhausted themselves. But the robust moralizing continued unabated, and was joined by Shaw's own "incorrigible propensity for preaching"[27] in his next play, *Candida*.

Shaw's disdain for the anti-Parnell zealots was shared by Christian Socialist Stewart Headlam, who was "enraged [by the] Nonconformist moralizing"[28] of Clifford and Hughes.[29] Fabian, Guild of St. Matthew founder, and Church and Stage Guild host, Reverend Headlam was a great friend of Shaw.[30] In the preface to *Candida*, Shaw considers their shared appreciation for minimizing the hyperbole that often made its way to public debate: "members of the Guild of St. Matthew were no more 'High Church clergymen,' Dr. Clifford no more 'an eminent Nonconformist divine,' than I was to them 'an infidel.'"[31] Although Shaw said on more than one occasion that Stopford Brooke was a model for *Candida*'s Reverend James Morell, Headlam is very much present from the opening act, where, as Peter Gahan observes, "in the first scene of the play the Christian Socialist clergyman Morell reads an article by Headlam and news about the Guild of St. Matthew in *The Church Reformer*, and the lecture Morell gives to the Guild [offstage] between acts II and III becomes pivotal to the action."[32]

Morell's Guild lecture is deemed a "noble, splendid, inspired address"[33] by the curate Alexander Mill, whose innate kindness is matched by Morell's. For all of Morell's foolishness—which is nothing more than a bit of mid-life madness in worry of losing his wife's affections—his verbosity and self-assuredness are the result of being a well-loved son and brother who was "spoiled from his cradle."[34] The love that raised him, his wife argues, is what engenders his ability to be loved (Prossy's complaint), which is posited as an equally—if not more—generous act than loving others. Demonstrating here that he will not stereotype; Shaw's Morell is the antithesis of the pretentious and emotionally stingy Gardner. Morell is "robust and good-looking, full of energy, with pleasant, hearty, consider-ate manners...a first-rate clergyman"[35] who is capable of seeing his own foolishness: a charming quality sorely lacking in Morell's foil, the poet Eugene Marchbanks. Marchbanks also struggles with listening and lan-guage, unable to assess Morell's sermons as anything other than "words! words! words!"[36] Shaw's note in the preface to *Three Plays for Puritans* that "critics, like other people, see what they look for, not what is actually before them,"[37] is more direct, but Marchbanks is an early embodiment of the conceit.

The Devil's Disciple (1896), *Captain Brassbound's Conversion* (1899), *John Bull's Other Island* (1904) and *Getting Married* (1908), were also composed prior to the Kiddie's Scheme and contain memorable clerics who are emblematic of Shaw's refusal to wrap cliché in a collar. Sometimes these plays, like *Mrs. Warren's Profession* and *Candida*, contain contempo-rary references, but, broadly speaking, these preachers are those earlier characters writ small. Neither as foolish as Gardner nor as verbose as Morell, they show Shaw well on his way to "perhaps put[ting] more cler-gymen on the stage than any other playwright of any period"[38] and dis-playing increased depth of characterization in the process.

The principal clergy of *Three Plays for Puritans*—Anderson in *The Devil's Disciple* and Rankin in *Captain Brassbound's Conversion*—are unsentimental foils to their respective Shavian protagonist counterparts. Anthony Anderson, the American minister of *The Devil's Disciple*, is "a man capable of making the most of this world, and perhaps a little apolo-getically conscious of getting on better with it than a sound Presbyterian ought."[39] He is at his most Shavian—and something of a match for *Candida*'s Morell—in his philosophical moments, as when he claims that "the worst sin towards our fellow creatures is not to hate them, but to be indifferent to them; that's the essence of inhumanity."[40] Richard Dudgeon, Anderson's counterpart and the self-proclaimed devil's disciple, is the more influential preacher in this play: freely spouting his ideology and handily winning converts. Attention to his natural gifts is reinforced when Dudgeon, wearing Anderson's coat, is mistaken for the minister by soldiers looking to arrest him for treason (a charge of which he is not guilty). All that separates the rascal from the minister is high-quality cloth. When Anderson learns that Richard was taken in his place in jail, "his eyes become injected with hot blood; the man of peace vanishes, transfigured into a choleric and formidable man of war"[41] who rides off to battle. It took a non-congregant to deliver the parson to his true calling as a "man of action."[42] The ease with which Anderson adapts to his military vocation makes him believe that the devil's disciple "will start presently as the Reverend Richard Dudgeon, and wag his pow in my old pulpit, and give good advice to this silly sentimental little wife of mine."[43] In the end, Anderson's mirth allows him to consider a most material method of transubstantiation. Disguise and transformation also figure in *Captain Brassbound's Conversion*, but, as the title suggests, it is contained within the buccaneer Brassbound. Rankin, the aging Scottish missionary, is a minor character. But his common sense and practical nature make him yet another admirable Shavian cleric. His quarter-century of service has netted zero conversions, but he takes comfort in being known among the locals as "the Christian who is not a thief," which, as he notes, "is something."[44]

No such peace of mind is afforded to Peter Keegan, the missionary of *John Bull's Other Island*. Prone to melancholy and lamenting the misery of Ireland in communion with a grasshopper, Keegan was removed from his duties after ministering to "an elderly Hindoo" whose death revealed for Keegan that the world "is very clearly a place of torment and penance, a place where the fool flourishes and the good and wise are hated and persecuted."[45] The result was his being deemed mad and marginalized by his church. By contrast, the play's Father Dempsey—"a priest neither by vocation nor ambition, but because the life suits him"[46]—is in very good standing. But Shaw does not write him as an entirely one-dimensional corporate figure, he maintains "boundless authority over his flock, and taxes them stiffly enough to be a rich man…[but] on the whole, [he is an] easygoing, amiable, even modest man as long as his dues are paid and his authority and dignity fully admitted."[47] Class snobbery does assert itself, however, the locals still call Keegan "father," much to the chagrin of Dempsey, who is frustrated by their inability to "tell the difference between [a] priest and any old madman in a black coat."[48] Dempsey holding a profession rather than vocation is more a commentary on community naiveté than on clergymen. There is a suggestion here that parishioners are unable to see the man behind the collar, much like the locals who still call Keegan "father."

The first by-the-book Shavian protagonist to sport a collar is Bishop Alfred Bridgenorth of *Getting Married*.[49] Bridgenorth joins Oliver Cromwell Soames (aka Father Anthony) and greengrocer-Alderman George Collins in comprising the play's advisory triumvirate who are tasked with sorting out the ethics of marriage. His "humorous eyes," like Rankin's, are "not without a glint of mischief."[50] He does not reflect the snobbish reverend of *Mrs. Warren's*, the verbose-to-the-point-of-cliché Christian Socialist of *Candida*, the quixotic minister of *The Devil's Disciple*, or the community entrenchment (for better or worse) of *John Bull's Other Island*. Rather, at the centre of a cast that risks being seen as "a row of Shaws"[51] and in a play written some five years prior to Shaw's dismay at the clerical response to the Kiddies Scheme, Bridgenorth seems to be a combination of that which came before, culminating as possibly the most Shavian cleric of them all.

Shaw's objections to marriage and divorce laws go back at least as far as the Parnell case and are referenced to one degree or another in many of his plays, but *Getting Married* is his high-water mark on the subject and the self-proclaimed "very funny Bishop"[52] among his most eloquent preachers:

> If we are going to discuss ethical questions we must begin by giving the devil fair play…we always assume the devil is guilty: and we wont allow him to prove his innocence, because it would be against public morals if he succeeded. We used to do the same with prisoners accused of high treason. And the consequence is that we overreach ourselves; and the devil gets the better of us after all. Perhaps thats what most of us intend him to do.[53]

Soames's father "was an eminent Nonconformist divine who habitually spoke of the Church of England as The Scarlet Woman."[54] Soames's conversion to Anglicanism while still a teenager attacks his father's religious and political positions simultaneously, and when baptized into his new

faith, he did so under a new name. The younger Soames had been chris-
tened Oliver Cromwell, but changed his name to Anthony and advises the
grooms-to-be that when they become fathers they should "be very careful
not to label a helpless child with views which it may come to hold in
abhorrence."[55]

Bridgenorth maintains an even-handedness and repeatedly does so in
response to the traditional (or devilish) position. He regularly reminds the
debaters that they "must give the devil fair play" and not to do so risks
displaying "a very unchristian"[56] disposition, as if Richard Dudgeon was
given a sequel to *The Devil's Disciple* and it showed him living the life
Anderson predicted for him. The Bishop encourages drafting a contract of
marriage in which the women have some say as an effort to do "the greatest possible service to morality,"[57] and which reflects the play's position
that the "central horror of the dependence of women on men…reduces
the difference between marriage and prostitution to the difference between
Trade Unionism and unorganized casual labour: a huge difference, no
doubt, as to order and comfort, but not a difference in kind."[58] Granted,
trade unionism had been raised in earlier plays through socialist clerics,
but never so centrally. Bridgenorth, written and performed well before the
Lockout, would turn out to be the last labour-focused—as well as the last
truly multifaceted—clergyman in the Shaw canon.

Generally, the post-Kiddies Scheme plays—particularly *Back to
Methuselah* (1921), *Saint Joan* (1923), *The Simpleton of the Unexpected
Isles* (1934), *Geneva* (1938) and *In Good King Charles's Golden Days*
(1935)—contain less complex clerics. They also share a "fundamental pessimism"[59] that was not previously overt and the "willingness to take risks
as a means of conceiving a more socially useful morality [that] character-
izes all of Shaw's religious heroes and heroines in varying degrees"[60] is not
as robustly on display as in the pre-Lockout works.

The clerical pessimism of the Swiftian *Back to Methuselah* is embodied
in William Haslam. A spirited debate early in the play centres on the prop-
osition that men can live to 300 if introduced to the notion that it was
possible. It is central to the plot and shows a gentle community naiveté of
earlier works having evolved to a harsher community gullibility. The parson offers no insights or opinions of any consequence, and recalling that
moment more than a century later, the now 200-year-old archbishop
Haslam recalls that he was "not conscious of sharing [their opinion on the
power of suggestion]: I thought I was only amused by it. To me my father-
in-law and his brother were a pair of clever cranks who had talked one

another into a fixed idea which had become a monomania with them."[61] He only realizes he is living longer than usual when he tries applying for a pension. His fate is to live in Galway among people who have "lost all their political faculties by disuse except that of nationalist agitation"[62] until set to rights by Haslam sometime in the past, but by then any sense of imagination had evolved out of them and this led to their extinction. The cleric here is essentially a pawn in the hands of bigger brains, not unlike the Christian clergyman who is the titular fool of *The Simpleton of the Unexpected Isles.*

Saint Joan and *Geneva* offer perhaps the best examples of a decline in rich clerical characterization. The monks in *Saint Joan* embody a sort of mute Greek chorus rather than being figures of agency, and the failing bishop of *Geneva* drops dead when confronted with his obsolescence. The figures in both plays are entirely devoid of the gumption expected of a Shavian cleric after *Getting Married.* As in Shaw's earlier history play, *Caesar and Cleopatra*, the named clerical figures of *Saint Joan* (particularly Bishop Peter Cauchon and Brother John) exist solely in dramatic relationship to the titled character(s). *"In Good King Charles's Golden Days"* is the one history play where the cleric, Society of Friends founder George Fox, is more than a foil.

One of Shaw's last plays and the final one to have a clerical figure central to its cast, *"In Good King Charles's Golden Days"* speaks back to the issue of concealment that appeared in *The Devil's Disciple* and *Captain Brassbound's Conversion.* However, here it is addressed entirely by characters—Fox and King Charles—that maintain a religious authority that goes quite against their better instincts. When Fox laments the pressure he feels to "unmask" the "pitiful rascal twaddling in his pulpit,"[63] he receives only a miniscule amount of understanding because the cry of false clerics is trite. Charles recognizes the falseness in his own role as head of the church but in doing so absolves himself of any hypocrisy. Rather, he laments how easy it is to deceive the public, particularly if the one espousing policy or doctrine is speaking from a pulpit: "the clergy are mostly dull dogs; but with a little disguise and ritual they will pass as holy men with the ignorant."[64] This notion of interchangeability between rascal and cleric getting by the "ignorant" man of the crowd displays a mean-spiritedness that was entirely absent from those early works, where the target was an authority figure rather than the common punter. That targeting of religious authority is, one might conclude, the most unique shift in Shaw's post-Lockout clerical characterizations.

It seems 1913 represents a tipping point at which Shaw becomes less inclined to give characters in religious authority any benefit of the doubt. They cease being humorously and humanely flawed, and are instead not quite worth the bother. It is as if Shaw's interaction with the Nonconformists over the Parnell affair piqued his curiosity and motivated his engagement with religious themes and characters: safe to do when it is all politics and posturing with no lives at stake. But when it came to the Kiddies Scheme and religious officials standing in the way of tenement children receiving relief, the stakes were rather too high to keep the jokes flowing, and the Church behaviour beyond the range of humour.

NOTES

1. Larkin was sentenced on October 27 and would be released (early) on November 13. The charges stemmed from a speech he delivered August 31 from an Imperial Hotel balcony on O'Connell Street. Police charged the crowd that was listening to Larkin, and hundreds were injured.
2. Semantics pivot on the position taken: the business owners would refer to the event that lasted through December as a strike; but those supportive of the workers—and indeed the historical record—use the term Lockout, which was coined by Larkin from the first day.
3. Peter Gahan, "Bernard Shaw: Dégringolade and Derision in Dublin City," *SHAW: The Annual of Bernard Shaw Studies* 32 (2012), 44.
4. Qtd. in Pádraig Yeates, *Lockout: Dublin 1913* (New York: Palgrave, 2000), 343.
5. Dora B. Montefiore, *From a Victorian to a Modern* ([London]: E. Archer, 1927), 156.
6. Nelson O'Ceallaigh Ritschel, *Shaw, Synge, Connolly, and Socialist Provocation* (Gainesville, FL: Univ. Press of Florida, 2011), 139–140.
7. Mary Diskin, "Dora Montefiore: An Unwitting Victim of Propaganda," in *Lockout Centenary: Dun Laoghaire 1913–2013*, ed. Padraig Mannion (Dublin: 1913 Commemorative Committee, 2013), 29.
8. Ritschel, *Shaw, Synge, Connolly, and Socialist Provocation*, 148.
9. Lucy McDiarmid, *The Irish Art of Controversy* (Ithaca, NY: Cornell Univ. Press, 2005), 125.
10. Dora Montefiore, "Our Fight...," in https://www.marxists.org/archive/montefiore/1913/kiddies.htm
11. George William Russell (AE), "An Open Letter to Employers," in *The Dublin Strike* (Dublin: Irish Worker Press, [1913]), 4.
12. Russell, "A Plea for the Workers," in *The Dublin Strike*, 1.
13. Russell, "An Appeal to Dublin Citizens," in *The Dublin Strike*, 7.

14. Yeates, *Lockout: Dublin 1913*, 343.
15. Ritschel, *Shaw, Synge, Connolly, and Socialist Provocation*, 153.
16. Nonconformist was an umbrella term for non-Anglican denominations that joined forces to counter their individual minority statuses when supporting or opposing select social and political issues.
17. Robert Pope, "The Nonconformist Conscience," in *The Oxford Companion to Twentieth-Century British Politics* (Oxford: Oxford University Press, 2002), 474.
18. Shaw, "Shall Parnell Go? I," in *The Matter with Ireland* (New York: Hill and Wang, 1962), 25.
19. Shaw, "Shall Parnell Go? I," in *The Matter with Ireland*, 25.
20. Shaw, Preface to *Getting Married*, in *Collected Plays, Vol. III*, ed. Dan H. Laurence (New York: Dodd, Mead, 1972), 452–453.
21. Shaw, Preface to *Getting Married*, 462.
22. The parenthetical dates within this essay refer to the year Shaw completed his MS; the dates in the Bibliography refer to year of first publication.
23. There is a clergyman in *Widowers' Houses* (1892), but he never appears on stage.
24. Shaw, *Mrs. Warren's Profession*, in *George Bernard Shaw's Plays*, ed. Sandie Byrne (New York and London: W.W. Norton, 2002), 24.
25. Shaw, "Shall Parnell Go? II," in *The Matter with Ireland*, 26–28.
26. Shaw, "Shall Parnell Go? I," in *The Matter with Ireland*, 25.
27. Shaw, "Acting, By One Who Does Not Believe in It," in *Platform and Pulpit* (New York: Hill and Wang, 1961), 20.
28. John Richard Orens, *Stewart Headlam's Radical Anglicanism: The Mass, the Masses, and the Music Hall* (Urbana and Chicago: University of Illinois Press, 2003), 119.
29. Fabian references—including Sidney Webb (*Getting Married*) and H.G. Wells (*Back to Methuselah*)—are not uncommon in Shaw's clerical plays and even more so in the prefaces.
30. Their friendship, however, was tested in 1896 when they disagreed vehemently over the position that the Fabian Society should take against the Tories regarding the Boer War.
31. Shaw, Preface to *Candida* (New York: Penguin, 2006), xxv.
32. Peter Gahan, introduction to *Candida* (New York: Penguin, 2006), xii.
33. Shaw, *Candida*, 60.
34. Shaw, *Candida*, 67.
35. Shaw, *Candida*, 3.
36. Shaw, *Candida*, 37.
37. Shaw, "Why for Puritans?," in *Three Plays for Puritans* (New York: Penguin, 1957), 25.
38. Eric Bentley, *Bernard Shaw* (New York: Applause, 2002), 91.

39. Shaw, *The Devil's Disciple*, 47.

40. Shaw, *The Devil's Disciple*, in *Three Plays for Puritans* (New York: Penguin, 1957), 72.

41. Shaw, *The Devil's Disciple*, 87.

42. Shaw, *The Devil's Disciple*, 117.

43. Shaw, *The Devil's Disciple*, 117.

44. Shaw, *Captain Brassbound's Conversion*, in *Three Plays for Puritans* (New York: Penguin, 1957), 260.

45. Shaw, *John Bull's Other Island*, in *Modern and Contemporary Irish Drama*, 2nd ed., ed. John P. Harrington (New York and London: W.W. Norton, 2009), 176.

46. Shaw, *John Bull's Other Island*, 138.

47. Shaw, *John Bull's Other Island*, 138.

48. Shaw, *John Bull's Other Island*, 141.

49. He is not the sole Shavian protagonist in *Getting Married*, however; the position is shared with Hotchkiss, who shares the Shaw family nickname of Sonny and asserts that he does not "believe in anything but [his] own will, pride and honor." See p. 658 of *Collected Plays, Vol. III* for his most Shavian rant and its reflection of Shaw's comments regarding his being the result of a specifically "Irish eighteenth centuryism" as discussed in the "My Own Part in the Matter" portion of the preface to *Back to Methuselah*.

50. Shaw, *Getting Married*, in *Collected Plays, Vol. III* (New York: Dodd, Mead, 1975), 573.

51. Shaw, "Mr. Bernard Shaw on his New Play" in *Collected Plays, Vol. III*, ed. Dan H. Laurence (New York: Dodd, Mead, 1975), 665.

52. Shaw, *Getting Married*, 640.

53. Shaw, *Getting Married*, 574.

54. Shaw, *Getting Married*, 609.

55. Shaw, *Getting Married*, 609.

56. Shaw, *Getting Married*, 621.

57. Shaw, *Getting Married*, 601.

58. Shaw, Preface to *Getting Married*, 501.

59. Alfred Turco Jr., *Shaw's Moral Vision* (Ithaca and London: Cornell University Press, 1976), 268.

60. Anthony S. Abbott, *Shaw and Christianity* (New York: The Seabury Press, 1965), 183.

61. Shaw, *Back to Methuselah* (New York and London: Oxford University Press, 1947), 102.

62. Shaw, *Back to Methuselah*, 144.

63. Bernard Shaw, "In Good King Charles's Golden Days," in *Bernard Shaw Collected Plays, Vol. VII* (New York, Dodd, Mead, 1974), 234.

64. Shaw, "In Good King Charles's Golden Days," 234.

REFERENCES

Abbott, Anthony S. 1965. *Shaw and Christianity.* New York: The Seabury Press.

Bentley, Eric. 2002. *Bernard Shaw.* New York: Applause.

Diskin, Mary. 2013. *Dora Montefiore: An Unwitting Victim of Propaganda.* Ed. Padraig Mannion. Lockout Centenary: Dun Laoghaire 1913–2013. Dublin: 1913 Commemorative Committee.

Dora Montefiore Archive, *Manchester Guardian.* http://www.marxists.org/archive/montefiore/1913/10/guardian.htm

Gahan, Peter. 2006. *Introduction to Candida*, vii–xxi. New York: Penguin.

———. 2012. Bernard Shaw: Dégringolade and Derision in Dublin City. *SHAW: The Annual of Bernard Shaw Studies* 32: 39–58.

McDiarmid, Lucy. 2005. *The Irish Art of Controversy.* Ithaca: Cornell University Press.

Montefiore, Dora B. 1927. *From a Victorian to a Modern.* London: E. Archer.

———. Our Fight to Save the Kiddies in Dublin: Smouldering Fires of the Inquisition. https://www.marxists.org/archive/montefiore/1913/kiddies.htm

Orens, John Richard. 2003. *Stewart Headlam's Radical Anglicanism: The Mass, the Masses, and the Music Hall.* Urbana/Chicago: University of Illinois Press.

Ramsden, John, ed. 2002. *The Oxford Companion to Twentieth-Century British Politics.* Oxford: Oxford University Press.

Ritschel, Nelson O'Ceallaigh. 2011. *Shaw, Synge, Connolly, and Socialist Provocation.* Gainesville: University Press of Florida.

Russell, George William (AE). 1913. *The Dublin Strike.* Dublin: Irish Worker Press.

Shaw, Bernard. 1947. *Back to Methuselah.*1921. New York/London: Oxford University Press.

———. 1957. *Three Plays for Puritans: The Devil's Disciple, Caesar and Cleopatra, and Captain Brassbound's Conversion.* 1901. Ed. Dan H. Laurence. London/New York: Penguin.

———. 1961. *Platform and Pulpit.*Ed. Dan H. Laurence. New York: Hill and Wang.

———. 1962. *The Matter with Ireland.* Ed. Dan H. Laurence and David H. Greene. New York: Hill and Wang.

———. 1967. *Shaw on Religion.* Ed. Warren Sylvester Smith. New York: Dodd, Mead.

———. 1972. *Getting Married: A Disquisitory Play.* 1911. *Collected Plays Vol. III*, ed.Dan H. Laurence, 449–668. New York: Dodd, Mead.

———. 1973. *The Simpleton of the Unexpected Isles.* 1936. Ed. Dan H. Laurence. *The Bodley Head Bernard Shaw, Vol. VI*, 741–846.London: The Bodley Head.

———. 1974. In Good King Charles's Golden Days. 1939. *Collected Plays Vol. VII*, ed. Dan H. Laurence, 201–301. New York: Dodd, Mead.

————. 1975. Mister Bernard Shaw on his New Play.1908. *Collected Plays, Vol. III*,ed. Dan H. Laurence, 663–668. New York: Dodd, Mead.

————. 1985. *Bernard Shaw Collected Letters, Vol. 3: 1911–1925*. Ed. Dan H. Laurence. New York: Viking.

————. 2002. *Mrs. Warren's Profession*. 1898. *George Bernard Shaw's Plays*, ed. Sandie Byrne, 3–66. New York/London: W.W. Norton.

————. 2006. *Candida*. 1898. Ed. Dan H. Laurence, Introduction by Peter Gahan. New York:Penguin.

————. 2009. *John Bull's Other Island*. 1907. In *Modern and Contemporary Irish Drama*, ed. John P. Harrington, 2nd ed., 113–196. New York: W.W. Norton.

Turco, Alfred Jr. 1976. *Shaw's Moral Vision*. Ithaca/London: Cornell University Press.

Yeates, Padraig. 2000. *Lockout: Dublin 1913*. New York: Palgrave.

CHAPTER 6

Bernard Shaw and Sean O'Casey: Remembering James Connolly

Nelson O'Ceallaigh Ritschel

The focus of this chapter is an exploration of the parallel tracks of Ireland's prominent socialistic authors from 1915 through the 1920s, Bernard Shaw and Sean O'Casey. This examination will demonstrate that these parallel tracks were influenced, even shaped, by Shaw's and O'Casey's respective perceptions of the militant socialist and trade unionist James Connolly, Commandant of the Dublin rebel forces during the Easter Rising, which saw his execution by a British firing squad on 12 May 1916. While Shaw would develop much admiration for O'Casey by the late 1920s, and O'Casey adamantly claimed to have been much influenced by Shaw, their socialistic literary tracks were at first distinctly separate—as separate as each chose to remember Connolly. And for his part, Connolly in early 1916 would react to Shaw's then recent Irish recruitment efforts for the Great War that would, in turn, be responded to ten years later by O'Casey. A glimpse at these complicated directions of Shaw and O'Casey

N. O'Ceallaigh Ritschel (✉)
Massachusetts Maritime Academy, Pocasset, MA, USA
e-mail: nritschel@maritime.edu

© The Author(s) 2020
A. McNamara, N. O'Ceallaigh Ritschel (eds.), *Bernard Shaw and the Making of Modern Ireland*, Bernard Shaw and His Contemporaries, https://doi.org/10.1007/978-3-030-42113-7_6

is discernible in three key plays from Shaw, O'Casey, and Connolly that reveal the parallel, yet distinctive tracks that the former two pursued within Connolly's shadow. The rails for these tracks, particularly for Shaw and the influence O'Casey mined from Shaw's works, were forged during the eventful years prior to 1916.

The 2011 monograph *Shaw, Synge, Connolly, and Socialist Provocation* details a stage dialogue between George Bernard Shaw and John Millington Synge, along with Shaw's indirect and direct involvement in Irish socialism from 1899–1916 that included crossings with the militant socialist James Connolly. Part of the dialogue between Shaw and Synge stemmed from Synge's 1903 one-act play *In the Shadow of the Glen*, which at the very least upended the stranger in the house motif that Lady Augusta Gregory and William Butler Yeats employed in their 1902 *Cathleen Ni Houlihan*. In 1904, specifically on 26 March, Shaw attended the performances, matinee and evening, of the Irish National Theatre Society in London—a one-day engagement that included *In the Shadow of the Glen*. Three months later, Shaw would begin writing his master Irish play *John Bull's Other Island*, which, like Synge's play, presented a critical view of rural Ireland, complete with the petty greed of its folk—but on a grander scale, which furthered the stranger's presence in the form of the English civil engineer Tom Broadbent. Within days of reading Shaw's manuscript on a train to Belmullet, north County Mayo, Synge began drafting the play that would premier, in 1907, as *The Playboy of the Western World*— arguably a rewrite of Acts 2, 3, and 4 of Shaw's play. This time, instead of an English capitalist who follows the model of efficiency, the stranger visitor is, essentially, a Munster lad with a "gallous story".[1] As Synge was dying of cancer in early March 1909, Shaw wrote *The Shewing-up of Blanco Posnet* as a jab at the British censor within the Lord Chamberlain's Office—a play owing much to Synge's *Playboy*.[2] This was fitting since some of *Playboy*'s dialogue had been censored by the Lord Chamberlain's office before the Abbey Theatre performed it in London in June 1907. And as the Lord Chamberlain's censorship powers did not carry to Ireland, Shaw, Gregory, and Yeats elected to premier *Blanco Posnet* at the Abbey in Dublin in August 1909, months after Synge's death.

Drawing on Synge's work did not end for Shaw in 1909, but instead would be taken further six years later. But by then, Ireland had gone through the 1913 Dublin Lockout, which witnessed Shaw sharing the speakers' platform with James Connolly at a London rally on 1 November on behalf of the then imprisoned labour leader James Larkin and locked out Dublin workers, and within a year's time in 1914 the Great War was under way, which, together with the workers' defeat in the Lockout, placed Connolly on the road to 1916 and again interlocking him with Shaw—and with an out-of-work labourer whom Connolly may never have personally known, named John Casey, who in turn would become Sean O'Casey. Shaw and O'Casey would come to represent, even attempt to define, socialistic Irish drama and thought from the Great War years into the 1920s, all within the shadow of Connolly as expanding from three plays: Shaw's *O'Flaherty, V. C.*, Connolly's *Under Which Flag?*, and O'Casey's *The Plough and the Stars*—with repercussions into 1927–1928.

At the end of 1911, John Casey was sacked by the Great Northern Railway without an official explanation. After exchanging several letters with the Railway's secretary regarding his termination, O'Casey submitted the correspondence to the *Irish Worker*, the recently formed paper of the Irish Transport and General Workers' Union (ITGWU) edited by the union's General Secretary, James Larkin.[3] In early 1912, a green-paper-covered edition of *John Bull's Other Island* was published to coincide with the Home Rule Bill then in Parliament. Known as the Home Rule edition, Shaw arranged its price at six pennies, making it affordable to all classes. In 1938, O'Casey would recall in a letter to Charlotte Shaw, Shaw's wife and partner, that a "Dublin comrade ... first put the green-covered copy of 'John Bull's Other Island' into my then reluctant hand" (*O'Casey Letters*, I, 742).[4] In 1945, O'Casey recalled further that on reading the play for the first time in 1912, he was led to see Ireland as "being hitched to a power and will to face the facts. And this Irishman Shaw, was helping us to do it" (*Drums*, 257).[5] So began O'Casey's admiration for Shaw, and, presumably, Shaw's influence on O'Casey. But in 1912, O'Casey was still finding his way, which included a prolonged debate in the *Irish Worker* with A. Patrick Wilson, a fellow ITGWU member who would in a year's time become manager of the Abbey Theatre.[6] Their debate was over whether Gaelic and nationalism had any relevance for labour—with O'Casey arguing on behalf of Gaelic and nationalism. Wilson's argument that Ireland's next fight was to be over labour's rights proved prophetic with the next year's Lockout.

The flashpoint for the Lockout's beginning in August 1913 was with the trams of the Dublin United Tramways Company. When William Martin Murphy, Chairman of the Tramways Company (among other business concerns such as owner of the *Irish Independent* newspapers), sacked known ITGWU organizers in his employ, the ITGWU under Larkin responded with tramway drivers walking off their assigned trams on 26 August. Events escalated into the Murphy-led Employers' Federation locking out all employees suspected of ITGWU membership throughout most large-scale Dublin employers. Locking out ITGWU members was answered by strikes from sympathizing unions, which led the Dublin Metropolitan Police to respond by baton charging congregating workers over the weekend of 30 and 31 August. The resultant carnage pulled literary Dublin into the fray, as W. B. Yeats rushed his poem, eventually to be titled "September 1913", into print in the *Irish Times*. Originally written to protest Murphy's leading role in opposing the Municipal Art Gallery to house Hugh Lane's Impressionist paintings collection, the poem took on new relevance within the Lockout.[7] In October, James Connolly published "Labour in Dublin" in the *Irish Review*, edited then by pro-labour Thomas MacDonagh. Connolly called for more from literary Dublin on behalf of the down trodden during the Lockout.[8] When Larkin was arrested and imprisoned, Connolly, who was then the ITGWU's Belfast organizer, began to fill in for Larkin in Dublin during the crisis. London's leftist *Daily Herald*, a newspaper launched in 1912 with some financial assistance from Shaw, organized the London rally for Larkin and Dublin workers. Connolly's speech at the rally included, "If there is nothing in your stomach it matters mighty little what flag is flying".[9] Shaw immediately followed Connolly on the speakers' platform. He began by vocally jabbing the Dublin priests who had blocked the plan to send children of locked out workers to England for care during the crisis as their parents faced starvation without incomes. Next Shaw criticized the British Government for charging Larkin with sedition for saying that Dublin employers "lived on profits". Then Shaw, no doubt remembering London's 1887 Trafalgar Square riots where he witnessed police attacking labourers and protestors, voiced the most radical statement of the rally as he addressed the recent police baton attacks in Dublin:

> If you once let loose your physical force without careful supervision and order you may as well let loose in the streets a parcel of mad dogs as a parcel of policemen. It has been the practice, ever since the modern police were established, in difficulties with the working class to let loose the police and tell them to go and do their worst to the people. Now, if you put the police on the footing of a mad dog, it can end in one way—that all respectable men will have to arm themselves. ("Mad Dogs", 97)[10]

Two weeks later in Dublin, Connolly addressed workers outside Liberty Hall and called for the organization of what became the Irish Citizen Army (ICA): "See if the police will clear us off the street [now] as they [have] threatened".[11] In two further weeks, on 30 November, the ICA began to train under Jack White, a former British army Captain turned political radical from Ulster, who in the previous year shared the speakers' platform with Shaw at a London rally of Irish Protestants for Home Rule. On beginning his training of the ICA, White recalled to the crowd a conversation he recently had with a Jesuit Priest in which they discussed Shaw. The priest, according to the *Irish Times*, responded to White by saying, "he wrote Socialism". White then asked the priest "if the democracy of Ireland was not fit for the socialistic life, and the priest replied that they were not".[12] In another two weeks, mid-December, in an article with a title borrowed from Shaw's 1894 play *Arms and the Man*, Connolly reported that the ICA was already having an effect as the Police were backing away from confrontations with Dublin labour.[13] Yet despite such direct and indirect—indeed important—ties between Shaw and the ICA, O'Casey, when he published his 1919 book *The Story of the Irish Citizen Army*, made no references to Shaw's role in the early formation of what historian D. R. O'Connor Lysaght has labelled Europe's first "Red Guard" (21).[14] While O'Casey was not in London for the 1 November rally, it was extensively covered in Dublin and London papers, with much on Shaw's incendiary speech.[15] Even White's opening training comments on 30 November with his Shaw reference, received coverage in Dublin papers.

After the Lockout ended in workers' defeat in January 1914, O'Casey became involved in strengthening the ICA's organization. By this time, Connolly had returned to his union duties in Belfast. O'Casey, as the ICA's secretary, drafted the ICA's constitution in Dublin, adapting a quotation from 1840s Fenian James Fintan Lalor for the ICA's first principle: "That the first and last principle of the Irish Citizen Army is the avowal that the ownership of Ireland, moral and material, is vested in the right of the people of Ireland".[16] O'Casey had borrowed the quotation from the masthead of the *Irish Worker*, edited by James Larkin. Larkin's idea to use the Fintan Lalor quote most likely came from Connolly, who in his important 1910 book *Labour in Irish History*, wrote that Fintan Lalor "advocated his principles as of the creed of the world, and not merely only to the incidents of the struggle of Ireland against England".[17] Connolly had taken the republican Lalor's philosophy and interpreted it—or spun it—in the terms of international socialism. At this point, it appears that Connolly

and O'Casey were both seeing Irish labour within a socialism with republican leanings—as was the case with the ITGWU under Larkin's leadership, as Adrian Grant argues in *Irish Socialist Republicanism 1909–36*.[18]
However, much would change when the Great War erupted in August
1914—including the immediate suspension of the Home Rule Act on the
eve of its implementation.

In August 1914, with Connolly still in Belfast, O'Casey had generated
controversy within the ICA by demanding that aristocratic-born member
Constance Markievicz resign either from the ICA or from Cumann na
mBan, the women's wing of the Irish Volunteers. O'Casey argued that the
bourgeois make-up of the Volunteers was not conducive to the working-
class affiliation of the ICA. This stance by O'Casey first appeared in the
wake of Labour's Lockout defeat in early 1914. In the 21 February *Irish
Worker*, O'Casey attacked numerous Volunteers for being bourgeoisie,
specifically claiming that Padraic Pearse, who would emerge as a prominent
Volunteer leader in the 1916 Rising, was "the worse of all", stating that
Pearse "constantly used the trams on every possible occasion during the
Lockout" (O'Cathasaigh [O'Casey], "Volunteers and Workers", *Irish
Worker*; *Sean O'Casey Letters, Vol. I*, 40–41).[19] What O'Casey appears to
have been unaware of, was the fact that during the height of the Lockout
in fall 1913, Pearse published pro-labour articles in *Irish Freedom*, a republican paper edited by Tom Clarke and Sean MacDiarmada, both prominent
republicans. Specifically, Pearse wrote: "My instinct is with the landless
man against the master of millions. I may be wrong, but I do hold it a most
terrible sin that there be landless men in this island of waste yet fertile val-
leys, and that there should be breadless men in this city where great for-
tunes are made and enjoyed".[20] Pearse also sarcastically proposed that
employers should live up to their claim that £1 per week was sufficient "to
sustain a Dublin family in honest hunger" and step into the "shoes of our
hungry citizens. ... I am quite certain they will enjoy their poverty and
hunger".[21] So, O'Casey remained fixated in August 1914 on the non-
working class Volunteers of Pearse and Markievicz, being his antithesis of
the working-class ICA., Connolly, like Shaw, was more immediately focused
on the War that threatened to engulf Europe and beyond in August 1914.

In the first issue of the *Irish Worker* published after Britain declared War
on 3 August, Connolly asked:

> What should be the attitude of the working-class of Europe in the face of the
> present crisis? ... Should the working class of Europe, rather than slaughter

each other for the benefit of kings and financiers, proceed tomorrow to erect barricades all over Europe, to break up bridges and destroy the transport services that war might be abolished, we would be perfectly justified in following such a glorious example and contributing our aid to the final dethronement of the vulture classes that rule and rob the world. … Starting thus, Ireland may yet set the torch to a European conflagration that will not burn out until the last throne and the last capitalist bond and debenture will be shriveled on the funeral pyre of the last war lord.[22]

At roughly this time, Connolly commented to his socialist and labour comrade William O'Brien, "I will not miss this opportunity" (as quoted in O'Brien, *Forth*, 269).[23]

Shaw, within days of the War beginning, began writing *Common Sense About the War*, published in the *New Statesman* on 14 November 1914, arguably a most potent example of modern journalism and a testament to the free press, the cornerstone of democracy. In its first paragraphs Shaw stated that"until Home Rule emerges from its present suspended animation, I shall retain my Irish capacity for criticising England with something of the detachment of a foreigner, and perhaps with a certain slightly malicious taste for taking the conceit out of her".[24] Shaw, with great courage, criticized the aristocratic foreign policy of Britain's Liberal Government led by Herbert Asquith, with Sir Edward Grey as Foreign Secretary, as well as the British execution of the War during its early months—also led by aristocrats within the British military. Unlike Connolly, Shaw, now that Britain was in the War, committed himself to Britain and France's victory—provided that the War was fought to end all militarism, not just Germany's. Shaw also responded to militant revolutionaries such as Connolly, and warned the warring governments:

No doubt the heroic remedy for this tragic misunderstanding is that both armies should shoot their officers and go home to gather in their harvests in the villages and make revolution in the towns; and though this is not at present a practicable solution, it must be frankly mentioned, because it or something like it is always a possibility.[25]

The backlash against Shaw for *Common Sense About the War*, which the popular and sensationalizing press condemned as unpatriotic and treasonous, was immediate and exhaustive. Theatres chose not to perform Shaw's plays, as his books were removed from shop inventories. Undeterred, Shaw wrote a letter to Dublin's *Freeman's Journal* in the same month,

November 1914, calling for the Irish to fight against Germany, adding: "If they will not join the French army as volunteers, or the British army as regulars, they can, nonetheless, understand that the one thing they must not do if they are good Irishmen is to join the Germans or help the Germans against the French" ("Ireland and the First", 103).[26] For Shaw, it needed to be a war for greater democracy, despite England being allied to autocratic Russia—which Connolly also extensively criticized.

On 12 December 1914, Shaw's essay "The Last Spring of the Old Lion", which compared Britain at War to an old lion springing on whom it thinks is challenging its superiority, was also published in the *New Stateman*. After the *Irish Worker* was suppressed by the British military under the Defence of the Realm Act (DORA) due to the paper's anti-recruitment stance, Connolly started a short-lived weekly named *The Worker*. In its 2 January 1915 edition, Connolly published excerpts from Shaw's "The Last Spring of the Old Lion" in order to bypass censorship with previously published material that criticized Britain's War Government. While they disagreed on the Irish role in the War, Connolly continued to monitor and draw on Shaw—which in June 1915, after women's suffrage activist and socialist Francis Sheehy-Skeffington was arrested and imprisoned for an anti-recruitment speech, Connolly published a letter Shaw wrote in response to Sheehy-Skeffington's imprisonment, along with Sheehy-Skeffington's speech from the dock, in a Liberty Hall pamphlet printed on the newly acquired antiquated printing press; in ten months the press would print the Easter Proclamation.

But during the 1915 spring, Shaw and wife Charlotte visited Ireland and stayed for more than a week with Sir Horace Plunkett, the great co-operator and organizer for improving working and living conditions in rural Ireland. Hosting dinners where people from various political and cultural persuasions frequently attended, Plunkett's home outside Dublin, Kilteragh, was in many ways, an institution. Joining the Shaws and others for dinner, as revealed by Peter Gahan, on 3 April, was Sir Matthew Nathan, the British Undersecretary for Ireland.[27] Before leaving Dublin, the Shaws followed up with a meeting with Nathan on 10 April, possibly at the Undersecretary's home in Phoenix Park. Part of the conversation presumably, and maybe inevitably, turned to the War, with Nathan asking Shaw for help in recruiting Irishmen for the British military, particularly working-class Irish.

Within days the Shaws were visiting Lady Gregory at Coole Parke, County Galway, where they heard of the Abbey Theatre's financial difficulties because of night-time curfews in the city due to the War. German U-Boats threatened sea routes in the Atlantic and on 7 May 1915, the British Cunard passenger ship *Lusitania* was torpedoed and sunk off County Cork, Ireland, with the loss of at least 1119 people, which included Gregory's nephew Hugh Lane.[28] Such prevented the Abbey from undertaking another American tour as they had done in 1911 and 1913 to significant financial rewards.[29] Still, the Abbey was maintaining its regular two to three-week June engagement in London, which the Theatre had been doing since 1907. Yet during a clash with Yeats in the spring of 1915 over the scheduling and rehearsing for the London run, O'Casey's former adversary A. Patrick Wilson resigned as the Abbey's manager. The internal turmoil only added to the Theatre's difficulties in 1915—as did the toll of the War on London audiences. This spurred Shaw on to write his second Irish play for the Abbey Theatre, which as its subtitle "a recruiting pamphlet" suggests, was also his response in part to Matthew Nathan's request for help in recruiting working-class Irish for the British army. A possible added benefit for the play, which Shaw was most likely not aiming for, was some repair to Shaw's reputation following the press backlash against *Common Sense About the War*. The play was *O'Flaherty, V. C.*, which was slated for rehearsals at the Abbey in late October and scheduled to premiere on 23 November.[30]

While it is true that Shaw's play was being rehearsed to premier at the Abbey, an important aspect of that first production is often overlooked, that it would be included in the English music hall circuit for the 1916 summer. Since 1912, the Abbey, following its June London engagements, booked one of its one-act plays from the June run in the music hall circuit—a short play on a music hall bill that included an assortment of entertainments: comic routines, acrobats, films, risqué and romantic songs. Such bookings created revenue for the Abbey during its inactive summers and allowed some of its actors much needed income. This arguably was a significant aspect of the planned Abbey premier of *O'Flaherty, V. C.*, which would have addressed Shaw's prominent reasons for writing the play: provide funding for the Abbey and appeal to working-class Irish audiences within Britain's industrial cities along the music hall circuit to enlist. The music hall circuit the Abbey booked its selected one-act plays since 1912 included London's premier music hall, the Coliseum Theatre. On 12 October 1915, Shaw wrote to Lady Gregory about his concern over whether the play would be approved by the Lord Chamberlain's office in London for the English music hall performances: "It is by no means sure that it will be licensed in England; and a few preliminary trials in Dublin might do no harm".[31] In early November, with the play in rehearsals, Yeats sent a copy of the script to the Abbey's London agent who booked their forays in the music hall circuit, to which Yeats then wrote to Shaw saying that the agent could see nothing in the play that could be objected to by the English censor (*Shaw, Lady Gregory, and the Abbey: A Correspondence and a Record*, 107).[32] Shaw's, Gregory's, and Yeats' concern about whether *O'Flaherty, V. C.* would receive a license in England reflects their focus on the music hall booking (which for Shaw might have also repaired some of the damage to his career since *Common Sense About the War*), as well as concern for the official opposition to the play that emerged in Dublin. But before such opposition appeared, the ITGWU's Liberty Hall, under Connolly, responded.

The ITGWU's amateur theatre company, the Irish Workers' Dramatic Company, also called the Liberty Hall Players, had been organized in 1912 by Delia Larkin, sister to James Larkin. After Delia Larkin's departure during the 1915 summer, Connolly placed the Workers' Dramatic Company under his comrade Helena Molony. Being a trade union activist and socialist since at least 1910, Molony was also an Abbey Theatre actor. In addition, Molony was a member of the Irish Citizen Army, as was another socialist and Abbey actor, Sean Connolly, no relation to James. Since both Molony and Sean Connolly were Abbey actors by autumn 1915, with the latter emerging as an important company actor, it is possible that one or both were in the cast when *O'Flaherty, V. C.* entered rehearsals.[33] For someone who had maintained a keen interest in Shaw's work as James Connolly had, he no doubt received word of Shaw's new play being rehearsed at the Abbey from Molony and Sean Connolly, whether they were in the cast or not given the Abbey's small company of actors. And since James Connolly had used the ITGWU's newpaper *The Workers' Republic* to preach anti-recruitment, a recruiting play by Shaw at the Abbey had to have been astutely considered. Molony quickly inaugurated her leadership of the Workers' Dramatic Company by staging, on 7 November, George Farquhar's 1706 satirical comedy *The Recruiting Officer* at Liberty Hall. Only two weeks earlier in the *Workers' Republic*, Connolly lamented the British "recruiting sergeant" ("Notes on the Front",4).[34] The stage was being set.

In writing his second Irish play, Shaw chose to link *O'Flaherty, V. C.* more closely to the Abbey Theatre's repertoire than he had with his 1904 *John Bull's Other Island*, in which he did quite the opposite.

Specifically, and no doubt mindful of the intention of running the play in the music hall circuit, Shaw turned to Synge, who's 1903 one-act *In the Shadow of the Glen* had proved popular in the music hall circuit since 1912. In writing to Lady Gregory once his play was completed, Shaw suggested that its length would be similar to Gregory's *The Workhouse Ward* but its "picture of the Irish character will make the Playboy seem a patriotic rhapsody by comparison. The ending is cynical to the last possible degree. The idea is that O'Flaherty's experience in the trenches [of the Great War] has induced [in] him a terrible realism and an unbearable candour".[35] Shaw's allusion to *The Playboy of the Western World* was an indication of the play's potential for controversy. But contemplating Shaw's play with *Playboy* in mind, reflects some of Shaw's direction. The last name of Synge's Pegeen Flaherty becomes O'Flaherty in Shaw's play, and the dialogue in *O'Flaherty, V. C.* comes closer to Synge's than *John Bull's*.

The language and gruff character of Mrs. O'Flaherty recalls *Playboy*'s Old Mahon, with both characters portrayed as bullying and abusive parents who, at one point or another, have driven their sons from their homes. In addition, O'Flaherty and Synge's Christy Mahon are both braggarts, as Shaw's Madigan remarks to O'Flaherty, "I think that story about you fighting the Kaiser and the twelve giants of the Prussian guard single-handed would be better for a little toning down".[36] Such subtly connects O'Flaherty's gallous story of killing twelve German soldiers to Christy's false tale, told first in the shebeen, of killing his father. Furthermore, Shaw turns the backyard squabble behind the shebeen in *Playboy*'s Act III into a vocal spat before the landlord's front door as Mrs. O'Flaherty and Tessie incessantly argue, democracy for peasant and landlord. But there was more borrowing from Synge.

The most significant Syngean elements employed by Shaw in *O'Flaherty, V. C.* are from *In the Shadow of the Glen*, again a popular play within the English music hall circuit. When Shaw's Teresa questions O'Flaherty about the gold chain he gave her and about his military V.C. pension, she appears callous, much the same as *Shadow*'s Michael Dara, who thinking Nora's husband dead, counts the money he thinks is now hers and states his intent to marry her. The petty greed is the same, and as in *Shadow*, the loveless marriage to Teresa is avoided by O'Flaherty, a marriage that would have entrapped him as much as Nora's marriage to Dan Burke enslaved her. Both plays also follow a similar structure in reaching their conclusions. In Synge's *Shadow*, the denouement is set into motion by the Tramp offering Nora an escape: "Come with me now, lady of the house, and it's not my blather you'll be hearing only, but you'll be hearing the grouse and the owls with them, and the larks and the big thrushes when the days are warm".[37] The idealism of the speech leads Nora away from her husband and her drudgery. Similarly, at the end of Shaw's play, O'Flaherty tells Madigan of the ideal which he craves and hence will go to in order to escape his abusive home: "Only a month ago, I was in the quiet of the country out at the front, with not a sound except the birds and the bellow of a cow in the distance as it might be, and the shrapnel making little clouds in the heavens, and the shells whistling, and may be a yell or two when one of us was hit".[38] O'Flaherty's speech expresses its idealism buy touching on the images and sounds of nature and war at the front, just as the Tramp's speech touches on images and sounds of nature. In a 14 September letter to Lady Gregory about *O'Flaherty, V. C.*, Shaw writes that there is an important part "played by a thrush"[39] The play opens with a thrush singing until it "utters a note of alarm and flies away", and after Mrs. O'Flaherty and Teresa are pushed into the house near play's end, Shaw's stage direction announces: "the thrush begins to sing melodiously".[40] As the thrush is included in the Tramp's speech in Synge's play representing an escape for Nora, the thrush—of all the birds Shaw could have selected—is actually heard and signals O'Flaherty's escape.

In addition, *O'Flaherty, V. C.* portrays the disruption within O'Flaherty's home life, even though his mother's home is not physically portrayed, as coming not from a nationalist icon like Cathleen Ni Houlihan as in Gregory and Yeats' play, but from the stranger that O'Flaherty now represents—changed due to his experience and worldliness acquired from the War and his time in France. Tellingly, when asked by his mother what has happened to him, O'Flaherty responds: "What's happened to everybody? That's what I want to know. Whats happened to you that I thought all the world of and was afeared of? Whats happened to Sir Pearce, that I thought was a great general, and that I now see to be no more fit to command an army than an old hen? Whats happened to Tessie, that I was mad to marry a year ago, and that I wouldn't take now with all Ireland for her fortune? I tell you the world's creation is crumbling in ruins about me; and then you come and ask whats happened to me?".[41] In his September letter to Lady Gregory about his play, in which Shaw states that the War, in inducing into O'Flaherty "a terrible realism and an unbearable candour", allows O'Flaherty to see "Ireland as it is, his mother as she is, his sweetheart as she is; and he goes back to the dreaded [War] trenches for the sake of peace and quietness".[42] Interestingly, this ability for O'Flaherty to see

Ireland as it, as if the play could instil the same into its audiences, is similar to O'Casey's 1945 comments about his first reactions to reading *John Bull's Other Island* in 1912, that the play led him and Ireland "to face the fact[s]".[43] Facing the facts in *O'Flaherty, V. C.* not only illuminates O'Flaherty, it reveals the cursed agony of his mother's and Teresa's respective plights during the War, as separation allowances and pensions introduced steady cash into the hands of Ireland's destitute, which is an aspect of the play that demands attention.[44] Ireland's economic reality is revealed in the span of the thirty- to forty-minute play.

Despite all of this, *O'Flaherty, V. C.*, as we know, did not premier in Dublin in November 1915 as planned, and the Abbey did not book it into the music hall circuit in summer 1916. The British military pressured Dublin Castle, which in turn pressured the Abbey's management to withdraw the play. The military was concerned that if performed, it would have disrupted their recruiting efforts in Dublin, and their need for more troops was unrelenting given the horrific casualty numbers—especially in 1915 following the two failed Gallipoli campaigns, combined with the slugging western front. This concern was coupled by the many placards then in Dublin celebrating an Irish soldier in the British army who did receive the Victoria Cross, V. C., Michael O'Leary. (At the time Shaw denied that he drew anything in his play from O'Leary, but in 1921 admitted that he did take the idea of the V. C. from O'Leary: "His [O'Leary's] exploit created the situation I dramatized; but my play is entirely fictitious".[45]) However, the play's impact in late 1915 and during the early months into 1916, was still to be felt, thanks to Helena Molony and Sean Connolly, James Connolly's trusted comrades. It is unlikely that Shaw, never one to be politically naïve, was unaware of how the militant socialist Connolly would respond to a play portraying a preference for Britain's War trenches to addressing the poverty at home.

When *O'Flaherty, V. C.* was in rehearsals in November 1915, Matthew Nathan asked the Dublin Employers' Federation for help in recruiting more labourers for the War. This Federation, which had forced the Dublin Lockout, now pressured their military-age labourers to enlist in the military or be sacked. James Connolly responded in the *Workers' Republic* by noting that the Federation's leader, William Martin Murphy, was "ever prominent in anything that savours of an attack upon popular rights".[46] Also during this same month, Connolly met with each member of the ICA, and informed them that they would soon be called on to fight, and wanted no one in the ICA who was not prepared to do so.[47] Connolly was on the path to 1916, which led him to meet in January of that year with Padraic Pearse, Tom Clarke, Joseph Plunkett, Eamonn Ceannt, and Sean MacDiarmada—not only were they on the Irish Republican Brotherhood's military council, each had publicly supported labour during the Dublin Lockout, and, therefore, had built bridges towards Connolly. They set the date for the Rising, of course, on Easter.

Also, in early 1916, the Irish Workers' Dramatic Company entered its most active period, performing a play on Sunday evenings, roughly every two weeks. In the 19 February 1916 *Workers' Republic*, Connolly ran an advertisement announcing that a space within Liberty Hall had been "fitted up as a Theatre to Accommodate the Huge Crowds for which the Front Room is insufficient". A Workers' Orchestra was now to accompany every production, under the direction of Michael Mallin, the ICA's Chief of Staff. Tellingly, the header for the advertisement read: "Next to the Revolution/ The Greatest Event of 1916".[48] A month later, the *Workers' Republic* included an advert for the next evening's performance of the Workers' Dramatic Company: "UNDER WHICH FLAG/A New Play dealing with the '67 Movement in Three Acts, BY JAMES CONNOLLY".[49] Connolly had written his own recruiting play, with the knowledge of Shaw's *O'Flaherty, V. C.*

While not on the literary level of Shaw's play, *Under Which Flag?* counters aspects of *O'Flaherty, V. C.* Set within a rural cottage during the 1867 Fenian risings, not unlike Gregory and Yeats' 1798 set *Cathleen Ni Houlihan*—but without the allegorical fantasy of the Cathleen myth—Connolly sets out to answer Shaw's portrait of O'Flaherty's acquired knowledge from his War experiences that disrupts the domestic proletariat home-life as he sees Ireland as it is, which Shaw portrayed as riddled with the ignorance and poverty epitomized by O'Flaherty's mother and Teresa. First, *Under Which Flag?* opens with the mother figure Ellen O'Donnell conversing with the young woman Mary O'Neill, an orphan who had been taken in by the O'Donnells, as Mary states: "who reared me all these years when they had enough to do to rear their own".[50] The camaraderie between the two is clear, as is the generosity of the O'Donnells—clearly in opposition to the greed of Shaw's Mrs. O'Flaherty but reminiscent, as Peter Gahan suggests, to the Doyles having taken in Nora O'Reilly years prior to the action in *John Bull's Other Island*. And as the action reveals, Mary O'Neill is romantically linked to Ellen's son Frank O'Donnell, echoing Shaw's Teresa.

As the family gathers, the domestic tranquillity is not stirred until Mary asks how the family friend Dan McMahon came to be blind, to which is reported that it was due to an English incarceration. John O'Donnell, one of the sons, then openly disrupts the home by challenging the idea that getting out of Ireland educates: "I'm for America, …Ireland is only fit for slaves. America is the place where a man is a man, a free man".[51] Ellen responds as a character with an internationalist class sense who has presumably never left Ireland: "Always slaving for other people, … And do you think you will get out of that by going to America? …The poor of the world are always slaving for other people, always going hungry that others may be clothed, badly housed that others may live in palaces. 'Tis the way of the world in America as well as in Ireland".[52] The notion of Shaw's O'Flaherty gaining a world view outside of Ireland in the British army is further challenged when son Frank in Connolly's play announces that he intends to enlist in the British army for opportunity and the financial benefits: "I will see the world, be well taken care of, and after my time is done, retire on a pension, and come home and spend my days in Ireland".[53]

Just as O'Flaherty's mother in Shaw's play is appalled that her son wishes, after his military service, to live in France, Shaw's then ideal of republicanism, so Frank O'Donnell's father is horrified by his son's intention of enlisting in the British army. Despite her nationalist flourishes, Mrs. O'Flaherty's objection to France is over a perception of the risqué life offered by French women, not his service in the British army that earns her the separation allowance. In Connolly's play, the father states: "A pension is blood money got from the British government, and every bit of food that's bought with a soldier's money has blood on it, the blood of the people murdered to keep the bloody empire going!".[54] The contrast between O'Flaherty's mother wanting the separation allowance to O'Donnell's father is clear. If such was not enough, and Connolly's play is often not subtle, the character McMahon states: "Ireland has many curses, but the worse curse of all are the poor amadams [i.e. fools] who take the blood money of the enemy, and imagines that they could eat and drink at England's expense without being corrupted".[55] Thus domestic harmony is not destroyed by a character's elevated perspective gained from British military service out of Ireland, as in *O'Flaherty, V. C.*, but by characters who mistakenly believe that out of Ireland the army can elevate their lives to escape their poverty in Connolly's play. By that play's end, Frank O'Donnell having enlisted in the British army, deserts to join an Irish revolution, hence the play's title—all of which points to Connolly' embrace of the idea of revolution in Ireland right on the eve of the 1916 Rising.

In 1945, O'Casey wrote that the 1916 production of Connolly's *Under Which Flag?* in Liberty Hall, which featured the Abbey actor and ICA Captain Sean Connolly in the cast, meant that "the labor movement was flying under false colours".[56]Two years later, O'Casey privately commented that the play was "a terrible, silly, sentimental thing".[57] Such views were in the same vein as O'Casey's first book, *The Story of the Irish Citizen Army*, in 1919, in which he wrote:

> A well-known author has declared that Connolly was the first martyr for Irish Socialism; but Connolly was no more an Irish Socialist martyr than was Robert Emmett, P. H. Pearse, or Theobald Wolfe Tone.[58]

The well-known author was the leftist essayist and ulster-born journalist, and Shaw friend, Robert Lynd, who in 1917 wrote the Introduction to a reprinting of Connolly's last two major theoretical works: *Labour in Irish History* (1910) and *The Re-Conquest of Ireland* (1915). Lynd opened with:

> James Connolly is Ireland's first Socialist martyr. To say so is not arhetorical flourish. It is a simple historical fact that must be admitted even by those who dispute the wisdom of his actions and the excellence of his ideas.[59]

O'Casey, in turn, would strive to create the impression over decades that he opposed Connolly, as his words indicate, because he considered the Easter Rising as a bourgeois exercise to create a bourgeois independent Ireland—despite the evidence to the contrary, which includes Vladimir Lenin's favourable assessment of Connolly's 1916 revolution. Lenin, cognizant of Marx and Engels' 1871 *Ireland and the Irish Question*, which argued that the solution of the Irish question [... was] the solution of the English, and the English as the solution of the European",[60] defended the Dublin Rising against those who dismissed Connolly's efforts: "Whoever expects a 'pure' social revolution will never live to see it. Such a person pays lip service to revolution without understanding what revolution is".[61] But even O'Casey, who in his numerous writings on the ICA never alluded to Shaw's ties to the ICA's formation, had a very different view of Connolly immediately following the Rising and into the early months of 1918, at least publicly. O'Casey had written a number of songs on Connolly in which he endeavoured to interest Dublin publisher

Fergus O'Connor, such as "Voices from the Dead Connolly" and "The Bonnie Bunch of Roses O" in February 1918. James Moran explains that the latter song "castigates England … and puts Connolly on a pedestal".[62] A question that arises then, is what changed O'Casey's public view of Connolly? The answer was rooted in developments that O'Casey probably knew little of at the time, at least not until mid-1918.

When James Larkin accepted an invitation to lecture in the United States after the ITGWU's devastating defeat during the Lockout, leaving Ireland in October 1914, Larkin asked Connolly to lead the union's insurance division and edit the *Irish Worker*, with union official P. T. Daly taking over for Larkin as the ITGWU's Acting General Secretary. Connolly, who had grown to dislike Larkin, as many within the union's leadership had—believing Larkin had pushed its membership against the transport companies before it was ready—asked comrade William O'Brien to recruit the ITGWU's President Tom Foran to convince Larkin to name Connolly as the Acting General Secretary over Daly, who was a firm follower of Larkin's. Of course, Connolly had a point in that when Larkin was in England during the Lockout in December 1913, Connolly was the Acting General Secretary.[63] Foran agreed, resulting in Connolly becoming the Acting General Secretary, as well as the *Irish Worker*'s editor, and Daly was relegated to the insurance division. Obviously, this had significant consequences for Ireland with regard to Connolly who, as the Acting General Secretary, took over as Commandant of the Irish Citizen Army. So, while these machinations helped to set the stage for 1916, they also led to divided camps within the ITGWU after the Rising, which would eventually impact O'Casey.

After the ITGWU officials who had been arrested and interned following the Rising, returned to Dublin, the divided camps began to emerge over the union's leadership. Those who had worked closely with Connolly, such as William O'Brien (then of the tailors' union), Tom Foran, and Cathal O'Shannon, were mindful of the fact that Larkin, at some point, would return from the United States. As such, they again moved against Daly as O'Brien joined the ITGWU. Rumours surfaced that Daly was a Government informer, which began to reach the press. In the 7 March 1918 edition of the *Evening Telegraph*, O'Casey, who had been fairly seemingly inactive within the ITGWU after resigning from the ICA in August 1914 followed by illnesses and then efforts as a writer, wrote in Daly's defence. O'Casey argued that he personally knew that Tom Clarke and Sean Mac Diarmada, both executed 1916 leaders, were close friends with Daly over "many years".[64] Clarke's widow Kathleen Clarke, who was Mac Diarmada's sister, wrote to the paper refuting O'Casey—which prompted O'Casey to write again, this time alluding to a public meeting that Tom Clarke participated in and Daly chaired, "If P. T. Daly did not have the confidence of the militant leaders of the Volunteers, why was he allowed to preside at this meeting?".[65]

At the same time, O'Brien delivered an address at the Trades Union Congress, that was reported in Dublin papers, in which O'Brien attempted to strengthen his position within the Labour movement by drawing on "Connolly, one of whose oldest friends in the labour movement I can proudly claim to be. ... His are the ideals we follow, his principles we adopt, his memory and inspiration from which we draw our strength and our place in the forefront of the fighting army of Labour and in the battle for freedom and justice in this and all other lands".[66] As O'Brien and his allies within Labour, regardless of the fact that they drifted away from Connolly's socialism and radical trade unionism, drew on the memory of Connolly as they endeavoured to push Daly aside, O'Casey steadily slanted himself against Connolly—especially as he interpreted correctly that machinations against Daly were machinations against Larkin. The last development that O'Brien and Foran wanted was Larkin's return to the ITGWU and his role as General Secretary.

Yet in the same year, 1918, as the Great War slugged on (and Bolsheviks waged Russian civil war to consolidate revolution), Shaw again endeavoured to encourage Irish enlistment in the British army by writing *War Issues for Irishmen*. In the small book, Shaw, like O'Brien, drew on James Connolly to make his case—almost echoing O'Brien's public admiration for Connolly's socialist principles. That Shaw did so, seemed on the surface to be at odds with Connolly's anti-recruitment efforts, but it was Connolly's internationalism that Shaw enlisted to his cause, writing:

> But at least they [the Irish] must be dimly conscious that there was anattempt made in Dublin in the Easter of 1916 to establish an independent Irish Republic, and that one of its leaders was a noted Socialist trade unionist named James Connolly who, being captured by the British troops, was denied the right of a prisoner of war, and shot. Now Connolly owed his positionand influence as an Irish Nationalist leader to the part he had taken in organizing the great strike of the transport workers in Dublin in 1913 [the Lockout], and the remains of his organization was the nucleus of thelittle army of the Irish Republican Brotherhood. (*War Issues*, 196–197)

Shaw was not alone in thinking that Connolly was instrumental for bringing the Rising into reality.[67] And in stating that Connolly's Irish Citizen Army, formed during the Lockout, was the "nucleus" of the Rising's rebel army, Shaw was, of course, cognizant of his role in the ICA's formation. Shaw continued by reminding the 1918 Irish that locked out labourers in 1913 were assisted by English workers:

> The strike was sustained for many months after it would have exhausted the resources of the Irish workers [ITGWU] had they not been aided from abroad. Where did the aid come from? From the reckless generosity of the English unions. The English worker fed, out of their own scanty wages, the Irish strikers and their families for months.

English labour unions had provided food relief for locked out workers in Dublin. Next Shaw recalled his stand with Connolly during the 1 November 1913 rally in London, where he, Shaw, had called for locked out Dublin workers to "arm themselves", to which Connolly two weeks later announced the formation of what became the Irish Citizen Army[68]:

> I myself, with Connolly and Mr. George Russell, was among the speakers at a huge meeting got up in aid of the strike by Mr. James Larkin in London[69].... Connolly got the money [raised at the London rally] by the plea that the cause of Labour was the cause all the world over, and that as against the idler and the profiteer England and Ireland were "members one of another".... It is only through Connolly and the international solidarity that Connolly stood for that the Irish worker can be made to feel that his cause and that of the English worker is a common cause. (*War Issues*, 196–197)[70]

It appears (perhaps) that Shaw had read or knew of Connolly's article "The Irish Flag" in the 8 April 1916 *Workers' Republic*, two weeks prior to the Rising, in which Connolly stated: "The cause of labour is the cause of Ireland, the cause of Ireland is the cause of labour".[71] Indeed, Shaw's portrait of Connolly in *War Issues* arguably recognized that Connolly was foremost an internationalist, which was also testified to by Connolly's first article published after the Great War was declared in August 1914, in which he wrote, quoted above, of Ireland lighting the European conflagration of an international or European socialist revolution. And November 1914, in *Common Sense About the War*, Shaw anticipated Connolly's reaction and such conflagrations as he warned the warring capitalist and imperialist governments that such revolutions were possible during the War, which proved prophetic after the Easter Rising with Russian Bolsheviks seizing Petrograd (St. Petersburg) and Moscow during their October 1917 Revolution. While Shaw was not a Connolly-ite, he could sympathize with Connolly's means in 1916, as he did in 1917 with Lenin's means in Petrograd when he scolded a Fabian Society meeting when objections to Bolshevik violence were expressed: "We are socialists".[72]

In the year following Shaw's *War Issues for Irishmen*, 1919, O'Casey published his history of the Irish Citizen Army, and attempted a second book that he titled "Three Shouts on a Hill", which included three essays: one on labour, a second on nationalism, and a third on Gaelic.[73] O'Casey sent his manuscript to Shaw, and asked Shaw to write a preface for the book. Shaw, who did not then know O'Casey or anything about him, replied on 3 December: "Of course the publishers will publish it with a preface by me; but how will that advance you as an author? ... You must go through the mill like the rest and get published for your own sake, not mine". But with regard to O'Casey's three essays in his manuscript, Shaw asked: "Why do you not come out definitely on the side of Labour & the English language? ... You ought to work out your position positively & definitely. This objecting to everyone else is Irish, but useless".[74] Perhaps taking Shaw's advice, O'Casey began refining his focus, which positioned him for the 1920s—and for Larkin's return.

James Larkin returned to Dublin in 1923, after serving a prison sentence in the United States for sedition due to his work on behalf of American labour. While O'Brien and Foran, treasurer and president of the ITGWU, respectively, were still not favouring Larkin's return as the union's General Secretary, Larkin hurt his cause before even leaving New York. He cabled Foran "for £5,000 to buy a steamer" ship.[75] While offering little by way of an explanation or rationale as to why the ITGWU needed a ship, Foran refused the request.[76] Emmet O'Connor notes that the "self-seeking demands on the union's purse" incensed O'Brien (83).[77] O'Brien and Foran then moved to restrict the General Secretary's powers by proposing a five-person leadership team.[78] But in 1924, Larkin attempted to regain his control of the ITGWU, which O'Brien aggressively countered by focusing on the Rapid Transit Company breaking an ITGWU picket line at the Kingsbridge Rail Station. The Rapid Transit Company was owned by Delia Larkin's husband Patrick Colgan, where there was an insinuation that Larkin himself was an investor in the company—Colgan and Delia lived in the same Dublin house as Larkin.[79] O'Brien, whom O'Casey would remember as "the mangy rat", moved quickly and managed to expel Larkin from the ITGWU. O'Casey, along with Larkin's other friends and supporters, was extremely embittered over O'Brien's consolidation of autonomy within the ITGWU that orchestrated Larkin's expulsion, especially as Larkin was still officially the General Secretary when expelled. But by this time, O'Casey had emerged as an Abbey playwright, most notably with *The Shadow of the Gunman* in 1923 and *Juno and the Paycock* the following year—establishing O'Casey's focus on the Dublin proletariat paying a cost of republican violence. But the ascent of O'Brien in the ITGWU, and Larkin's expulsion, sharpened O'Casey's focus against Connolly as, arguably, a way to strike at O'Brien, who continued to portray himself as Connolly's close comrade and friend. This focus is embodied in *The Plough and the Stars*, a play which O'Casey biographer Christopher Murray suggests had "more to do with Dublin 1924 than with Dublin 1916" (163).[80]

Despite being a tightly constructed drama, *Plough's* historical inaccuracies cannot be denied. Moving Padraic Pearse's dramatic end of his speech delivered at Jeremiah O'Donovan Rossa's burial site in Glasnevin Cemetery on 1 August 1915 to the outside of a Dublin pub while Pearse, as well as Connolly and many of their followers, actively advocated abstinence, leans to an unfair portrait. This is loudly echoed by the play's ICA officers entering the pub for drinks or stiffeners during the speech. However, despite republicans who objected during the play's premier to a prostitute's presence amid Pearse's iconic words leading to the Rising, Connolly, so conscious of the plight of his class and women's plights within that class, arguably would not have objected to Rosie Redmond's presence—and we know that Shaw definitely would not have objected, given *Mrs Warren's Profession*, as well as the character Feemy Evans in *The Shewing-up of Blanco Posnet* (which was still a staple in the Abbey's 1926 repertoire). More importantly, as James Moran points out in *The Theatre of Sean O'Casey*, Connolly is portrayed in *Plough* as "the figure who directly coaxes men to their death, away from the love and comfort of home life".[81] In fact, in a seeming response to Connolly's *Under Which Flag?*, O'Casey portrays Connolly, who does not appear in the play, as the force that disrupts the tranquillity of the home in *The Plough and the Stars*, rather than the young men seeking work and opportunity through emigration and British army enlistment, as in Connolly's play, or O'Flaherty's acquired knowledge from the Great War that allows him to see Ireland for what it is in Shaw's play. Scathingly, Nora Clitheroe in Act I of *The Plough and the Stars* asks her husband, once he commits himself to the Irish Citizen Army: "Is

General Connolly an' the Citizen Army goin' to be your only care?" (quoted in Moran, 38).[82] And while Clitheroe's involvement in Connolly's ICA indeed leads to his death, to Nora's loss of their child, and to Nora's madness—not to mention the horrors that befall the other folk living within the portrayed Dublin tenement—Nora continues her speech, breaching a deeper portrait:

> Is your home goin' to be only a place of merry-makin' at night for you? Your vanity'll be th' ruin of you an' me yet.... That's what's movin' you: because they made an officer of you, you'll make a glorious cause of what you're doin', while your little red-lipped Nora can go on sitting here, makin' a companion of th' loneliness of th' night' (O'Casey, 92).[83]

Nora's words play into Clitheroe's desire for importance, arguably representing such desire within the working and sweated classes. O'Casey not only portrays the cost of Connolly's revolution on impoverished Dubliners, but, like Shaw and Connolly in *O'Flaherty, V. C.* and *Under Which Flag?*, respectively, touches on—perhaps more effectively than in the two previous plays—the desperation of the poor for relevance, which makes *Plough*, despite its historical liberties, a great play.[84]

O'Casey would next write one of the greatest of internationalist Irish dramas when he directly drew again from *O'Flaherty, V. C.* for his 1927 *The Silver Tassie*, itself a play of the Great War that arguably also echoes Shaw's *Common Sense About the War* with regard to the proletarian class. As Anthony Roche argues in his encompassing *The Irish Dramatic Revival 1899–1939*, O'Casey pulls from Shaw's Mrs. O'Flaherty in the form of his Mrs. Heegan., Portraying further the working-class desperation generated by the British Separation Allowance during the War. As Mrs. O'Flaherty desires the War to continue to maintain her separation allowance—clearly a priority that negates any concern for her son's welfare at War—is matched by Mrs. Heegan's anxiety to see her son Harry board the ship that will return him to the War so her same allowance continues.[85] By the time he wrote *The Silver Tassie*, O'Casey was well on his way to internationalizing his own socialist perspective as reflected in his growing interest in Soviet Russia, as Susan Cannon Harris reflects in *Irish Drama and the Other Revolutions*.[86] Two years after completing the play, O'Casey would declare that the work "is the best play I have written".[87] And on reading it, Shaw famously reacted with: "What a hell of a play!".[88] Of course, the greed for the separation allowance during the War as portrayed by Shaw and

O'Casey, again indicative of the economic difficulties facing the working-class, was also an issue Connolly addressed in his anti-recruitment editorials and articles, and in the desire of his play's Frank O'Donnell for the army pension, selling himself for the steady income—an income unknown for too many trapped within the excessive poverty.

The Abbey Theatre rejected *The Silver Tassie* in 1928, unable to reconcile itself to the play's internationalism as War imaging. That same year, Shaw published his long gestating *The Intelligent Woman's Guide to Socialism and Capitalism*, in which he arguably and consciously echoed Connolly's *The Re-Conquest of Ireland* in considering the condition of women under capitalism: where "she becomes the slave of a slave".[89] Shaw's access to Connolly's *Re-Conquest* most likely was through its 1917 reprint in *Labour in Ireland: Labour in Irish History, The Re-Conquest of Ireland*, in which Shaw's friend Robert Lynd contributed the Introduction—the introduction O'Casey had refuted in his *The Story of the Irish Citizen Army*. Lynd, like Shaw and Horace Plunkett, contributed to the fund to assist Connolly's widow Lily Connolly and family after his execution, which had been organized by George Russell and the surgeon who treated Connolly's wounds after the Rising, while held in Dublin Castle, Richard Tobin. While Shaw contributed the most, Russell and Tobin maintained a direct interest in Connolly's son Roderic.[90] The socialist Connolly had made an impression, and the shared internationalist convictions between Shaw and Connolly on the plight of proletariat women remains, obviously, abundantly relevant—while the brilliant *The Silver Tassie* allowed its author the continued internationalist mantle, if briefly.[91]

NOTES

1. John Millington Synge, *The Playboy of the Western World*, 116.
2. See Anthony Roche's excellent *The Irish Dramatic Revival 1899–1939* and the above *Synge, Connolly, and Socialist Provocation* for more on the ties between *The Shewing-up of BlancoPosnet* and *The Playboy of the Western World* (Roche, 90–91; O'Ceallaigh Ritschel, 80–85).
3. See O'Casey's 1911 correspondence with the Great Northern Railway's secretary in *The Collected Letters of Sean O'Casey, Vol. I, 1910–1941*, edited by David Krause.
4. Sean O'Casey, *The Collected Letters of Sean O'Casey, Vol. I*, 742.
5. Sean O'Casey, *Drums Under the Window*, 257.

6. A. Patrick Wilson (who used the name Andrew P. Wilson in Scotland) was a regular contributor to the *Irish Worker* prior to 1915 and often used the pseudonym "Euchan", as he did in the debate with O'Casey—a debate O'Casey initiated. See O'Casey's published debate with Wilson in the *Irish Worker*, 8 February to 8 March 1913 in *The Letters of Sean O'Casey, Vol. I, 1910–1941*, edited by David Krause.

7. Lane offered to donate his collection of Impressionist paintings to Dublin if the city provided a suitable gallery to house the collection. While there was much support for providing a gallery, there was significant opposition, as by William Martin Murphy who objected to using public funds for the project.

8. James Connolly, "Labour in Dublin", 387.

9. James Connolly, quoted in Francis Sheehy-Skeffington, "London's Magnificent Rally to the Dublin Rebels", 1.

10. Shaw, George Bernard, "Mad Dogs in Uniform", 97. Perhaps it should be stated that Shaw's call for Dublin labour to "arm themselves" refers to the arming of the working class against the physical oppression from by the state, in this case through the Dublin Metropolitan Police. Shaw's call was decidedly not a call to arm individuals as in a right to arm for the sake of arming. Shaw's political call for arming the working class was also made on 1 February 1905 at a meeting of the Society of the Friends of Russian Freedom, which was itself in response to Russian workers who were fired on by Tsar Nicholas II's troops on 9 January 1905. Hundreds of workers and their families had marched in procession to the Winter Palace in St. Petersburg in order to present petitions for social improvements to Nicholas. Shaw stated, as reported by London's *Times*: "until all the working-class populations of the world understood that when they stirred out of their ordinary round to oppose the state they must do it with arms in their hands or it would be understood that none of them really meant business" ("The Crisis in Russia", *The Times*, 2 February 1905, quoted in Soboleva and Wrenn, 113).

11. James Connolly, quoted in Donal Nevin, *James Connolly: 'A Full Life'*, 463.

12. "In Croyden Park", 6.

13. In his 2017 book *Judging Shaw*, Fintan O'Toole makes the same point about James Connolly using the title from Shaw's *Arms and the Man* for his 13 December article in the *Irish Worker* on the Irish Citizen Army (114). This connection and point was first made in *Shaw, Synge, Connolly, and Socialist Provocation* in 2011 (155).

14. D. R. O'Connor Lysaght, "The Irish Citizen Army, 1913–1916: White, Larkin, and Connolly", 21.

15. The London press that was pro-employers and against labour and social-ism, like the *Daily Sketch*, reacted strongly to Shaw's 1 November speech

by calling for his arrest for "inciting armed revolt" (Laurence and Grene, "Introduction and Notes", 96). The reaction of the pro-employers press in Dublin was much different. Rather than add credence to Shaw in Ireland by calling for his arrest, the Dublin commercial bourgeois press sought to undermine and dismiss Shaw. The *Irish Times*: "[Shaw] boasts that he left Ireland at the age of twenty, and has not lived here since. As a licensed buffoon and consecrated prophet of the patently absurd, he has to support his reputation by insisting that what is obviously wrong is quite clearly right" ("Mr. Bernard Shaw on the Strike",6). The *Sunday Independent* (the Sunday version of William Martin Murphy's *Irish Independent*) struck a similar tone as it published a cartoon depicting Shaw as"G. B. S., the Buffoon". James Connolly, at the time handling the editor's duties of *The Irish Worker* while James Larkin was imprisoned, published a cartoon by Ernest Kavanagh on 9 November that depicted Murphy cast on to rocks by other members of the Employers Federation, which Murphy led against workers. Titled "On the Rocks", the cartoon suggested that a split was possible within the Federation given Murphy's "obsession with destroying Larkin and the ITGWU, i.e., that their relationship could be 'on the rocks'" (Curry, 78).

16. Irish Citizen Army Constitution, quoted in Arrington, Lauren. *Revolutionary Lives: Constance and Casimir Markievicz*, 102.
17. James Connolly, *Labour in Irish History*, 188.
18. Adrian Grant, *Irish Socialist Republicanism 1909–36*, 37.
19. Sean O'Casey (P. O'Cathasaigh), "Volunteers and Workers", *Irish Worker*, in *Sean O'Casey Letters, Vol. I*, 40–41.
20. Padraig Pearse, quoted in Peter Berresford, Ellis, *A History of the Irish Working Class*, 223–224.
21. Padraig Pearse, quoted in Padraig Yeates, *Lockout Dublin 1913*, 220.
22. James Connolly, "Our Duty in the Crisis", 4.
23. Quoted in William O'Brien, *Forth the Banners Go: Reminiscences of William O'Brien as Told to Edward MacLysaght*, 4.
24. George Bernard Shaw, *Common Sense About the War*, 16–17.
25. Ibid., 17.
26. George Bernard Shaw, "Ireland and the First World War", 103.
27. Peter Gahan, "Bernard Shaw in Two Great Irish Houses: Kilteragh and Coole" (in this Volume).
28. The Shaws encountered some of the *Lusitania*'s survivors during their return voyage to England from Ireland. In his Preface to *Heartbreak House*, Shaw recalled: "To me, with my mindfull of the hideous cost of Neuve, Chapelle, Ypres, and the Gallipoli landing, the fuss about the Lusitania [sic] seemed almost a heartless impertinence, though I was well acquainted personally with [...] and understood better perhaps than most

people, the misfortune of the death of [Hugh] Lane" (34). The ship sank in less than eighteen minutes. The imprecise number of lives lost is due to the fact that not all servants traveling with First Class passengers were listed among the passengers. This was the practice at the time, and between competing passenger liners. The White Star's *Titanic* also has an imprecise number for those lost with the ship.

29. However, the dangers crossing the Atlantic in 1915 did not prevent Lady Gregory from traveling to the United States for a lecture tour in the 1915 autumn.

30. Dan H. Laurence and Nicholas Grene, "Notes", *Shaw, Lady Gregory, and the Abbey: A Correspondence and a Record*, 105.

31. George Bernard Shaw, *Shaw, Lady Gregory, and the Abbey: A Correspondence and a Record*, 104.

32. William Butler Yeats, *Shaw, Lady Gregory, and the Abbey: A Correspondence and a Record*, 107. Dan H. Laurence and Nicholas Grene indicate that *O'Flaherty, V. C.* was in rehearsals by the second week of November 1915 ("Notes". 106).

33. Shaw had requested Abbey actors Arthur Sinclair and Sara Allgood for the cast of *O'Flaherty, V. C.*; both were not then with the Abbey. However, Sinclair was rehired but Allgood was then in Australia and unavailable. Helen Molony, like Allgood, was often cast in older roles. In the previous year, Sean Connolly played the lead in Edward McNulty's *The Lord Mayor*. McNulty was a childhood friend of Shaw's, which both continued as adults.

34. James Connolly, "Notes on the Front", 4.

35. Shaw, *Shaw, Lady Gregory, and the Abbey: A Correspondence and a Record*, 95.

36. George Bernard Shaw, *O'Flaherty, V. C.*, 261.

37. John Millington Synge, *In the Shadow of the Glen*, 43.

38. Shaw, *O'Flaherty, V. C.*, 276.

39. Shaw, *Shaw, Lady Gregory, and the Abbey: A Correspondence and a Record*, 94.

40. Shaw, *O'Flaherty, V. C.*, 258; 276.

41. Shaw, *O'Flaherty, V. C.*, 273.

42. Shaw, *Lady Gregory, and the Abbey: A Correspondence and a Record*, 95.

43. O'Casey, *Drums Under the Windows*, 257.

44. In the 5 February 1916 *Workers' Republic*, Connolly lamented the financial enticements the British army offered the working class: "For the sake of a few paltry shillings per week thousands of Irish workers have sold their country in the hour of their country's greatest need and hope. For the sake of a few paltry shillings Separation Allowance thousands of Irish women have made life miserable for their husbands with entreaties to join the British Army" ("Ties ThatBind", 1).

45. George Bernard Shaw, *Bernard Shaw Collected Letters, 1911–1925, Vol. 3*, 717.

46. James Connolly, "Enlist or Starve", 1. Shaw, also at this time, provided Nathan with a poster-text on how to more effectively recruit working-class Irishmen. In February 1916, the British issued a recruiting pamphlet from Dublin Castle, stating that "the Dublin slums were more unhealthy than the trenches in Flanders"(quoted in Nevin, 615). Arguably, this sentiment was in Shaw's poster-text as he re-uses it in *War Issues for Irishmen* in 1918, specifically as: "A Trench is a safer place than a Dublin slum"(*War Issues*, 198). Undoubtedly, Shaw did not retrieve the idea from the British recruiting pamphlet, which he probably never saw. Connolly responded to the British pamphlet in February 1916, writing: "You can die honourably in a Dublin slum,...if you die of fever orwant, rather than sell your soul to the enemies of your class and country" (quoted in Nevin,616).

47. O'Brien, *Forth the Banners Go: Reminiscences of William O'Brien as Told to Edward MacLysaght*, 195.

48. James Connolly, "Next to the Revolution" Advert, 4.

49. James Connolly, *Under Which Flag?* Advert, 4.

50. James Connolly, *Under Which Flag?* 106.

51. Ibid., 112.

52. Ibid., 112. As Ellen O'Donnell's internationalist class perception reflects Connolly's seven years in America as a labour organizer and socialist, as well as his socialistic background in Scotland, Connolly inadvertently—through Ellen's perspective—reinforces Shaw's point about gaining a world perspective once outside of Ireland.

53. Ibid., 113.

54. Ibid., 114.

55. Ibid., 115.

56. Sean O'Casey, quoted in Christopher Murray, *Sean O'Casey: Writer at Work*, 97.

57. Sean O'Casey, *The Letters of Sean O'Casey, 1942–1954, Vol. II*, 438.

58. Sean O'Casey, *The Story of the Irish Citizen Army*, 52.

59. Robert Lynd, Introduction, James Connolly, *Labour in Ireland: Labour in Irish History, The Re-Conquest of Ireland*, vii.

60. Karl Marx and Frederick Engels, *Ireland and the Irish Question*, 251.

61. Vladimir Lenin, *The Discussion of Self-Determination Summed Up*. In January 1918, only months after Russia's October Revolution in which Bolsheviks seized Petrograd (St. Petersburg) and Moscow, Connolly's colleagues William O'Brien and Cathal O'Shannon met Maxim Litvinov, the Soviet plenipotentiary in London. O'Shannon recalled the meeting: "It was a great pleasure for us to hear him speak of James Connolly, and as he spoke I thought how Connolly's heart would have rejoiced at the success

of the Bolsheviks, and how he would have handled the situation. In Russian, Litvinoff told us, they had heard of Connolly and his work years ago, even before 1913" (quoted in O'Connor, 14). When Connolly's son Roderic travelled to Petrograd in 1920 and was introduced to Lenin by radical American journalist John Reed, Lenin told Roderic that he had read Connolly's *Labour in Irish History* and described James Connolly as "'head and shoulders' above his contemporaries in the European socialist movement" (quoted in Charlie McGuire, *Roddy Connolly and the Struggle for Socialism in Ireland*, 36).

62. James Moran, *The Theatre of Sean O'Casey*, 37.

63. In December 1913, Connolly maintained crucial ITGWU correspondence and signed the letters as "Acting General Secretary" (as in letter to G. Sherlock, Lord Mayor, 11 December1913, http://catalogue.nli.ie/Record/vtls000626661).

64. O'Casey, *The Letters of Sean O'Casey, 1910–1941, Vol. I*, 74.

65. Ibid., 78.

66. William O'Brien, quoted in Barry Desmond, *No Workers' Republic: Reflections on Labour and Ireland, 1913–1967*, 31. William O'Brien also in early 1917 was instrumental in reviving the Socialist Party of Ireland (SPI), and was elected its chairman. The SPI had roots with Connolly on his return from the United States in 1910, but an earlier party of the same name was formed in1904 after Connolly had emigrated—but was defunct before 1909. The resurgent SPI of 1910, faded once Connolly became Acting General Secretary of the ITGWU, and Commandant of the ICA in October 1914. Under O'Brien's leadership, the resurfaced SPI in 1917 "advertised itself as founded by Connolly" (quoted in O'Connor, 19). Emmet O'Connor argues that O'Brien used the SPI in order "to place himself at the heart of the resurgent ITGWU" (17).

67. Shaw's friend, the Dublin poet George Russell who knew Connolly well and who had also been on the speakers' platform on 1 November 1913 with Connolly and Shaw, stated in his post-1916 poem "To the Memory of Some I knew Who Are Dead" that Connolly "cast the last torch on the pile" that ignited the Rising, as in a conflagration (as quoted in Nevin, 704).

68. Shaw, "Mad Dogs in Uniform", 97; Nevin, *James Connolly: 'A Full Life'*, 463.

69. Among the English socialists and suffragettes who also spoke at the 1 November 1913 London rally on behalf of Larkin and locked out Dublin workers was Silvia Pankhurst. In 1920, Pankhurst assisted Connolly's son Roderic in traveling to Russia, where Roderic met Lenin and attended the Second Comiterm Congress (McGuire, 32).

70. George Bernard Shaw, *War Issues for Irishmen*, 196–197.

71. James Connolly, "The Irish Flag", 1.

72. Olga Soboleva and Angus Wrenn, *The Only Hope of the World: George Bernard Shaw and Russia*, 119.

73. David Krause, "Notes", *The Letters of Sean O'Casey, 1910–1941, Vol. I*, 87.

74. George Bernard Shaw, in *The Letters of Sean O'Casey, 1910–1941, Vol. I*, 88.

75. Emmet O'Connor, *The Reds and the Green: Ireland, Russia and the Communist Internationals,1919–43*, 83.

76. Ibid., 83.

77. Ibid.

78. Ibid., 84.

79. Gerry Watts, "Delia Larkin and the Game of 'House'", 37–38.

80. Murray, *Sean O'Casey: Writer at Work*, 163. While *The Plough and the Stars* premiered in 1926, O'Casey began writing it in 1924.

81. Moran, *The Theatre of Sean O'Casey*, 38.

82. Quoted in Ibid., 38.

83. Sean O'Casey, *The Plough and the Stars*, 92.

84. The same desperation for relevance is seen throughout *The Plough and the Stars*, as in Peter Flynn in his Foresters' uniform, in The Covey with his copy of the fictitious Jenersky's *Thesis on the Origin, Development, an' Consolidation of the Evolutionary Idea of the Proletariat*, and even in Nora's desire for a loving husband.

85. Anthony Roche, *The Irish Dramatic Revival, 1899–1939*, 95–96; 141.

86. Susan Cannon Harris, *Irish Drama and the Other Revolution*, 173.

87. O'Casey, *The Letters of Sean O'Casey, 1910–1941, Vol. I*, 329.

88. Ibid., 284.

89. George Bernard Shaw, *The Intelligent Woman's Guide to Socialism and Capitalism*, 197; James Connolly, *The Re-Conquest of Ireland*, 38. In *The Re-Conquest of Ireland*, Connolly stated the above as: "The worker is the slave of capitalist society, the female is the slave of that slave"(38). In 1972, John Lennon and Yoko Ono wrote and released their song "Woman is the Nigger of the World", which included the lyrics "Woman is the slave to the slave". In an American television interview with Dick Cavett, also in 1972, Lennon, with Ono seated next to him, explained the song and defended its title. In his comments, Lennon stated that they included the idea of "woman is slave of a slave, that is what Connolly said, the great Irishman"(https://www.youtube.com/watch?v=iOu7QtVLfJQ). This is an interesting notion on many levels, not the least of which indicates that Lennon too read Connolly's *The Re-Conquest of Ireland*, in part or whole. This might lead to the speculation of that the inclusion of Shaw's image on the cover of the Beatle's 1967 *Sgt. Pepper* album was Lennon's idea. Lennon often linked himself towards socialist ideas in his work, such as in his 1970 song "Working Class Hero". In his contributed dramatic sketch "James Connolly" in the 2016 theatrical literary response to the centennial

of the 1916 Easter Rising, *Signatories*, that was staged within Dublin's Kilmainham Goal (where the seven signatories of the Easter Proclamation were executed, along with seven other rebel combatants), Hugo Hamilton ends with an economically marginalized immigrant woman singing Lennon's "Working Class Hero" in Britain (40).

90. Peter Grogan Rare Books, *Catalogue Four*. Perhaps if Plunkett's contribution to the fund for Connolly's family had been public knowledge, Plunkett's home Kilteragh might not have been burned by Republicans during the Irish Civil War—although that is by no means a surety given that Connolly's radicalism and socialism was not shared by many Republicans.

91. A fuller and more nuanced consideration of the post-1916 parallel tracks of Shaw and O'Casey, in the shadow of Connolly, will be in my forthcoming monograph, *Bernard Shaw, Sean O'Casey, and the Dead James Connolly*.

REFERENCES

Arrington, Lauren. 2016. *Revolutionary Lives: Constance and Casimir Markievicz*. Princeton: Princeton University Press.

Barton, Brian. 2010. *The Secret Court Martial Records of the 1916 Easter Rising*. Stroud: The History Press.

Boyd, Andrew. 2003. Robert Lynd: Essayist and Irishman.*History Ireland* Issue 2 (Summer). http://www.historyireland.com/20th-century-contemporary-history/robert-lynd-essayist-and-irishman/.Accessed 7 July 2017.

Connell, Joseph E.A., Jr. 2006. *Where's Where in Dublin: A Dictionary of Historic Locations, 1913–1923*. Dublin: Dublin City Council.

Connolly, James. 1913. Letter to Lorcan G. Sherlock, Lord Mayor, December 11.catalogue.nli.ie/Record/vtis000626661. Accessed 29 Jan 2018.

———.1914a.The Isolation of Dublin.*Forward*, February 9, 4.

———. 1914b. Our Duty in the Crisis.*Irish Worker*, August 8, 4.

———. 1915a. Enlist or Starve.*Workers' Republic*, November 27, 1.

———.1915b.Notes on the Front.*Workers' Republic*, October 16, 4.

———. 1915c. *The Re-Conquest of Ireland*. Dublin: Liberty Hall.

———. 1916a. The Irish Flag.*Workers' Republic*. April 8.

———. 1916b. "Next to the Revolution" Advert. *Workers' Republic*, February 19, 4.

———. 1916c. The Ties That Bind.*The Workers Republic*, February 5, 1.

———. 1916d. *Under Which Flag?* Advert. *Workers' Republic*, March 25, 4.

———. 1917. *"Labour in Irish History." Labour in Ireland: Labour in Irish History, the Re-Conquest of Ireland*. Dublin: Maunsell.

———. 1973. A Continental Revolution. In *James Connolly's Selected Writings*, ed. P. Berresford Ellis, 239–242. London: Pluto Press.

———. 2007a. *Between Comrades: James Connolly, Letters and Correspondence 1889–1916*.Ed. Donal Nevin. Dublin: Gill and Macmillan.

———. 2007b. Under Which Flag? In *Four Irish Rebel Plays*, ed. James Moran, 105–132. Dublin: Irish Academic Press.

Curry, James. 2012. *Artist of the Revolution: The Cartoons of Ernest Kavanagh (1884–1916)*. Cork: Mercier Press.

———. 2014. The Worker: James Connolly's 'Organ of the Irish Working Class'. In *Periodicals and Journalism in Twentieth-Century Ireland: Writing Against the Grain*, ed. Mark O'Brien and Felix M. Larkin, 75–88. Dublin: Four Courts Press.

Desmond, Barry. 2009. *No Workers' Republic: Reflections on Labour and Ireland, 1913–1967*. Dublin: Watchword.

Ellis, Peter Berresford. 1972. *A History of the Irish Working Class*. London: Pluto Press.

English, Richard. 2007. *Irish Freedom: The History of Nationalism in Ireland*. London: Pan Books.

Ferriter, Diarmaid. 2005. *The Transformation of Ireland*. London: Profile Books.

Figes, Orlando. 2017. 1917: Russia's Year of Revolution.*National Geographic History*, September/October,70–89.

Gahan, Peter. 2008. John Bull's Other War: Bernard Shaw and the Anglo-Irish War, 1918. In *SHAW: The Annual of Bernard Shaw Studies*, Volume 28, Shaw and War, ed. Lagretta Tallent Lanker, 209–238. University Park: Pennsylvania State University Press.

———. 2017. Bernard Shaw and the Irish Convention.*History Ireland: Ireland After the Rising 1916–1918 Changed Utterly*, a *History Ireland* Annual, 81–85.

———. 2020. Bernard Shaw in Two Great Irish Houses: Kilteragh and Coole.*Bernard Shaw and the Making of Modern Ireland*. Cham: Palgrave Macmillan.

Gibbs, A.M. 2005. *Bernard Shaw: A Life*. Gainesville: University Press of Florida.

Grant, Adrian. 2012. *Irish Socialist Republicanism 1909–36*. Dublin: Four Courts Press.

Grogan, Peter. 2017. Rare Books. *Catalogue Four*. Autumn.

Hamilton, Hugo. 2016. James Connolly. In *Signatories*, 29–42. Dublin: University College Dublin Press.

Harris, Susan Cannon. 2017. *Irish Drama and the Other Revolutions*. Edinburg: Edinburg University Press.

Holroyd, Michael. 1988. *Bernard Shaw: Volume I, 1856–1898, the Search for Love*. New York: Random.

"In Croyden Park". 1913. *Irish Times*, December 1, 6.

Krause, David. 1975. Notes. In *The Letters of Sean O'Casey, 1910–1941, Vol. 1*, ed. David Krause, 87, 183. New York: Macmillan.

Laurence, Dan H., and Nicholas Grene. 1993. Notes. In *Shaw, Lady Gregory, and the Abbey: A Correspondence and a Record*, ed. Dan H. Laurence and Nicholas Grene, 106. Gerrards Cross: Colin Smythe.

Lenin, Vladimir. The Discussion of Self-Determination Summed Up. https://www.marxists.org/archive/lenin/works/1916/jul/x01.htm.   Accessed 27 Dec 2017.

———. The Socialist Revolution and the Right of Nations to Self-Determination. https://www.marxists.org/archive/lenin/works/1916/jan/x01.htm. Accessed 27 Dec 2017.

Lennon, John and Yoko Ono Television Interview with Dick Cavett.1972. https://www.youtube.com/watch?v=iOu7QtVLfJQ

Lynd, Robert. 1916a. If the Germans Conquered England. *Irish War News*, April 25, 1–2.

———.1916b. If the Germans Conquered England. *New Statesman*, April.

———. 1917. Introduction: James Connolly. In *Labour in Ireland: Labour in Irish History, the Re-Conquest of Ireland*, vii–xxvi. Dublin: Maunsell.

MacLochlainn, Piaras F. 2005. *Last Words*. Dublin: Office of Public Works.

Marx, Karl, and Frederick Engels. 1971. *Ireland and the Irish Question*. Moscow: Progress Publishers.

McGeever, Brendan. The Easter Rising and the Soviet Union: An Untold Chapter in Ireland's Great Rebellion. www.opendemocracy.net/uk/brendan-mcgeever/easter-rising-and-soviet-union-untold-chapter-in-ireland-s-great-rebellion. Accessed 30 Dec 2017.

McGuire, Charlie. 2008. *Roddy Connolly and the Struggle for Socialism in Ireland*. Cork: Cork University Press.

Moran, James. 2013. *The Theatre of Sean O'Casey*. London: Bloomsbury Methuen.

Morrissey, Thomas, S. J. 2007. *William O'Brien, 1881–1968: Socialist, Republican, Dail Deputy, Editor, and Trade Union Leader*. Dublin: Four Courts Press.

Murphy, Paul. 2013. O'Casey and Class. In *The Theatre of Sean O'Casey*, ed. James Moran, 227–242. London: Bloomsbury Methuen.

Murray, Christopher. 2004. *Sean O'Casey: Writer at Work*. Dublin: Gill and Macmillan.

Nevin, Donal. 2005. *James Connolly: 'A Full Life'*. Dublin: Gill and Macmillan.

"Nora Connolly O'Brien and Leon Trotsky Correspondence (1936)." www.marxist.org/history/etol/document/Ireland-fi/norac.htm. Accessed 30 Dec 2017.

O'Brien, William. 1969. *Forth the Banners Go: Reminiscences of William O'Brien as Told to Edward MacLysaght*. Dublin: Three Candles Press.

O'Casey, Sean. 1919. (P. O'Cathasaigh). *The Story of the Irish Citizen Army*. London: The Journeyman Press.

———. 1928. *The Silver Tassie*. New York: Macmillan.

———. 1956. *Drums Under the Windows. Mirror in My House: The Autobiographies of Sean O'Casey, Volume I*, 375–431. New York: Macmillan.

————.1975a. *The Letters of Sean O'Casey, 1910–1941, Vol. 1*. Ed. David Krause. New York: Macmillan.

————. 1975b. Volunteers and Workers. In *Sean O'Casey Letters, Vol. I*, ed. David Krause. New York: Macmillan.

————.1980. *The Letters of Sean O'Casey, 1942–1954, Vol. II*. Ed. David Krause. New York: Macmillan.

————. 1988. *The Plough and the Stars. Sean O'Casey: Plays, 2*, 63–161. London: Faber and Faber.

O'Connell, Joseph E.A. 2006. *Where's Where in Dublin: A Directory of Historic Locations 1913–1923*. Dublin: Dublin City Council.

O'Connor, Emmet. 2004. *Reds and the Green: Ireland, Russia, and the Communist Internationals, 1919–43*. Dublin: University College Dublin Press.

O'Connor Lysaght, D. R.2006. The Irish Citizen Army, 1913–1916: White, Larkin, and Connolly.*History Ireland*, March-April,19–23.

O'Toole, Fintan. 2017. *Judging Shaw*. Dublin: Royal Irish Academy.

Ritschel, Nelson O'Ceallaigh. 2011. *Shaw, Synge, Connolly, and Socialist Provocation*. Gainesville: University Press of Florida.

————. 2015. Shaw and the Dublin Repertory Theatre. *SHAW: The Journal of Bernard Shaw Studies* 35 (2): 168–184. University Park: Pennsylvania State University Press.

————. 2017. *Bernard Shaw, W. T. Stead, and the New Journalism: Whitechapel, Parnell, Titanic and the Great War*. Cham: Palgrave Macmillan.

Roche, Anthony. 2015. *The Irish Dramatic Revival 1899–1939*. London: Bloomsbury Methuen.

Russell, George. *Peter Grogan Rare Books, Catalogue Four, Autumn 2017*, item number 254.

Shaw, George Bernard. 1928. *The Intelligent Woman's Guide to Socialism and Capitalism*. New York: Brentano's.

————. 1972. Preface to Heartbreak House. In *The Bodley Head Bernard Shaw Collected Plays with Their Prefaces, Volume V*, 12–58. London: Max Reinhardt, Bodley Head.

————. 1985. *Bernard Shaw Collected Letters, 1911–1925, Vol. 3*.Ed. DanH. Laurence. New York: Viking Penguin.

————. 1993. *Shaw, Lady Gregory, and the Abbey: A Correspondence and a Record*. Ed. Dan H. Laurence and Nicholas Grene. Gerrards Cross: Colin Smythe.

————. 2001a. The Easter Week Executions. In *The Matter with Ireland*, ed. Dan H. Laurence and David H. Greene, 2nd ed., 69–70. Gainesville: University Press of Florida. 124–26.

————. 2001b. Ireland and the First World War. In *The Matter with Ireland*, ed. Dan H. Laurence and David H. Greene, 2nd ed., 101–104. Gainesville: University Press of Florida.

———. 2001c. Mad Dogs in Uniform. In *The Matter with Ireland*, ed. Dan H. Laurence and David H. Greene, 2nd ed., 95–97. Gainesville: University Press of Florida.

———. 2001d. Neglected Morals of the Irish Rising. In *The Matter with Ireland*, ed. Dan H. Laurence and David H. Greene, 2nd ed., 69–70. Gainesville: University Press of Florida. 120–23.

Sheehy-Skeffington, Francis. 1913. London's Magnificent Rally to the Dublin Rebels. *The Daily Herald*, November 3, 1.

Soboleva, Olga, and Angus Wrenn. 2012. *The Only Hope of the World: George Bernard Shaw and Russia*. New York: Peter Lang.

Spainneach, Liam. 2005. Irish Socialist Party. *History Ireland*, November–December, 16.

"Stop Press! The Irish Republic." 1916. *Irish War News*, April 25, 4.

Synge, John Millington. 1904. *In the Shadow of the Glen, Samhain*, 34–44.

———. 1991. The Playboy of the Western World. In *Modern Irish Drama*, ed. John P. Harrington, 73–118. New York: Norton.

"The Crisis in Russia". 1905. *The Times*, February 2, 6.

Townshend, Charles. 2005. *Easter 1916: The Irish Rebellion*. London: Allan Lane.

Watts, Gerry. 2017. Delia Larkin and the Game of 'House'! *History Ireland*, September/October, 35–38.

Yeates, Padraig. 2000. *Lockout Dublin 1913*. Dublin: Gill and Macmillan.

CHAPTER 7

The Economics of Identity: *John Bull's Other Island* and the Creation of Modern Ireland

Aileen R. Ruane

Staging cultural identity presents problems for theatrical practitioners, especially when it concerns staging the colonial/colonised Other, because it raises serious questions about the perspective from which that identity is observed, and who profits from such representations. It also highlights the immediacy of the theatrical medium; globally, the theatre is an optic through which audience members can identify with and observe their own cultures, and do the same for others, without, as Patrick Lonergan notes, implicating themselves in those cultures.[1] Postcolonial theatrical criticism regards with some scepticism any attempt by the coloniser to circumvent this process, that is to say, efforts by the coloniser to either garner sympathy for himself or offer substantive commentary regarding the colonised's identity.[2] The establishment of an identity apart from the one that has been imposed by the coloniser on the colonised is therefore a crucial step in the evolution towards a new society. In the twentieth and twenty-first centuries, depictions of nations that had emerged from colonial settings have given rise to criticism regarding who has a right to tell these stories

A. R. Ruane (✉)
Université Laval, Laval, QC, Canada
e-mail: Aileen.Ruane@lit.ulavel.ca

and, indeed, their very nature.[3] The purpose, then, of staging them tends to be the transmission of a previously neglected or hidden reality or perspective on the part of the colonised. However, the tension between coloniser and colonised is often presented in black-and-white terms, irrespective of economic and historical nuance.

Bernard Shaw's relationship with Ireland, as well as his socialist beliefs, set the stage for an investigation not only of what it means to be "authentically" Irish, but also of what should be done in order to ensure that Irish identity does not shackle the country to a romanticised past.[4] In *John Bull's Other Island*, Shaw presents different stereotypes of Irish and English figures, blending them with hard realities about colonial Irish life. It is through a juxtaposition of national caricatures and uncompromising economic reality that Shaw is able to produce a reflection on why notions of cultural and national authenticity distract from progress, and new direction in which to emphasise that cultural identity. Shaw urges action, which parallels the very nature of his theatre, in lieu of the kind of discussion he decries in "Socialism and Ireland," his address to the Fabian Society on November 28, 1919.Whereas other plays of the Gaelic revival staged "aspirational" models of citizenship to follow, *John Bull's Other Island* critically challenges deeply rooted, and indeed individual attachments to the land. It is this connection that Shaw seeks to disrupt, for as J.H. Whyte notes:

> Irish problems existed in plenty. The most serious of these problems, we can now see on looking back, was the question of the land. The land of Ireland was simply not sufficient to feed all those who were trying to get a living off it. Population was increasing rapidly. This led to competition for land, and drove up rents, thus reducing still further the people's resources.[5]

Through a postcolonial approach that will take into consideration the active nature of theatre, this chapterwill investigate how Shaw uses his stereotypes to promote an economic agenda as a fundamental marker of identity. It is this step that Shaw highlights as the right direction in which to conduct a modern Irish Society.

POSTCOLONIALISM AND IRELAND

The controversial relationship between Postcolonial Studies and Ireland helps to situate Shaw's exploration of English dominance and Irish acquiescence, both in terms of culture and in terms of economics.[6] The primary relationship from which all others spring between the coloniser and the colonised is manifested in who controls and profits from natural resources. The Marxist-materialist branch of postcolonial theory thus provides the means with which to understand how English economic domination continued well after Ireland's independence. As a proponent of this branch of postcolonial theory, Ania Loomba notes that we must consider the historical circumstances of an area or region in order to properly deploy the terms colonialism, imperialism, and neo-colonialism, which will subsequently allow for a more nuanced view of economic identity.[7] In the case of England and Ireland, their histories have been linked for a considerable period of time, thus these terms take on new importance along with added complications. Victor Merriman notes that in this struggle, particularly for Ireland, material ownership of the land was paramount.[8]The English presence in the Irish question that Shaw notes in his address to the Fabian Society persisted long after the Westminster parliament had partitioned Ireland into North and South, eventually leading to the establishment of the Irish Free State, which points to their colonial relationship via geography. This Irish question is essentially a national one, and, as Shaw notes, should be resolved in a simple manner—Ireland is being abused and should be given the chance to self-govern.[9]

A direct consequence of England's lengthy colonial presence in Ireland was the subsequent parcelling of territory to the landed English aristocracy that had previously belonged to Gaelic clans, which themselves maintained complex interrelationships of distinct, yet mutable allegiances that were dominated by family lines as opposed to individual ownership. This action fits in line with what Loomba has described as *"unforming* or reforming the communities that existed there already."[10] If we can say that the English coloniser was reforming a complicated system previously regulated via the old Gaelic land laws, the Brehon Laws, it is necessary to ask why those communities were being *re-formed.*[11] Aidan Clarke argues that following the execution of Charles I in 1649, "[i]t was the wealth of the land of Ireland that the government of England was interested in. And it reserved its special fury for those who owned that land."[12] The main issue with settlement thus became the reforming of territory in favour of a

Protestant upper class that had been transplanted to Ireland as a result of this colonisation. In the years that would follow the Restoration of the monarchy and the coming of William of Orange, Catholics in Ireland would bounce between marginal gains and losses with regard to the ability to own land and practise their religion.

The latter half of the seventeenth and the eighteenth centuries saw legislation enacted, the Penal Laws, that resulted in the exclusion of Irish Catholics from participation in government and from land ownership. When the relief act for English Catholics was passed in parliament in 1778, it provided an opportunity for Catholics in Ireland to press for similar integration and equality, and allowed for some parity on a religious and economic level. However, as R.B. McDowell cautions, this in no way implied a share in political power and representation.[13] Indeed, leaders like Wolfe Tone argued passionately for Catholic Emancipation on the grounds that Ireland had no quarrel with countries that provoked the ire of England, but it was not until Daniel O'Connell's successful campaign for full Catholic emancipation in the 1820s that real progress was seen. The passage of the Catholic Emancipation Act in 1829 finally allowed Catholics to hold political office and, according to J.H. Whyte, "the whole body gained in morale from the removal of the taint of inequality."[14]

The year 1870 gave rise to the Home Rule movement, which was conceived of by Isaac Butt. Butt envisioned Home Rule as providing the necessary structures to allow Ireland to be governed by the Irish, but did not imply complete independence. Instead, it offered a way for Ireland to remain associated with the larger political and economic power of England. While not conceived of as a permanent solution by the Irish, and certainly not prior to 1916, many who were sympathetic to Britain viewed this in terms of other major, former colonies, such as Canada. Apart from highlighting the lengths to which certain parties went to attain some semblance of independence, as well as the exploitation of the Irish by the English, these measures demonstrate the economic complexity of the Irish-English relationship.

"The Irish question," which Shaw addresses in his lecture to the Fabian Society on Socialism and Ireland, concerns this larger association with England. More importantly, it directly implicates how and why the land in Ireland was used.[15] Organisations such as the Land League supported the rights of tenants to have more control and security over the land on which they lived. Many different land acts subsequently paved the way for greater individual ownership of the land, but it was the Wyndham Land Act of

1903, which, in the words of Donal McCartney, "eventually abolish[ed] the old landlordism and turn[ed] Ireland into a land of owner occupiers."[16] Brad Kent also notes that one of the primary consequences of this legislation was that the government "made up for the gap between the price at which the land was valued and what the people could afford to pay for it."[17] However, years of abuse by the landlord system instead seemed to go against the principles of the founder of the Land League, Michael Davitt. Davitt envisioned a system that was closer to what Shaw sought: national ownership.[18]

Another important date that Shaw references is the failed 1916 rebellion, the Easter Rising, in which Nationalists attempted to seize the central post office and other important institutions in Dublin and declare an Irish state. More than its historic significance, the symbolism of the Easter rebellion created a mystique around the men and women involved and thus their place in Irish history. Of the ninety rebels charged and court-martialled for participation in the Rising, fifteen were executed, with additional citizens, numbering approximately 1500, arrested once martial law was imposed.[19] However, the effort to wrest control from England was, to paraphrase Dan H. Laurence and David H. Greene, futile if not dramatic.[20] This was the kind of imagery that fuelled the nationalistic theatre prior to, and directly after, independence. Indeed, with theatre taking an important role in discussions about Irish culture and politics, its subject matter, and how the latter could form the national consciousness, was of particular interest to all parties involved.[21] Shaun Richards goes so far as to argue that introducing the issues of social class and economics would "have shattered the necessary fiction of an undivided people directed to the goal of national liberation."[22]

John Bull's Other Island exists as an intermediary space where Shaw attempts to bridge the gap with the postcolonial world that Ireland desires to inhabit. In introducing a social class optic, Shaw reminds the reader and theatregoer of what the Marxist school in postcolonial theory consistently highlights: the economic ramifications of colonialism. Loomba describes colonialism as "the conquest and control of other people's land and goods," which mirrors England's historical relationship with Ireland.[23] "Colonialism" provides the structure in which to situate discourse regarding cultural differences, but it is primarily rooted in economic distinctions. Another proponent of the Marxist branch, Joe Cleary, situates the importance of considering this approach with regard to the inclusion of Ireland in Postcolonial Studies:

To determine how Irish social and cultural development was mediated by colonial capitalism must be the goal of any materialist postcolonial studies. From its inception, the colonial process was never simply a matter of the subjugation of this or that territory. It was, rather, an international process through which different parts of the globe were differentially integrated into an emergent world capitalist system.[24]

We are only able to recognise the presence of colonialism through stereotypes used to categorise the colonised, and political/economic oppression.[25]

In writing a play that predates Irish independence by over fifteen years, Shaw warns of another grey area between being colonised and having independence. In confronting those who would obfuscate economic liberty solely in favour of Revivalist cultural attachments, Shaw in fact anticipates the emergence of another significant concept, "neo-colonialism." With regard to this notion, Loomba notes that "a country may be both postcolonial (in the sense of being formally independent) and neo-colonial (in the sense of remaining economically and/or culturally dependent) at the same time."[26] Shaw's Ireland is still far from this state, but the danger of becoming remains. Indeed, to be "neo-colonial" implies that a culture has not truly decolonised; formal independence is not really so if it has been stripped of the capacity to ensure financial independence and the egalitarian distribution of capital. The interrelatedness of the postcolonial and the neo-colonial exemplifies the tension that exists between the two principle branches of postcolonial theory. Shaw's ideological approach fits in line more with the Marxist-materialist branch that appeals to the need for economic equality and fairness. This is what Shaw seems to be trying to avoid: a neo-colonial Irish Society that has not been completely liberated from the economic inequities and injustices of British rule, and that finally perpetuates the old system on its citizens.

IDENTITY AND STEREOTYPES

Stuart Hall posits that there are two ways of considering cultural identity. The first of these is that there is one, true, shared identity within a common culture. It is the second way, however, that will be considered here in light of Shaw's use of stereotypes and economic reality. Hall writes that it "recognises that, as well as the many points of similarity, there are also critical points of deep and significant difference which constitute 'what we really are'; or rather – since history has intervened – 'what we have become.'"[27] Cultural identity is therefore an action that is continually rec-reating itself, not just a static essence. As Shaw diverges from other propo-nents of the Gaelic revival, like W.B. Yeats, his view of the former position is clear: there is no one, singular Irish identity to which the Irish people must cling in order to ensure survival of the culture. If Shaw is correct, then this calls into question the very need to establish such a concrete identity.[28]

Homi Bhabha creates the link between stereotyping and postcolonial-ism when he argues that "the stereotype, which is its [colonialism's] major discursive strategy, is a form of knowledge and identification that vacillates between what is always 'in place', already known, and something that must be anxiously repeated."[29] The stereotype assumes a fixity that is somehow also uncertain due to the fact that it is continually repeated within the colonial discourse. Shaw anticipates this as well when he writes, "The worst of it is, that when a spurious type gets into literature, it strikes the imagination of boys and girls. They form themselves by playing up to it; and thus the unsubstantial fancies of the novelists and music-hall song-writers of one generation are apt to become the unpleasant and mis-chievous realities of the next."[30] At first glance, Shaw is speaking of English writers, but on a more profound level, Shaw is also addressing Irish writers so that they do not fall into the temptation of resorting to one-dimensional versions of themselves in order to promote their culture as a product. Bhabha's admonition for postcolonial discourse to shift from simply ana-lysing stereotypical images as good or bad, to instead evaluating the pro-cesses by which these images are constructed relates to Shaw's work in *John Bull's Other Island* through the character of Larry Doyle. Doyle acts a conduit through which images of the Irish are rejected and accepted. Therefore, the "otherness" of the colonial subject is seen as a historical fact that will make its presence known in the future.

Shaw understands how a stereotype, even in the service of achieving independence,[31] can undermine the economic security of Ireland, which relates to Ireland's obsessively complex relationship with the land. The ruse that is the stereotyped image, even when reappropriated by the colo-nised, does little more than romanticise attachment to physical space. This is where a poststructuralist-based postcolonial approach, as outlined by Bhabha, can no longer be said to suit Shaw's argument; recognising the dangers of stereotypes does little if the structure onto which they are superimposed remains the same. Similarly, Merriman draws attention to the fact that "Shaw dramatizes the land as public property, 'native home,' and political territory."[32] This seems to be supported by what Loomba affirms with regard to the relationship between coloniser/colonised in the modern sense: "Modern colonialism [...] restructured the economies of the latter [the colonised], drawing them into a complex relationship with their own, so that there was a flow of human and natural resources between colonised and colonial countries. This flow worked in both directions."[33]

IMAGINING IRELAND ON STAGE

Postcolonial discourse takes on a particular resonance on stage because the stereotypes that are part of that discourse are inherently performative, just as is identity, which further complicates the playwright's task—the performativity of these stereotypes is inherent, whether intended or not.[34] The cause for concern is a result of perception on the part of the audience/reader, which is largely out of the playwright's hands. Shaw, however, knew how to manipulate the theatrical environment in order to encourage discussion of a given topic, rather than passive iteration. More important than this, though, was Shaw's ability to observe and critique what he called the "Stage Irishman" stereotype, a caricatured fixture of the nineteenth-century stage that reduced Irish characters to drunk, child-like, or lazy Celts, who needed a firm hand in terms of leadership. While not every character is a stereotype, as Martin Meisel notes, "the contrasts are made explicit [...] between the Stage Irishman and the real peasant, with his real virtues and vice."[35] Indeed, it is Shaw's "Stage Irishman" Tim Haffigan who fulfils the stereotype of the Irish drunkard, whilst the rest of the Irish characters rarely mention or exhibit a particular affinity for or addiction to alcohol; Haffigan is all vice and vaudevillian comedy, with no nuance—and is indeed only of Irish descent by way of Glasgow. Not to be one-dimensional, Shaw's other Haffigan in the play, Matthew, presents the audience with an archetype of Ireland's new class of landowners who "do not seek to help raise up their fellow countrymen, but rather watch them anxiously, keep them in their places, and exploit them mercilessly."[36]

Shaw's February 1896 review of Dion Boucicault's *The Colleen Bawn* provides more insight into the economic and cultural critiques against stereotypes.[37] For instance, Shaw opens his review of the play by writing that "I have lived to see *The Colleen Bawn* with real water in it; and perhaps I shall live to see it some day with real Irishmen in it, though I doubt if that will heighten its popularity much."[38] This commentary is pure critique; as the play is set in Ireland and peopled entirely by Irish characters,

Shaw essentially dismisses any merit the work may have on both a cultural level and a theatrical level. This two-tiered dismissal both highlights the general problems with Irish stereotypes and points to the effects of casting English actors to personify those stereotypes; the deformed notion of one's own self, as presented by the colonial power to its own constituents as well as the colonised, is not simply a question of necessity, rather, it hints at missed opportunities to create something more profound.[39]

However, Shaw's review of Boucicault's play goes beyond a critique of staged stereotypes. In his preface to *John Bull's Other Island*, Shaw writes that he intended his play for an Irish audience. Though clearly intended for a more international one, this admission is telling due to the staging of Irish and English characters. As Shaw is quite cognisant of this,[40] it is necessary to focus attention on the effects of these stereotypes on the Irish and English through an examination of several principal characters. With regard to this, Declan Kiberd remarks: "at root the English and Irish are rather similar peoples, who have nonetheless decided to perform versions of Englishness and Irishness to one another, in the attempt to wrest a material advantage from the unsuspecting audience of each performance."[41] Performativity thus presents the opportunity for agency on the part of the person being stereotyped. With commentary offered on all sides regarding the state of affairs in Rosscullen, Shaw sets the conditions necessary to discuss and debate what modernising Ireland really means.

According to Martin Meisel, it is somewhat contradictory to speak of *John Bull's Other Island* as "a discussion of the realities of Irish life and character in terms of their theatrical conventions," while also highlighting the presence of stereotypes.[42] We should thus consider what Hall writes regarding cultural practices and forms of representation: "Practices of representation always implicate the positions from which we speak or write – the positions of enunciation."[43]Considering that theatrical representation both speaks (the orality of the performance) and writes (the dramatic text), its value in terms of representing postcolonial cultural identity is exceedingly important. Furthermore, Hall's emphasis on "becoming" as well as "being" confirms the notion that theatrical representation provides a physical space in which these multiple identities within a culture can be investigated.

In *The Quintessence of Ibsenism*, Shaw defines and delineates his idea of the discussion play, which he contrasts with the well-made play of the nineteenth century.[44] Shaw describes the discussion aspect of the play as being a technical and integral part of popular theatre. Therefore, a key part of the investigation into the representation of cultural identities on stage is Shaw's choice of the discussion play. Again, this presents itself in a counterintuitive fashion, but viewed in light of what theatre actually accomplishes, Shaw's choice of genre serves to encourage action. Shaw himself saw this as a bit of bargaining on the part of the audience members who have "a thrifty sense of taking away something from such plays: they not only have had something for their money, but they retain that something as a permanent possession."[45] Through this combination of discussion and history on the stage, Shaw challenges the idea that "discussion" implies passive inactivity.[46] In staging this discussion of identity and economics, Shaw subverts both English and Irish audiences' expectations through theatrical practices that, as Brad Kent notes, "overtly challenge their norms while holding their attention despite themselves through the palliative of his comedic wit."[47]

Therefore, as the discursive aspects of *John Bull's Other Island* happen on stage, they take on an active, performative quality that is difficult to achieve in a medium other than theatre. In addition, Shaw understands this inherent performative quality when he describes that the attraction that the theatre should hold for the mature theatre-goer lays not in action for the sake of action, but in: "the exhibition and discussion of the character and conduct of stage figures who are made to appear real by the art of the playwright and the performers."[48] Theatre serves a voyeuristic function, one in which art and activity are already implied, so it is the responsibility of the playwright, in Shaw's mind, to influence that medium for a purpose beyond entertainment or art for art's sake.

Discussion, of course, implies talking, but when such posturing is moved to the stage, it also demands action on the part of the actors. For Shaw, the dramatic action is in the discussion itself:

> In the new plays, the drama arises through a conflict of unsettled ideals rather than through vulgar attachments, rapacities, generosities, resentments, ambitions, misunderstanding, oddities and so forth as to which no moral question is raised. The conflict is not between clear right and wrong: the villain is as conscientious as the hero, if not more so: in fact, the question which makes the play interesting (when it *is* interesting) is which is the villain and which the hero. Or, to put it another way, there are no villains and no heroes.[49]

It is up to the actors, then, to stage these discussions in a way that fosters debate. Indeed, the intersection of these discursive qualities with the action of the stage is seen in the play's final scene between Broadbent, Doyle, and Keegan. The conversation between these three characters is at once dense and highly charged, defining and arguing different political and economic philosophies. Shaw is able to translate this into a kind of action through his detailed use of stage directions; while *John Bull's Other Island* is typical of Shaw in that it offers the spectators no relief in the form of what to do and in whom to put their trust, Shaw's stage directions (whether during private reading or public performance) assist in presenting interpretations of the characters. Much critical attention is paid to the length of these directions; however, the focus here is on the directions as they relate to the actors. In one key stage direction for Broadbent and Doyle, Shaw at once communicates a psychological undertone whilst referencing an economic reality. As Keegan utters the phrase, "You will recognize the scheme efficiently; you will liquidate its second bankruptcy efficiently," Shaw's stage direction indicates that "BROADBENT and LARRY look quickly at one another; for this, unless the priest is an old financial hand, must be inspiration."[50] Thus, while it is true that Shaw does not provide straightforward heroes or villains, he does indicate in so many words the morality towards which the actors must direct the audience.

As an Irishman who spent his formative years in Ireland Shaw is poised to observe Irish identity.[51] Certain characterisations of Irish figures in this play are of particular interest, as they inhabit two worlds, much like Shaw. The character that exemplifies this intermediary space is Larry Doyle. While at first glance Doyle appears to be a mouthpiece for Shaw, he instead serves as a lens through which the audience member can more clearly recognise the presence of cultural stereotypes. It is Doyle after all, who alerts Tom Broadbent to Tim Haffigan's scheme: "don't you know that all this top-o-the-morning and broth-of-a-boy and more-power-to-your-elbow business is got up in England to fool you."[52] Doyle is quick to notice Haffigan's scheme to trick Broadbent into giving him money without having actually completed his task, and then spend that money at the local pub to boot.

Shaw takes this a step further, again through the character of Doyle, to examine the effect of accents on stage. In his critique of *The Colleen Bawn*, Shaw remarks that "with such opportunities Mr Purdon, having a strong sense of fun, and being a born mimic, has no difficulty in producing a brogue; but it is not a pretty one."[53] In referring to the accent in this way, Shaw not only critiques the actor's performance, but he also stages both a judgement of Irish identity for Irish audiences and expectations regarding this same identity for English audiences. His intermittent use of stereotypes reflects Shaw's own utilitarianism. The outright critique of stereotypes instead is surpassed by a kind of pragmatic acknowledgement of the truth behind these stereotypes. Shaw writes that Nora's "Irish peevishness" is an attempt to confront Broadbent's overpowering English charm.[54] However, he hints at its contrived nature when a character as trustworthy as Peter Keegan drops "the broad Irish vernacular of his speech to Patsy."[55]

The character of Broadbent most aptly represents one aspect of the English coloniser. Kathleen Ochshorn writes that through him, Shaw "ridicules England's self-righteous justification for colonial rule through Broadbent's remarks about the virtues of English efficiency, anticipates the international marketing of Ireland's beauty and the exploitation of its rural landscape, and sets the stage for the empire of multinational syndicates."[56] Indeed, the effect of this is to highlight Shaw's push for economic change as opposed to romanticism. Shaw is clearly not a proponent of English imperialism, but Broadbent's practicality, the same practicality that Shaw lauds, wins the day. Broadbent's is a more insidious image than a simple stereotype of the over-bearing, vicious occupier—Broadbent seems indeed to have only the best of intentions with regard to Ireland and Irishmen and women. However, even if Home Rule passes, Broadbent's syndicate will still remain, thus highlighting the importance of a Marxist-materialist perspective that seeks to alert folks to the fact that in spite of any supposed economic "benefits" or cultural uniqueness, the presence of the syndicate *is* the colonial power and will continue to poorly distribute land and capital. Through isolating one aspect of the coloniser, Shaw stages an image that, for the alert audience member, is surprisingly attractive, yet is tantamount to predatory capitalism.

This charm that Broadbent projects also quickly overpowers Nora, who not only cannot escape it, but must indeed join with it through marriage.[57] While Nora is not a stereotype, she is an archetype, that is to say, a character that represents for Shaw an image of Ireland. Her plain and unremarkable nature to her compatriots is twisted into the stereotype par excellence of the exotic Irishwoman for Broadbent. Kent notes that Broadbent falls in love "with the *idea* of Nora," which not only demonstrates Shaw's use of the fixed image in the service of colonised, but also points to how

Broadbent wishes to exploit all aspects of the island.[58] This is indicative of both the wilful ignorance of the coloniser towards the people it hopes to rule and the preconceived notions that come as a result of essentialised images.

Another character whose presence on stage suggests a more global vision for Shaw's part is Broadbent's servant Hodson. He in particular presents two faces, both of which would be familiar for English audiences of the time: the stodgy, uptight servant, and the coarse, cockney lower class. Kiberd argues that Shaw uses this character to point to the common cause of the dispossessed Irish labourer and the exploited English proletariat.[59] The staging of this stereotype thus demonstrates a latent effect of colonialism that goes beyond religious or ethnic discrimination: the oppression of the working class, regardless of origin. The presence of an Englishman, albeit one from a lower class, demonstrates the systemic inequities of British rule. Seen on stage before various audiences, Shaw wants to challenge assumptions that even the colonised might have regarding their colonisers. Not all Englishmen are the oppressor, and many others are oppressed within the context of their own economy.

Shaw's dual images of Ireland—the stereotypical figures alongside the realities of country life—work well within this space. Similar to Kiberd's previous statement, Ochshorn hints at this duality when she argues that "characters put on masks – adopting and dropping brogues, for example – and they neatly divide the world into how the English or the Irish are expected to behave."[60] Given the effect of stereotypes on stage, this statement takes on a meta-theatrical tone; after all, if the characters are performing for each other, they are also performing for an audience. This mixing, blending, and blurring of the lines produces a distance by which the audience can "read" and process Shaw's juxtaposition of stereotypes and reality. Bertolt Brecht confirms this in writing that "probably every single feature of all Shaw's characters can be attributed to his delight in dislocating our stock associations."[61] This distance and dislocation is seen on stage and serves as a complement to Shaw's Fabian socialism.

FABIAN SOCIALISM: A CALL TO ACTION

It is in Shaw's preface where we can perceive the synthesis of stereotypes in a colonial setting with economic discourse regarding the real Ireland. This is yet another way in which we can see how Shaw integrates stereotypes, performance, and discussion whilst predicting Loomba's "neo-colonial" designation as a consequence of acquiescence. As Ochshorn notes, "Shaw manages to define and ridicule colonialism; anticipate the nature of a postcolonial Ireland; and imply the difficulties of a free trade, neo-colonial economy, where individual and national interests are subverted by the all-powerful forces of development and transnational commerce."[62] While no one, singular character embodies a call to pure Socialism, this ideology is reflected as a response to Doyle and Broadbent's plans.

What Shaw proposes via this play is essentially a dramatisation of aesthetics versus pragmatics. The proponents of the Gaelic Revival perceived Ireland's salvation to be of a different nature. Donal McCartney notes: "In Yeats's vision the poets and the dramatists and the writers would cater for the intellectual, as distinct from the material, needs of Ireland."[63] Ironically, without an economic identity, which is the end result of a functioning economy, this esotericism would do neither. It also sheds light on the vacuum being created by the removal of Ireland's colonial overlord. The resulting void is something that poetry and theatre alone cannot fill. Economic stability in a postcolonial setting is thus something that romantic notions of a heroic past cannot fix. Ochshorn confirms this by writing that Shaw saw that the real problem facing Ireland at the dawn of the twentieth century was "how to become an independent yet economically viable nation. The backwardness engendered by centuries of exploitation rendered the country vulnerable to new and unseemly capitalist enterprises."[64]

A character not yet discussed at length here is Peter Keegan, whose non-stereotypically Irish nature (that is to say, as a stage figure, he does not fit within "classic" Irish types like the Stage Irishman, yet he does appear to be a "classic yogi type") merits a place in this last section. Keegan's perceptiveness is a key aspect of Fabian socialism, where it relies on a hope that intellectual perception of economic issues will lead to their alleviation. As Shaw says: "you will see that a country like this is not ripe for Socialism. It is still very largely an agricultural country."[65] Keegan's observations are the other side of the coin, so to speak, of Larry Doyle. If Doyle is the lens through which the spectator realises the effects of stereotypes, then Keegan points to political and economic irregularities. Even though Keegan's eloquence and intelligence differ greatly from the stereotype of the Stage Irishman, he is ineffectual in the face of Broadbent's pragmatism. He is able to intellectualise this conflict, but he is unable or unwilling to act on it.

Political and social currents as complex as Socialism and Capitalism do not necessarily lend themselves well to the stage, at least not exactly in the way that the theatrical medium demands. However, Shaw seems to predict Jean-Paul Sartre's ideas concerning an engaged theatre. Sartre regarded the theatre as place where humanity could ponder and then contest its rights.[66] Through what we have seen of Shaw's views regarding the discussion play, gratuitous entertainment does not have a place in serious theatre. Like Sartre, Shaw saw the theatre as a staging ground for his philosophy. Also like Sartre, Shaw saw the inherent difficulty in this when he writes, concerning Ibsen, that "the dual aspect of his [Ibsen's] idealist figures, who are at once higher and more mischievous than the ordinary figures, puzzles the conventional actor, who persists in assuming that if he is to be selfish on the stage he must be villainous. [...] Hence the difficulty of getting Ibsen's works fairly treated on the stage, where alone that can make their full effect."[67] In Shaw's point of view, the stage is the conduit, albeit a challenging one, through which political and philosophical ideals are most effectively translated.

Peter Gahan notes that Shaw seems to support contradicting ideologies, such as imperialism in the service of socialism's over-arching goals. However, when it is viewed in light of *John Bull's Other Island*, Shaw's purpose becomes clearer. Gahan notes that "for Shaw, Marxist to the extent of understanding socialism as having to emerge from a highly developed industrial Society, the imperial project was a possible vehicle for the advance of civilization, of socialism, but only if that advance was conducted in line with the precepts of civilization."[68] The complexity of this uneasy alliance is evident in the play to the extent that Shaw wished for Ireland to remain aligned to England so that England would need to take responsibility for its colonial territories. This course of action would help to avoid the exploitation that would follow a capitalist approach. Indeed, the British Empire, as Shaw points out in his preface, not only negatively affected the colonised, but the English people as well: "Bermondsey [a district in London] goes to the dogs whilst those whose business it is to govern it are sitting on Bengal; and the more Bengal kicks, the more Bermondsey is neglected, except by the tax collector."[69] Therefore, the staging of this play is especially important with regard to its audience; as previously discussed, Shaw's global aspirations for this play are clear. The economic inequities that face Ireland also affect the poor English labourer.

CONCLUSION

In conclusion, what Shaw promotes on stage in *John Bull's Other Island* is not just a timely critique of English imperialism, but rather a call to action for Ireland to create and assume an economic identity, which is to say, a concrete sense of a functioning, equitable economy, before becoming locked into a cycle of one-sided cultural essentialismand continued economic exploitation, as previously perpetrated by the coloniser. This type of identity must be concrete and practical, and actually take steps to prevent a regression into neo-colonialism: in contrast, a focus on the romanticised past is akin to putting a bandage on a gaping wound created by colonisation.[70] We can read Shaw's fears for Ireland through postcolonialism's inherent contradictions: "'Colonialism' is not just something that happens from outside a country or a people, not just something that operates with the collusion of forces inside, but a version of it can be duplicated from within."[71] Stereotypes, being a way of duplicating ideas regarding a colonised people, thus shackle the latter to their former economic state through their constant repetition. Duplication and iteration, once set in motion in a theatrical context, take on a life of their own—Shaw recognised the power of this in his own work and thus could warn of the effects of their long-term abuse.

Shaw's vision for Ireland is not a series of essentialised images, however useful they may be for rallying around the Irish cause. His comment in his 1906 "Preface for Politicians" lays out this distinction in clear terms: "It [*John Bull's Other Island*] was uncongenial to the whole spirit of the neo-Gaelic movement, which is bent on creating a new Ireland after its own ideal, whereas my play is a very uncompromising presentment of the real old Ireland."[72] Shaw juxtaposes stereotypes and economic realities to warn that without solid and equitable economic groundwork in place, aesthetic aspirations of Irish identity are completely irrelevant. The stereotypes themselves are not altogether important, which can be seen in their fluid nature in this play. Peter Gahan points this out when he writes that "Whether Haffigan fails to recognize Doyle as Irish because he can only recognize the stereotypical Irish characteristics he is mimicking for the benefit of Broadbent or whether Larry seems to Haffigan to have all too successfully mimicked the native characteristics of his adopted country is difficult to decide."[73] Instead, Shaw asks his audience to question how they are being used and to what end. For his own part, Shaw seems to provide no solid solutions as to how this economic identity should be achieved. However, it is important to acknowledge that *John Bull's Other Island* as a whole represents Shaw's evolving sensibilities as they concern British colonialism's relationship to the rest of its empire and Ireland, as evidenced by the changes Shaw enacted to his 1912 Home Rule edition preface, as well as its 1931 version. These prefaces are thus not indictments; as important as the plays, they allow the debate to continue, evolving in such a way as to engender the kind of discussion Shaw sought from the theatre. Shaw's complex politics are thoroughly modern in terms of their capacity to process and integrate new, sometimes paradoxical, information, and the play and prefaces reflect this progression.[74]

Frantz Fanon warned that "colonisation is not satisfied merely with holding a people in its grip and emptying the native's brain of all form and content. By a kind of perverted logic, it turns to the past of oppressed people, and distorts, disfigures and destroys it."[75] Shaw anticipates this process, and takes it one step further; it is not just England that holds Ireland under its sway, but the Irish themselves who distort their own past through reverting to an image of an Ireland that has no place in the future. "I am quite ready to help the saving work of reducing the sham Ireland of romance to a heap of unsightly ruins," he writes. "When this is done, my countrymen can consider the relative merits of building something real in the old country."[76] Shaw comes down firmly on the side of modernisation, but asks his audience to question its costs and the ideology that inspires it. In the case of *John Bull's Other Island*, Shaw warns that debates about what it means to be "authentically" Irish serve only to distract from the real problem, a neo-colonial Ireland that memorialises the past to profit from it, thus ensuring that the colonised never escape their master.

NOTES

1. Lonergan specifically notes this with regard to how Irish theatre is interpreted by the communities that translate it: "The inherent otherness of much Irish drama allows other cultures to answer their own questions creatively, without having to merge or mix with Irish culture itself." See Patrick Lonergan. "'The Laughter Will Come of Itself. The Tears Are Inevitable': Martin McDonagh, Globalization, and Irish Theatre Criticism." *Modern Drama*, 47.4 (Winter 2004), p. 647.
2. Critics who have explored the importance of a postcolonial perspective in the realm of Theatre Studies are Victor Merriman (2009), Mark Fortier (2002), Jane Dunnett (2006), and Dawn Duncan (2004). Of these,

Merriman and Duncan examine the particularly contentious issue of post-colonialism and Ireland.

3. In particular, critics and theoreticians such as Mark Fortier (2002), Frantz Fanon (2004), Dwight Conquergood (1992), Feroza Jussawalla and Reed Way Dasenbrock (1992), and Janelle Reinelt (1992) discuss the need for a greater presence on the part of the colonised or formerly colonised person's perspective in order to avoid careless or reckless appropriation by the coloniser. Fortier, for example, cites the example of Aimé Césaire's *Une Tempête* as an example of a postcolonial reappropriation of Shakespeare's *The Tempest*.

4. [iv] Shaw remarks that, "one of the advantages that I have as a student of history from having been born in Ireland is that I was literally born in the XVII century [...] If you go from here to Ireland you get back into the XVII and XVIII century atmosphere." (Bernard Shaw. "Socialism and Ireland." In *The Matter with Ireland*. Ed. Dan H. Laurence and David H. Greene. 2nd ed. Gainesville: University Press of Florida, 2001. 236).

5. J.H. Whyte. "The Age of Daniel O'Connell (1800–47)." In *The Course of Irish History*. Ed. T.W. Moody and F.X. Martin. Cork: Roberts Rinehart Publishers, 1964. 248–249.

6. For detailed accounts of why Ireland is perceived differently than other British colonial possessions, see Joe Cleary. *Outrageous Fortune, capital and culture in modern Ireland*. Dublin: Field Day Publications, 2007; "Misplaced ideas? Locating and Dislocating Ireland in Colonial and Postcolonial Studies." In *Marxism, Modernity and Postcolonial Studies*. Ed. Crystal Bartolovich and Neil Lazarus. Cambridge: Cambridge University Press, 2002. 101–124.

7. Ania Loomba. *Colonialism/Postcolonialism*. New York: Routledge, 1998. 6.

8. Victor Merriman. "Bernard Shaw in Contemporary Irish Studies: 'Passé and Contemptible'?" *SHAW: The Annual of Bernard Shaw Studies* 30 (2010). 217.

9. Shaw addresses this question in two letters, the first being part of a series of articles written in November of 1917 titled "How to Settle the Irish Question" and his lecture to the Fabian society on 28 November 1919 titled "Socialism and Ireland." Whilst written for exceptionally different audiences, both letters focus on Ireland's relationship to the land, capital, and nationhood.

10. Loomba, *Colonialism/Postcolonialism*, 2.

11. F.J. Byrne provides a brief summary of just how complex this system was, as it allowed for different relationship schemes on the male side of families, encompassing up to five generations, in his chapter "Early Irish Society

(1st-9th Century)." In *The Course of Irish History*. Ed. T.W. Moody and F.X. Martin. Cork: Roberts Rinehart Publishers, 1964.43–60.

12. Aidan Clarke. "The Colonisation of Ulster and the Rebellion of 1641." In *The Course of Irish History*. Ed. T.W. Moody and F.X. Martin. Cork: Roberts Rinehart Publishers, 1964.203.

13. R.B. McDowell. "The Protestant Nation (1775–1800)." In *The Course of Irish History*. Ed. T.W. Moody and F.X. Martin. Cork: Roberts Rinehart Publishers, 1964. 234.

14. J.H. Whyte, "The Age of Daniel O'Connell (1800–47)," 255.

15. Donal McCartney. "From Parnell to Pearse (1891–1921)." In *The Course of Irish History*. Ed. T.W. Moody and F.X. Martin. Cork: Roberts Rinehart Publishers, 1964. 280–281.

16. McCartney, "From Parnell to Pearse (1891–1921)," 289.

17. Brad Kent, "Shaw's Everyday Emergency: Commodification in and of *John Bull's Other Island*," *SHAW: The Annual of Bernard Shaw Studies* 26 (2006): 168.

18. McCartney, "From Parnell to Pearse (1891–1921)," 289.

19. More arrests would follow, with the majority of these not facing formal charges or court-martial. McCartney, "From Parnell to Pearse (1891–1921)," 307–310.

20. Dan H. Lawrence and David H. Greene. "Introduction." In *The Matter with Ireland*. Ed. Dan H. Laurence and David H. Greene. 2nd ed. Gainesville: University Press of Florida, 2001. xviii.

21. Shaun Richards discusses this idea with regard to the debate about the use of realism in Irish theatre. Setting aside the debate pitting realism against symbolism, we can still see the role that politically active, consciousness raising theatre played in the development of a national theatre in Ireland. Shaun Richards, "'We were very young and we shrank from nothing': Realism and Early Twentieth-Century Irish Drama." In *The Oxford Handbook of Modern Irish Theatre*. Ed. Nicholas Grene and Chris Morash. Oxford: Oxford University Press, 2016. 105–120.

22. Shaun Richards, "'We were very young and we shrank from nothing': Realism and Early Twentieth-Century Irish Drama," 107.

23. Loomba, *Colonialism/Postcolonialism*, 2.

24. Joe Cleary, "Misplaced ideas? Locating and Dislocating Ireland in Colonial and Postcolonial Studies," 121.

25. Other leading proponents of the Marxist-materialist branch of Postcolonial Studies include Neil Lazarus (2002), Benita Parry (2002), and Crystal Bartolovich (2002).

26. Loomba, *Colonialism/Postcolonialism*, 7.

27. Stuart Hall. "Cultural Identity and Diaspora." In *Identity: Community, Culture, Difference*. Ed. Jonathan Rutherford. London: Lawrence and Wishart, 1990.225.

28. Shaw's notion of what constitutes Irishness and Irish identity is of course quite nuanced. His appeal to the Irish climate as indicative of this identity is much less rigid than the geographical notions upheld by other Gaelic Revivalists. Appeals to climate, in Shaw's typically artful fashion, evoke an attitude or a sensibility that is more inclusive than views such as that of W.B. Yeats, which obliged an author to explicitly territorialise a play in Ireland in order to benefit from the designation of "Irish."

29. Homi K. Bhabha. *The Location of Culture*. New York: Routledge Classics, 1994. 94.

30. Shaw places the blame for this on the Irish, too—immediately prior, he writes, "Of all the tricks which the Irish nation have played on the slow-witted Saxon, the most outrageous is the palming off on him of the imaginary Irishman of romance" (Shaw, "Dear Harp of my Country!" 29–30).

31. The strategic essentialism spoken of by Gayatri Chakravorty Spivak (amongst others) risks becoming implacable, as the reaction and perception of the coloniser cannot be predicted or controlled thereafter, endangering the neo- or postcolonial society's opportunities to not only differentiate themselves in terms of cultural identity, but also in terms of economic systems.

32. Victor Merriman, "Bernard Shaw in Contemporary Irish Studies: 'Passé and Contemptible'?" 218.

33. Loomba, *Colonialism/Postcolonialism*, 3.

34. Brad Kent acknowledges this: "Shaw himself gets sublimated into the process of postcoloniality despite his challenge to the more facile and readily commodifiable images of Irishness presented by many other dramatists. But what Root describes as the 'commodification of the proper name,' the branding of artists, cultures, and places, suggests that the play was increasingly commodifiable as soon as Irishness became attached to it and, even more subtly, as soon as it was known that Shaw was its author. That this process occurs despite the play's themes and the ways in which they are treated creates a dilemma for a Fabian Socialist such as Shaw." Brad Kent. "Shaw's Everyday Emergency: Commodification in and of *John Bull's Other Island*," 163.

35. Martin Meisel. "Irish Romance." In *Shaw and the Nineteenth Century Theatre*. Princeton: Princeton University Press, 1991.487.

36. Brad Kent goes on to note that, in spite of their newly acquired land and supposed control over their affairs, they "allow themselves to be bamboozled by the soft-nationalist rhetoric of Broadbent. Failing to realize that Broadbent's liberalism allows for multinational corporations and transna-

tional capital to move freely across borders, they are in the process of having their recently won freedom taken away." Brad Kent. "Missing Links, Bernard Shaw and the Discussion Play." In *The Oxford Handbook of Modern Irish Theatre*. Ed. Nicholas Grene and Chris Morash. Oxford: Oxford University Press, 2016. 142.

37. Shaw's review of Boucicault's play appeared in *The Saturday Review* on 1 February 1896. These reviews are compiled in *Our Theatre in the Nineties*, which appears in three volumes.

38. Shaw, "Dear Harp of My Country!" 28.

39. In this same article, Shaw goes on to write, "Fortunately, the same talent that enabled Ireland to lead the way in inventing and dramatizing national types now keeps her to the front in the more salutary work of picking them to pieces, a process which appeals to her barbarous humor on the one hand, and on the other to her keen common sense and intelligent appreciation of reality." Shaw, "Dear Harp of My Country!" 30.

40. Shaw's connection to England and his arrangement with Vedrenne-Barker to have the play premiered at the Royal Court Theatre suggest that Shaw was also well aware of the fact that his audience was truly two-fold, British and Irish alike. Indeed, just after stating that the intended audience is that of Ireland, Shaw goes on to acknowledge the wider scope of his project when he writes "The next thing that happened was the production of the play in London at the Court Theatre by Messrs. Vedrenne and Barker, and its immediate and enormous popularity with delighted and flattered English audiences." After allowing for differences in reactions to the play, he writes: "English audiences very naturally swallowed it eagerly and smacked their lips over it, laughing all the more heartily because they felt that they were taking a caricature of themselves with the most tolerant and large-minded goodhumor" (Shaw, "A Preface for Politicians," 808–809).

41. Kiberd, "John Bull's Other Islander – Bernard Shaw," 54.

42. Meisel, "Irish Romance," 486.

43. Hall, "Cultural Identity and Diaspora," 222.

44. Brad Kent addresses this very issue in "Missing Links, Bernard Shaw and the Discussion Play" (Oxford University Press, 2016, 138–151), noting that in the case of Shaw, the discussion play evolved from the play of ideas and provoked the need of the spectator to debate and discuss possible resolutions for the play in question, as Shaw rarely provided any clear-cut ones himself.

45. Shaw, *The Quintessence of Ibsenism*, 212.

46. [44] In *The Quintessence of Ibsenism*, Shaw describes initial critical reception of this genre in the following terms: "They [the critics] declare that discussions are not dramatic, and that art should not be didactic (Shaw, *The Quintessence of Ibsenism*, 210).

140 A. R. RUANE

47. Brad Kent. "The Politics of Shaw's Irish Women in *John Bull's Other Island*." In *Shaw and Feminisms On Stage and Off*. Ed. D.A. Hadfield and Jean Reynolds. Gainesville: University Press of Florida, 2013. 74.

48. Shaw, *The Quintessence of Ibsenism*, 212.

49. Shaw, *The Quintessence of Ibsenism*, 214.

50. Bernard Shaw. *John Bull's Other Island*. In *The Bodley Head Bernard Shaw Collected Plays with Their Prefaces*. Ed. Dan H. Laurence. London: The Bodley Head Ltd., 1971. 1017.

51. Kathleen Ochshorn. "Colonialism, Postcolonialism, And the Shadow of a New Empire: *John Bull's Other Island*." *SHAW: The Annual of Bernard Shaw Studies* 26 (2006):191.

52. Shaw, *John Bull's Other Island*, 905.

53. Shaw, "Dear Harp of My Country!" 32.

54. Shaw, *John Bull's Other Island*, 1005.

55. Shaw, *John Bull's Other Island*, 928.

56. Kathleen Ochshorn, "Colonialism, Postcolonialism, And the Shadow of a New Empire: *John Bull's Other Island*," 192.

57. There is, of course, evidence to support the fact that Nora is a much more complex character here, especially given the fact that she is faced with a rather certain future (marriage), but one in which she might be able to exercise power. As with much of Shaw's work, the ambiguity here leaves the audience with little means of pigeon-holing characters in stereotypical roles. For a more detailed, nuanced discussion of Nora's roll in *John Bull's Other Island*. See Brad Kent. "The Politics of Shaw's Irish Women in *John Bull's Other Island*." In *Shaw and Feminisms On Stage and Off*. Ed. D.A. Hadfield and Jean Reynolds. Gainesville: University Press of Florida, 2013.

58. Kent, "The Politics of Shaw's Irish Women in *John Bull's Other Island*," 80.

59. Kiberd, "John Bull's Other Islander – Bernard Shaw," 54.

60. Ochshorn, "Colonialism, Postcolonialism, And the Shadow of a New Empire: *John Bull's Other Island*," 184.

61. Bertolt Brecht. "Three Cheers for Shaw." In *Brecht on Theatre, The Development of an Aesthetic*. Ed. John Willett. London: Methuen & Co ltd, 1964.11.

62. Ochshorn cites Tracy C. Davis's assessment that Shaw never truly makes it to the postcolonial stage. Kathleen Ochshorn, "Colonialism, Postcolonialism, and the Shadow of a New Empire: *John Bull's Other Island*," 181.

63. McCartney, "From Parnell to Pearse (1891–1921)," 295.

64. Ochshorn, "Colonialism, Postcolonialism, And the Shadow of a New Empire: *John Bull's Other Island*," 192.

65. Shaw, "Socialism and Ireland," 238.

66. Jean-Paul Sartre. *Un théâtre de Situations.* Paris: Gallimard, 1973. 31.
67. Shaw, "Fragments of a Fabian Lecture 1890," 94.
68. Peter Gahan. "Colonial Locations of Contested Space and *John Bull's Other Island.*" *Shaw: The Annual of Bernard Shaw Studies* 26 (2006): 197.
69. Shaw, "Preface to the Home Rule Edition of 1912," 883.
70. Shaw's article appearing in *The Star* posits an even more sinister, ominous take on the real effects of bourgeois charity, essentially arguing that those charitable efforts themselves are tainted and largely one-sided: "Charity is only a poisoned dressing on a malignant sore. If we are callous enough and silly enough to let that easily preventable sore occur, the only remedy is the knife; and if it is too long delayed, the knife may take a triangular shape and slide in a tall wooden frame over-hanging a Procrustean bed. Starved children always revenge themselves one way or another." Shaw, "The Children of the Dublin Slums," 182.
71. Loomba, *Colonialism/Postcolonialism*, 12.
72. Shaw, "Preface for Politicians," 808.
73. Peter Gahan, "Colonial Locations of Contested Space and *John Bull's Other Island*," 209.
74. Shaw's disappointment registers in the explanatory note added to his 1930 reprinted "Preface to the Home Rule Edition of 1912": "Readers who skip to that [the 1906 "Preface for Politicians"] preface will lose nothing by missing this one except a possibly instructive example of how our eternal march into the future must always be a blindfold march. I guessed ahead, and guessed wrongly, whilst stupider and more ignorant fellow-pilgrims guessed rightly." Shaw "Preface to the Home Rule Edition of 1912," 874.
75. Frantz Fanon. *The Wretched of the Earth.* London: Paladin, 1963. 170.
76. Shaw, "Dear Harp of My Country!" 31.

REFERENCES

Bartolovich, Crystal. 2002. Introduction. In *Marxism, Modernity and Postcolonial Studies*, ed. Crystal Bartolovich and Neil Lazarus, 1–17. Cambridge: Cambridge University Press. Print.

Bhabha, Homi K. 1994. *The Location of Culture*. New York: Routledge Classics. Print.

Brecht, Bertolt. 1964. Three Cheers for Shaw. In *Brecht on Theatre, the Development of an Aesthetic*, ed. John Willett, 10–11. London: Methuen & Co ltd. Print.

Byrne, F.J. 1964. Early Irish Society (1st-9th Century). In *The Course of Irish History*, ed. T.W. Moody and F.X. Martin, 43–60. Cork: Roberts Rinehart Publishers. Print.

Clarke, Aidan. 1964. The Colonisation of Ulster and the Rebellion of 1641. In *The Course of Irish History*, ed. T.W. Moody and F.X. Martin, 189–203. Cork: Roberts Rinehart Publishers. Print.

Cleary, Joe. 2002. Misplaced Ideas? Locating and Dislocating Ireland in Colonial and Postcolonial Studies. In *Marxism, Modernity and Postcolonial Studies*, ed. Crystal Bartolovich and Neil Lazarus, 101–124. Cambridge: Cambridge University Press. Print.

———. 2007. *Outrageous Fortune, Capital and Culture in Modern Ireland*. Dublin: Field Day Publications. Print.

Conquergood, Dwight. 1992. Performance Theory, Hmong Shamans, and Cultural Politics. In *Critical Theory and Performance*, ed. Janelle Reinelt and Joseph R. Roach, 41–62. Ann Arbor: University of Michigan Press. Print.

Duncan, Dawn. 2004. *Postcolonial Theory in Irish Drama from 1800–2000*. Queenston: The Edwin Mellen Press. Print.

Dunnett, Jane. 2006. Postcolonial Constructions in Québécois Theatre of the 1970s: The Example of *Mistero Buffo*. *Romance Studies* 24 (2): 117–131.

Fanon, Frantz. 1963. *The Wretched of the Earth*. London: Paladin. Print.

Fortier, Mark. 2002. *Theory/Theatre: An Introduction*. 2nd ed. New York: Routledge.

Gahan, Peter. 2006. Colonial Locations of Contested Space and *John Bull's Other Island*. *SHAW: The Annual of Bernard Shaw Studies* 26: 194–221. *Academic Search Complete*. Web. 8 Nov. 2014.

Hall, Stuart. 1990. Cultural Identity and Diaspora. In *Identity: Community, Culture, Difference*, ed. Jonathan Rutherford, 222–237. London: Lawrence and Wishart. Print.

Jussawalla, Feroza, and Reed Way Dasenbrock. 1992. *Interviews with Writers of the Post-Colonial World*. Jackson: University Press of Mississippi. Print.

Kent, Brad. 2013. The Politics of Shaw's Irish Women in *John Bull's Other Island*. In *Shaw and Feminisms on Stage and off*, ed. D.A. Hadfield and Jean Reynolds, 73–91. Gainesville: University Press of Florida. Print.

———. 2006. Shaw's Everyday Emergency: Commodification in and of *John Bull's Other Island*. *SHAW: The Annual of Bernard Shaw Studies* 26: 162–179. *Academic Search Complete*. Web. 8 Nov. 2014.

———. 2016. Missing Links, Bernard Shaw and the Discussion Play. In *The Oxford Handbook of Modern Irish Theatre*, ed. Nicholas Grene and Chris Morash, 138–151. Oxford: Oxford University Press. Print.

Kiberd, Declan. 1996. John Bull's Other Islander – Bernard Shaw. In *Inventing Ireland*, 51–63. Cambridge: Harvard University Press. Print.

Lazarus, Neil. 2004. Introduction. In *The Cambridge Companion to Postcolonial Literary Studies*, ed. Neil Lazarus, 1–16. Cambridge: Cambridge University Press. Print.

Laurence, Dan H., and David H. Greene. 2001. Introduction. In *The Matter with Ireland*, ed. Dan H. Laurence and David H. Greene, 2nd ed., xv–xxiv. Gainesville: University Press of Florida. Print.

Lonergan, Patrick. 2004. The Laughter Will Come of Itself. The Tears Are Inevitable': Martin McDonagh, Globalization, and Irish Theatre Criticism. *Modern Drama* 47 (4, Winter): 636–657. Print.

Loomba, Ania. 1998. *Colonialism/Postcolonialism*. New York: Routledge. Print.

McCartney, Donal. 1964. From Parnell to Pearse (1891–1921). In *The Course of Irish History*, ed. T.W. Moody and F.X. Martin, 294–312. Cork: Roberts Rinehart Publishers. Print.

McDowell, R.B. 1964. The Protestant Nation (1775–1800). In *The Course of Irish History*, ed. T.W. Moody and F.X. Martin, 232–247. Cork: Roberts Rinehart Publishers. Print.

Meisel, Martin. 1991. Irish Romance. In *Shaw and the Nineteenth Century Theatre*, 269–289. Princeton: Princeton University Press. Print.

Merriman, Victor. 2010. Bernard Shaw in Contemporary Irish Studies: 'Passé and Contemptible'? *SHAW: The Annual of Bernard Shaw Studies* 30: 216–235. *Academic Search Complete*. Web. 8 Nov. 2014.

Ochshorn, Kathleen. 2006. Colonialism, Postcolonialism, and the Shadow of a New Empire: *John Bull's Other Island*. *SHAW: The Annual of Bernard Shaw Studies* 26: 180–193. *Academic Search Complete*. Web. 8 Nov. 2014.

Parry, Benita. 2004. The Institutionalization of Postcolonial Studies. In *The Cambridge Companion to Postcolonial Literary Studies*, ed. Neil Lazarus, 66–80. Cambridge: Cambridge University Press. Print.

Reinelt, Janelle. 1992. Introduction to 'after Marx'. In *Critical Theory and Performance*, ed. Janelle G. Reinelt and Joseph R. Roach, 109–116. Ann Arbor: University of Michigan Press. Print.

Richards, Shaun. 2016. 'We Were Very Young and we Shrank from Nothing': Realism and Early Twentieth-Century Irish Drama. In *The Oxford Handbook of Modern Irish Theatre*, ed. Nicholas Grene and Chris Morash, 105–120. Oxford: Oxford University Press. Print.

Sartre, Jean-Paul. 1973. *Un théâtre de Situations*. Paris: Gallimard.

Shaw, Bernard. 1932. Dear Harp of my Country! In *Our Theatre in the Nineties*, 28–34. London: Constable and Company. Print.

———. 1979a. Fragments of a Fabian Lecture 1890. In *Bernard Shaw'sthe Quintessence of Ibsenism and Related Writings*, ed. J.L. Wisenthal. Toronto: University of Toronto Press. Print.

———. 1971a. John Bull's Other Island. In *The Bodley Head Bernard Shaw Collected Plays with Their Prefaces*, ed. Dan H. Laurence, 893–1022. London: The Bodley Head Ltd. Print.

———. 1979b. The Quintessence of Ibsenism. In *Bernard Shaw'sthe Quintessence of Ibsenism and Related Writings*, ed. J.L. Wisenthal. Toronto: University of Toronto Press. Print.

———. 1971b. A Preface for Politicians. In *The Bodley Head Bernard Shaw Collected Plays with their Prefaces*, ed. Dan H. Laurence, 807–872. London: The Bodley Head Ltd. Print.

———. 1971c. Preface to the Home Rule Edition of 1912. In *The Bodley Head Bernard Shaw Collected Plays with Their Prefaces*, ed. Dan H. Laurence, 873–892. London: The Bodley Head Ltd. Print.

———. 2001a. How to Settle the Irish Question (1917). In *The Matter with Ireland*, ed. Dan H. Laurence and David H. Greene, 2nd ed., 153–173. Gainesville: University Press of Florida. Print.

———. 2001b. The Children of the Dublin Slums. In *The Matter with Ireland*, ed. Dan H. Laurence and David H. Greene, 2nd ed., 180–183. Gainesville: University Press of Florida. Print.

———. 2001c. Socialism and Ireland (1919). In *The Matter with Ireland*, ed. Dan H. Laurence and David H. Greene, 2nd ed., 233–249. Gainesville: University Press of Florida. Print.

Whyte, J.H. 1964. The Age of Daniel O'Connell (1800-47). In *The Course of Irish History*, ed. T.W. Moody and F.X. Martin, 248–262. Cork: Roberts Rinehart Publishers. Print.

CHAPTER 8

O'Flaherty V.C.: Satire as Shavian Agenda

Susanne Colleary

There is no doubt that *O'Flaherty V.C.* caused quite a stir. As is well known, the one act play was written for Dublin's Abbey Theatre in 1915, as part of the autumn schedule. The playwas also intended for a run through the English music hall circuit during the following summer. Since the loss of Horniman's fiscal support in 1910, the Abbey's dire financial circumstances made touring integral to the theatre's coffers.[1] However, the play never saw the Abbey stage that year, with opposition to its production coming from many quarters. Significantly, Ireland's involvement in the Great War was a deeply contentious issue. In the autumn of 1915, tensions amplified; the British army's aggressive recruitment tactics ensured that the focus of Shaw's play was cause for anxiety in Dublin Castle. Equally, Shaw's concerns for the play's reception on tour across the water were clear. He wrote to Yeats, 'it is by no means sure that it will be licensed in England and a few preliminary trials in Dublin might do no harm.'[2] Yeats duly sent a copy to the theatre's agent in London, who speculated that it would not offend the censor.[3] In Dublin, Matthew Nathan, then undersecretary to chief secretary Augustine Birrell, brought the point home. He reported in unequivocal terms: 'Bernard Shaw has

S. Colleary (✉)
Trinity College Dublin, Dublin, Ireland

© The Author(s) 2020
A. McNamara, N. O'Ceallaigh Ritschel (eds.), *Bernard Shaw and the Making of Modern Ireland*, Bernard Shaw and His Contemporaries, https://doi.org/10.1007/978-3-030-42113-7_8

sent a play to the Abbey Theatre which will be looked upon as too much a recruiting play by the Irish and as an anti-recruiting play by the English.'[4] Christopher Morash deepens the point by noting that the play was 'so subversive of ideas of family and home – dear to both Irish republicans and supporters of the British war effort, that the Abbey would have found few supporters in the controversy...all concerned (Shaw excepted) were glad when it sunk away quietly.'[5] Amid the flurry of correspondence that passed between the theatre and the Castle leading up to the play's ultimate containment, Shaw had his own set of concerns.Writing to Lady Gregory, he articulated his expectation:

> The picture of the Irish character will make the Playboy seem a patriotic rhapsody by comparison...The idea is that O'Flaherty's experience in the trenches has induced in him a terrible realism and an unbearable candour. He sees Ireland as it is, his mother as she is, his sweetheart as she is; and he goes back to the dreaded trenches joyfully for the sake of peace and quietness.[6]

Shaw's suggestion that *O'Flaherty V.C.* would be divisive enough to incite riots as with Synge's *Playboy* at the Abbey in 1907 is perhaps stretching the point. Many commentators have noted that the play was not likely to draw such a hue and cry from the people of Dublin. That said, it does indicate Shaw's concern for the fervid political atmosphere percolating beyond the walls of the theatre. In the end the curtain did not rise for *O'Flaherty V.C.*, with Shaw's pen doing little to stem the tide. Although he consented to change 'any lines that may jar on the military staff' and was at pains via the *Freeman's Journal* (among others) to 'make it clear that the author has no more desire to discourage recruiting in Ireland than the military authorities themselves,' it made little difference.[7]Despite all the talks between Castle, theatre and author, the play was 'postponed,' and inevitably, dropped.

A SHAVIAN AGENDA

Shaw's concern about what a Dublin audience might think of the 'Irish character,' applies equally not only toO'Flaherty but to the others in the play. All are held up to comic scrutiny. Peter Berger describes satire as a broad church; that which can be understood as the 'deliberate use of the comic for purposes of attack' [and that whatever the degree], 'satire is present in almost all forms of comic expression.'[8] Such attacks 'are part of *an agenda* on the part of the satirist.'[9] Andrew Stott argues that satire is 'the most directly political of comic forms and the one that has caused the majority of censorious government interventions.' He adds:

> Satire aims to renounce folly and vice and urge ethical and political reform by the subjection of ideas to humorous analysis…it takes its subject matter from the heart of political life or cultural anxiety, reframing issues at an ironic distance that enables us to revisit fundamental questions that have been obscured by rhetoric, personal interests or realpolitik.[10]

Clearly then, satire can be understood as a weapon of attack, usually underscored by degrees of ironic intent, and fuelled by an author's *agenda*.Its useis often driven by the desire to censure the target however seamed through with ambivalent qualities, so that 'by exposing that which is denounced however ambiguously, such satire is able to take on the quality of corrective moral comedy.'[11] Bearing this thinking in mind, I want to add the idea of comic exaggeration to the discussion. Comic exaggeration works whereby 'anyone or anything is held up to ridicule through exaggeration of their outstanding weakness…this is based on distortion…that [which] create[s] a ludicrous impression for the reader.'[12] In order to examine how Shaw is utilising satire in the work; I want to briefly describe the play's recurrent motifs, before examining how the play's characters can be read as comic exaggeration.I then want to connect those character amplifications to Shaw's satirical *agenda* as the play takes account of the patriot, the nationalist and the materiality of family life during World War I in Ireland.[13]

DISTORTIONS

Sir Pearce Madigan is a baronet of O'Flaherty's 'native place' and having gained the rank of General, is a loyal soldier to the Crown.O'Flaherty is a tenant on the Baronet's land, and has been fighting at the front in France. Having just received the Victoria Cross from King George, he has returned home to help with enlistment.We first meet Sir Pearce and O'Flaherty as they come back from a recruiting drive in the locality. Sir Pearce talks in satisfied tones of fighting for one's King and country, (a notion that itself was satirized by Shaw in other works; he was scathing of the aristocratic officer class as incapable of leading the war effort).[14] Accordingly *O'Flaherty* deflates the notion with immediacy:

> Well sir, to you that have an estate in it, it would feel like your country. But the divil a perch of it I ever owned.' And as to the king; God help him, my mother would have taken the skin off my back if I'd ever let on to have any other king than Parnell.'

Sir Pearce is overcome by the idea that O'Flaherty or his mother could have any feeling other than patriotism for the King. Moreover, he is shocked when O'Flaherty informs him that his mother thinks her son is fighting '*agen* the English.' He is emphatic that the King's war is everyone's war and, in the face of O'Flaherty's continued equivocation, blurts out, 'Does patriotism mean nothing to you?' O'Flaherty replies:

> To me and the likes of me, it means talking about the English just the way the English papers talk about the boshes. And what good has it ever done here in Ireland? It's kept me ignorant because it filled up my mother's mind and she thought to fill up mine too. It's kept Ireland poor because instead of trying to better ourselves we thought we was the fine fellows of patriots when we were speaking evil of Englishmen that was as poor as ourselves and maybe as good as ourselves. (5).

Sir Pearse holds strong for the cause of the patriot, and binds O'Flaherty to king and country. O'Flaherty levels the field by talking of English patriotism and its Irish echo in one breath. He accuses nationalistic ideals of keeping Irish people poor by filling Irish minds with English evil rather than economic growth and social progression.

Before long the General again returns to his grandiose feelings for the war. And again O'Flaherty is pragmatic in the face of English patriotism:

> They never thought of being patriotic until the war broke out; and now the patriotism has took them so sudden and come so strange to them that they run about liked frightened chickens, uttering all manner of nonsense. (6)

Sir Pearse reacts with the necessary fervour; the war has 'uplifted' the English people in a 'wonderful way' and 'the world will never be the same again.' And again O'Flaherty takes the wind out of the bombast; he equates patriotism to a parasitic infestation that with some application will eventually wash off. Ultimately O'Flaherty questions killing in the name of any country, and starkly depicts the horrific reality of war:

[W]hen the day comes to you that your comrade is killed in the trench beside you... all you say is to ask why the hell the stretcher-bearers don't take it out of the way...No war is right; and all the holy water that Father Quinlan ever blessed couldn't make one right. (5)

Sir Pearce has little by way of response. The Baronet, who reacts emotionally when O'Flaherty makes his opinions frank, also sidesteps being drawn into any deeper consideration of O'Flaherty's moral or ethical points of view throughout the play.

The conversation turns towards the imminent arrival of O'Flaherty's mother. Sir Pearce makes apology for his wife's being in London and O'Flaherty recalls how he and his mother used to pray for her and the baronet's conversion to the true faith:

And...call down the blessing of God on your head when she was selling you your own three geese that you though had been ate by the fox the day after you'd finished fattening them, sir.

Sir Pearce is astounded (again) at the revelation and O'Flaherty is not surprisingly matter-of-fact:

Sure we needed them sir. Often and often we had to sell our own geese to pay you the rent to satisfy your needs, and why shouldn't we sell your geese to satisfy ours...sure you had to get what you could out of us; and we had to get what we could out of you. God forgive us both!

Sir Pearce flatly suggests that O'Flaherty seems somewhat upset by the war, again skirting O'Flaherty's realistic portrayal of the power relations at play with the baronet from his 'weeshy' childhood. He returns again to O'Flaherty's deception and insists that Mrs. O'Flaherty *must* be told of her son's fighting for the English side in the War. O'Flaherty remains unmoved, and instead builds an elaborate version of Mrs. O'Flaherty's character. She is depicted as the 'wildest Fenian and rebel,' who declares 'Gladstone...an Irishman' and more:

She says all the English generals is Irish. She says all the English poets and great men was Irish. She says the English never know how to read their own books until we taught them. She says we're the lost tribes of the house of

Israel and the chosen people of God...the goddess Venus...came up out of
the water in Killiney Bay...and that Lazarus was buried in Glasnevin. (6)

The fearsome description anticipates Mrs. O'Flaherty's entrance finally
and in full Sunday-best peasant costume. She is obsequiousness and polite
to the overwrought General. She tells him that it's no wonder her son
grew up such a fine solder with 'you before his eyes for a pattern of the
finest soldier in Ireland' (7). Sir Pearce takes the compliments 'with
extreme geniality' and soon takes his leave, entering his house to order tea.
   When gone, Mrs. O'Flaherty assails her son, 'scalding' him for deceiv-
ing her about fighting for the English side, 'did you take me for a fool that
couldn't find out, and the papers all full of you shaking hands with the
English king at Buckingham Palace?' However, when Mrs. O'Flaherty
hears that the English pay better than both the German and the French
army, she exclaims 'Oh murder! They must be a mean lot, Denny.' Denny
makes it clear to his mother that he did his best for her, 'I went where I
could to get the biggest allowance for you; and little thanks I get for it!'
He is furious when he learns that she has been docked some of the separation allowance 'do you tell me they knocked ten shilling off you for my
keep?' Although his mother assures him that she has fooled the 'black-
guards' by other means, Denny is critical of the British Government who
have short-changed his mother, stating, 'it's in the nature of governments
to tell lies.'[15] Yet if Mrs. O'Flaherty and Denny spend some of their time
together necessarily discussing money, O'Flaherty's relationship with
Tessie is defined by it. Teresa O'Driscoll is a parlour maid in the Madigan
house, and is O'Flaherty's sweetheart. As Mrs. O'Flaherty is leaving her
boy to go in for tea in the drawing room with the General, Tessie comes
to Denny. Almost immediately he produces a gold chain for her, which he
tells Tessie he stole from a German prisoner-of-war. Tessie takes little time
recovering from the thought and wants to have the chain appraised. Her
mercenary attitude upsets Denny; however, it is forgotten momentarily as
they embrace. She thanks God that the priest cannot see them, to which
he replies, 'it's little they care for priests in France alanna.' The taking of
the gold chain and the sexual insinuations of his time in France are the first
real glimpses of a darker, more practical realism shaded in O'Flaherty's
character. In the short time that Tessie spends with Denny; she talks of the
meagre size of his pension, and the hope of more money if O'Flaherty is
wounded. She makes sure he is going back to the front and once again
assures herself that the pension will be forthcoming 'you'll have a pension

anyhow Denny, won't you, whether you're wounded or not'? With that she enters the house and Denny spits out 'if I do get a pension itself, the divil a penny of it you'll ever have the spending of.' O'Flaherty's passion has cooled in the face of Tessie's clear mercenary motives.

In the final scene, Mrs. O'Flaherty berates her son for speaking ill of Tessie, who has a dowry of ten pounds. He responds bitterly, 'she's thinking of nothing but to get me out there agin to be wounded so that she may spend my pension…I've been made a fool of an imposed upon all my life.' But O'Flaherty has gained 'knowledge and wisdom,' through his time away from home, and now threatens his mother with the marrying of a Frenchwoman and of living in that country. For Denny will not 'stick in this place…among a lot of good-for-nothing devils that'll not do a hands turn but watch the grass growing and build up the stone wall where the cow walked through it.' Sparks fly between the two women over Denny's upset, descending into a vicious argument while (alerted by the commotion) an exasperated Sir Pearce and Denny *drive* (my emphasis) them into the house. Sir Pearce slams the door on the two women, at which 'a heavenly silence falls.' O'Flaherty speaks fondly of getting back to the trenches; 'Some like war's alarums; and some likes home life. I've tried both, sir, and I'm for war's alarums now.' A thrush sings. A jay laughs. An easy quiet descends.

EXAGGERATIONS

In *O'Flaherty V.C.*, there are a series of comic exaggerations at work though the broadly stock characterisations of Sir Pearce, Mrs. O'Flaherty and Tessie. Within the conventions of a one-act play, Sir Pearce is depicted as a one-dimensional character; an enthusiastic, if gullible, ascendancy class landlord.His stock-in-tradeis to persistently and misguidedly extol the virtues of patriotism to a clearly resistant O'Flaherty. He also seems blind to the nature of the power relations at play between him and his tenants in O'Flaherty's native place.He is, however intentionally, naive to the heavily stacked, symbiotic nature of that relationship. While Denny tries at times to redress the power balance, through his newly found acquired knowledge as an accomplished soldier, his 'unbearable candour' and attempt at honest exchange with Sir Pearce, is unlikely to change neither the material nature of their relationship nor the reality of everyday life, for those living on the Baronet's estate.Sir Pearce's obliviousness to O'Flaherty's views then, on patriotism, nationalism, the futility of war and everyday reality for the O'Flahertys as tenants on his estate, distorts his character through comic exaggeration, exposing his outstanding weaknesses to ridicule.As the inverted image, Mrs. O'Flaherty is unequivocally depicted as a fervid nationalist who initially equates any and all worth exclusively to an Irish identity. Her ratcheting nationalist fervour is as absurd as Sir Pearce's grandiloquent avowals for monarch and nation. Her bizarre declarations and nationalist zeal emphasise the flaws in her character even before she sets foot on the stage.However, her character is described through the mouth of her son in anticipation of her arrival. Although of necessity, flattering to the baronet, and scalding to her son at times, she is not as overblown as the reputation that preceded her. She is in fact something of a more nuanced character for a time at least. She may seem fiery in the face of Denny's fighting for the English, however, it's possible she already knew, as the wrangling with the British over the separation allowance may suggest. While reliant on Denny for her survival, their frank conversations are those between a mother and son on money matters and she in fact tries to comfort him with the thought that she outdid the British with her financial wrangling.Her grief at the prospect of losing her son to a French land and wife depict a heightened sense of worry for her son and for herself should he abandon her. In this respect at least Mrs. O'Flaherty does not deviate from other portrayals of Irish mothers on Irish stages. However, the row between Mrs. O'Flaherty and Tessie is the most distorted aspect of Mrs. O'Flaherty's behaviour in the play. Her descending into 'an appalling tempest of wordy wrath' with the servant girl, depicts her as a shrew, and an ignorant old countrywoman who never put her nose beyond the barony. Mrs. O'Flaherty's behaviour here above any other in the play, distorts her, exaggerating her flaws to the ridicule of her son and the General.

It may well be Tessie who comes off the worst in this play. She is diamond-cut; as Denny's sweetheart there are some momentary glimpses of the couple's romantic relationship; however; her fixation on Denny's pension reverberates through the text. As the shortest character sketch in the play, her function is apparent. She is wholly concerned with money and Denny's potential worth in separation allowances, including the value of his battle scars. Tessie's obsession with Denny's worth and her reiteration of those sentiments exposes her outstanding weakness as a highly mercenary young woman, and paints an absurdly distorted picture of Tessie's character for an audience.But what of O'Flaherty himself?He is the most well-drawn character and at first blush he is the character with which an audience may feel most empathy for. War has made him both pragmatic and philosophical; he confounds Sir Pearce, yet holds him in some lessening respect while recognising his flaws. He clearly loves his mother, yet he is more than aware of and speaks plainly to her failings, which seem to him to be more pronounced now than ever before. If he is no longer 'afeard' of his Mother's fierceness, he seems angry and hurt by Tessie's clearly drawn motives for courting him. O'Flaherty understands himself as an accomplished soldier despite his resistance to the General's rhetoric; as an experienced man with knowledge of the world, marking him out from those around him. He hints at his own sexual adventures in France, his behaviour to the German solider over the gold chain is dubious and his subtle disavowal of his religion is clear. He seems unaware of his own character failings even he is clear eyed in his summary judgement of those around him. At the end of the play, and having dispatched the brawling women, O'Flaherty and the General sit outside enjoying the silence. O' Flaherty adopts the pastoral mode; he describes the French countryside, and the machinery of war in idyllic tones. He speaks of his once longed for wish for home. After a short time with his Mother and Tessie, O'Flaherty chooses to escape towards the battlefront and away from hearth and home, as he is a 'quiet lad by natural disposition.' Finally, the absurd notion that the front is a more peaceful place, distorts the plays ending, and exposes Denny's comic-ironic view of family life to scrutiny. Is this O'Flaherty's outstanding weakness after all?

Comic Tears of the Brain…

Shaw's use of satire to distort some if not all of the characters in the play opens up the gap of critical distance in the work.[16] In Brechtian terms (interestingly Brecht was an admirer of Shaw's proclivity for 'intellectual attack on his audience')[17] that gap can be described as *Verfremdungseffekt*, which works by 'turning the object…to which one's attention is to be drawn, from something ordinary, familiar…into something peculiar, striking, and unexpected.'[18] Another way to describe making the familiar seem strange is Simon Critchley's concept of humour as *sensus* and *dissensuscommunis*. Critchley describes a *sensus communis* as that which[19]

> [m]akes explicit the enormous commonality that is implicit in [our] social life… this is what Shaftsbury had in mind…when he spoke of humour as a form of *sensus communis*. So, humour reveals the depth of what we share.[20]

Critchley argues that humour *returns* people to a shared common sense. But it does so by creating a temporary distance, by de-familiarising the world before returning us to that familiarity.[21] In other words the *sensus communis* is returned by temporarily estranging the world, or by creating moments of *dissensus communis*, 'distinct from the dominant common sense,'which throws light on everyday practices. By doing so the *dissensus communis* may hint at or signify how 'things might be otherwise.'[22] Both Brecht's *Verfremdungseffekt* and Crichley's *sensus communis* can, however ambivalently, point at another common sense or new awareness, with an audience somehow made aware of differing possibilities.

Shaw's satire works in *O'Flaherty V.C.* by means of distortion; that is the comic exaggeration of flaws lay bare the characters' outstanding weaknesses in the play. Those failings expose the character to ridicule and produce a comic effect that makes for moments of *dissensus communis*, making that which is familiar, seem strange. Those moments occur across the play of ideas in *O'Flaherty V.C.* In those moments Shaw collapses difference between ideas of patriotic zeal and national fervour to draw attention to the similarities that exist between the two seemingly opposed ideologies. Drawing such comparisons also highlights the fallacies when held up against the grim realities of the Great War and the bleak depiction of everyday life in Ireland. Yet, despite this play of ideas there is a Shavian ambivalence at work here; for even as the ideological fallacy is advanced, it is clear that Shaw draws out a life for O'Flaherty, even in war torn France that seems a better prospect than returning home. With 'terrible realism,' Shaw points to 'Ireland as it really is.'[23] A place stymied by nationalist politics, thwarting the country's socio-economic growth and progression. In the final moments of the play in particular, Shaw bends the function of the female characters in his satirical agenda in order to drive home the point. For the women and the lessons they have taught him, above all else, turn the soldier's face from home, driving him back to the front.

Allowances

Then as now, a number of debates circle around the playwright's 'two thinks' about the Great War.[24] Nicholas Grene notes that Shaw's earlier essay 'Common Sense About the War' garnered him very little favour with the British public.[25] The essay 'won him widespread notoriety and hostility for its cool analysis of the origins of the war and resistance to the fervid patriotism of the time.'[26] Yet, Grene argues that despite the unpopular reaction to the piece, Shaw did in fact support the allied war effort and he specifically connects this view to the play.Further, Shaw's replacing of the play's original tag line with a *'Recruiting Pamphlet,'* mirrors the first line of the prologue (also added after 1915), as a 'recruiting poster in disguise.'[27] There are those who disagree. Lauren Arrington argues that Shaw's 'opposition to the war was well known' and that 'the censorship of *O'Flaherty V.C.* was a product of Shaw's protagonist's stance that'no war is right.'[28] However, Arrington's argument does not fully take into account Shaw's belief that once in the War, it was imperative to win, in that sense Arrington's argument can only go so far.[29] Shaw does take aim at Dublin Castle for bungling the British Army's recruitment drive in 1915. As perplexing as it may be to Englishmen 'Irish patriotism does not take the form of devotion to…England's king.' The Castle would have more success had they appealed to an adventurous spirit and the ambition to leave Ireland, 'which is a dull place to live in' and where there was something worth fighting for if the place was not to submit to the threatened jack boot of German rule. Declan Kiberd makes the point that in Shaw's plays 'the Irish have become the fact-facers through harsh poverty, while the English have enjoyed a scale of wealth so great that it allows them to indulge their victims with expansively sentimental gestures.'[30] On one level, the point defines *O'Flaherty V.C.* very well in that the relationship between rhetoric and harsh reality materially underscores the world of the play. O'Flaherty is the pragmatic philosopher played against the sentimental gesturing of the landlord class. Without doubt the world of harsh poverty permeates the work as a whole but extends in particular to how the women are depicted in the play. If some years later, O'Casey depicted the women in the *Silver Tassie* as enjoying separation money, Shaw marks out Mrs. O'Flaherty and Tessie in the same way.[31] If not by their acts alone, then out of the mouth of O'Flaherty himself.Arguably the women are utilised by Shaw as ironic stereotypes used to critique Ireland's insularity; that which stunts Irish progress and keeps the women tied to the petty jealousies of town land politics and penurious states. They are bent to the author's agenda.

Peter Berger argues that satire 'more than other expression of the comic, is bound by its social context…it is time-bound, at its best it leads beyond the immediate object of its attack and gives a sense of liberation beyond the particular historical moment.'[32] In that sense and as reformist or progressive comedy, Shaw reframeshis subject matter from 'the heart of political life or cultural anxiety,'[33] beyond the separatist forces at work in the play. Shaw was confident 'in the power of progressive intellectual enlightenment'[34] which self-supported his 'conviction of the need for a closer relationship, conducted on a voluntary basis between the two island peoples.[35] However, the depiction of the women and by extension that of home and family in this play is unsympathetic to the broader contexts and harsh realities of Irish life at that time. As Foster notes thousands of men signed up'often encouraged by unemployment at home and a generous separation allowance for their families.'[36] People must live, and the women who are in certain respects no less pragmatic then O'Flaherty must also live. A separation allowance or a Victoria Cross pension would have made material differences to the everyday lives of these women and in that respect the satire employed by Shaw is utilised for the purpose of a call to arms. Those moments in the play speak to the harshly drawn outlines of the women and the misappropriation of the comic for purposes of attack. If there is an outstanding weakness in *O'Flaherty V.C.*, then it lies here.

In the end, the satire in the play interrogated the tensions of the time; ideas of the patriot, of the nationalist and of the realities of lived experience both for those who left to fight and for those left behind to fight for their daily bread in Ireland. Ultimately the play could not escape the particular historical moment; Shaw knew he had written a play that at the time was utterly inadmissible, 'what can I do but apologize, and publish the play now that it can no longer do any good.'[37] Foster notes that 'independent Ireland would later adopt a policy of intentional amnesia about the extent of Irish commitment to the War effort before 1916.'[38] Kiberd also observes that for decades after the war these soldiers were expunged from the record for fighting 'for the rights of small nations and for Home Rule after the cessation of hostilities.'[39] In post-independent Ireland this cultural anxiety, which led to intentional cultural forgetting, is bound to the unpalatable notion of having been part of a British war where Irishmen fought and died for a shilling king. Now that Ireland is in the decade of centenaries, the play can be re-imagined to speak to a newly receptive audience. For now, it can add to the present historical moment as Irish voices begin to redress their amnesia; a cultural memory loss that silenced Irish soldiers far away from the battles of the Somme, or Verdun or Passchendaele—much worse than that, a cultural memory loss that silenced Irish soldiers on their own soil.

NOTES

1. Nelson O'Ceallaigh Ritschel, 'Irish Politics' in *George Bernard Shaw in Context*, ed. Brad Kent (Cambridge: Cambridge University Press, 2015), 227.
2. George Bernard Shaw cited in Lucy McDiarmid, 'The Abbey and the Theatrics of Controversy 1909–1915' in *A Century of Irish Drama: Widening the Stage*, ed. Stephen Watt, Eileen Morgan, and Shakir Mustafa (Indiana: Indiana University Press, 2000), 70.
3. See *Shaw, Lady Gregory and the Abbey: A Correspondence and a Record*, ed. Dan H. Laurence and Nicholas Grene (Britain: Colin Smythe Ltd., 1990), 107.
4. Matthew Nathan cited in Lauren Arrington, 'The Censorship of *O'Flaherty V.C.*,' *SHAW: Annual of Bernard Shaw Studies,* 28 (2008),89.
5. Christopher Morash, *A History of Irish Theatre: 1601–2000* (Cambridge: Cambridge University Press, 2002), 158.
6. Arrington, 'The Censorship of *O'Flaherty V.C.*,' 90.
7. Arrington, 'The Censorship of *O'Flaherty V.C.*,' 97–99.
8. Peter L. Berger, *Redeeming Laughter: The Comic Dimension of Human Experience* (Berlin and New York: De Gruyter, 1997), 157.
9. Berger, *Redeeming Laughter*, 157.
10. Andrew Stott, *Comedy: The New Critical Idiom* (Oxon: Routledge, 2005), 109.
11. Susanne Colleary, 'The Savage Eye Sees Far: 'Militant Irony' and the Jacobean Corrective in Contemporary Irish Satire' in *For the Sake of Sanity: Doing Things with Humour in Irish Performance*, ed. Eric Weitz (Dublin: Carysfort Press, 2014), 208.
12. Andrew Davis, *Baggy Pants Comedy: Burlesque and the Oral Tradition* (New York: Palgrave Macmillan, 2014), 119.
13. All direct quotations are taken from George Bernard Shaw, *O'Flaherty V.C.: A Recruiting Pamphlet* https://www.gutenberg.org/files/3484/3484-h/3484-h.htm
14. See George Bernard Shaw, 'Common Sense Aboutthe War,' *in Current History of the European War, Vol. I – No I* (New York: New York Times, December 1914) In the brief preface to his other one-act War play *Augustus Does His Bit,* Shaw portrays this idea with great comic effect.
15. Shaw made no bones about this sentiment, which is repeated many times in'Common Sense About the War'and in much of his journalism during the early months of the War.See George Bernard Shaw, 'Common Sense Aboutthe War,' and Nelson O'Ceallaigh Ritschel, *Bernard Shaw, W.T. Stead, and the New Journalism; Bernard Shaw and his Contemporaries* (Switzerland: Springer International Publishing, 2017).

16. I have spoken elsewhere (and am not alone) of the ironic detachment at play in the world of comedy and have linked that sense of ironic detachment to de-familiarisation processes. See Susanne Colleary, *The Comic 'i': Performance and Identity in Irish Stand-Up Comedy* (Hampshire: Palgrave Macmillan, 2015).

17. See T.F. Evans, *George Bernard Shaw* (Collected Critical Heritage) (Oxon: Routledge, 1997), 29.

18. Bertolt Brecht, cited in Oliver Double and Michael Wilson, 'Karl Valentin's Illogical Subversion, Stand-Up Comedy and the Alienation Effect,' NTQ 20, no.3 (2004),214. In his discussion of ideas of the comic and religious experience, Peter Berger also points to Brecht's technique of *Verfremdung* and Eugène Ionesco's concept of *depaysement*,which literally means 'losing one's country.' Berger argues that the comic transcends the reality of the familiar world, transforming reality into something strange and unfamiliar; in other words, 'it relativizes paramount reality.' See Berger, *Redeeming Laughter*, 207.

19. Simon Critchley talks of the *sensus communis* as a Roman concept that was first linked to the idea of humour by the Earl of Shaftsbury in 1709. See Simon Critchley, *On Humour, Thinking in Action*, ed. Simon Critchley and Robert Kearney (Oxon: Routledge, 2002), 80.

20. Critchley's formulation does fly in the face somewhat of other theorists who believe that modern relativism has taken the arguments of Shaftsbury (and others) out of their original contexts, using 'bits and pieces' of the original in order to celebrate the positive aspects of humour over and above the negative. See Michael Billig, *Laughter and Ridicule: Towards a Social Critique of Humour* (London: Sage Publications, 2005).

21. Critchley, *On Humour*, 18.

22. Critchley, *On Humour*, 18–90, 90.

23. A point Shaw also made in the 1907 'Preface for Politicians,' the preface for *John Bull's Other Island (1904)*.

24. James Joyce quoted in *The Irish Mind: Exploring Intellectual Traditions*, ed. Richard Kearney (Dublin: Wolfhound Press, 1985), 10.

25. The essay was written for the *New Statesman* in October 1914. Shaw was also involved in the creation of the periodical.

26. Nicholas Grene, 'Writers in the DIB: George Bernard Shaw (1856–1950),'*Royal Irish Academy* (2015), accessed August 3, 2015,https://www.ria.ie/research/dib/writers-in-the-dib%2D%2Dgeorge-bernard-shaw-(1856-1950.aspx

27. The subtitle was added in 1930 for the authorised version of the play; see Arrington, 'The Censorship of *O'Flaherty V.C.*,' 103.

28. Arrington also argues that 'the Abbey Theatre's state of financial crisis, brought on by the war, […] prevented the theatre's directors from risking the production.' See Arrington, 'The Censorship of O'Flaherty V.C.,' 85.
29. See George Bernard Shaw, 'Common Sense Aboutthe War.'
30. Declan Kiberd is discussing *John Bull's Other Island* in this instance. See Declan Kiberd, *Inventing Ireland, The Literature of the Modern Nation* (London: Vintage, 1996), 52.
31. Kiberd, *Inventing Ireland*, 242.
32. Berger, *Redeeming Laughter*, 158.
33. Stott, *Comedy*, 109.
34. Christoper Innes cited in *Clare Wallace, Suspect Cultures: Narrative, Identity & Citation in 1990sNew Drama* (Czech Republic: Litteraria Pragensia, 2006), 92.
35. Kiberd, *Inventing Ireland*, 63.
36. R.F. Foster, *Modern Ireland: 1600–1972* (London: Penguin, 1989),471.
37. George Bernard Shaw, Prologue, *O'Flaherty V.C.: A Recruiting Pamphlet* https://www.gutenberg.org/files/3484/3484-h/3484-h.htm
38. Foster, *Modern Ireland*,472.
39. Declan Kiberd, *Inventing Ireland*, 239.

REFERENCES

Arrington, Lauren. 2008. The Censorship of O'Flaherty V.C. *SHAW: Annual of Bernard Shaw Studies* 28: 85–106.
Berger, L. Peter. 1997. *Redeeming Laughter: The Comic Dimension of Human Experience*. Berlin/New York: De Gruyter.
Billig, Michael. 2005. *Laughter and Ridicule: Towards a Social Critique of Humour*. London: Sage Publications.
Colleary, Susanne. 2014. The Savage Eye Sees Far: 'Militant Irony' and the Jacobean Corrective in Contemporary Irish Satire. In *For the Sake of Sanity: Doing Things with Humour in Irish Performance*, ed. Eric Weitz. Dublin: Carysfort.
———. 2015. *The Comic 'I': Performance and Identity in Irish Stand-Up Comedy*. Hampshire: Palgrave Macmillan.
Crtichley, Simon. 2002. In *On Humour, Thinking in Action*, ed. Simon Critchley and Robert Kearney. Oxon: Routledge.
Davis, Andrew. 2014. *Baggy Pants Comedy: Burlesque and the Oral Tradition*. New York: Palgrave Macmillan.
Double, Oliver, and Michael Wilson. 2004. Karl Valentin's Illogical Subversion: Stand-Up Comedy and Alienation Effect. *NTQ* 20 (3): 203–215.
Evans, T.F.1997. *George Bernard Shaw* (Collected Critical Heritage).Oxon: Routledge.

Foster, R.F. 1989. *Modern Ireland: 1600–1972*. London: Penguin.

Grene, Nicholas. 2015. Writers in the DIB: George Bernard Shaw (1856–1950). In *Royal Irish Academy*. https://dib.cambridge.org/viewReadPage.do? articleId=a8004. Accessed 3 Aug 2015.

Kiberd, Declan. 1996. *Inventing Ireland: The Literature of the Modern Nation*. London: Vintage.

McDiarmid, Lucy. 2000. The Abbey and the Theatrics of Controversy 1909–1915. In *A Century of Irish Drama: Widening the Stage*, ed. Stephen Watt, Eileen Morgan, and Shakir Mustafa. Indiana: Indiana University Press.

Morash, Christopher. 2002. *A History of Irish Theatre: 1601–2000*. Cambridge: Cambridge University Press.

CHAPTER 9

Shaw, Women and the Dramatising of Modern Ireland

Audrey McNamara

A series of letters on events in Ireland, the first one a review on J. A Partridge's "The Making of an Irish Nation", written in 1886, to *The Pall Mall Gazette,* indicates Shaw's interest and engagement with Irish affairs. He wrote prolifically on Ireland's political situation until 1928 and this interest manifests itself in his growing body of dramatic work. It is also quite clear that Shaw's affiliation with the social and political affairs of Ireland is without the extreme nationalism often associated with the period. He had very little time for the romanticised version of Irish nationalism that he felt was put forward by the progenitors of the National Irish theatre, and what Dan. H. Laurence described as "the pathetic slavery of the Irish to romantic illusion, to a mystic mirage conjuring up the harp, the hound, and the round tower".[1] He objected to the symbolism of Kathleen ni Houlihan as a redemptive figure of "mother Ireland". In correspondence with Horace Plunkett in 1917, he speaks about the illusory nature of the Irish question and maintains that "nothing less than a congress of the human race called 'The Peace Conference' is worthy to

A. McNamara (✉)
School of English, Drama and Film, University College Dublin, Dublin, Ireland

© The Author(s) 2020
A. McNamara, N. O'Ceallaigh Ritschel (eds.), *Bernard Shaw and the Making of Modern Ireland,* Bernard Shaw and His Contemporaries, https://doi.org/10.1007/978-3-030-42113-7_9

redress the wrongs of Kathleen ni Houlihan".[2] Interpreting this literally as the wrongs *of* rather than the wrongs *to*, as there might be a temptation to, helps to highlight Shaw's search for a practical solution to the Irish problem. Elizabeth Cullingford argues:

> The identification of Ireland with a woman, variously personified as the Shan Van Vocht, Cathleen ni Houlihan, and Mother Ireland, is like all political deployments of the female symbol, strategic and constructed.[3]

This chapter argues that Shaw subverts this personification of Ireland by deconstructing the romantic notion of the helpless and dependent female. Shavian women were for the most part shrewd, strong and articulate. His creations, Blanche Sartorius (*Widower's Houses* 1892), Mrs. Warren and her daughter Vivie (*Mrs Warren's Profession* 1893), Candida (*Candida* 1894) and Mrs. George (*Getting Married* 1908), are shown to be middle-class women who share a lower-class status in their backgrounds. The money they come from is "new money", so this separates them immediately from the aristocracy where women were educated to be wives, mothers and hostesses for their husbands. The notion of "new money" works to demonstrate a greater female engagement in the public sphere of the male characters. Blanche Sartorius becomes interested and involved in the business world of her father and her fiancé, Harry Trench. Mrs. Warren is a self-made wealthy woman who made her money through a somewhat risqué profession, and her daughter Vivie, who although she does not desire to follow her mother's business route, takes up a profession that was male dominated. Candida, though portrayed as the mother figure, emerges as the controlling figure in her household, and Mrs. George as the presence of wisdom in the Bridgenorth home. Feemy Evans (*The Shewing Up of Blanco Posnet* 1909), and Eliza Doolittle (*Pygmalion* 1912) are two female characters from the lower stratum of society that appear to have little going for them. This, however, is not a negative in regard to the way Shaw develops their characters as the progression of their characters serves to mark an improvement in social acceptance. Though Eliza fares better on an economic social scale through education than Feemy Evans, Feemy's acceptance as part of a community was a relatively new dramatic departure for a lower—class female character, even for Shaw who was not afraid to push social boundaries. Nora Reilly's character (*John Bull's Other Island* 1904) is considered an "heiress" in relation to the other inhabitants of Rosscullen and her shrewdness pays off when she captures the imagination of the conquering Englishman, Tom Broadbent. Bearing in mind how the social, economic and political atmosphere of the times resonates in the creation of Shaw's characters, the chapter examines how Shaw's take on the Irish question resonates through his construction of the female protagonists in three major plays, *John Bull's Other Island* (1904), *Pygmalion* (1912) and *Heartbreak House* (1916).

There is no doubt that Bernard Shaw's definitive Irish play *John Bull's Other Island* was influenced by Irish historical factors at the turn of the twentieth century. However, while contentious issues of the Irish political scene inspired Shaw to address such matters in dramatic form, it was what Holroyd terms as the "renaissance in Irish theatre"[4] that prompted Shaw to write *John Bull's Other Island*. He was impressed by the productions of the early Irish dramatic movement and was determined to contribute one of his plays to their burgeoning repertory. In watching Irish plays at the Theatre Royal off Shaftsbury Avenue in London on 24 March 1904—a one-day run of matinee and evening performances, Shaw identified a niche in the Irish repertoire that he felt compelled to fulfil. While the newly formed Irish National Theatre Society performed in London in 1903 and 1904, Shaw missed the former but attended the matinee and evening performances in 1904. The matinee ran "[a] bill of fare that included Synge's *In the Shadow of the Glen* and *Riders to the Sea*".[5] Bearing in mind Shaw's fascination with Women's suffrage, the marriage question "can be no coincidence". As Nelson O'Ceallaigh Ritschel argues, "Shaw named his main Irish woman character Nora after seeing J.M. Synge's Nora in London, as both Noras leave with intruding strangers,[6] though he goes on to argue that though she is important to the play, 'she is not the central character'".[7] On the opposite end of the spectrum Fredrick McDowell asserts, "She is the Kathleen ni Houlihan figure whom Shaw views sardonically: she lacks the spiritual force associated with such a female symbol of Ireland by the authors of the Celtic Revival and is, instead, a parasitic and ineffectual lady".[8] While McDowell is quite right that Shaw held a sardonic view of Kathleen ni Houlihan, the mythic spirit of Ireland and the title character in W.B. Yeats and Lady Gregory's 1902 play, McDowell has missed the point of Shaw's Nora Reilly.

Shaw created Nora to be a more pragmatic character than Synge's Nora, who although obtaining a degree of autonomy, leaves for a life of poverty. In setting her against the "spiritual" ideal of freedom at any price or "for no price" in the case of Nora Burke, it is quite possible that Shaw now saw the opportunity through his Nora character to openly challenge

the notional ideal of Kathleen ni Houlihan who had become the nationalist symbol of the Irish National Theatre Society, dating from the 1902
production of the Yeats/Gregory play *Kathleen ni Houlihan*. Nora Reilly
might, rather, be read as *central* to the plot as the creation of her character
is in essence the very antithesis of Kathleen ni Houlihan. In fact, Shaw
"fashioned the play to prove a point: the unifying vision of a dreamy,
romantic Ireland was invented by the Celtic Renaissance",[9] and as such
bore no resemblance to reality.

As for the fantasy of Kathleen, Declan Kiberd argues that the architects
of the neo-Gaelic movement were not the only ones with a hand in its
construction for "if Ireland never existed, the English would have invented
it".[10] While this may have been so, Ireland *did* exist, so arguably, what was
actually happening within the neo-Gaelic movement was a *re-invention* of
Ireland to counteract the perceived homelessness of the Ascendancy class.
This narrative of an imagined Ireland was born out of a class awareness of
being "English to the Irish" and "Irish to the English". It is probable that
Shaw set about exposing the reality that Ireland as an imagined space
would never survive and needed to see beyond its own borders and seek a
more international perspective; a perspective he himself had achieved.
Otherwise the fate of the play's rural village of Rosscullen, held back by
the small and stunted minds of its inhabitants, might become a reality for
Ireland as a nation. Shaw's Nora subverts and exposes the Yeats/Gregory
Kathleen as a so-called femme fatale that draws the nation's menfolk into
a stagnant quagmire that lacks resolution. In Act I of *John Bull's Other
Island*, Tom Broadbent, the soon-to-be realised conquering Englishman,
challenges Larry Doyle, the self-exiled Irishman, wondering if she [Nora]
is the "reason for your reluctance to come to Ireland with me" (CP II,
522). There is a shared history between Nora and Doyle that he (Doyle)
appears loath to revisit. The implication is that what Doyle (and perhaps
Shaw) is resisting is the mythical call to the young men of Ireland for the
so-called greater sacrifice to the Sean van Vocht, the Kathleen ni Houlihan
figure, to restore her "four green fields" in order to achieve independence
for Ireland. Shaw's view is that it is not "the old" that is needed for restoration but "the new"' and "the young". He reveals a pattern of stagnation
in *John Bull's Other Island* through Doyle's return to Rosscullen and how
the mythical symbolism of Kathleen ni Houlihan, perpetrates that
stagnation.

Through the union of Tom Broadbent and Nora Reilly and her rejection by Larry Doyle, Shaw explores the Irish political situation of the first

decade of the twentieth century. The idea of a failed love story and seemingly successful future marriage transects notions of colonisation and nationalism. There are patterns of exchange evident in this play that are reminiscent of *Widower's Houses* where marriage, property and social position become the primary reason for marriage. However, Nora, like Blanche and Ellie, takes some control over her own agency and appears to make a calculated decision to marry Broadbent in order to change her status when she perceived she is rejected by Doyle through his inability to effectively interact with her. One fact that emerges is that Nora *wants* to be married; her acceptance of Broadbent's proposal, when she will wait no further for Doyle, demonstrates that there is always more than one choice. Bearing this in mind, the question posed by Doyle's romantic ineptness towards her takes on a more nationalistic nuance when considering the implication that a marriage between the two could have signified a "united" Irish marriage, but Doyle's failure to express his love for her through eighteen years and in their first scene together in Act III, forces an English and Irish union, echoing the Home Rule versus Independence for Ireland debate. Nora's character though faced with a similar dilemma to Blanche Sartorius's character in relation to class and property, moves one step further to represent woman as nation being married to a future Liberal MP—the Pro-Home Rule English Party since 1886 and was on the political threshold to return to power in late 1905, which Shaw and many most likely anticipated after the long years of Conservative governments.

In taking the opportunity to dramatically interrogate the state of the relationship between Ireland and England in 1904, Shaw demonstrated how little sympathy he had for the romantic Ireland of Yeats, and felt that Yeats's use of the Irish myth of Kathleen ní Houlihan was outdated and unrealistic. It is in Act I that Larry Doyle dismisses the reliance on the Kathleen myth: "An Irishman […] dreams of what the Shan van Vocht said in ninety-eight. If you want to interest him in Ireland youve got to call the unfortunate island Kathleen ni Houlihan and pretend she's a little old woman" (CPII 517). Shaw, in correspondence with J.L. Shine, who played Doyle in the 1904 Royal Court production, stated that of this particular speech, that the audience "will perhaps laugh at Yeats's expense when you mention Kathleen ni Houlihan".[11]

Shaw's portrayal of Nora Reilly acts as the link between fantasy and reality. Nora may seem to be insulated from any exterior influences as she has never left Rosscullen, however, she is not blinded to an exterior opportunity when it is presented to her in the form of Broadbent. The Shavian message is that the insular blindness that has been adopted by the idealists needs to extend its reach into a more international forum for true independence to be achieved. Nora Reilly makes her appearance in the second scene of Act II when she locates Keegan. Nora is a woman in waiting and is apprehensive about meeting Larry Doyle with whom she had a past relationship—and possibly an understanding with—before he settled in London. Shaw designed Nora to be the antithesis to Kathleen ni Houlihan. The Yeatsian use of the Kathleen myth presents the old hag who bewitches young men to fight for Irish independence, which romantically transforms her into a beautiful young woman. Shaw, in response, turns the Yeats image on its head by the presenting of a woman approaching middle-age whose actions are self-serving and practical, suggesting a much different Ireland with different needs in 1904 than the Yeats-Gregory Ireland presented in 1902 but set within the failed 1798 Irish rebellion. One recalls a mythic fantasy within the litany of Irish political disasters; the other presents a practical and realist approach to Ireland on the threshold of modernisation.

The Act II meeting between Nora and Broadbent introduces a semblance of a love theme to the proceedings, but this is reduced to a farce by Broadbent's nonsensical proposal to a woman he had only just met. The pragmatic Irish nature presents itself once more when Nora tells Broadbent "Oh, get along with you, Mr. Broadbent! You're breaking your heart about me already, I daresay, after seeing me in the dark for two minutes" (CP II 543). Excusing him for being drunk, she tells him that he will think the better of it in the morning. Shaw's stage directions at this point amount to a running commentary on the difference between an Englishman and an Irishman: "*And he has no suspicion of the fact or of her ignorance of it, that when an Englishman is sentimental he behaves very much as an Irishman does when he is drunk*" (CP II 546). The proposal is very much a commentary on the colonisation of Ireland. Shaw spins a new take on colonisation, as it is Nora who not only does not swoon at Broadbent's feet, with his marriage proposal, which the English coloniser in him expects, but rather dismisses him and then undermines his self-perceived superiority by deflecting him and his proposal to own her by informing him that he is drunk—which, in turn, transforms the old English colonising stereotype of the Irish as being drunk. Not only has Nora become the benchmark of control and power, but she takes on the role of coloniser over Broadbent—just as Shaw came to see himself in London as colonising the English.

The character of Nora Reilly is indicative of her time and by the end of the play has proven herself open to the best opportunities that are presented—embracing Shaw's realist over idealism philosophy. To be considered now, of course, is how Nora appears in marrying Broadbent, to be subsumed into the patriarchal union of England and Ireland. However, the choice to marry Broadbent is Nora's, and she demonstrates through this choice that she is not prepared to wait around in the hope that something better may come along, such as the ineffective Larry or any of his similarly ineffective countrymen who have never appealed to Nora in eighteen years. Larry, in telling Nora that "I don't want his [Broadbent] marriage to you to be his divorce from me" (CP II 600), is making quite an arrogant statement. He is not willing to make a commitment and, as such, represents the indecisiveness that accompanies the Home Rule debate among the different factions involved in Irish politics since the majority of the Irish Party voted Parnell out of leadership in 1890 for the sake of the archaic English divorce law generated by Britain's 1890 popular press that forced the Liberal Party to insist on Parnell's removal from leadership of the Irish Party.[12] As Nelson O'Ceallaigh Ritschel argues, "the insinuation is that Nora's marriage to Broadbent will be profitable, marrying for wealth and attention".[13] This certainly holds true in the light of the capitalist venture to be undertaken in Rosscullen by Broadbent and his syndicate, but, to further the analysis, the other question to be considered on foot of Nora's decision is whether it will be better for Ireland to be a willing partner in Broadbent's capitalist venture, or to sit back and let it happen. Shaw does not provide an answer to that in the play, but he does address Nora's—and thematically Ireland's—future in her matrimonial tie to Broadbent.

The primary theme of Shaw's 1912 play *Pygmalion* deals with language as a social discourse in order to assimilate Eliza Doolittle into polite society. However, a sub-textual examination opens up another possibility of a nationalist reading of the play. Awam Amkpa maintains that

> a colonising dominant culture firstly imposes an ideological strain on language where it not simply as a frontier of making meaning but a process of socialising people into a dominant discourse.[14]

This allows a debate on *Pygmalion* to suggest that Shaw could have constructed the character of Eliza to act as a metaphor for a colonised Ireland, an Ireland that is dominated by her richer and more powerful neighbour.

Kimberly Bohman-Kalaja maintains that "Eliza, [...] the cockney-flower-girl-turned-English-fine-lady complicates and reworks the Saxon-Celt divide".[15] Through an analysis of Eliza's character, it appears that Shaw again denounces the idealistic picture of Ireland as portrayed by the Yeats/ Gregory character, Kathleen ni Houlihan. Eliza's character can be read as representing how, through language, a nation can reclaim its identity from a conquering empire. Shaw knew that importance of language to a colonised country. During an interview for an Irish newspaper in 1946, Shaw replied to the reporter's question on how much being Irish had coloured his mental makeup by stating that it made him a foreigner in every other country but went on to say that "the position of a foreigner with complete command of the same language has great advantages".[16]

On the notion of colonialism, there is one overriding and vital question posed on three occasions in *Pygmalion*, firstly by Mrs. Pearce, secondly by Mrs. Higgins and finally by Eliza herself, that resonates with Britain's exasperation with Ireland. As Mrs. Pearce so succinctly asks Higgins,

> And what is to become of her when you have finished your teaching? You must look a little ahead. (CPI 218)

Later Mrs. Higgins referred to "the problem of what is to be done with her afterwards" (CPI 250). There is no doubt that the question of Eliza's future is huge and alludes to the bigger question that was a political hotbed at that time between England and Ireland. Shaw, though he had left Ireland at twenty years of age, had always maintained his sense of Irishness, stating that he "was Irish, typically Irish".[17] It stands to reason that this sense of Irishness manifests itself in his writings and subtly underscores the obvious with a layered undercurrent. Eliza represents that ever changing aspect of "the question". The only way that Higgins could respond to the question posed was in a flippant manner, telling Mrs. Pearce:

> Well, when I've done with her, we can throw her back into the gutter; then it'll be her own business again; so that's all right. (CPI 218)

Through this callous reply which infers superiority, Shaw was highlighting British indecisiveness and, it should be added, indifference about how to handle its Irish colony. Later, in 1913, Shaw was to write an essay titled "Why Devolution Will Not Do". In it he states: "It is our [the Irish] business to demand a National Parliament and a Federal Parliament; but we

want the National Parliament first".[18] He was aware of the English ineptitude when dealing with Irish affairs and was quite categorically stating his
allegiance to his Irish roots. In giving Higgins a "laboratory" rather than
a study he directs the theme of the play towards experimentation rather
than education.

These ideas of imperialism and colonisation are inherent throughout
the play and are highlighted from the very first stage directions. The
notion of Irishness is present through the questions of identity that
Higgins poses and his concentration on language and dialect as a means of
identity. Eliza, in dismissing her birthplace, highlights a signal for change.
She knows that change should come through language and realises that in
order to be accepted in a class-driven society, she must learn to "talk more
genteel" (CPI 212). Even though it was Higgins who introduces the subject of language in Act I:

> You see this creature with her kerbstone English: the English that will keep
> her in the gutter to the end of her days. Well, sir, in three months I could
> pass that girl off as a duchess at an ambassador's garden party. I could even
> get her a place as a lady's maid or shop assistant, which requires better
> English. (CPI 206)

it is Eliza who knocks on Higgins's door seeking to learn the language of
commerce.

Shaw has played very cleverly with the character of Eliza in the way that
has presented her needs as language driven. In the letter to *The Freeman's
Journal* in October 1910, Shaw wrote quite succinctly about his opinion
on the many perceptions of Irish language and it was his opinion that the
Gaelic league were manufacturing a brand of Irish that was not in sync
with how Irish was really spoken. He stated that

> some of our Gaelic League enthusiasts are trying hard, by setting native Irish
> speakers to work on their literary exercises, to produce a sort of Gaelic
> Esperanto which can be imposed on us as our native language.[19]

Shaw's argument is that if another form of language is to be introduced it
may as well be something that will be beneficial to the nation and allow
Ireland to take her proper place on the word stage. Bohman-Kalaja argues
that "images of the Irish as a race of savages with incomprehensible speech
abound in the popular Victorian Press", and she quotes from *Punch
Magazine*:

> It comes from Ireland, whence it has contrived to migrate; it belongs in fact
> to a tribe of Irish savages: the lowest species of the Irish Yahoo. When con-
> versing with its kind, it talks a sort of gibberish.[20]

Just as Higgins recognises the fact that Eliza has "had to learn a complete new language" (CPI 238) to fit in with society's perception of what is acceptable, likewise, the Irish had to adopt the language of the coloniser in order to take control of their own future. Brian Friel deals with this subject succinctly in his play *Translations* (1980). The character Máire in *Translations* concentrates on the need to learn English to progress as she argues that Daniel O'Connell said that "the old language is a barrier to modern progress". She goes on to state that "he is right" and that she "wants English".[21] Máire, like Eliza displays a drive for her own agency and independence. Following on from the question posed by both Mrs. Pearce and Mrs. Higgins, Eliza, with new-found self-awareness, asks of Higgins: "Why did you take my independence from me? Why did I let you?" (CP1 277). Shaw here is posing the bigger question than what was to be done with Eliza when Higgins has finished with her; it is a question of what Eliza is to do with herself. There is a mirroring here of Ireland's political struggle. Shaw answers the question by empowering Eliza with the knowledge that she has been educated and that no matter what, this cannot be taken back or away from her. It is her moment of anagnorisis:

> Aha! Now I know how to deal with you. What a fool I was not to think of
> it before! You cant take away the knowledge you gave me. You said I had a
> finer ear than you. And I can be civil and kind to people, which is more than
> you can. Aha! That's done you Henry Higgins, it has. Now I dont care
> (*snapping her fingers*) for your bullying and big talk. (CP1 280)

What becomes obvious from this speech of Eliza's is that although he has taught her to pronounce correctly, he has not succeeded in changing her dialectical nuances, a fact he references in conversation with his mother just before her "at home" in Act III when Higgins tells his mother:

> You see, Ive got her pronunciation all right: but you have to consider not
> only *how* a girl pronounces, but *what* she pronounces. (238/39)

Shaw is cognisant of the fact, that although Irish people learned to speak English, they applied their own dialectical translation and in doing so created a hybrid version of the English language. Kiberd argues of the Irish nation's approach to English:

> That once Anglicization is achieved the Irish and the English, instead of speaking a truly identical tongue, will be divided most treacherously by a common language.[22]

Shaw plays beautifully with these dialectical differences through Eliza's dialogue during the "at home" in Act III. Her conversation about how her Aunt died is full of anomalies. Sentences like "them as pinched it done her in" (CP1 243) is passed off by Higgins as the new small talk; he is able to do so because her diction is perfect, though her syntax leaves a lot to be desired. In fact, what is happening is that Shaw is very aware of the dramatic writings of Lady Augusta Gregory and the late J.M. Synge and how they utilise the speech patterns of the native Irish which demonstrated how the English language had been adopted but adapted to suit the Irish speaker. In other words, the Irish had taken the English language and made it their own. It was to become known as Hiberno-English and Shaw employs it pointedly in his 1916 play *Heartbreak House* through the character of Nurse Guinness. Shaw goes one step further in exposing how, when something is created in a laboratory, it may not necessarily survive outside it. Eliza's education in Higgins's laboratory bears testament to the fact that when she tries to survive in the "real" world she has not been necessarily equipped with the proper tools.

Shaw is highlighting what is needed for Ireland if it, as nation, is to succeed as an independent entity. Through Eliza, he demonstrates how "project Ireland" does not possess the necessary tools to govern itself. He argues in his essay "How to Settle the Irish Question":

> Surely, of all sorts of dependence, the most abjectly wretched is that in which a minor State is helplessly dependent on a powerful neighbour, who accepts no responsibility for her and shares nothing with her, but makes her soil the no-man's-land between two frontiers when war breaks out.[23]

Eliza's situation mirrors that of Ireland. She is once again in "no-[wo]man's-land", possessing a skill acquired that is not fit for purpose as she was not given the necessary tools to utilise her new-found skill. However, Eliza has realised what she has been given cannot be taken back from her, but without the necessary support and training to enhance this skill, she knows there will be no progress. As with *The Shewing Up of Blanco Posnet,* the question of marriage rears its head in the final scene of the final act. Higgins renounces the idea of marrying Eliza telling her "I'll adopt you as my daughter and settle money on you if you like. Or would you rather marry Pickering?" (CP1 277). Eliza completely rejects the notion, telling Higgins, "I wouldn't marry *you* if you asked me; and youre nearer my age than what he is" (CP1 277). What Eliza is rejecting here is the subservience expected of her if she were to marry either of the older men. She knows that in order to progress she has to be on an equal footing with her partner. Her parting retort to Higgins was that she was going to "marry Freddy, I will as soon as he's able to support me" (CP1 279).[24] This speaks to the English and Irish situation and the Home Rule Bill (1912) that, at the time of writing of the play, had been passed and was due to be enacted in 1914. However, the outbreak of World War 1 in 1914 put paid to that enactment.

Although *Heartbreak House* is set in the English countryside during World War I, Shaw obviously intended that a more international analysis of the play be taken. For instance, his allusion to Chekov and Ibsen in his preface to the play, along with his statement that "Heartbreak House is not merely the name of the play […]. It is cultured leisured Europe before the war" (CP1 449), encourages this interpretation. However, the preface, written in June 1919 when the Irish War of Independence was in full swing, begs a closer look at the Shavian mind-set. Titled *Heartbreak House and Horseback Hall,* Shaw maps out the futility of the lives of those within *Heartbreak House.* His portrayal of *Horseback Hall,* "a prison for horses" (CP1 450), as an equally futile alternative to the house speaks to the colonial relationship between Ireland and England; the lands of the former commandeered by the aristocracy in England. Considering his engagement and interest in Irish affairs, Shaw most likely became preoccupied with the 1916 Easter Rising in Dublin during the writing of the play. Nicholas Grene speaks of Shaw's preoccupation not only with the war but "the Easter 1916 rebellion in Ireland and its aftermath, which deeply shocked him and involved him in a series of public controversies".[25] Grene argues that "to view it wholly as a war play is to misunderstand it".[26] I have discussed in other essays, as has David Clare, that naming proves crucial in Shaw's work and all the more so in this particular play beginning with the fact that the name *Heartbreak House* could be interpreted a way of imagining a repressed Ireland. Act II opens with the first interaction witnessed between Boss Mangan and Ellie Dunne. This central act of the three-act play draws all the elements of the fantasy life of *Heartbreak House* together. It is also the act where Ellie takes centre-stage in terms of the dramatic impetus and in doing so becomes a catalyst in identifying the change so badly needed in the house. She emerges as the Shavian version in opposition to Yeats/Gregory's Kathleen ní Houlihan. She is the breath of life so desperately needed in *Heartbreak House* as Shotover states, "Youth! Beauty! Novelty! They are badly wanted in this house" (CP1 497). She, however, does not appear as an old woman drawing young men to their death, rather as a young woman breathing life into an aging establishment. Shaw described Ellie as "the heavy lead in the play",[27] and it is no coincidence that he wrote the part with the Irish actress Ellen O'Malley in mind, of whom he said that she "presents Ellie Dunne, exactly as I planned her; as the strong respectable woman of the play … audaciously passionate and imaginative".[28] In fact, Sybil Thorndike maintained that Ellen O'Malley "was Shaw's favourite actress".[29]

Hesione Hushabye has never left *Heartbreak House* while Lady Utterword has lived away for more than two decades. A nod to colonialism is present through Lady Utterword's absent husband, Sir Hastings Utterword, of whom she states that he "has been governor of all the crown colonies in succession" and she has "always been the mistress of Government house" (CP1 495). Shotover's cry for youth is sinister as it is known throughout the play that both Mrs. Hushabye and Ariadne Utterword are mothers. Another sinister note is struck in Mrs. Hushabye's reply to Mazzini Dunn when he thanks her for inviting Ellie to the house: "Not at all. Very nice of her to come and attract young people to the house for us" (CP1 501). It has to be argued, therefore, that Ellie, for the residents of *Heartbreak House* and for Shaw, signifies the need for change. Shaw's construction of "the stranger" acts against the Yeatsian infiltrator. Ellie, as the Shavian stranger, offers a future by her very youth. The development of Ellie as a character is a driving force in the play. She appears naive and immature at the onset but as the dramatic events unfold and revelations occur, she can be seen to toughen and become more self-confident. She makes her own decisions and does not seek approval. She becomes the antithesis of her father whose ineptitude at decision making with regard to his own autonomy is marked conversely by her new-found assertiveness as the play progresses. Her interaction with Mangan reveals an inner strength that had not been hither-to-fore acknowledged. The verbal tennis which ensues reduces Mangan to insignificance as Ellie demonstrates how well she has thought out her marriage to him and how to capitalise on the benefits of the marriage arrangement. Mangan reveals to Ellie that he deliberately ruined her father though it is not until Act III that events take a distinct twist and the real truth about Mangan is revealed; a revelation which compounds the illusory appearances that are integral to *Heartbreak House*. Ellie's reaction to Mangan's confession is one of indifference as she uses emotional blackmail in order to prevent Mangan from backing out of their arrangement. He had revealed that he was in love with Hesione expecting to shock her but Ellie retained the upper hand in revealing that she was in love with Hector and what was even more astonishing to Mangan was that Hesione knew about Ellie's infatuation. Mangan had been under the impression that he had been dealing with a naïve "child" (84) as he referred to her youth frequently in their interchange. Ellie's control of the situation discombobulated Mangan and she soothed him by hypnotising him and leaving the room.

Ellie once again takes centre-stage in this penultimate act. Her newly acquired assertive attitude is marked when in conversation with Hesione she notes:

Ellie.	Perhaps you don't understand why I was a nice girl this morning, and am now neither a girl nor particularly nice.
Hesione.	Oh yes I do. It's because you have made up your mind to do something despicable and wicked.
Ellie.	I don't think so, Hesione. I must make the best of my ruined house. (CP1 546/47)

She rejects the revengeful and self-pitying path and adopts an air of acceptance and fortitude. By developing Ellie's character so, Shaw has demonstrated the type of attitude needed to eliminate the lethargy that permeates a society especially an oppressed one such as Ireland was. Kathleen ní Houlihan appeared as an old woman calling for the young men of Ireland to follow her to fight for freedom and only changes into a young woman when the young men follow her. Shaw has played with that notion by presenting a young woman who captures the imagination of an old man. Their dialogue is the crux of this second act. Following the comedic incident with the burglar who turns out to be Shotover's bosun and Nurse Guinness's erstwhile husband and not to be a burglar at all but rather a confidence trickster, not unlike Mangan, all retire to bed leaving the Captain and Ellie alone together. Their ensuing conversation on the pros and cons for marrying for money or love reveals Ellie's pragmatic nature. She admits to Shotover that her marriage to Mangan is revenge for the way he treated her father rather than the gratitude that had been implied earlier. She tells him:

> Mangan robbed my father and my father's friends. I should rob all the money back from Mangan if the police would let me. As they wont, I must get it back by marrying him. (CP1 565)

Shotover warns her:

> If you sell yourself, you deal your soul a blow that all the books and pictures and concerts and scenery in the world wont heal. (CP1 565)

The Shavian message here is very clear; the incentive to act and take control of a situation has to have a higher motive than revenge in order for there to be equality otherwise the vicious cycle of futility and ineffective living that is innate in the inhabitants of *Heartbreak House* will continue to fester. Ellie, as the antithesis to the Kathleen ní Houlihan figure breathes new life into the house by aligning herself with the old man in order to bring about change. She tells Shotover that "I should like to marry you. I would rather marry you than Mangan" (CP1 568). It becomes a case of youth bringing the past to the present rather than living in a fractured, invented bygone era. By ending act II with a fractious exchange between Hector, Randall and Ariadne, Shaw has strengthened the perception of the lack of direction and purpose in the lives of the inhabitants of *Heartbreak House* by exposing their shallowness.

Act III opens with a scene of lethargy and foreboding. The night is "moonless" (CP1 577) intimating a darkening situation; a sense of stagnation prevails in the stillness and in the inactivity of the residents of the house. The discussion revolves around the house and what the problem with it is. Lady Utterword maintains that the absence of horses contributes to the inability of the house to be a "sensible, healthy and pleasant house" (CP1 579). Hector Hushabye is the only character that recognises that the building is not the problem, that it is the occupants who are causing the decay. He states quite categorically:

> We are wrong with it. There is no sense in us. We are useless, dangerous and ought to be abolished. (CP1 578)

Once again, central to this the final act, Ellie commands the attention of the other members of the house. She announces her marriage to Shotover, stating that it is a spiritual union "made in heaven, where all true marriages are made" (CP1 586). The implication of the word marriage implies a consensual union. Shaw, in a letter to the *Irish Statesman* in October 1919 stated of Ireland:

> If we are to remain in the British Commonwealth voluntarily, we will remain on exactly the same terms as England. First, we must be free as England is free: that is, we shall order our national life in our own way to our own taste over the whole range of it that is not touched by our treaty with the commonwealth.[30]

As can be seen through this statement, Shaw's vision for the Irish question was one of independence—both socially and politically.

The case of Nora and Broadbent's union in *John Bull's Other Island* was a marriage noted for the purpose of financial gain on Nora's part and acceptance of community on the part of Broadbent, underscored with the notion of equality. Eliza, in stating she was going to marry Freddy, a member of the upper middle class, if he could support her, highlighted the need for a common language and how, once acquired, served to strengthen an independent relationship. Ellie, on the other hand, rejected any notion of materialism with Mangan and opted for a union that looked beyond the immediate, a union that would merge wisdom, experience and enthusiasm. Significantly, Shaw is intimating that in order for there to be progress, there needs to be freedom of agency, education and equality. The creation of the characters of Nora, Eliza and Ellie encapsulate the Shavian way of thinking of Ireland as a progressive nation. As representative Irish characters, these women control their destiny by asserting their equality rather than continue to be subservient within the British Imperial system, and at the same time they debunk the Irish national myth of Kathleen ni Houlihan by becoming self-reliant in order to obtain their goals.

NOTES

1. Bernard Shaw, *Collected Letters 1911–1925*, ed. Dan H. Laurence, (USA: Viking 1985) p. 582.
2. Bernard Shaw, *Collected Letters 1911–1925*, p. 488.
3. Elizabeth Cullingford, *Gender and History in Yeats's Love Poetry*, (USA: Syracuse University Press 1996) p. 55.

4. Michael Holroyd, *Bernard Shaw: The Pursuit*, p. 82.
5. Ben Levitas, "These Island's Others: *John Bull*, the Abbey and the Royal Court," *Irish Theatre in England*, ed. Richard Cave & Ben Levitas, (Ireland: Carysfort Press 2007) p. 19.
6. Nelson O'Ceallaigh Ritschel, *Shaw, Synge, Connolly, and the Socialist Provocation*, (USA: University of Florida Press 2011) p. 38.
7. Nelson O'Ceallaigh Ritschel, *Shaw, Synge, Connolly and the Socialist Provocation*, p. 41.
8. Fredrick P.W. McDowell, "The Shavian World of *John Bull's Other Island*," *Modern Critical Views: George Bernard Shaw*, ed. Harold Bloom, (New York: Chelsea House Publishers 1987) p. 66.
9. Audrey McNamara, "John Bull's Other Island: Taking the Bull to Ireland," *Shaw (32): Shaw and the City*, ed. Desmond Harding, (USA: Penn State University Press 2012) p. 135.
10. Declan Kiberd, *Inventing Ireland: The Literature of a Modern Nation*, (London: Vintage 1996) p. 9.
11. Bernard Shaw, *Collected Letters 1898–1910*, ed. Dan H. Laurence, (London: Max Reinhardt 1972) p. 460.
12. See chapter 3, "Parnell, Disarmament, and the Morality Frenzy," in Nelson O'Ceallaigh Ritschel's *Bernard Shaw, W.T. Stead, and the New Journalism*, (USA: Palgrave Macmillan 2017).
13. Nelson O'Ceallaigh Ritschel, *Shaw, Synge, Connolly, and the Socialist Provocation*, p. 40.
14. Amkpa, Awam. "Drama and the Languages of Postcolonial Desire: Bernard Shaw's 'Pygmalion,'" *Irish University Review* 29, no. 2 (1999) p. 294.
15. Kimberly Bohman-Kalaja, "Undoing Identities in *Two* Irish Shaw Plays: *John Bull's Other Island* and *Pygmalion*, *Shaw 30: Shaw and the Irish Literary Tradition*, ed. Peter Gahan, (USA: Penn State University Press 2010) p. 118.
16. Bernard Shaw, *The Matter with Ireland*, ed. David H. Greene & Dan H. Laurence, (London: Rupert Hart-Davis 1962) p. ix.
17. Bernard Shaw, "The Irish Players," *The Matter with Ireland*, p. 63.
18. Bernard Shaw, "Why Devolution Will Not Do," *The Matter with Ireland*, p. 204.
19. Bernard Shaw, "The Gaelic League," *The Matter with Ireland*, p. 60.
20. Kimberly Boham-Kalaja, "Undoing Identities in *Two* Irish Shaw Plays: *John Bull's Other Island* and *Pygmalion*," p. 120.
21. Brian Friel, "Translations," *Plays 1*, (London: Faber & Faber 1984) p. 400.
22. Declan Kiberd, *Inventing Ireland: The Literature of a Modern*, p. 622.
23. Bernard Shaw, "How to Settle the Irish Question," *The Matter with Ireland*, p. 148.

24. This dialogue is from the C1916 and C1931 versions of the play. This piece was changed to "as soon as I am able to support him" in 1941. See Leonard Conolly's edited version published by Meuthen Drama, 2008.
25. Nicholas Grene, *Bernard Shaw: A Critical View,* (New York: St Martin's Press 1984) p. 118.
26. Nicholas Grene, *Bernard Shaw: A Critical View,* p. 121.
27. Bernard Shaw, *Collected Letters 1911–1925,* ed. Dan H. Laurence, (USA: Viking 1985) p. 741.
28. Shaw in a series of letters to Arnold Bennet and St John Ervine is very emphatic as to his reasoning for choosing Ellen O'Malley for the role, not least because she was an Irishwoman; comparing the role to that of Lady Macbeth. See Bernard Shaw, *Collected Letters 1898–1910,* pp. 740–745.
29. Basil Langton, "Shaw's Stagecraft," *Shaw: The Annual of Bernard Shaw Studies Vol 21,* (Pennsylvania. Pennsylvania University Press 2001) p. 25.
30. Bernard Shaw, "Why Devolution Will Not Do," *The Matter with Ireland,* p. 204.

REFERENCES

Amkpa, Awam. 1999. Drama and the Languages of Postcolonial Desire: Bernard Shaw's 'Pygmalion,'. *Irish University Review* 29 (2): 294–304.

Bohman-Kalaja, Kimberly. 2010. Undoing Identities. In *Two Irish Shaw Plays: John Bull's Other Island and Pygmalion Shaw 30: Shaw and the Irish Literary Tradition,* ed. Peter Gahan. University Park: Penn State University Press.

Cullingford, Elizabeth. 1996. *Gender and History in Yeats's Love Poetry.* Syracuse: Syracuse University Press.

Friel, Brian. 1984. Translations. In *Plays 1.* London: Faber & Faber.

Grene, Nicholas. 1984. *Bernard Shaw: A Critical View.* New York: St Martin's Press.

Holroyd, Michael. 1989. *Bernard Shaw: The Pursuit of Power 1898–1918.* London: Chatto & Windus.

Kiberd, Declan. 1996. *Inventing Ireland: The Literature of a Modern Nation.* London: Vintage.

Langton, Basil. 2001. Shaw's Stagecraft. In *Shaw: The Annual of Bernard Shaw Studies,* vol. 21. Pennsylvania: Pennsylvania University Press.

Levitas, Ben. 2007. These Island's Others: *John Bull,* the Abbey and the Royal Court. In *Irish Theatre in England,* ed. Richard Cave and Ben Levitas. Dublin: Carysfort Press.

McDowell, Fredrick P.W. 1987. The Shavian World of *John Bull's Other Island.* In *Modern Critical Views: George Bernard Shaw,* ed. Harold Bloom. New York: Chelsea House Publishers.

McNamara, Audrey. 2012. John Bull's Other Island: Taking the Bull to Ireland. In *Shaw (32): Shaw and the City*, ed. Desmond Harding. University Park: Penn State University Press.

Nelson O'Ceallaigh, Ritschel. 2011. *Shaw, Synge, Connolly, and the Socialist Provocation*. Florida: University of Florida Press.

Shaw, Bernard. 1962. *The Matter with Ireland*, ed. David H. Greene and Dan H. Laurence. London: Rupert Hart-Davis.

———. 1972. *Collected Letters 1898–1910*, ed. Dan H. Laurence. London: Max Reinhardt.

———. 1985. *Collected Letters 1911–1925*, ed. Dan H. Laurence. New York: Viking.

CHAPTER 10

WWI, Common Sense, and *O'Flaherty V.C.*: Shaw Advocates a New Modernist Outlook for Ireland

Aisling Smith

> *The very words nation, nationality, our country, patriotism fill me with loathing. Why do you want to stimulate a self-consciousness which is already morbidly excessive in our wretched island, and is deluging Europe with blood? If we could only forget for a moment that we are British, and become really catholic Europeans, there would be some hope for us.*
>
> Shaw, personal letter to Lady Gregory, Dec 1917 (*Bernard Shaw and Augusta Gregory*. Shaw, Lady Gregory and the Abbey: A Correspondence and a Record, *ed. Dan H Laurence and Nicholas Grene [Buckinghamshire, Gerrards Cross: Colin Smyth, 1993], 136*)

Composed months prior to the 1916 Easter Rising, Shaw's *O'Flaherty V.C.* is markedly one of only three dramatic Shaw texts set in, and concerned with, Ireland. Encompassing national identity as a central

A. Smith (✉)
National University of Ireland Galway, Galway, Ireland

© The Author(s) 2020
A. McNamara, N. O'Ceallaigh Ritschel (eds.), *Bernard Shaw and the Making of Modern Ireland*, Bernard Shaw and His Contemporaries, https://doi.org/10.1007/978-3-030-42113-7_10

theme, the play directly addresses the unfixed nature of Ireland's future and the Irish nation's involvement in World War I (WWI). Reacting against both the extreme elements of the nationalist movement in Ireland and the surge of patriotic propaganda precipitated by the outbreak of WWI in the United Kingdom (that carried into Ireland), Shaw advocates for the Irish public to face the uncertain future with a new international mindset. This is a call which would be echoed some fifty years later by the Taoiseach Seán Lemass, who in 1966 publicly asserted that it was time for Ireland to leave behind the country of the Shan Van Vocht and focus on the Ireland of the future. Though importantly, Lemass's policies would not ascribe to Shaw's overall socialist agenda.

Originally subtitled "An Interlude in the Great War of 1914", Shaw wrote *O'Flaherty V.C.* in response to the social and political context of 1915. At this time, the question of Ireland's future autonomy had gotten inextricably bound to the ongoing world war, due to the expected implementation of Home Rule having been postponed on Britain's entrance to the conflict. Undoubtedly inspired by Corporal Micheal O'Leary, the idea for *O'Flaherty V.C.* had germinated with Shaw while he and his wife Charlotte were visiting Lady Gregory at Coole Park, Co. Galway, in April 1915. O'Leary was the Corconian who, having been awarded the Victoria Cross for his heroic exploits in the war, had become the new poster boy for the war office's recruitment efforts in Ireland.[1]

Within the play, Shaw identifies nationalism as the common thread by which to discuss and navigate social issues arising from the Irish nationalist movement and WWI in detail. Thereby dramatising, and making more palatable, many of the ideas he had previously put forward in his widely condemned manuscript: "Common Sense About the War" in 1914. Furthermore, by setting his war-time play in rural Ireland and centring it on Ireland's involvement in the war, Shaw was simultaneously participating in, and critiquing, the Irish literary and dramatic revival. Ultimately, *O'Flaherty V.C.* advocates for Ireland to adopt a new modern outlook based on economic realities, and abandoning nationalist conceits of the past. Though the Easter Rising would seemingly render this social message moot before the play was ever publicly performed, the themes of national patriotism and identity explored within *O'Flaherty V.C.* have proved prevailing issues, which not only influenced the founding of modern Ireland, but continue to be of concern to contemporary society.

Shaw had three motivations for writing *O'Flaherty V.C.* Firstly, his belief that increased enlistment was vital for the war effort; secondly, he had been personally asked to produce an Irish centric recruiting play by Sir Matthew Nathan, Undersecretary of Ireland[2]; and thirdly, the play was to be a means by which to help raise money for the financially troubled Abbey Theatre.[3] Shaw's desire to highlight the conflicting politics of these two institutions, the Abbey and Dublin Castle, where Irish involvement in WWI was concerned, is reflected in the play. He strongly attacks both fervent Irish nationalism and British patriotism, in an effort to nullify them as mitigating factors in the minds of Irishmen with regard to enlistment and future life choices.

In 1915, Shaw was not a popular public figure; due to condemnation of his lengthy manuscript "Common Sense About the War", published in both *The New Statesman* and *The New York Times* the year before. Divided into three sections—an untitled introduction, "Recruiting" and "The Terms of Peace", the wide-ranging manuscript castigated the role of the press and the government (via the British Foreign Office and the War Office), had played in the war to date. Asserting that the war had been caused by junkerism and militarism on both sides, the manuscript contended that the conflict could have been averted had England pledged allegiance to France before the outbreak of war proper. Moreover, it identified fervent patriotism and nationalism as a precursor to the war, and a threat to future peace. Internationally denounced, the document earned Shaw very negative press and even inspired the false rumour that he was pro-German. However, despite this condemnation of the document, Shaw arguably dramatised many of the ideas from "Common Sense About the War" in *O'Flaherty V.C.*, believing perhaps, the ideas, along with his sardonic and facetious humour, would be more palatable in a character-driven play than they had been in manuscript form.

Since the Great famine, Irish nationalists saw England's control of Ireland as being directly linked to the country's social problems and impoverished condition. This view of the Irish question became the centre of a progressively urgent national cultural debate that consumed all spheres of social life. In 1915 Ireland, emigration was high, and Dublin in particular was still recovering from the effects of the 1913 Lockout. Though second city of The Empire, Dublin had one of the biggest slums in Europe; with over a third of the population (120,000 out of 305,000) living in tenement buildings.[4] Furthermore, the postponement in implementing the long-anticipated Home Rule Bill in 1914 had made the international war and the Irish question inextricably linked. Tensions had already been running high within the nationalist ranks prior to this, as many had become disillusioned by parliamentary politics; but the issue of Irish enlistment into the British Army to fight in WWI was completely divisive.

On Britain's joining of the war, the Irish Volunteers divided their loyalties between Owen Mac Neil and John Redmond; the majority joining the latter, who advocated Irish enlistment as a means to secure English good faith and ensure future autonomy. Those that sided with Mac Neil stayed in Ireland. Notably, though united in their opposition to Ireland's involvement in the war, the remaining nationalists were still divided with respect to the confidence they held in the effectiveness of parliamentary nationalism. After the first wave of recruitment in Ireland in 1914, enlistment dropped substantially, and was very low in 1915. This was partly due to an ill managed recruitment campaign in Ireland by the Home Office (as discussed by Shaw in the later written preface to *O'Flaherty V.C.*), as well as the prevalence of strong anti-enlistment feeling in the Irish capital from the outset of the war. Early recruitment rallies saw anti-recruitment protestations, and in September 1914, the Irish neutrality league was founded, with James Connolly as its president.[5] A key objective of *O'Flaherty V.C.* for Shaw was to help improve enlistment in Ireland. In "Common Sense About the War" he had declared that though as a socialist he was against war in principle, he believed the current war needed to be fought and won by the Allies to protect democracy and future peace. The fortification of democracy would, Shaw believed, lead to social reform in the long term, promising a say for all regardless of class.

While "Common Sense About the War" had been published internationally by Shaw, *O'Flaherty V.C.* was written to be produced at the Abbey Theatre, followed by a music hall tour in England.[6] In writing *O'Flaherty V.C.* Shaw created a recruitment play based on terms to which he felt the Irish labouring class would relate. The play centres on Private Dennis O'Flaherty, a member of the Irish peasantry, who having been awarded the Victoria Cross, returns to his home village in rural Ireland on a recruitment drive. The action of the play takes place in front of the home of O'Flaherty's local landlord, and commanding officer, General Sir Pearce Madigan, who has invited O'Flaherty and his mother to tea (a new occurrence given O'Flaherty's new war-hero status, which, at least for the moment, breaks down class barriers). Exploring the theme of nationalism throughout the play, Shaw analyses and effectively demonstrates how the issues of Ireland's continued poverty; the country's uncertain political future; and WWI, were all ideologically bound together for the Irish public. Within this context Shaw decisively promotes enlistment and the adoption of a future orientated, internationally minded, perspective by the Irish public, as the best means to ensure their future peace and prosperity.

Within *O'Flaherty V.C.*, Shaw creates in Sir Pearce the epitome of an English Junker, as characterised by him in "Common Sense About the War". For all intents and purposes, the patriotic and imperialist Sir Pearce, as a member of the landed gentry, represents England within the play. In the first scene, Shaw introduces the themes of national patriotism and nationalism by highlighting that Sir Pearce's ideological reasons for fighting in the war are not those held by O'Flaherty:

SIR PEARCE   I've been dog tired myself on parade many a time. But still, you know, there's a gratifying side to it, too. After all, he is our king; and it's our own country, isn't it?

O'FLAHERTY.   Well, sir, to you that have an estate in it, it would feel like your country. But the divil a perch of it ever I owned. And as to the king: God help him, my mother would have taken the skin off my back if I'd ever let on to have any other king than Parnell.[7]

With this introduction to the themes of national patriotism and nationalism, Shaw achieves several things. Firstly, Shaw acknowledges that loyalty to the crown is not a motivating factor for enlistment for the majority of the Irish peasantry. In fact, the prospect of supporting the crown would be a deterring factor for someone raised as an Irish nationalist, such as O'Flaherty. Secondly, Shaw broaches the nationalist contention that English occupation of Ireland continues the subjectification and impoverishment of the Irish people. O'Flaherty and the native Irish do not own the land they work and live on, but are paying tenants to the landed gentry, and are therefore unable to rise in wealth or stature. The third point that Shaw succeeds in making, is that O'Flaherty, because he does not own any land, does not feel like Ireland is really *his* country. This is the most significant point put forward in the exchange, as it serves to reveal the paradox of nationalism; that the sense of ownership of place which nationalism promotes is imaginary. Nationalism contradictorily instils a feeling of ownership within citizens over their country of birth, when in reality, the majority of individuals do not have any legal claim to the physical land of the nation. By revealing this paradox, Shaw sequentially intimates to the prospective audience that, while British patriotism may not be a motivating factor to join the British army, neither should Irish nationalism be a deterrent from joining. As nationalism is itself an inherently flawed concept.

While writing the play, Shaw wrote to Lady Gregory that the work was a "comedy of disillusionment".[8] Since leaving Ireland, O'Flaherty has re-evaluated his former existence through the lens of his international experiences and returned from the front line with a new more worldly perspective. No longer the "poor, ignorant, conceited creature"[9] he recognises himself to have been on leaving; he now has with a fresh understanding and awareness of his upbringing, and life, in Ireland. This awareness has rendered him utterly disillusioned by his home country and what he now sees as the insular mindsets retained by his Irish nationalist mother and imperialist landlord General Sir Pearce. Setting these insular mindsets in stark contrast to O'Flaherty's international future orientated outlook; Shaw presents O'Flaherty's new perspective as an empowered force, which has enabled O'Flaherty to throw off the old demoralising behaviours of his past.

Throughout his conversations with Sir Pearce and his mother, O'Flaherty re-writes the unwritten rules of their relationships; which had dictated their interactions up until this point. Speaking honestly and directly to Sir Pearce, for the first time, it is with great comic effect that O'Flaherty relays some home truths to the general regarding how he and his wife are viewed by their tenants. With great candour, O'Flaherty informs the general that all of the local tenants behave falsely to him, admitting to the astonished general, that he and his mother have themselves deceived him on multiple occasions. O'Flaherty's revelation that his mother, Mrs. O'Flaherty, is not an imperialist, but "the wildest fenian and rebel, and always has been"[10] aptly illustrates the depth of Sir Pearce's past ignorance. This serves to make Mrs. O'Flaherty's later sycophancy towards Sir Pearce, all the more amusing.

O'Flaherty's time away from Ireland has resulted in him having the space to critically examine, and form a new understanding of, his homeland, and his relationship to it. Comforting Sir Pearce, O'Flaherty acknowledges that they had up until now been operating by the standard system which, though not of their creation, had dictated their false relationship and behaviours towards one another; as it did with all landlords and tenants:

Sure you had to get what you could out of us; and we had to get what we could out of you. God forgive us both![11]

Within the play O'Flaherty renegotiates not only his relationship with Sir Pearce, but also that which he shares with his mother—by determinedly asserting himself as her equal. In their first scene alone together, Mrs. O'Flaherty continuously attempts to shame and scold her son. He however, refuses to cower down to her, and instead resolutely defends his decision to join the British army. There is a sense that this exchange is not the status quo, when Mrs. O'Flaherty challengingly asks, "Why wouldnt I know better than you? Amment I your mother?"[12] However, owing to O'Flaherty's wartime experiences, the unconditional subordination Mrs. O'Flaherty expects from her son is no longer possible, leading O'Flaherty to swiftly and triumphantly rebuke her attempted assertion of all-encompassing authority.

Within the play, Shaw suggests that O'Flaherty's previously subjugated status and dishonest relationships with both Sir Pearce and his mother, emanated from inherited anti-English feeling, and a harsh rural upbringing. The returned O'Flaherty however, endowed with a wider more informed perspective, is no longer a product of his upbringing. It is such a perspective that Shaw wished to inspire in the whole of the nation. Noting that "democracy is what O'Flaherty gains by achieving his own voice while at war",[13] Ritschel writes that Shaw envisioned the enlistment and exodus from Ireland by the uneducated labouring class would open the social faction's eyes to the unacceptable nature of their current condition. With experience of the outside world enabling the realisation that their quality of life in Ireland could, and should, be better. Thus empowered, they would then be capable of enacting real social change, such as that enacted by O'Flaherty within the play; but on a mass scale. Setting up O'Flaherty as an aspirational example, Shaw encourages the Irish public to cut the apron strings tying them to old Ireland nationalism, and adopt a new internationally minded perspective. This would allow them to renegotiate their ideological and working relationship with Britain and leave behind old attitudes, behaviours, and beliefs, for the sake of future prosperity.

In "Common Sense About the War", Shaw had steadfastly refused to engage in partisanship. Furthermore, identifying nationalism, and the insularism which it breeds, as being a threat to future peace, he maintained it should play no role in recruitment. It is not surprising therefore, that in *O'Flaherty V.C.,* his recruiting play, Shaw created characters whose opinions are skewed and dominated by nationalist and patriotic beliefs. Countering Sir Pearce's role as a type of British Junker, Mrs. O'Flaherty plays the part of the zealous nationalist as characterised in "Common Sense About the War". One of the most comical episodes of the play occurs when O'Flaherty explains the depth of his mother's nationalist sensibilities to Sir Pearce by listing the people and events she has assimilated into Irish history. This list builds in a crescendo to her apparent convictions: the Irish are the lost tribes of the house of Israel, Venus was born out of Killiney Bay (specifically off Bray Head), Moses built the seven churches on Inís Mór, and Lazarus is buried in Glasnevin Cemetery.[14] It is, however, her apparent conviction that Shakespeare was from Cork which finally breaks Sir Pearce's spirit. His mother's brand of delusional nationalism is the same, O'Flaherty asserts, as the patriotism currently being displayed throughout Europe:

> She's like the English: they think theres no one like themselves. It's the same with the Germans, though theyre educated and ought to know better.[15]

Likening Mrs. O'Flaherty's brand of nationalism to that of the British, and of the Germans, Shaw widens his argument. He demonstrates that it is not Irish nationalism specifically which he aims to ridicule, but the very concept of national patriotism, promoting O'Flaherty's internationally informed perspective in its place.

Consistently refusing to be drawn into anti-partisan rhetoric during the play, O'Flaherty does not claim moral superiority over Britain's war-time enemies. Speaking to Sir Pearce he shows his distaste for the current practices of vilifying the Germans, and glorifying the war, in the name of so called patriotism:

O'FLAHERTY.   The Boshes I kilt was more knowledgeable men than me: and what better am I now that I've kilt them? What better is anybody?

SIR PEARCE   *[huffed, turning a cold shoulder to him]*. I am sorry the terrible experience of this war—the greatest war ever fought—has taught you no better, O'Flaherty.

O'FLAHERTY   *[preserving his dignity]*. I dont know about it's being a great war, sir. It's a big war; but thats not the same thing.[16]

Shaw's stage directions here are demonstrative of the play's intended message regarding partisanship and national patriotism. Sir Pearce as a supporter of British patriotism becomes huffy and petulant, while conversely O'Flaherty remains dignified throughout the exchange. It is O'Flaherty's unbiased objective outlook which Shaw is promoting to the Irish public; an outlook grounded in reality and direct experiences, not one contrived by propaganda and nationalist rhetoric.

Presenting Sir Pearce and Mrs. O'Flaherty as mere surface manifestations of a more systemic problem, Shaw fastidiously exposes the effects of nationalism to be deeply consequential. He achieves this early in the play, by implicating nationalism as being at the root of Ireland's continued poverty. When asked by an affronted Sir Pearce, during the opening dialogue of the play, if patriotism means anything to him, O'Flaherty responds:

> It means different to me than what it would to you, sir. It means England and England's king to you. To me and the like of me, it means talking about the English just the way the English papers talk about the Boshes. And what good has it ever done here in Ireland? It's kept me ignorant because it filled up my mother's mind, and she thought it ought to fill up mine too. It's kept Ireland poor, because instead of trying to better ourselves we thought we was the fine fellows of patriots when we were speaking evil of Englishmen that was as poor as ourselves and maybe as good as ourselves. The Boshes I kilt was more knowledgable men than me: and what better am I now that Ive kilt them? What better is anybody?[17]

Through O'Flaherty's sincere and direct reply, Shaw proposes that the insular Irish nationalist agenda has stunted Ireland's development. He suggests that the following of Irish nationalism has resulted in a collective concentration on the past, and has thus held back economic and social progress. O'Flaherty's final question hangs in the air; motivating the audience to consider who may be gaining financially from the war.[18] By including the Germans in this sentiment of solidarity, Shaw widens the perspective. He is perhaps suggesting that the lower classes should not allow themselves to be pitted against each other, out of a sense of patriotism.

Phillips maintains that the above lines can be read as a charge against nationalist literature of the period, which as well as narrowing Irishmen's vision, idealised peasant-life and kept the suffering caused by acute poverty hidden and thereby aided the English exoticisation and romanticising of the Irish peasantry. This made nationalist writers, to an extent, complicit in Ireland's continued repression. Phillips writes:

> Ironically it was their [sections of the Gaelic movement] very nationalism, not only cultural nationalism, … but the strongly anti-English tone of physical-force nationalism that resulted in their own complicity.[19]

Witnessing society in the grip of war hysteria, Shaw could see that heightened national patriotism was breeding increased fear and hatred among the British for their European counterparts. He believed this was being fuelled by partisan propaganda, a by-product of extreme nationalism and patriotism. Partisan discourse, he felt, had paved the way for the current war and was socially damaging. Both "Common Sense About the War" and *O'Flaherty V.C.* look at the culpability of the printed press where partisan propaganda is concerned. In "Common Sense About the War" Shaw critiqued newspapers' propagation of war hysteria and what he deemed hypocritical British rhetoric about Belgian. He also attacked journalistic standards, calling into question the calibre of person contributing articles[20] in the British press. Furthermore, Shaw stated that widespread anti-German feeling had been purposefully created and contrived in England through militarist propaganda. He declared that he could remember the beginning of the endeavour occurring after the Franco-Prussian War of 1870–1891, with Germany's decisive defeat over France "by the exercise of an organized efficiency in war of which nobody up to then had any conception".[21] This, according to Shaw, sparked a lineage of pro-war literature and behaviours in England. Beginning with the anonymously written *Battle of Dorking* booklet,[22] and ending with the launch of the Dreadnoughts warships by the navy in 1906:

> Throughout all these agitations the enemy, the villain of the piece, the White Peril, was Prussia and her millions of German conscripts[23]

When O'Flaherty tells Sir Pearce that he does not know what the war is about, the aged General is shocked and asks whether O'Flaherty does not "read the papers". The implication here being, that if he did, he would have been provided with all the necessary information to understand the causes and intricacies of the international conflict. O'Flaherty answers that he has little to no access to newspapers in the trenches.[24] However,

O'Flaherty reveals his scorn towards what is written in the press regarding the war when he returns to the subject unprompted later in their conversation:

> Why should I read the papers to be humbugged and lied to by them that had the cunning to stay at home and send me to fight for them?[25]

Calling out the culpability of the British press, Shaw charges them with intensifying the partisan propaganda during the war, creating a cultural climate of war hysteria, and publishing inflammatory prejudicial articles under the banner of patriotism.

In "Common Sense About the War", Shaw had taken particular issue with the fact that no credentials were required to author a newspaper column. With the result that one-sided partisan opinions were printed as facts. This, he felt, was a threat to the security of British democracy:

> A far graver doubt is raised by the susceptibility of the masses to war fever, and the appalling danger of a daily deluge of cheap newspapers written by nameless men and women whose scandalously low payment is a guarantee of their ignorance and their servility to the financial department, controlled by a moneyed class which not only curries favour with the military caste for social reasons, but has large direct interests in war as a method of raising the price of money, the only commodity the moneyed class has to sell.[26]

Shaw believed the press' substandard reporting and fuelling of war hysteria, had its origins in financial concerns. The sustainment of a zealous patriotic commitment to the war among the public, was in favour of the capitalist war mongers who were profiting from it. As far as he was concerned, the plutocracy was successfully controlling the newspapers and in turn, the masses.

In "Common Sense About the War" and *O'Flaherty V.C.* Shaw communicates that zealous nationalism and national patriotism was being systematically foisted upon the general public by the governing class to further their own interests. In *O'Flaherty V.C.* Shaw encourages the public to follow O'Flaherty's example, and recognise the biased and exploitative nature of the press' fuelling of war hysteria; nationalism; and national patriotism. This again is an advocation for the adoption of a non-partisan mindset, like that demonstrated by O'Flaherty, as Shaw believed only such an outlook would secure future peace and prosperity within Ireland and across nations.

Shaw's commitment to social reform, and his will to improve conditions for the Irish working class and peasantry, as demonstrated in *O'Flaherty V.C.*, was not a new phenomenon. As Nelson O'Ceallaigh Ritschel details, Shaw had already proven he had a genuine concern for Irish economic affairs through his support of the workers during the 1913 Dublin Lockout.[27] Ritschel surmises that Shaw aspired for an enlightened democratic government to be established in Ireland, before old reductive nationalist animosities intensified. Indeed, Shaw had for some time been of the opinion, that Ireland could only achieve prosperity if it adopted a more international outlook. In a letter to Mabel Fitzgerald in 1914 Shaw had expressed this belief in no uncertain terms, writing:

> The days of small nations is past, indeed, except for nations `still denied self-government, nationalism is a dead horse…Only as a member of a great commonwealth is there any future for us. We are a wretched little clod, broken off a bigger clod, broken off the west end of Europe, full of extraordinary beautiful but damnably barren places, with a strange climate that degrades base people hideously and clears the souls of noble people wonderfully.[28]

While this passage from Shaw hints toward his position during the 1917 Irish Convention, when he advocated for Home Rule but within a Commonwealth of Ireland, Scotland, and England, in *O'Flaherty V.C.* Shaw advocates for the Irish public to replace their insular nationalist beliefs with a modern worldly perspective based in economic realities, as a means to combat against Ireland's continued poverty. He created O'Flaherty's character to show how such an outlook could empower them by allowing them to break free from their oppressive past rather than be beholden to it.

As part of his assault against the insular and parochial Irish nationalist mindset within *O'Flaherty V.C.*, Shaw goes as far as to challenge the role of the church in rural life. He does this by highlighting, what he deems, the church's hypocritical support of the war effort; a point he had previously addressed in "Common Sense About the War". In the 1914 document, he had described the condition of churches remaining open during war time, while the stock exchange closed, as a "top note of keen irony".[29] Shaw displays his dissatisfaction with the church's stance on the war in *O'Flaherty V.C.* through O'Flaherty's recounting of his visit to the local priest, Father Quinlan, to Sir Pearce:

O'FLAHERTY. He says "You know, don't you," he says, "that it's your duty, as a Christian and a good son of the Holy Church, to love your enemies?" he says. "I know it's my juty as a soldier to kill them" I says. "That's right, Dinny," he says: "quite right. But" says he, "you can kill them and do them a good turn afterward to shew your love for them" he says; "and it's your duty to have a mass said for the souls of the hundreds of Germans you say you killed" says he; "for many and many of them were Bavarians and good Catholics" he says. "Is it me that must pay for masses for the souls of the Boshes?" I says. "Let the King of England pay for them" I says; "for it was his quarrel and not mine."[30]

Shaw successfully portrays Father Quinlan's main concern to be financial not spiritual, and makes him an object of ridicule within the play. By highlighting the priest's insular take on the war, Shaw challenges an important norm of Irish parochial society: unquestioning devotion to the church. This challenge however, is notably softened by Shaw's decision to have O'Flaherty relay the conversation he had with the priest. As the priest is not present he is being mocked indirectly; allowing the audience to laugh at the idea of father Quinlan, not an actual priest on stage, which is reminiscent of J. M. Synge's treatment of a priest in *The Playboy of the Western World* (1907), but unlike Father Dempsey in Shaw's *John Bull's Other Island* (1904), who is very much onstage. Through this exposition of the church's hypocritical support of the war, Shaw advocates a re-evaluation of all insular nationalist cultural norms.

In creating a play concerned with Ireland's current and future social and political position, to be produced by the Abbey Theatre, Shaw positioned *O'Flaherty V.C.* within the ongoing National Irish Literary Revival movement; which incidentally, was famed for creating the very nationalist literature Shaw criticises as having a negative impact on Ireland's development within the play, as discussed earlier. Often referred to as the Irish dramatic and literary revival, the movement saw the development and staging of plays as well as the production of nationalist writings. Marvin Carlson points out that the wave of modern nationalist thinking which swept across Europe immediately after the Napoleonic era (1799–1815) saw theatre being utilised for nationalist purposes in many countries.[31]

Spearheaded by Yeats and Gregory, the Irish literary and dramatic revival, like the rest of the Gaelic Revival Movement, followed Douglas Hyde's belief that the public enactment of Irish identity would further the campaign for Irish national autonomy.[32] At the heart of the Irish literary revival was Irish nationalism. The Irish revivalists sought to publicly perform native Irish identity to further the quest for national independence and debate Ireland's political and social future. Paige Reynolds argues that by taking the power of spectacle from the British, the national literary and dramatic revivalists sought to further the interests of Irish nationalism:

> Performance provided a compelling tool in the construction and consolidation of Irish national identity by encouraging all citizens to act out their political and cultural affiliations through gesture, costume and dialogue. It furnished a model of identity.[33]

Roche maintains that though Shaw had a sustained involvement with the Irish Literary Revival, since his introduction to it in 1904, his role in it has historically been diminished.[34] Within *O'Flaherty V.C.*, Shaw comments directly on the works of the national literary revivalists and other nationalist dramatists; by subverting their tropes, such as, the keening woman, the peasant figure, and the motif of self-sacrifice they used to frame their discussion of Ireland's political and cultural future. More subtly perhaps, is Shaw's engagement with existing revivalist texts through the form of *O'Flaherty V.C.*, as discussed by Roche and O'Ceallaigh Ritschel. Roche proposes that the play can be seen as a comic subversion of Yeats's and Gregory's *Kathleen Ní Houlihan* (at the time attributed solely to Yeats), a seminal piece of the movement.[35] While Nelson O'Ceallaigh Ritschel, details how Shaw borrows and utilises a number of conventions from the plays of deceased revivalist Synge within the work. This manner of engagement with revivalist works enabled Shaw to both ingratiate his play to the Abbey audience and critique the nationalist movement.[36]

Like many revivalist plays, Shaw has a male member of the Irish peasantry as the play's hero. Not so usual however, is that Shaw's peasant, O'Flaherty, is also a WWI soldier who has earned one of the British army's highest accolades: The Victoria Cross. In addition, instead of presenting the traditional and iconic keening Irish woman, Shaw presents Mrs. O'Flaherty as blubbering disingenuously, while attempting to emotionally blackmail her son and curry favour with Sir Pearce. Providing an altogether unfavourable representation of the female Irish peasantry throughout the play, Mrs. O'Flaherty and Tessie exhibit mercenary values and manipulative behaviours indicative of their marginalised and impoverished position in society as both women attempt to safeguard their future survival via

O'Flaherty. It is through this portrayal of Mrs. O'Flaherty and young Tessie that Shaw successfully parodies Yeats's and Gregory's literary creation of the regenerating Kathleen Ní Houlihan (the female embodiment of Ireland). Where *Kathleen Ní Houlihan* ends with Michael (mesmerised by the keening old woman's call to arms) going to war and sacrificing himself for her, *O'Flaherty V.C.* sees O'Flaherty (endowed with "knowledge and wisdom" born from "pain and fear and trouble"[37]) refusing to be emotionally manipulated by his mother. Chastising his mother and branding Tessie a "covetious sthreal",[38] O'Flaherty ultimately declares his intention to pursue a better quality of life in France after the war:

MRS O'FLAHERTY.   Ask me to die out of Ireland, is it? and the angels not to find me when they come for me!

O'FLAHERTY.   And would you ask me to live in Ireland where I've been imposed on and kept in ignorance, and to die where the divil himself wouldnt take me as a gift, let alone the blessed angels? You can come or stay. You can take your old way or take my young way. But stick in this place I will not among a lot of good-for-nothing divils thatll not do a hand's turn but watch the grass growing and build up the stone wall where the cow walked through it. And Sir Horace Plunkett breaking his heart all the time telling them how they might put the land into decent tillage like the French and Belgians.[39]

Through O'Flaherty's actions, Shaw intended to present a rejection of past-focused nationalist ideals, in favour of a more individualistic attitude to the Abbey audience. O'Flaherty's "young way" is a new modern way of living, centred on the pursuit of progress and not being beholden to a sense of duty to either the past or one's country of birth. By having O'Flaherty consider his future in this manner, Shaw can also be seen to encourage the envisioning of a time when the war is over. Suggesting that If the Irish public wish to see themselves as part of a collective at this point, it should be as O'Flaherty does; as part of the international working class, with the whole of Europe at his feet. In "Common Sense About the War", Shaw had devoted a whole section to the end of the war titled "The Terms of Peace". He can be seen in this final section to advocate for the

European powers to adopt a future-orientated mindset much like that which he promotes in *O'Flaherty V.C.*

Due largely to its non-partisan stance and denouncement of national patriotism, Shaw's far-ranging "Common Sense About the War" was internationally condemned when published in 1914.[40] Though Shaw's ideas concerning the war may have been more palatable in play form, it will never be known how *O'Flaherty V.C.* would have been received by a 1915, Irish audience; as it was effectively cancelled when its planned run in the Abbey Theatre in November 1915 was indefinitely postponed. Lauren Arrington argues that this decision, taken by Dublin Castle, was due to the even-handed nature with which Shaw had critiqued nationalism within the play. Shaw's dramatic offering to support the recruitment effort risked sparking trouble, as it would potentially be too much of a recruiting play for the nationalists, and too much of an anti-war play for Irish militarists.[41] Shaw, for his part, endeavoured to minimise the potential fallout for Dublin Castle; publicly denying that the play's run was stopped due to censorship. Keeping good relations with Shaw, Sir Matthew Nathan, the undersecretary of Ireland stationed in Dublin Castle,[42] visited him in London the following month and enlisted his help in curbing the generation of pro-German feeling in Ireland by Sinn Féin.[43] Moreover in 1918, Shaw would compose a pamphlet designed to encourage voluntary enlistment in Ireland at the bequest of the authorities in Dublin.[44]

Though Shaw explores the issues arising from WWI, extreme Irish nationalism, and Ireland's involvement in the war from a number of perspectives, the play does not address the prospect of Irish nationalists using "England's difficulty as Ireland's opportunity".[45] That is, the possibility of extreme nationalists staging an armed insurrection in Ireland while Britain were engaged in the war. In a *New York Times* magazine article on April 9, 1916, just two weeks before the rebellion, Shaw did mention that the threat of insurrection was being voiced in Ireland. However, he did not give it much credence; dismissing it as illogical, owing to it not being in Ireland's best long-term interests:

> The cry that "England's difficulty is Ireland's opportunity" is raised in the old senseless, spiteful way as a recommendation to stab England in the back when she is fighting someone else and to kick her when she is down, instead of in the intelligent and large minded modern way which sees in England's difficulty the opportunity of showing her what a friendly alliance with Ireland can do for her in return for the indispensable things it can do for Ireland.[46]

However, unbeknown to Shaw, an armed Irish insurrection was imminent. The initial decision to stage an armed rising while Britain was at war had been made by the IRB and other extreme republican nationalists in September 1914. Furthermore, it was in August 1915, a month before Shaw had finished writing *O'Flaherty V.C.*, that the funeral of Jeremiah O'Donovan Rossa took place. This was a key event in the build-up to the Rising, which saw Pearse give his rousing graveside speech evoking the Fenian dead, and a contingent of the Irish Citizens Army march in the funeral procession.[47]

The imminent rebellion, now known commonly as the 1916 Easter Rising, would directly render Shaw's advocacy for a new non-partisan and internationally focused perspective for the Irish public, as put forward in *O'Flaherty V.C.*, a moot point. This is due to the fact that the Rising, and the British government's extreme and violent response to it, had a profound effect on the Irish psyche. This effect saw a hostile attitude towards Britain become ingrained in the mindsets of the Irish public; making the internationalist socialistic message of *O'Flaherty V.C.* an impossible one to heed. Historian Thomas Hennessy notes that for Ireland, WWI "created the circumstances which led to a form of psychological partition which could not have been predicted before the war".[48]

In the preface to *O'Flaherty V.C.*, added later, Shaw discusses the rebellion and Britain's response to it, namely their reducing "Dublin to ruins" and execution of the rebel leaders "in cold blood morning after morning with an effect of long-drawn-out ferocity".[49] Shaw suggests that the British government's rash actions during and after the Rising, will have longer lasting effects than they may realise. He sees that English-Irish relations have soured, and anticipates the permanent animosity on the part of the Irish public towards England. In conjuring the image of the "smouldering ruins of Dublin", he even hints that the fire of revolution has not yet been fully extinguished.

The preface ends as follows:

> War is not a sharpener of wits; and I am afraid I gave great offence by keeping my head in this matter of Irish recruiting. What can I do but apologize, and publish the play now that it can no longer do any good?[50]

Shaw's assertion here that the play "can no longer do any good" is ambiguous. He may be referring to the fact that now the war is over its objective as a recruitment play is defunct. Alternatively, he may be acknowledging that after the 1916 Rising and its aftermath, the Irish public will not be receptive to his advocation of a new non-partisan and internationally minded cultural outlook. The manner in which he phrases the last sentence, posing it as a question however, suggests that he believed something may be done to improve English-Irish relations, or perhaps even counteract narrow-minded nationalism, in the future.

Though not in line with his overall socialist ideology, Shaw's hope for Ireland to adopt a more internationally minded and future focused outlook did come to fruition some fifty years later. This was through the modernising policies of Seán Lemass; first in his role as Minister of Industry and Commerce, and then as Taoiseach from 1959 to 1966 (in combination with the influential Ken Whitaker, then secretary of the Department of Finance). Echoing the ethos of Shaw's international socialist messages in "Common Sense About the War" and *O'Flaherty V.C.*, Martin Mansergh notes that government policies during Lemass's tenure as Taoiseach focused on "[o]pening a hitherto protectionist and relatively isolated Ireland to the world",[51] which included improving English-Irish relations through the Anglo-Irish Free Trade Area Agreement.[52] Moreover, internal policies were enacted which opened up society in many ways, regarding education, the role and status of women, and censorship,[53] all issues Shaw wrote extensively about.

In 1966, the bi-centennial year of the Easter Rising, Lemass echoed Shaw's 1915 advocation of a more international outlook based in economic realities for Ireland, proclaiming:

We have to forget the Ireland of the Sean Bhean Bhocht and think of the Ireland of the technological expert.[54]

Ireland was now ready to receive the same message Shaw had tried to give in 1915, with regard to the repressive effect of insular nationalism at least. Lemass had been a volunteer stationed in the GPO during the week of the Easter Rising, and his brother had been violently killed during the Civil War. His past, steeped in dedication and sacrifice, undoubtedly gave his vision for Ireland's future authority and legitimacy in the eyes of the public. It is striking that Lemass evoked the image of the Sean Bhean Bhocht, referencing Yeats and Gregory's nationalist play *Kathleen Ní Houlihan*, when calling for an ideological shift forward; just as Shaw had done in *O'Flaherty V.C.* However, it must be noted that while Lemass shared Shaw's ambitions to see Ireland gain economic prosperity, adopt a future orientated outlook, and embrace a role on the international stage; his social ideology was not one of socialism as Shaw's had been. While Shaw championed modernisation and internationalism in the pursuit of an equal socialist society, Lemass's core goal was economic gain within the existing global capitalist system. As noted by Bryce Evans, Lemass "envisioned Irish development through a capitalist economy".[55]

O'Flaherty V.C. eventually received its premier performance at the Theatre Royal, on the Royal Flying Corps base, in Treizennes France; on February 21st 1917. Produced as entertainment for the soldiers, it was performed by the 40th squadron and was directed by Shaw's friend Robert Lorraine, with Robert Gregory, Lady Gregory's son, playing the role of Tessie. Shaw himself attended a full dress rehearsal of the performance during his tour of the Western Front, just under three weeks before the performance.[56] Though *O'Flaherty V.C.* would not be performed in Ireland till 1924 (when it was performed by a visiting company at the Abbey), Shaw continued to be concerned with recruitment in Ireland for the remainder of the war, penning his "War Issues for Irishmen" in 1918.

Both "Common Sense About the War" and *O'Flaherty V.C.* reflect the complicated and interwoven nature of world, European, and Irish politics during WWI. Dramatising points he had previously made in "Common Sense About the War", Shaw promoted Irish enlistment in the context of Ireland's turbulent political situation. Seeing the war as an opportunity for the Irish labour class to become more internationally aware, he contrasted the enlightened and socially empowered O'Flaherty with the military patriotism of Sir Pearce, and Mrs. O'Flaherty's extreme nationalism. Overall, the play comprehensively damns nationalism as a reductive ideal contributing to Ireland's prevailing impoverished state. For this reason, throughout the play Shaw advocates for the Irish public to adopt a more international perspective, and to reconfigure their relationship with Britain; for the sake of their own future economic prosperity. At this time however, radical nationalists, believing there was no hope of social reform for Ireland while under British rule, saw the war as an opportunity to claim immediate democracy through rebellion.[57] The armed insurrection of the Easter Rising, and its traumatic aftermath, rendered the international socialistic message contained in *O'Flaherty V.C.* redundant to the Irish public for the foreseeable future. In 1966, Taoiseach Seán Lemass, echoing Shaw's call for Ireland to think internationally and look towards the future, heralded in a new era of broad-minded Irish politics. This era however, saw an internationalism based on capitalist principles, not aligned with

Shaw's socialist ideology. Now, in today's political climate of populism, mass migration, ethnocentrism, and Euroscepticism; Shaw's international socialistic message, contained in *O'Flaherty V.C.*, seems as relevant to our society as it ever has been.

NOTES

1. Nelson O'Ceallaigh Ritschel. *Shaw, Synge, Connolly, and Socialist Provocation*. (Florida: University Press of Florida, 2012), 184.
2. Murray Biggs. "Shaw's Recruiting Pamphlet" *SHAW The Annual of Bernard Shaw Studies* Vol. 28 (2008): 107–111.
3. Lauren Arrington. "The Censorship of O'Flaherty V.C." SHAW *The Annual of Bernard Shaw Studies* Vol. 28 (2008): 85–106.
4. "John Cooke "Darkest Dublin"". *Tríd and Lionsa*, Season 2, episode no. 14. (Galway: TG4, 1 February 2018). Television.
5. Micheál Mac Donncha. "The Irish Neutrality League: Remembering the Past". *Anpholbalacht*, 2 November, 2014: www.anphobalacht.com/contents/24531
6. Nelson O'Ceallaigh Ritschel. *Shaw, Synge, Connolly, and Socialist Provocation*. (Florida: University Press of Florida, 2012), 188.
7. Shaw, Bernard. O'Flaherty V.C. *The Works of Bernard Shaw Volume II*. (London: Constable and Co. LTD, 1930), 206–207.
8. Bernard Shaw and Augusta Gregory. *Shaw, Lady Gregory and the Abbey: A Correspondence and a Record*, ed. Dan H Laurence and Nicholas Grene (Buckinghamshire: Gerrards Cross: Colin Smyth, 1993), 105.
9. Shaw, Bernard. O'Flaherty V.C. *The Works of Bernard Shaw Volume II*. (London: Constable and Co. LTD, 1930), 212.
10. Shaw, Bernard. O'Flaherty V.C. *The Works of Bernard Shaw Volume II*. (London: Constable and Co. LTD, 1930), 207.
11. Shaw, Bernard. O'Flaherty V.C. *The Works of Bernard Shaw Volume II*. (London: Constable and Co. LTD, 1930), 214.
12. Shaw, Bernard. O'Flaherty V.C. *The Works of Bernard Shaw Volume II*. (London: Constable and Co. LTD, 1930), 218.
13. Nelson O'Ceallaigh Ritschel. *Shaw, Synge, Connolly, and Socialist Provocation*. (Florida: University Press of Florida, 2012), 187.
14. Shaw, Bernard. O'Flaherty V.C. *The Works of Bernard Shaw Volume II*. (London: Constable and Co. LTD, 1930), 215.
15. Ibid., 215–216.
16. Ibid., 211.
17. Ibid., 211.

18. Terry Phillips. "Shaw, Ireland, and World War I: *O'Flaherty V.C.*, an Unlikely Recruiting Play". *SHAW The Annual of Bernard Shaw Studies* Vol 30 (2010): https://muse.jhu.edu/article/392186
19. Ibid.
20. Shaw, Bernard. "Common Sense About the War". (1914) *The New York Times Current History*, Vol 1. (Urbana Illinois: Project Gutenberg, 5 October, 2004) 11–59. www.gutenbberg.org/files/13635/13635-h/13635-h.htm
21. Ibid.
22. Authored by George Tomkyns Chesney in 1871, the booklet contained a fictional story in which Germany invaded England; and gained control of the country in a decisive final battle at Dorking. Mark Astley writes that Chesney's alarmist story caused uproar when it was published and "catapulted the genre of future war fiction into the public arena". Astley, Mike. 'The Fear of Invasion'. *The British Library*. 2014. www.bl.uk/romantics-and-victorians/articles/the-fear-of-invasion
23. Ibid.
24. Shaw, Bernard. O'Flaherty V.C. *The Works of Bernard Shaw Volume II*. (London: Constable and Co. LTD, 1930), 210.
25. Ibid., 212.
26. Shaw, Bernard. "Common Sense About the War". (1914) *The New York Times Current History*, Vol 1. (Urbana Illinois: Project Gutenberg, 5 October, 2004) 11–59. www.gutenbberg.org/files/13635/13635-h/13635-h.htm
27. Nelson O'Ceallaigh Ritschel. *Shaw, Synge, Connolly, and Socialist Provocation*. (Florida: University Press of Florida, 2012), 147–151.
28. Ed Mulhall. "'Common Sense' and the War: George Bernard Shaw in 1914", RTE. 2014. http://www.rte.ie/centuryireland/index.php/articles/common-sense-and-the-war-george-bernard-shaw-in-1914
29. Shaw, Bernard. "Common Sense About the War". (1914) *The New York Times Current History*, Vol 1. (Urbana Illinois: Project Gutenberg, 5 October, 2004) 11–59. www.gutenbberg.org/files/13635/13635-h/13635-h.htm
30. Shaw, Bernard. O'Flaherty V.C. *The Works of Bernard Shaw Volume II*. (London: Constable and Co. LTD, 1930), 209.
31. Marvin Carlson. *The Haunted Stage: Theatre as Memory Machine*. (Ann Arbor: The University of Michigan Press, 2011), 33.
32. Douglas Hyde. "The Necessity for De-Anglicising Ireland". (1892) Gaeilge. (Accessed February 14, 2018). www.gaeilge.org/deanglicising.html

33. Paige Reynolds, "Performance and Spectacle in (and out) of Modern Irish Theatre", in *The Irish Dramatic Revival 1899–1939*, ed. Anthony Roche (London: Bloomsbury Methuen Drama, 2015), 161.

34. Anthony Roche. *The Irish Dramatic Revival 1899–1939*. (London: Bloomsbury Methuen Drama, 2015), 80.

35. Ibid., 94.

36. Nelson O'Ceallaigh Ritschel. *Shaw, Synge, Connolly, and Socialist Provocation*. (Florida: University Press of Florida, 2012), 189.

37. Shaw, Bernard. O'Flaherty V.C. *The Works of Bernard Shaw Volume II*. (London: Constable and Co. LTD, 1930), 222.

38. Ibid.

39. Ibid., 224.

40. Terry Phillips. "Shaw, Ireland, and World War I: *O'Flaherty V.C.*, an Unlikely Recruiting Play". *SHAW The Annual of Bernard Shaw Studies* Vol 30 (2010): https://muse.jhu.edu/article/392186

41. Terry Phillips. "Shaw, Ireland, and World War I: *O'Flaherty V.C.*, an Unlikely Recruiting Play". *SHAW The Annual of Bernard Shaw Studies* Vol 30 (2010).

42. A. M Gibbs. *A Bernard Shaw Chronology*. (New York: Palgrave, 2001), 216.

43. Bernard Shaw and Augusta Gregory. *Shaw, Lady Gregory and the Abbey: A Correspondence and a Record*, ed. Dan H Laurence and Nicholas Grene (Buckinghamshire: Gerrards Cross: Colin Smyth, 1993), 116.

44. Xliv Ibid., 117.

45. *Oxford Dictionary of Proverbs, s.v.* "England's difficulty is Ireland's opportunity". February 6, 2018. http://www.oxfordreference.com/view/10.1093/acref/9780198734901.001.0001/acref-9780198734901-e-666

46. Shaw, Bernard. "George Bernard Shaw on "Irish Nonsense About Ireland"". *The New York Times*, April 9, 1916.

47. Nelson O'Ceallaigh Ritschel. *Shaw, Synge, Connolly, and Socialist Provocation*. (Florida: University Press of Florida, 2012), 180–181.

48. Terry Phillips. "Shaw, Ireland, and World War I: *O'Flaherty V.C.*, an Unlikely Recruiting Play". *SHAW The Annual of Bernard Shaw Studies* Vol 30 (2010): https://muse.jhu.edu/article/392186

49. Shaw, Bernard. O'Flaherty V.C. *The Works of Bernard Shaw Volume II*. (London: Constable and Co. LTD, 1930), 201.

50. Ibid., 203.

51. Martin Mansergh. "The Political Legacy of Seán Lemass". Etudes irlandaises Vol 25, No. 1 (2000), 141–172. www.persee.fr/doc/irlan_0183-973x_2000_num_25_1_1540

52. Ibid.

53. Ibid.

54. Speeches and newspaper reports relating to Seán Lemass when Taoiseach. 1959–1966. NAI GIS 1/216-222. Government Information Service Papers. Dublin: National Archives of Ireland.
55. Evans, Bryce. *Sean Lemass: Democratic Dictator.* (Cork: The Collins Press, 2011).
56. David Gunby. "The First Night of O'Flaherty V.C." SHAW *The Annual of Bernard Shaw Studies* Vol 19 (1999), 85–97. www.jstor.org/stable/40681594
57. Nelson O'Ceallaigh Ritschel. *Shaw, Synge, Connolly, and Socialist Provocation.* (Florida: University Press of Florida, 2012), 175.

REFERENCES

Arrington, Lauren. 2008. The Censorship of O'Flaherty V.C. *SHAW The Annual of Bernard Shaw Studies* 28: 85–106.

Astley, Mike. 2014. The Fear of Invasion. *The British Library.* www.bl.uk/romantics-and-victorians/articles/the-fear-of-invasion

Biggs, Murray. 2008. Shaw's Recruiting Pamphlet. *SHAW The Annual of Bernard Shaw Studies* 28: 107–111.

Carlson, Marvin. 2011. *The Haunted Stage: Theatre as Memory Machine*, 33. Ann Arbor: The University of Michigan Press.

Evans, Bryce. 2011. *Sean Lemass: Democratic Dictator.* Cork: The Collins Press.

Gibbs, A.M. 2001. *A Bernard Shaw Chronology.* New York: Palgrave.

Gunby, David. 1999. The First Night of O'Flaherty V.C. *SHAW The Annual of Bernard Shaw Studies* 19: 85–97. www.jstor.org/stable/40681594

Hyde, Douglas. 1892. The Necessity for De-Anglicising Ireland. Gaeilge. www.gaeilge.org/deanglicising.html. Accessed 14 Feb 2018.

"John Cooke "Darkest Dublin"". *Tríd and Lionsa*, Season 2, Episode No. 14. (Galway: TG4, 1 February 2018). Television.

Mac Donncha, Micheál. 2014. The Irish Neutrality League: Remembering the Past. *Anpholbalacht*, 2 November. www.anphobalacht.com/contents/24531

Mansergh, Martin. 2000. The Political Legacy of Seán Lemass. *Etudes irlandaises* 25(1): 141–172. www.persee.fr/doc.irlan_0183-973x_2000_num_25_1_1540

Mulhall, Ed. 2014 'Common Sense' and the War: George Bernard Shaw in 1914. RTE. http://www.rte.ie/centuryireland/index.php/articles/common-sense-and-the-war-george-bernard-shaw-in-1914

O'Ceallaigh Ritschel, Nelson. 2012. *Shaw, Synge, Connolly, and Socialist Provocation.* Florida: University Press of Florida.

Oxford Dictionary of Proverbs, s.v. "England's difficulty Is Ireland's Opportunity". February 6, 2018. http://www.oxfordreference.com/view/10.1093/acref/9780198734901.001.0001/acref-9780198734901-e-666

Phillips, Terry. 2010. Shaw, Ireland, and World War I: *O'Flaherty V.C.*, an Unlikely Recruiting Play. *SHAW The Annual of Bernard Shaw Studies* 30. https://muse.jhu.edu/article/392186

Reynolds, Paige. 2015. Performance and Spectacle in (and out) of Modern Irish Theatre. In *The Irish Dramatic Revival 1899–1939*, ed. Anthony Roche. London: Bloomsbury Methuen Drama.

Roche, Anthony. 2015. *The Irish Dramatic Revival 1899–1939*. London: Bloomsbury Methuen Drama.

Shaw, Bernard. 1914. Common Sense About the War. *The New York Times Current History*, vol. 1, 11–59. Urbana Illinois: Project Gutenberg, October 5, 2004. www.gutenberg.org/files/13635/13635-h/13635-h.htm

———. 1916. George Bernard Shaw on "Irish Nonsense About Ireland". *The New York Times*, April 9.

———. 1930. O'Flaherty V.C. In *The Works of Bernard Shaw Volume II*, 206–207. London: Constable.

Shaw, Bernard, and Augusta Gregory. 1993. *Shaw, Lady Gregory and the Abbey: A Correspondence and a Record*, ed. Dan H Laurence and Nicholas Grene. Buckinghamshire: Gerrards Cross: Colin Smyth.

Speeches and Newspaper Reports Relating to Sean Lemass When Taoiseach. 1959–1966. NAI GIS 1/216-222. Government Information Service Papers. Dublin: National Archives of Ireland.

CHAPTER 11

Bernard Shaw in Two Great Irish Houses: Kilteragh and Coole

Peter Gahan

In August 1922, Bernard Shaw and his wife, Charlotte, needed a short end-of-summer break away from their Hertfordshire home in Ayot St. Lawrence. They had passed the previous few summers in their native Ireland in spite of the Troubles (the 1919–1921 Irish War of Independence or Anglo-Irish War), mostly in Kerry. However, the Irish Civil War had broken out in June 1922 making the prospect of another summer there impossible, so they decided at the last-minute on a two-week vacation at the well-known Kelly's Hotel in Rosslare Strand, Co. Wexford, convenient to Rosslare Harbour, one of the closest Irish ports to Britain.[1]

During their final week, they received a dinner invitation at short notice from their Irish friend (Sir) Horace Plunkett for that Saturday, the day Shaw was due to travel back to England to attend the annual Fabian Summer School. On learning that Plunkett's chief guest would be General Michael Collins, commander-in-chief of the Irish Army, Irish guerrilla leader during the Irish War of Independence, chief negotiator on the Irish

P. Gahan (✉)
Independent Scholar, Los Angeles, CA, USA

© The Author(s) 2020
A. McNamara, N. O'Ceallaigh Ritschel (eds.), *Bernard Shaw and the Making of Modern Ireland*, Bernard Shaw and His Contemporaries, https://doi.org/10.1007/978-3-030-42113-7_11

side during the Treaty negotiations that established the Irish Free State, and, since the death of Arthur Griffith the previous week, President of the Dáil (Irish parliament), the Shaws happily accepted Plunkett's invitation.

Thus, on 19 August 1922 Bernard and Charlotte Shaw dined with Michael Collins at Kilteragh, Plunkett's home in Foxrock, Co. Dublin, where they had stayed many times over the previous ten years. Three days after the dinner Collins was killed in an ambush in his native West Cork by Irish Republicans opposed to the Treaty, and five months later Kilteragh itself was burned down by Republicans in the ongoing civil war.

While Horace Plunkett remains mostly unacknowledged as a founder of modern Ireland, Augusta Gregory (née Persse, widow of one-time Governor of Ceylon, [Sir] William Gregory, and so generally known as Lady Gregory), dramatist, Abbey Theatre director, writer on Irish myths and folktales, is more familiar from historical accounts. Her house at Coole Park in Co. Galway, was the second of two great Irish houses noted for the hospitality of their hosts that Bernard and Charlotte Shaw stayed at regularly between 1910 and 1922, that crucial period of Irish national self-determination. Both houses were central to the early-twentieth-century Irish cultural renaissance that extended beyond literature and the arts to agriculture and rural development, urban technical education and employment conditions, and, most immediately, the urgently required new political forms as Ireland detached itself from its long, largely involuntary association with the English monarch and the Westminster parliament. The late-eighteenth-century Coole House was old and traditional, situated deep in rural west of Ireland, which made it so important to W.B. Yeats, a frequent visitor who immortalized its swans and seven woods in his poetry, whereas Kilteragh, nestling at the foot of the Dublin mountains in a well-heeled suburb of the nation's capital, was modern—modernist even—built as recently as 1906 and convenient to the city railway line. Neither house long survived the birth of the new Irish state, but whereas Kilteragh is almost completely neglected in cultural and social histories of modern Ireland, Coole has long since assumed mythic proportions owing especially to its association with Yeats—and perhaps also due to the famous still-surviving copper-beech "Autograph" tree onto which leading contemporary writers—including Gregory, Violet Martin ("Martin Ross"), Yeats, John Synge, and Sean O'Casey—carved their initials, with those of Shaw—"GBS"—the most conspicuous.

From an old Irish Anglo-Norman family, Plunkett had been working tirelessly since the 1890s to improve the material well-being of Irish people, especially in rural Ireland. To this end he had founded the Irish Cooperative movement as the Irish Agricultural Organisation Society (IAOS) to develop Irish agriculture. He served as chairman of the 1895 Recess Committee that led to the establishment of both vocational schools and technical colleges in large towns and, most especially, the innovative Irish Department of Agriculture and Technology, for which he became first vice-chairman (in effect chief executive). He also served as chairman of both the Carnegie Trust in Ireland and the Irish Congested Districts Board, responsible for the extremely poor and underdeveloped areas along the western seaboard that provide settings for Synge's plays *Riders to the Sea* and *Playboy of the Western World*. The IAOS headquarters in Merrion Square, a large Georgian townhouse donated in November 1908 to the co-operative cause by friends of Plunkett and known as the Plunkett House, became the engine-house of his various activities on behalf of the nation, including providing a home for the journal the *Irish Homestead*, which published some of James Joyce's first short stories, and later the *Irish Statesman*, both edited by one of the other key figures of the Irish cultural renaissance, Æ, George Russell, and also a good friend of the Shaws.[2]

In the 1904 *Ireland in the New Century*, Plunkett set out his ideas for the development of modern Ireland, although his message was obscured by a controversy over perceived anti-Catholicism in spite of being fiercely interdenominational in public life, insisting that his associated organizations be non-denominational. A bachelor, he had nevertheless built Kilteragh on a large scale that would complement the great variety of work being done at the Plunkett House. Kilteragh, in effect functioned as a cultural centre, a residential meeting-place for people who could make a positive contribution to the New Ireland, whether Irish or non-Irish, of opposing or similar political or economic views, and irrespective of religious denomination or social class.

Plunkett first met the Shaws as he toured the congested districts of Mayo in September 1908. They all happened to stay at the Great Western Railway Hotel in Mulranny, close to Achill Island and the Shaws spent a day with Plunkett on his CDB rounds, which Plunkett described in his journal: "Sat., 19 Sept 1908: "Another delightful day with Bernard Shaw & his wife – both charming – studying congestion on mainland & Achill" (HP).[3] Shaw, however, was struck by Plunkett's lack of tact in dealing with local people, as he later told Plunkett's biographer, Margaret Digby: "He went round the Congested Districts to persuade Irish farmers whose farms were uneconomic to move into better holdings; a task which would have taxed the persuasive powers of a barrister earning £20,000 year, and took with him small schoolmasters of the £150 type, who could only make Plunkett's offer in the baldest terms, and when it was refused say no more than "Well, you are a very foolish man."[4]

The Shaws began their long friendship with Lady Gregory in early 1909, when she came to stay at their house in Ayot St. Lawrence seeking help for the Abbey Theatre following the death of John Millington Synge. As a result the Abbey Theatre in August 1909 staged Shaw's one-act Western *The Shewing-up of Blanco Posnet*, which had been banned in London for its religious theme. Gregory and Yeats put the play on in defiance of authorities in both Dublin and London: of the Irish Lord Lieutenant and of Dublin Castle as well as of the English stage censor and his superior the Lord Chamberlain. As both the Lord Lieutenant and the Lord Chamberlain acted officially in the person of the King, the Abbey's production amounted to treason. The theatre, therefore, scored a propagandist triumph irrespective of the artistic merits of the piece, restoring their legitimacy with Irish nationalists alienated by the production two years earlier of Synge's *The Playboy of the Western World*. Gregory invited the Shaws to Coole to celebrate their success, but although staying Kerry, they declined; their first visit came a year later.

COOLE: SUMMER 1910

As pioneers of the motoring holiday, the Shaws spent two and a half months touring the north and west of Ireland in the summer of 1910 (23 July—7 October): visiting Belfast and Derry before heading to Rosspenna in Co. Donegal on the north west coast of Ireland, and then driving down from Enniskillen following the Shannon through the middle of Ireland towards Athlone. In spite of wet weather, on 15 August they drove sixteen miles to visit the ruins of the great Irish medieval monastery, Clonmacnoise, before heading back west towards Coole Park, near Gort, Co. Galway, arriving in the evening. They stayed for ten days.

W.B. ("Willie") Yeats, who spent every summer at Coole before his marriage in 1917, was a fellow guest, and Yeats's biographer Roy Foster has written that when "Shaw came to stay [at Coole ... Yeats] felt their old antipathy begin to moderate."[5]

Despite habitual impatience with Shaw, since the London Avenue Theatre season of 1894 featuring plays from both Dublin writers, Yeats

always viewed Shaw as an important weapon at his disposal in his constant battles to improve Irish cultural life. And as for Yeats, so also for
Shaw as he explained later to Irish writer and politician Stephen Gwynn
(28 August 1940): "Not until I spent some time in the house with [Yeats]
at Lady Gregory's … did I learn what a penetrating critic and good talker
he was" (*SGA*, 62).[6]

Lady Gregory's only son, Robert, accomplished sportsman, artist, and
sometime theatre designer, and his wife Margaret, a fellow student at the
Slade Art School in London, were also in residence along with their one-
year-old son, Richard. The day after their arrival, the Shaws and the young
Gregory couple "drove over to tea" with the Goughs at Lough Cutra
Castle about six miles away (CFS).[7] The land all around had once belonged
to the Gaelic O'Shaughnessy clan before being supplanted in the early
seventeenth century by the Prendergasts, one of the old Irish Anglo-
Norman families. The Goughs, a distinguished British military family, had
bought the Lough Cutra estate in the late 1840s after Viscount Gort, a
descendant of the Prendergasts, bankrupted himself by providing famine
relief.[8] Margaret Gregory would marry Hugh Gough ten years after
Robert was killed in the Great War.

The following day, Shaw drove the young couple to see the famous
Cliffs of Moher in Co. Clare, taking in on the way (18 August 1910),
"Ennistymon, … Doolin, Lisdoonvarna & back here – Ballyvaughan &
Kinvarra" (GBS).[9] Charlotte remained behind in Coole and "walked in
park," noting that the sight-seers "came back very late for dinner" (CFS).
Shaw suffered one of his debilitating headaches the following day: "19,
Fri: Severe headache, began morning … bed afternoon, hideous night"
(GBS). Charlotte noted: "better in evening, he went for stroll." The
young Gregory couple then went off to "pay visits" to neighbours for a
few days. By Sunday Charlotte was able to report (21 August 1910):
"Bathing in lake with GBS in morning. Walk with him in afternoon." On
the Monday, with Lady Gregory now confined to bed with a "bad cold"
(CFS) the Shaws and Yeats made an "excursion … to Holy Island [Inis
Cealtra; also known as "the island of the seven churches"] Lough Derg.
Lunched at Mountshannon." From there they took a boat to the island,
and one can only imagine the conversation between Shaw and Yeats as
together they explored this famous sixth-century Irish Christian site. The
following day the Gregorys took the Shaw's car and chauffeur "to pay
visits" to neighbours, leaving Shaw and Charlotte behind to walk and talk
with Yeats (CFS). On Friday 26 August, they visited local churches and

went to the little harbour village Burrin, Co. Clare, to spend the day at Gregory's summerhouse, Mount Vernon, a Persse inheritance (GBS). Shaw later made the pier at Burrin (New Quay) his setting for the first act of *Tragedy of an Elderly Gentleman, Back to Methuselah: Part IV*, although on this trip he was working on *Fanny's First Play* (the eponymous Fanny O'Dowda being the daughter of an Irish papal count), and a short "Italian Play" (later *The Glimpse of Reality*), begun right after *Blanco Posnet* in 1909.[10] A short spoof of a miracle play, not without similarities to some of Yeats's and Gregory's short Abbey plays, Shaw read his "Italian Play" to the assembled company (although not to the still ill Lady Gregory). He completed the piece in Parknasilla, Kerry, three days after leaving Coole, on 30 August 1910.[11] From there, Shaw wrote thanking Gregory for her hospitality: "Coole must seem very quiet now that I have stopped talking" (*SGA*, 62). As Yeats was at least as loquacious as Shaw, it must have been a voluble ten days!

KILTERAGH 1913

The Shaws next return to Ireland came three years later, when they visited Kilteragh for the first time over Easter (28 March-11 April, 1913). Designed by English ecclesiastical architect of Danish descent belonging to the Arts and Crafts movement, W. D. Caröe, the building was completed in 1906. White-washed with granite dressings, The *Irish Builder* (8 January 1910) commented on its construction: "The design is a striking, and in many respects a peculiar, one. Many persons have adjudged it as an eccentric striving after originality, but everything considered, it presents many points of interest and cleverness… presents a gleaming and sparkling effect in the sunshine and at a distance extremely picturesque."[12] Æ adorned the interior with murals as he would the Plunkett House, and was more or less Kilteragh's resident sage although he lived contentedly with his wife in Rathmines. The driven, tireless, if somewhat eccentric and hypochondriac celibate, Plunkett slept in an eerie open to the elements on the roof of the house. Shaw described the house on this first visit as looking like a painting by Picasso.[13]

The Countess of Fingal, born Elizabeth "Daisy" Burke from one of the famous old Galway Norman "tribes" and wife of Plunkett's cousin, took care of the furnishings. She would come up to Dublin from Meath whenever Plunkett required her services as hostess, which was often as he was frequently away either in London or traveling. For over thirty years she served as first president of the United Irishwomen (later the Irish Countrywomen's Association) founded in 1911 along lines suggested by Plunkett and Æ to promote the well-being of rural Irish women, and was also president of the Irish Camogie (women's hurling) Association. Lady Fingal wrote of Kilteragh that Plunkett "had built the house for his friends and for Ireland. For as long as it stood, it was to be at the service of both" (West, 98).[14]

Over a period of ten years Kilteragh afforded the Shaws a base from which to get to know members of the Dublin intelligentsia whilst also exposing them, in a way otherwise impossible, to such contemporary Irish cultural movements as Plunkett and Æ's New Rural Civilization derived from their cooperative work in agriculture; Yeats and Lady Gregory's new national drama at the Abbey Theatre derived from stories of Irish peasant life in the rural west (as opposed to modern urban life associated with industrialized England); Douglas Hyde's Gaelic League; Arthur Griffith's Sinn Fein; John Redmond's Irish Parliamentary Party; Edward Carson's Ulster Volunteers; Bulmer Hobson and Eoin O'Neill's Irish Volunteers; James Larkin and the Trades Unions; James Connolly and Irish socialism; Childers and de Valera's Republicanism; and perhaps even that literary anarchist opposed to all allegiances, James Joyce, who preferred to forge "in the smithy of my soul the uncreated conscience of my race," as his fictional alter ego Stephan Dedalus famously put it. These diverse movements were locked in the same struggle for the so-called Irish soul, which with writing as the weapon of choice consequently led to an explosion of print outlets in Dublin: national newspapers, short-lived news sheets, reviews, or political, religious, and cultural journals—almost anyone of any consequence at the time edited at least one journal. Publishing houses like Maunsell's, the Talbot Press, Arthur Griffith's *Sinn Féin*, Connolly's ITGWU press, the Gaelic League's *An Claidheamh Soluis* edited by Patrick Pearce, the Yeats's sisters' Dun Emer Press and their later Cuala Press, all contributed to this bubbling Irish stew of national cultural and political discourse, in which everyone advocated their own particular (though not necessarily exclusive) vision of a new Ireland with a greater or lesser intensity in the short amount of time left before something *must* happen following the 1912 introduction of the third Home Rule bill at Westminster.

While Yeats and Gregory induced Shaw to contribute to the cultural side, especially on behalf of the Abbey Theatre and Hugh Lane's proposed gallery of modern art in Dublin, Plunkett and Æ worked on Shaw to contribute to the political-economic side. The Shaws became particularly close to Æ, who set out his ideas for the new Ireland as a cooperative civilization in *The National Being* (1916), and Susan Mitchell, his assistant on the *Irish Homestead*. A noted satirical poet and wit, Mitchell had lived for a time with the Yeats family in Bedford Park, London in the 1890s.

KILTERAGH, COOLE, AND THE SINKING OF THE *LUSITANIA*: 1915

With war breaking out in Europe, the Shaws did not stay in Ireland in 1914, but they accepted Plunkett's invitation to stay at Kilteragh the following year over Easter (1 to 12 April), which they followed up with a visit to Coole for almost a month (13 April to 10 May 1915). Charlotte wrote Plunkett about their impending trip to Ireland: "GBS is looking forward to the trip as much as I am … We thought, after spending about a week (or less as it suits you) with you, we would go for a few days tour in the country—perhaps getting as far as Lady Gregory's." Charlotte had been in communication with Plunkett about the precarious finances of the *Irish Homestead*, the co-operative newsletter edited by Æ: "we must settle something about that when we meet in Ireland" (Shaws-HP).[15] Charlotte used her private wealth to fund the causes she believed in.

At 8.30 am on Wednesday, 31 March 1915, the Shaws left London for Ireland. Despite Charlotte being "anxious about submarine attack!"—one of the hazards of wartime sea-travel, they had a "good passage." Lady Fingall was in residence at Kilteragh to greet them, and Æ came out from Dublin to dine (CFS). Plunkett, himself "was dog tired & don't know what I should have done without Daisy and Æ to entertain my guests" (HP). Next day, after spending the morning at work in Dublin, Plunkett had an "enjoyable day with the Shaws at Kilteragh" (HP). They all—including Charlotte—walked to the top of nearby Three Rock Mountain (CFS). Charlotte would stipulate in her will that her ashes be spread on top of Three Rock Mountain, from which you can see all of Dublin city and bay below (Shaw chose not to carry out her wish due to difficult wartime conditions at the time of her death in 1943).

Shaw's old Fabian colleague Sydney Olivier arrived from England, and the Rt. Hon. W.F. Bailey, one of the Irish Estates Commissioners and advisor to the Abbey directors, came out "to luncheon" (CFS) "to the edification of [Olivier] & G.B.S" (HP). Plunkett, Oliver, and Shaw again walked up Three Rock Mountain after Bailey and Lady Fingall departed. On Saturday, they drove "into Dublin. Long talk with Æ. Saw Mrs. Russell [Æ's wife] too" (CFS). In the afternoon, they all "Walked to top of Sugar Loaf Mountain [in nearby Co. Wicklow] ... Dined. A day of rest" (HP). The well-known physician and Dublin wit, Oliver St. John Gogarty, soon to be immortalized as Buck Mulligan in James Joyce's *Ulysses*, came to dine that evening (CFS). Shaw and Gogarty were wary of each other. When asked some years later by Irish artist Beatrice Campbell, (Lady Glenavy née Elvery), to comment on Gogarty's flow of conversation, Shaw retorted: "mere persiflage!"[16] "Prof. Mahaffy [the "Great Mahaffy," who had been Oscar Wilde's classics teacher at Trinity] came out, along with Prof. Lecky from T.C.D. for lunch, Easter Sunday" (HP). Lecky was son of the famous Trinity anti-Home Rule Whig historian, W.E.H. Lecky, who had died in 1903. Next day, Bank Holiday Monday, Plunkett noted, "delightful people in the house... To dinner, Under-Secretary Matthew Nathan, & Bailey brought Gregory. W.B. Yeats. An interesting conversation" (HP). Charlotte and a party that included Mrs. Alice Green (née Stopford, nationalist historian, whom Shaw had known since the 1890s as a good friend of Beatrice Webb and a cousin of Unitarian minister Stopford Brook, who chaired Yeats's Irish Literary Society in London, and whom Shaw had used as a model for the Christian Socialist Reverend Morell in *Candida*), drove to Glendalough, where "they saw another hawk" (HP). On Friday, Thomas Bodkin (son of a nationalist MP, nephew of Hugh Lane, and later director of the Dublin National Gallery) came out, and although GBS "was sick with a headache ... we had a great day" (HP). Plunkett noted a "long talk with G.B. Shaw" on Saturday 10 April, and next day they motored "to Dunsany & Kileen [the two neighbouring estates in Co. Meath belonging to the Protestant and Catholic branches respectively of the Plunkett family. Plunkett's brother was the present Lord Dunsany, while the Countess of Fingal lived in Kileen with her husband, the Earl of Fingal]. On their way back, they called on [Sir Matthew] Nathan [presumably at the Under-Secretary's Lodge in Phoenix Park]" (HP).

After lunch on Monday 12 April, the Shaws left Kilteragh for the West, traveling on "Very bad road to Kildare," where they had tea and saw St. Brigid's Cathedral, before making for Birr, Co. Offally, spending the night in Dooley's Hotel (GBS). "Very cold" next morning, they visited Birr Castle before taking to the road again to "drive over mountains" via Portumna and Derrybrien, arriving at Coole by lunchtime (GBS). In the afternoon, they walked "round [forestry] plantations with Lady G" (CFS). Charlotte wrote thanking Plunkett for their stay at Kilteragh (13 April 1915): "Our visit to you was a very great pleasure to us. The number of interesting people you collect round you is a great delight, & there is a happy stimulation, both mental & physical, about Kilteragh I have never met with anywhere else" (Shaws-HP).

From Coole, Gregory wrote to Yeats (16 April 1915): "The Shaws are here. They are very easy to entertain, he is so extraordinarily light in hand, a sort of kindly joyousness about him, and they have their motor so are independent." The cold Irish spring weather, however, had its effect on Charlotte, who quickly caught a cold. W. F. Bailey, who the Shaws had already met at Kilteragh, followed them on to Coole, where he took a series of photographs of Shaw writing in front of the house and its environs.

The next day, Saturday 17 April, the stricken Charlotte "stayed in house all day," while "all the others drove to the seaside and had tea" (CFS). On Monday, "Mr. Bailey left early," but Charlotte, whose cold was worse, stayed all day in her room, where "GBS & Lady G visited me" (CFS). Over the next couple of days she improved, but then Gregory's grand-daughter Ann became sick (Wed 21 April): "Dr came in afternoon (Dr. Foley) & stayed to tea. Ann better in evening. I took 2 short walks" (CFS).

Because of the Great War, and especially due to enforced curfews in Dublin, the Abbey's always precarious finances had reached breaking point. Shouldering the burden as best they could, Yeats and Gregory wondered if they should play in London for a few weeks. Gregory wrote to Yeats (21 April 1915): "A wire has come saying we must decide at once about taking the plays to London, followed by a letter today. I read it to G.B.S. He said decidedly we ought to go, and if we must die, die gloriously, and I was glad to have his definite opinion, for, of course, I realise the risk." Stepping into the breach, Shaw promised to write another play for them, *O'Flaherty V.C.*, for which he chose the front of Gregory's house as setting: not only a tribute to his hostess but a specific pointer to the location where both *O'Flaherty V.C.* as well as Yeats and Gregory's own *Cathleen Ni Houlihan* (1902)—that emblematic play of the Irish literary renaissance it satirizes—were conceived. Despite his own misgivings about the origins of the Great War, Shaw's play presented cogent, even Irish nationalist reasons for young Irishmen to fight in the British Army against militaristic Germany rather than for any necessarily bogus allegiance to England. Shaw also helped Gregory draw up a program for the Abbey's coming season.[17] She proudly reported to Yeats that Shaw thought her

Shanwalla, "the best ghost play he ever saw, and thinks Sinclair very fine in it."[18] Shaw, by now familiar with the Abbey actors, would want Sinclair to play O'Flaherty in his own new Irish play, but as it turned out, the Abbey withdrew the scheduled November 1915 production under threat of military censorship.

Friday 23 April 1915 was a "most Glorious Spring day" at Coole. Charlotte felt better, but "Children still unwell." Next day, however, "GBS bad headache. He went out in evening at 5.30. Got lost in the woods & did not come back till 11!" (CFS) On Sunday, Charlotte, Lady Gregory and her grandson, Richard, took the horse and side-car "to see woods where GBS got lost. Back by road. Lovely day" (CFS). Gregory relayed Shaw's misadventure to Yeats (Thursday 29 April): "Did I tell you of his being lost last Saturday in the woods, of which he declares there are seventy-seven. He didn't get home till 11.00 o'clock at night, having walked for five hours, when he got to Gort through Inchy, and took a car. The people all say already he was led "astray" [i.e. by the fairies]" (SGA, 91). Shaw's getting lost became part of local folklore as playwright Lennox Robinson discovered on a visit to Gort in 1943. Having known the Shaws since 1909, when he stayed with them to learn something about stage-management in London, he wrote asking Shaw if the story was true, Shaw confirmed it: "I have a very defective sense of direction, and thought I was making for Coole all the time until I found myself in Gort. I have no rec-ollection of their having sent out a searching party" (SGA, 90).

Their 1915 stay at Coole was prolonged waiting for English artist Augustus John, bohemian in time-keeping as in everything else, to appear. Gregory wrote in her journal: "Mrs Shaw was lamenting about not having him painted by a good artist and I suggested having John over, and she jumped at it." On Monday 26 April, Robert Gregory—supposed to be travelling with the artist—duly arrived, but "without Mr. Augustus John." Charlotte annotated her diary for the remaining days that week with, "Mr. John did not arrive!" (CFS) To fill in the time, they visited Gregory's sum-merhouse, Mount Vernon, near Burrin pier, with Robert: "Spent the whole day there by the sea; had picnic lunch" (CFS). On Wednesday, they went into Galway City with Lady Gregory, who records (April 1915): "Augustus John wired from Dublin yesterday that he would come on today. G.B.S. had his hair cut in Galway yesterday as a preliminary, but too much was taken off" (SGA, 90).[19] On Thursday, Charlotte went for "Long walk with GBS round lake. Hot & glorious." Friday, however, brought a change of weather: "Very wet in evening" (CFS).

John finally arrived at Coole on Sunday 2 May 1915, with Charlotte underlining the event in her diary for emphasis! Shaw, however, was now struck down by another headache, leaving John free to go off to Burrin with Robert Gregory (CFS). Next day, John himself succumbed to a bad cold, though "he did a sitting with GBS in the afternoon" (CFS). On Tuesday, Charlotte made Shaw take John to the doctor although: "They had a sitting in the afternoon (all yesterday's work was effaced)" (CFS). This last alludes to John's working method, where he would simply paint over an unsatisfactory version of the portrait rather than start afresh on a new canvas. Shaw wrote about Augustus John's technique to Frances Chesterton, wife of G.K. Chesterton: "I should have been back a week ago; but Lady Gregory insisted that Augustus John should paint a portrait of me. John exported himself for that purpose, but fell among convivial spirits and was lost on the way for a whole week. He arrived in a contrite and somewhat shattered condition on Sunday, and has since painted and obliterated no less than three masterpieces. Like Penelope, he gets up early and undoes the work of the day before. But the sitter will strike presently: besides, my vanity rebels against being immortalized as an elderly carica-ture of myself" (CL3, 294–5).

On Thursday 6 May, Charlotte commissioned John to paint a portrait of Robert Gregory's son, Richard, which then proceeded along with the Shaw portraits while Shaw himself used the extra time at Coole to write a follow-up essay (really a small book), "Uncommonsense About the War," to *Common Sense About the War*, his provocative anti-militarist, anti-British Foreign Office tract written the year before, Retitled "More Commonsense About the War," the *New Statesman* would refuse to pub-lish this even more stridently anti-British establishment sequel—and it remained unpublished until 2006.[20]

Catastrophe interrupted their already extended spring idyll. On Friday 7 May 1915, the luxury steamer the Lusitania—returning from New York—was torpedoed by a German U-boat just off the Kerry coast, one of the great civilian tragedies on the allied side during World War I. Gregory's nephew, art dealer Hugh Lane, was one of over a thousand people drowned. Charlotte noted: "Heard early of loss of Lusitania—Hugh Lane on board." When Shaw asked Gregory how he could help her, she replied: "I said I longed to be alone, to cry, to mourn, to scream if I wished. I wanted to be out of hearing and sight" (SGA, 91).[21] Next day, Sunday, Charlotte reported: "Terrible gloom … Lady Gregory left late at night." On Monday, John did the final sitting with Shaw, and they all left

Coole "after lunch. Taking Mr John" (CFS). After spending the night in Maryborough (Port Laoise), they headed for Dublin next morning, calling on Æ at the Plunkett House. They "brought him to luncheon at The Shelbourne," while John spent the afternoon with St John Gogarty. As Charlotte later explained to Plunkett (14 May 1915), John had ended up, "with a sprained knee, got, he informed us, "jumping over a gate at Gogarty's"!" (Shaws-HP) That night they all took the boat for Holyhead.

Many survivors of the Lusitania were on board, as Charlotte notes: "Crossed by night boat. Passengers from Lusitania on board. . . Slept at Holyhead" (CFS). After the war Shaw wrote about the sinking of the Lusitania in the preface to *Heartbreak House*, but more immediately in "More Commonsense about the War" he used it to illustrate the incapacity of civilians to comprehend the true scale of war-time horror: "I speak feelingly in this matter: for I had friends who went down with the Lusitania [Shaw had met Lane on a visit to his art gallery in Dublin in 1908]; and it happened that I had to cross the Irish Sea during the two main [German] submarine incursions, returning on the last occasion with the Lusitania survivors. ... [Yet] I found it impossible to persuade myself that I was entitled to any immunity from the destructive operations of the enemy. If I was not shooting, I was paying others to shoot, and *qui facit per alium facit per se* ... There can be no doubt that this comparatively trivial incident of the sinking of the Lusitania roused more fury in civilian England and civilian America than the sacrifice of a dozen army corps."[22]

KILTERAGH 1917 AND THE IRISH CONVENTION

Two years later, on Monday, 10 September 1917, Shaw arrived in Kerry to join Charlotte, who had already spent several weeks at Parknasilla. She went into Sneem to collect him off the train. Since early summer, Shaw had been acting as unofficial advisor to Plunkett, now chairman of the Irish Convention convened at the invitation of Prime Minister Lloyd George to decide on the future political constitution of Ireland. When Shaw informed Plunkett of his arrival in Kerry, Plunkett sent on to him there the first instalment of his report for the King on the Convention's proceedings, along with an invitation to Kilteragh (22 Sept 1917): "So near and yet so far! ... could you not both spend next week-end with me at Kilteragh on your way east?" Although Shaw responded in the negative, Plunkett did not give up: "I am very sorry we are not to meet this week-end but you will be better where you are .... Could you not lengthen your holiday in Ireland by taking another week when your hotel closes on the 8th, beginning with, say, three days at Killarney and ending with as many days as you can spare for Kilteragh?" Charlotte, always happy to spend more time in Ireland, responded more positively, while revealing a side to Shaw hardly ever glimpsed in his own ebullient letters: his periodic exhaustion resulting from an almost non-stop pursuit of so many different activities (27 September 1917): "If you really think it will be convenient for you to have us for a couple of nights about the 11th I think I can undertake to keep GBS in Ireland as long as that. There is nothing we should both of us like so much as a little quiet talking with you at Kilteragh before we go back with the not at all pleasant prospect of winter in London before us. I am most delighted with the effect Ireland has had upon GBS this time [he had been learning how to churn butter!]. He came over rather more than a fortnight ago looking about 80 & a perfect wreck! He was tired out & most despondent. Now he is more than himself again." Plunkett immediately replied (28 September 1917): "It will not only be convenient, but profitable in every way to have you both at Kilteragh, for as long as you can stay ... Do make this a definite fixture. I am delighted with your account of the rejuvenation of G.B.S. in his native air. One reason that I am anxious to get him here is that I feel it in my bones that the time has come for him to do his great service to Ireland" (Shaws-HP).

To prepare for the visit to Kilteragh and discussions on Ireland's future, Shaw had been boning up on the history of modern constitutions to figure out how his scheme of a federation of four nations in the two islands might best be advanced.[23] His notion that Ireland should enter into a Federation as a free independent nation co-equal with England and Scotland (and Wales, if it wanted a more clearly defined separation from England), meant that Ireland must first have national autonomy.

On 13 October, the Shaws left Parknasilla for Kilteragh, where they stayed a full ten days, 13–23 October 1917. Cold, bright weather had now set in (CFS). With Lady Fingall in attendance, several of the Convention's *dramatis personae* came out to Foxrock on Sunday 14 October, including Frank Cruise O'Brien and Shan Bullock, both of whom worked for Plunkett on the Convention's Dublin secretariat. "Mr. Murphy came to luncheon & Æ" (CFS & HP). Incongruously, but typical of Plunkett's Kilteragh, William Martin Murphy, the infamous newspaper proprietor, founder of the Dublin United Tramways Company, and employers' leader, had clashed violently with Æ during the 1913 Lock-out of Dublin workers, but now both were key delegates on the Convention.[24] Either at

Kilteragh or in Dublin, the Shaws met among others: Susan Mitchell, Gogarty, Stephen McKenna (friend of Synge's in Paris and translator of Plotinus), Mr. Smith (Gordon, later manager of the co-operative National Land Bank founded in August 1919),[25] and Mr. O'Brien (probably William O'Brien of the All-For-Ireland Party, who, though one of the promulgators of the Irish Convention idea, refused then to take part convinced it could only come up with "a hateful bargain for the partition of the country under a plausible disguise"),[26] Mr. Shaw (of the Convention secretariat in London), Col. Blackbourne, James Stephens, Lennox Robinson, Tim Healy, Mahaffy, now Provost of Trinity, which hosted the Convention, and poet Katherine Hinkson, née Tynan, Yeats's confidante during his youth in Dublin. On their last day, Shaw went with Plunkett to lunch in Phoenix Park with the heads of the two Irish police forces, the Royal Irish Constabulary and the Dublin Metropolitan Police, about which he had been so outspokenly critical during the 1913 Dublin Lockout. Shaw told Gregory (27 November 1917): "I ... quite enjoyed lunching at the R[oyal]. I[rish]. C[onstabulary]. depot in Phoenix Park with General Byrne and the chief of the [Dublin] metropolitan police, though I rather horrified them by my program of machine guns and Mills bombs." As for Plunkett, if the weather in Ireland was almost always wet, Plunkett was almost always ill. Charlotte noted (19 October 1917): "Friday. GBS spoke at dinner of Arts Club in place of [indisposed] Sir Horace" (CFS). Their old Mayo friend, the Rev. James Hannay (novelist "George Birmingham"), took the chair with many people from the arts scene in Dublin in attendance. Traveling back with Plunkett to England, they had a "Rough passage" across the Irish Sea (CFS).

COOLE AND KILTERAGH: OCTOBER 1918

Robert Gregory, who had become an air force pilot, was killed in action on 23 January 1918. Shaw wrote a letter of condolence to his mother (5 February 1918): "These things made me rage and swear once; now I have come to taking them quietly" (CL3, 527). Gregory replied (8 February): "I was hoping for a letter from you. I knew it would be helpful." Shaw's meeting with Robert on the Western Front the previous year would became part of Irish literary history after W. B. Yeats used Shaw's account of the young airman as source for several poems, including "In Memory of Robert Gregory" (1918), "An Irish Airman foresees his Death," (1918) and "Reprisals" (1920).[27] The main purpose of the Shaws's last visit to

Coole in October 1918 was to see how Gregory was coping after her son's death. After spending much of the summer in Parknasilla, they set out for Coole but a "tyre burst" in their car and their luggage was then delayed at Limerick Junction, so they spent two rainy days in Limerick city waiting for it to turn up (CFS). "Pouring" was Charlotte's consistent description of the weather for this visit to Coole (from 3 October to 11 October 1918). Robert had been very much alive during their last 1915 visit, but Charlotte judged their hostess as "rather well" (CFS). For distraction, they took short walks between the showers ("to see floods!"), and visited Edward Martyn, who had founded the Irish Literary Theatre with Yeats and Gregory in 1897, at nearby Tillyra.

After Coole, they visited Charlotte's niece, Cecily Colthurst, at Lucan House, outside Dublin. Cecily's husband Capt. Richard St. John Jefferyes Colthurst, last High Sheriff of Dublin before independence but who hailed from an old Cork family, had inherited Lucan House though a Vesey family connection. Cecily's eldest daughter, (Mary) Penelope (six years old in 1918), would eventually inherit Blarney Castle in Co. Cork owned by the Colthursts; the infamous Capt. John Bowen-Colthurst, responsible for the unwarranted execution of Francis Sheehy-Skeffington during the 1916 Rising, was from a junior branch of the Colthurst family living in Dripsey Castle, Cork.[28] From Lucan, the Shaws went on to visit Plunkett at Kilteragh for ten days (19–30 October 1918), with Shaw delivering a lecture on Equality (meaning economic equality) at the Abbey Theatre on Sunday, 20 October 1918. The question of equality had preoccupied him since writing *Major Barbara* at Charlotte's home in Castetownshend, West Cork, in 1905.[29] The previous week, also at the Abbey, he had engaged his old debating friend G.K. Chesterton, who delivered a lecture on private property (GBS). Charlotte attended Shaw's lecture with Cecily and Richard Colthurst (CFS). Plunkett took the chair, as he recounts (20 October 1918): "Sun: Bernard Shaw lectured on Equality at the Abbey Theatre. I presided & he talked all the time—answering questions the last hour. Left me nothing to do for which I am grateful. His thesis was the impossibility of any [social?] reform in a large way except on the basis of equality of income which means to all but the very poor the abolition of private property. He was vague & weak on the modus operandi of the reform but very good in his destructive criticism of the status quo" (HP). In questions from the audience Shaw adopted a deliberately antagonistic stance towards any display of Irish xenophobia. Joseph Holloway reported on the evening: "Sir Horace Plunkett briefly introduced Shaw, who, attired in blue, stood close to the chairman and commenced his delightful discourse on *Equality*, speaking without break or notes for an hour and a half. Shaw is hostile to the outlook of Irishmen and the words 'Sinn Fein' are his pet aversion. Yet all passed off delight-fully, although during question-time one felt that one was over a powder keg which would explode at any moment. It must have been a great physi-cal strain on Shaw, yet he came up smiling, eager to do battle with all-comers right up to the moment the chairman called halt at 10.30 pm."[30]

On 21 October, the Shaws lunched at Kilteragh with Lady Fingall, Plunkett, and Oliver St. John Gogarty, while afterwards Charlotte met Yeats to "talk about G.B.S. in Dublin" (CFS)—presumably future Abbey productions of Shaw's plays—and called on James Stephens, whom she knew from earlier Dublin visits. On Wednesday 23 October, Shaw had tea with his childhood friend Mrs. Ada Tyrell (1854–1955) in Hatch Street (GBS). Born Ada Shaw (no relation), her family had lived in Harrington Street, just around the corner from the Shaw family in Synge Street, and both families remained in contact after Bessie Shaw moved with her family to London in the 1870s.[31] Like her father, Ada's husband, Prof. Robert Tyrell (1844–1914), was a Classics don at Trinity College, who had taught, among others, Wilde, Synge, and Gogarty. On Thursday, the Shaws lunched with artist and stained-glass worker Sarah Purser (friend of Susan Mitchell) and her mother before going on to have tea with Æ (CFS). Friday was "pouring wet," leaving Charlotte struck down with the inevitable "cold + sore throat" (CFS).

Lady Gregory, having come up to Dublin, enlisted Shaw's help in a skirmish in the on-going war over Hugh Lane's bequest of modern art pictures to the nation. Gregory has left an intimate description of working closely with Shaw:

> I just thought of telephoning to [Kilteragh], where the Shaws were staying with Horace Plunkett, to ask if they would be in town during the day . . . The answer was that they would come between lunchtime and 4.30… I had just dropped asleep in my chair in the reading room, when I heard a friendly laugh, and there was G.B.S., and Charlotte. I said I wanted to consult him, and he at once sat down and gave his attention to my story [Gregory was trying to squash the idea that binding arbitration should be used to settle the Lane Pictures issue], and before I had gone far he exclaimed "Monstrous folly! Arbitration would be fatal!" Such a relief! … I said "Oh! If you could come to the meeting!" and he said "I should have no excuse for meddling."

> I saw then that he would come [along with Yeats]…[O]wing to G.B.S. every-
> one was in good humour. He had chaffed Bodkin a little, and been deferen-
> tial to the Chairman. I said, in saying goodbye, "When you're in doubt lead
> trumps say card players, and when I'm in doubt I lead G.B.S.," and he
> laughed and said to the others "She always tells me what to do, and I just do
> as I'm told." (Gregory *Journals 1*, 28–30)[32]

Shaw followed the matter up when he returned to London, writing to
Gregory (14 November 1918): "I think you may regard the arbitration
business as now finally shelved" (SGA, 140).

Charlotte spent the last two days at Kilteragh in bed with a cold while
Shaw went off to see a matinee performance on Saturday 26 October of
The Shewing-up of Blanco Posnet, which had become an Abbey staple—
along with *Kathleen Ni Houlihan* and Synge's *Playboy of the Western
World*—for tours to Britain and America. Fred O'Donovan both directed
and played Blanco, with Maire O'Neill as Feemy, with Abbey stalwarts
Arthur Shields and F. J. McCormack also in the cast. That evening Shaw
gave a lecture "Literature in Ireland" to the Dublin Literary Society at the
Little Theatre in O'Connell Street, where the Dublin Repertory theatre
had performed Shaw's *Mrs. Warren's Profession* in 1914 (CFS, GBS). The
Irish Times reported on 28 October 1918 that Shaw took aim at any
exclusively Gaelic notion of Irish literature, speaking of George Moore,
Synge and James Joyce having lived in Paris, and referred even to the latter's epic Dublin novel *Ulysses*, which would not be published until 1922
(Shaw had been reading the serialized chapters in Ezra Pound's *Little
Review*). Holloway again reported on Shaw's lecture, noting that the open
discussion after the talk was so extended that Shaw "became uneasy about
catching the last train at 10.30 pm from Harcourt Street Station."[33] After
the meeting, Holloway watched as Shaw took the Terenure tram up to
Harcourt Street railway station, from where he would take the last train
back to Foxrock.

Neither Shaw was well the following day, Sunday, 27 October 1918,
with Charlotte still in bed and Shaw suffering from a "bad headache!"
after his performance the previous evening (CFS). Plunkett, who had
spent most of the week in London, talked earnestly to Shaw on Tuesday,
29 October: "I tried to commit him to serious work for Ireland. I'm not
sure he takes her any more seriously than the country takes him. I believe
he has a heart but his pose is puzzling" (HP). Of all people, Plunkett
should have understood better Shaw's disappointment after the failure of
the Irish Convention (due not only to the Irish parties' inability to agree

on substantial matters, but more consequentially to Lloyd George sabo-
taging the Convention's recommendation of diluted Home Rule by linking its application to Irish conscription the very day Plunkett delivered the
final report to the Prime Minister). The Shaws returned to London next
day, with Shaw describing the journey to Gregory two weeks later (14
November): "We had a stormy voyage through the torpedoes: there was a
Westerly gale; and the ship kept standing on its head all the way. But we
got a cabin and were not sick" (CL3, 573). Shaw was not exaggerating
about the hazards of crossing the Irish Sea in war time: two weeks earlier
(10 October 1918) on the same route the *Leinster* mail boat had been
torpedoed and sunk with the loss of over 500 lives.

KILTERAGH 1920

Shaw did not visit Kilteragh in 1919, although Charlotte did after he
returned to England from Kerry for the Fabian Summer School. Arriving
on Saturday night 20 September, she found their Mayo friend Rev. James
Hannay ("George Birmingham") also in residence. In Dublin, she met the
usual round of people, as well as some new ones such as the Pope
Hennesseys and Lady Leslie, wife of writer Shane Leslie from an old
Monaghan Anglo-Irish family (Leslie, a Roman Catholic convert, was first
cousin of Winston Churchill through their American mothers).

In London the following March, Shaw went alone to visit his ailing
sister, Lucy, last surviving member of his immediate Dublin family. Lucy
died that afternoon when he was with her, and he wrote next day to his
Dublin childhood friend, Edward McNulty, who had once harboured
romantic notions about Lucy (28 March 1920): "Lucy died yesterday
afternoon at 5, practically in my arms … I was just starting for Ireland
when this occurred. When I have seen the cremation through ("no flow-
ers, no funeral, no mourning" says the will) I will resume my journey, and
will make some opportunity of seeing you and telling you more about it"
(*CL3*, 673). Lucy's death almost certainly had a greater effect on the now
sixty-three-year-old writer than he allowed. Shaw also wrote to Mrs.
Patrick Campbell, who had become a good friend of Lucy's when her
house had provided Shaw and the actress a refuge for assignations away
from Charlotte during their tumultuous 1912 affair. Shaw told Mrs.
Campbell that he was off to Ireland for a fortnight's stay at Kilteragh: "I
have been quite seriously ill (for *me*) for the last three weeks; and I must
have a recuperative change" (*CL3*, 674). "Dear Lucy," Mrs. Campbell
wrote back to Shaw, "I am glad I saw a little more of her these last

weeks—her suffering wrung my bosom—and how brave she was to be sure! I thanked heaven you were with her at the end."

The Shaws arrived at Kilteragh on 2 April 1920 for about ten days, followed by a couple of days at Lucan House with the Colthursts. While at Kilteragh Shaw helped Plunkett "very materially" in drafting a letter to raise money from American subscribers for the *Irish Statesman*, in severe danger of closing after only a year (HP). Although "Pouring rain" on Friday, 9 April 1920, they went into Dublin to see "Jack Yeats pictures, met Mr. Darrell Figgis, and to call on Mr. Martin [possibly, Edward Martyn]" (CFS). Darrrell Figgis, who they met several times during this period, was one of those troubled figures in Ireland's fight for Independence. Involved in the 1914 Howth gun-running, he became Honorary Secretary of the reconstituted Sinn Féin in 1917. Despite disagreements with Michael Collins, he reluctantly supported the Anglo-Irish Treaty but his personal life was unravelling, ultimately leading to his suicide in 1927.

That same day, which also saw the first of many attacks by British forces (known as "Black and Tans" and Auxiliaries) on Plunkett's IAOS cooperative creameries as reprisals for attacks on police barracks, Shaw met McNulty to talk about Lucy. Both Shaws attended a performance of *The Devil's Disciple* the following afternoon at the Abbey, leaving Shaw unimpressed. He offered Gregory his coruscating criticism of the production (12 April 1920): "An execrable performance, not improved by the hideous nervousness my presence set up. I can imagine that in the evening, with a less depressing audience and in finer weather, it goes better; but they are not up to my stage tricks anyhow, poor lambs!" (*SGA*, 150).

Charlotte noted on 12 April a "general strike in sympathy with the [IRA] prisoners on hunger strike at Mountjoy [Prison]," which continued next day (13 April 1920): "strike on—no one at work . . .. Punchestown [races] off in consequence of strike" (CFS). This strike proved successful, with the prisoners being awarded political or POW status with some hunger strikers were released (14 April): "Heard in Evening prisoners are released & strike is over" (CFS). The Shaws returned to England on 16 April. The British, however, withdraw political status from the IRA prisoners in August, provoking the more famous hunger strike in Cork prison by Sinn Féin Lord Mayor of Cork, Terence McSwiney, who was transferred to Brixton prison, London, where he died on October 1920.[34] Thousands of people lined the streets of Cork to pay their respects when his body was returned to Ireland.

KILTERAGH AUGUST 1922

Some influential people who had accepted administrative roles running the new Irish Free State were neighbours of Plunkett in the area around Kilteragh. They and their large houses were subjected to frequent Republican raids during the Civil War, as Charlotte notes in her diary the day they travelled up from Rosslare to Kilteragh to meet Michael Collins (19 August 1922): "Sat. Packed. Started in afternoon to Wexford. Dublin. Arrived Kilteragh 7.30. Sir H. met us, told us of raid [on a nearby house]. Found Lady Lavery & Collins. They stayed for dinner." The American-born beauty, socialite, and wife of famous Irish society painter John Lavery (and herself also an artist), Hazel Lavery née Martyn, of the same old Irish-Norman Martyn family—another of the Galway Tribes—as Edward Martyn, had in fact facilitated Collins's invitation to Kilteragh and accompanied him there. That Collins may have had an affair with her during the Treaty negotiations in London has been a subject of some speculation, not denied by the lady herself. Undoubtedly a flirtatious relationship existed on both sides, and the master-spy Collins probably used Hazel—with her acquiescence—as an informant on such personal contacts inside the British establishment as Winston Churchill, Austen Chamberlain, and Lords FitzAlan and Londonderry.[35] Plunkett left a fuller description of meeting Collins (19 August 1922): "Sat. G.B.S. & wife came in the evening and Lady Lavery brought Michael Collins to supper. This was my first talk with the Commander in Chief of the Army of the Provisional Government. He is an interesting personality. Too fat but virile. 32 years old. Amiable, direct, simple, and yet cunning. A bit crude (perhaps due to shyness) in the expression of his views. I got in my economic (agricultural) ideas … He took a risk in coming here without an escort. I fear he is too careless of his life. His car was bombed only yesterday when, luckily, he was not in it."[36] Collins was killed in an ambush in his native West Cork three days later. The battle-hardened commander-in-chief courted danger, which—with all the pressures of governing the new state—must have told on his nerves. Many years later, the observant Shaw described the Collins he met that evening: "His nerves were in rags: his hand kept slapping his revolver all the time he was talking pleasantly enough" (qtd. in *SGA*, 164). Also writing years afterwards, the somewhat less reliable Countess of Fingall conflates the Saturday evening dinner with Sunday's lunch, when she states that Plunkett also invited John Dillon, Irish Parliamentary Party leader, as well as W. T. Cosgrave, soon to be Collins's successor as President of the Dáil and Chairman of the Provisional Government. Plunkett had indeed written to Dillon the previous week inviting him to Kilteragh, adding that if he came on Sunday he would meet Bernard Shaw. It is practically certain that neither Cosgrave or Dillon was present with Collins on the Saturday evening, nor Sir John Lavery for that matter, as neither Charlotte's nor Plunkett's contemporary accounts mention them—though both Lavery and Cosgrave were at Kilteragh for lunch next day (HP). That the dinner with Collins was lively is evident from a letter of Hazel Lavery to Eddie Marsh (Sir Edward Marsh, Private Secretary to Winston Churchill) written during the course of the evening: "I am trying to write this with a babel of conversation which I dare not miss, going on around me."[37]

While at Kilteragh, Shaw wrote an article for *The Irish Times*, published two days later, on the stated position of Republicans Eamon de Valera and Erskine Childers in Ireland's ongoing Civil War. Plunkett presumably encouraged him to write it as well as supplying him with Childers and de Valera's pamphlets defending the Republican position against the Treaty.[38] Childers, who Shaw knew through his work with Plunkett on the Irish Convention secretariat, had definitively allied himself with de Valera in the Civil War, but Shaw was not persuaded by their arguments. He feigned incomprehension (21 August 1922): "I have a friendly personal regard for Mr Erskine Childers; but like all Englishmen, he is a born anarchist [Shaw was ironically making the point that many Irish nationalists, including Childers (born in England with an Irish mother and English father), Pearse, Connolly, and de Valera had either not been born in Ireland or had only one Irish parent] .... What chance against General Collins has Mr de Valera without military aptitude... Of course he can enjoy the luxury of dying for Ireland after doing Ireland all the damage he can... I suppose it will be settled, as usual, by another massacre of Irishmen by Irishmen" (MWI, 273–275). That the military hero Collins was killed the day after Shaw's article appeared proved a bitter irony.

That Sunday, the Kilteragh guests went to inspect the damage done to the house of Plunkett's neighbour, Sir Henry Lynch-Robinson, the Robinson (1857–1927), eminent Irish Civil Servant and member of the Irish Privy Council (20 August 1922): "To Sir H. _____'s house to see damage &c" (CFS). Charlotte adds that lunch guests included, "Sir J. & Lady Lavery, Bishop of Brisbane, Len[n]ox [Robinson], Mr. [Thomas] McGreevy [poet, later also a director of the National Gallery, and friend of Samuel Beckett], &c. for lunch & tea. GBS left after dinner" (CFS).[39]

Lennox Robinson informed Lady Gregory: "G.B.S. was in great form on Sunday afternoon."

Charlotte stayed on at Kilteragh after Shaw left. On Tuesday, Lynch-Robinson's house was again raided: "At 5 A.M. there was a terrible fusil-lade at Henry Robinson's House – machine gun, rifle & revolver. Daisy came up to my aerie on the roof in her 'nightie' as calm & brave as any man of my acquaintance. She also soothed Mrs. G.B.S. & the maids!" (HP). That day Collins was shot although news of the assassination did not reach Dublin till the following day, when Plunkett noted (23 August 1922): "Wed. Collins died in an ambush in a Co. Cork – a stunning blow" (HP), while Charlotte wrote (23 August 1922): "Wed: At home in morn-ing. Heard of shooting of Michael Collins. Into Dublin in afternoon. To see Æ & Susan [Mitchell] long talk" (CFS). On Wed, Plunkett went to meet Cosgrave, now acting head of the provisional government (HP). On Thursday, Charlotte accompanied Lady Lavery and Lady Fingall to see Collins's body, which had been bought back to Dublin (24 August 1922): "Thurs. Lady Lavery came in the morning. Went with McCormacks [the celebrated Irish tenor John McCormack and his wife] & Lady Fingall to see Michael C. in his coffin in the chapel of the St. Vincent Hospital" (CFS).[40]

Collins body would later be moved to City Hall for the lying-in-state, an image memorialized by John Lavery's painting as well as a much larger canvas of Collins's funeral (the following May, he painted a portrait of Shaw, exhibited at the Royal Academy).

Back in England, Shaw wrote his well-known letter of sympathy to Collins's sister, Johanna ("Hannie") Collins, who also lived in London. Shaw later explained to Hazel Lavery (7 October 1922): "a Fabian at the Summer School told me that Miss Collins was an old friend of his, and begged me to send her a line. I guessed that the line would get through, and sent it."[41] Flexible as ever in his language, Shaw's letter to Hannie characteristically reversed his sentiments about the same facts expressed five days earlier in his *Irish Times* article (24 August 1922): "How could a born soldier die better than at the victorious end of a good fight, falling to the shot of another Irishman—a damned fool, but all the same an Irishman who thought he was fighting for Ireland? … I met Michael for the first and last time on Saturday last, and am very glad I did. I rejoice in his memory, and will not be so disloyal to it as to snivel over his valiant death. So tear up your mourning and hang up your brightest colors in his honor" (*CL3*, 783). About this salute, John Lavery perceptively observed: "Of one thing

I am certain—Shaw has never written a letter to a bereaved person without giving courage, master of natural psychology that he is."[42]

Lady Fingall's embroidered account appeared in her memoir, *Seventy Years Young*: "On Wednesday, August 23, we read the morning papers with horror. Later Mrs Bernard Shaw and I were sitting together over the fire in the Kilteragh study, where Michael Collins had been with us such a short time ago. Suddenly the door opened and Hazel appeared, in deep mourning. She said: "I knew it before I saw the papers. I had seen him in a dream, his face covered with blood." ... Hazel and I went together to see him lying in state in that peaceful white chapel of the nuns at St. Vincent's Hospital, with the tall candles burning at his head and feet. Four splendid young men, in the still unfamiliar [Irish Army] green uniform, guarded him in his last sleep. Michael Collins lay in full uniform, and to him Death had given her full measure of beauty and dignity, increased by the effect of that white bandage around his head, which hid the wound..."[43] Hazel Lavery, according to her biographer, "wanted to wear widow's weeds, but Daisy [Fingall] restrained her. Gogarty [who had performed the autopsy and embalmment for Collins as he had for Arthur Griffith two weeks previously] commented, "We had Lady Lavery full of confidences of Collins. Lady Fingall made her go home and leave the arena to Kitty Kiernan [Collins's fiancée]." Shaw was perhaps the only person to write specifically of Hazel's affair with Collins when he replied to Hazel's letter of thanks for sending condolences to Hannie Collins (a friend of Hazel's). Shaw explained why he had not written earlier (7 October 1922): "I could not very well write to you directly without a certain indelicacy: I had no right to assume—though I knew—that Michael was what I call your Sunday husband [not necessarily implying a sexual liaison nor excluding one]. ... And so away with melancholy: you are a very lucky woman... Charlotte thought that the smile [of Collins] was that of a conqueror. The dead are always triumphant—if they were really alive before."

Charlotte recorded uncertainty in the country before Collins's funeral on Monday, Saturday 26 August 1922,: "Heard bridges, bikes, trains stopped ... Train service resumed in evening" (CFS). As for Arthur Griffith's a few weeks earlier, Plunkett attended the funeral of Michael Collins, one of the largest demonstrations ever in Ireland's capital city: "1922.08.28 Mon. A sad day. Went to Pro-Cathedral. Poor Collins had the biggest funeral I have seen. And the grief was wide and genuine, the vast crowd were marvelously self-disciplined & till I left Dublin (3.15) no shot or bomb was heard" (HP).[44] Plunkett went off to London after the funeral to raise funds for the *Irish Statesman* from wealthy and politically influential Americans while Charlotte spent the rest of the week meeting old Irish friends, her niece, and such Dublin cultural figures as Thomas McGreevy, Alice Green, and Æ. But, as had become almost routine, she fell ill for a couple of days before leaving Kilteragh for England on 2 September.

Sequel

That Plunkett became a Senator in the new Irish Free State having been a Unionist MP in the 1890s as well as having necessarily worked so much with the British government as the most notable Irish public servant in the quarter-century leading up to Irish independence was not to be forgiven by some Irish nationalists. As a result Kilteragh did not long survive this last visit of the Shaws. On 29 and 30 January 1923, with Plunkett away in the United States raising funds for the *Irish Statesman*, Kilteragh was burnt down over two nights by Republicans. Other homes destroyed belonging to those who accepted appointments as Senators of the new Irish Free State included Senator Oliver St. John Gogarty's Renvyle house in the west of Ireland and George Moore's "Moore Hall" on the shore of Lough Carra in Co. Mayo; his brother, Col. Maurice Moore, Roman Catholic, Republican in his political sympathies, and an Irish speaker, and who resided in the house had become an Irish Senator.[45] Even the four-arched bridge leading to Senator Yeats's famous tower house Thoor Ballylee near Coole was blown up; with Yeats away, his wife negotiated with the bombers to spare the tower itself. In practice, targets varied from case to case and locality to locality, often simply depending on how people got on with one another in ordinary civilian life. Because of her articles in *The Nation* documenting the Black and Tan terror around Coole during the Anglo-Irish War, Lady Gregory was assured by local Republicans that Coole would not be attacked although her Persse family home, Roxborough Co. Galway, was burnt down in 1922, as was (partially) Charlotte Shaw's old family home, "Derry," in Rosscarbery, West Cork.[46]

Susan Mitchell wrote that the burning of Kilteragh was an "ugly manifestation of the Irish character ... everything good and bad ... had boiled up ... we are under no illusions now; our vanity is punctured; we have seen our ugly faces in the glass" (qtd. in West, 205). At the time Kilteragh like Coole symbolized much of what was hopeful in early-twentieth-century Ireland. Its loss was a death blow to Plunkett's participation in Irish public life, but not to the work of those Irish organizations he had set in motion. In a letter to R.A. Anderson of the Co-Operative movement, Plunkett wrote (15 February 1923): "The priceless service of the house was the friends of Ireland it brought together—surely for the good of us all" (West, 205). As noted earlier, Shaw reflected to Plunkett's biographer Margaret Digby on Plunkett's propensity for tactless remarks: "Except within his own class he was a bad mixer. And yet with all this against him he was an amiable man whom nobody could dislike, a highly talented writer with a sense of humor, great political intelligence, and tireless public spirit, the greatest political Irishman of his time."[47]

Coole's fate was equally resonant of the birth pains, cultural conflicts, and short memory of the real new Ireland following independence that had failed, inevitably perhaps, to fulfil the high hopes held by many of the people Shaw had met in both houses earlier in the century. Much of the Coole estate had already been acquired by the Congested Districts Board before the house itself was eventually sold in 1927 by Robert Gregory's widow, Margaret, to the Land Commission (taking over the work of the CDB). Lady Gregory, however, continued her tenancy of the house until she died in 1932. Thereafter it quickly fell into disrepair, being demolished in 1941.

Notes

1. Shaw letter of 15 August 1922 from Kelly's Strand Hotel was written in response to the solicitor of two London IRA men, Dunn and O'Sullivan, following their execution on 12 August for the assassination (one of the sparks that ignited the Irish Civil War) on 22 June of Sir Henry Wilson, Irish Unionist and ex-British Army Chief of the Imperial General Staff. According to Whytes auction catalogue (8 November 2014): "1922 (15 August 1922). Manuscript letter written by George Bernard Shaw regarding Dunn and O'Sullivan, to their solicitor. Single octavo page of Kelly's Rosslare Strand Hotel notepaper, written on both sides in Shaw's own hand. Shaw had written in *The Guardian* and *The Nation* about the injustice of the trial of Dunn and O'Sullivan for the murder of Sir Henry Wilson. Here he repeats his view these men were simply lynched, though there was no difficulty in executing them legally." He is acknowledging receipt of the men's statements and approves of the publication of Dunn's but not of O'Sullivan: "if it is sincere he is an egotistical imbecile." Fascinating contribution to this intriguing and murky episode of Irish his-

tory by the Nobel Laureate." http://www.whytes.ie/Irish-Art/i2ArchivesResult.asp?Search=Shaw+Kelly%27s+Hotel

2. "Eveline," "The Sisters," and "After the Races," all later revised for *Dubliners,* were published in *The Irish Homestead* under the name "Stephen Daedalus."

3. The writer's great-grandfather, Frederick Townsend Gahan, chief inspector with the Congested Districts Board for Mayo (and incidentally a third cousin of Charlotte Shaw, née Townsend), travelled with Plunkett from Westport to "Mallaranny" that same day, Friday 18 September 1908; "The weather today was glorious," noted Plunkett (HP).

   HP in brackets here and elsewhere in the text refers to Horace Plunkett's Diaries available on microfilm at the National Library of Ireland, which provides online transcriptions, as in this instance for the year 1908: http://www.nli.ie/pdfs/diaries_of_sir_horace_curzon_plunkett/1908_diary_of_sir_horace_curzon_plunkett.pdf

4. From copy of 1949 letter from Bernard Shaw to Margaret Digby in the Plunkett Foundation, Oxford.

5. *W. B. Yeats: A Life: The Apprentice Mage (1865–1914)*, R.F. Foster (Oxford: Oxford University Press, 1998), 429.

6. SGA in brackets here and later in the text refers to *Shaw, Lady Gregory and the Abbey: A Correspondence and a Record* edited by Dan H. Laurence and Nicholas Grene. Gerrards Cross: Colin Smyth, 1993.

7. CFS in brackets here and elsewhere in the text refers to Charlotte Shaw's yearly engagement diaries, held in the British Library. Much of the information on places, names, and dates in this chapter comes from this source.

8. The distinguished Hugh, 1st Viscount Gough (1779–1869) may have in part inspired Col. Pearce Madigan in Shaw's *O'Flaherty V.C.* (1915). Both Madigan and O'Flaherty are old Gaelic family names associated with Galway, and Persse of course, was Augusta Gregory's maiden name; there had been earlier marriages between Perrse and Gough families!

9. GBS in brackets here and elsewhere in the text refers to Bernard Shaw's yearly engagement diaries, held in the Library of the London School of Economics. His information corroborates and supplements that found in Charlotte Shaw's diaries.

10. See Laurence, Dan H. *Shaw: An Exhibit* (Austin: Humanities Research Center, The University of Texas at Austin, 1977), item 340.

11. On 24 July 1926, Gregory wrote to Shaw: "No, you can't have read that play in my hearing; if you had done so there is no possible chance I should have forgotten it, and I have no memory of it at all." In fact, she had been sick in bed the evening Shaw read the play to Yeats and other guests at Coole; he may have wanted to get Yeats's opinion of the play. The short-

hand draft is misdated "Coole Park, Summer, 1909," when it should be 1910, corrected by Laurence in CL3, 835.

12. http://archiseek.com/2015/1905-kilteragh-foxrock-co-dublin/

13. In two letters in fact, one to Granville Barker on 31 March 1913 in *The Shaw-Barker Letters*, ed. C.B. Purdom (London: Phoenix, 1956), 188, and the other to Mrs. Patrick Campbell on 2 April 1913, in *Bernard Shaw Collected Letters: 1911–1925 Vol. 3* edited by Dan H. Laurence (London: Max Reinhardt, 1985), 164, designated hereafter in the text as CL3.

14. Trevor West, *Horace Plunkett, Co-operation and Politics: An Irish Biography*, (Gerrards Cross, Bucks.: Colin Smyth, 1986).

15. Shaws-HP in brackets here and elsewhere refers to copies of the correspondence between Bernard Shaw, Charlotte Shaw, and Horace Plunkett courtesy of the Plunkett Foundation, Oxford.

16. Their mutual dislike may have been due to shared similarities rather than differences. Gogarty with his derisive Dublin wit was an extreme manifestation of that part of his own personality Shaw was most ambivalent about, and so not predisposed to admire in a fellow Dubliner. See Peter Gahan "Bernard Shaw: Dégringolade and Derision in Dublin," in *Shaw and the City, SHAW 32: The Annual of Bernard Shaw Studies* ed. Desmond Harding (University Park: Pennsylvania State University Press, 2012).

17. Berg Collection, NYPL. Lady Gregory, TS n.d. [1915?] Programmes for three weeks "3 bills each week" for the Abbey Theatre: "Have drawn this up with G.B.S. AG." [in m.s.]

    1st Week: Kathleen ni Houlihan, Playboy; Minutes Wait, Maurice Harte, Workhouse; Mixed Marriage [St John Ervine, 1911], Rising [of the Moon].

    2nd Week: Shanwalla [Gregory, 1915], Sovereign Love; Playboy, or Well [of the Saints]; Riders to the Sea, Mineral Workers, "[m.s.] Minister was B____s Hyacinth."

    3rd Week: [On] Baile's Strand, Patriots [Lennox Robinson, 1912]; Playboy or Well (with Hyacinth [Halvey by Gregory]); [In the] Shadow of the Glen] (or Briary Gap), Birthright, Spreading [the News]

    Matinees. Slough, Deirdre of the Sorrows
    "Only one week to be announced at a time. Matinées (special) held back for the present."

18. See Gregory's letter to Arthur Sinclair, in which she quotes Shaw's high opinion of play and performance to persuade the actor—not as enamoured of Gregory's play as GBS—to tour in the play. Reprinted in Holloway, *Joseph Holloway's Abbey Theatre: a Selection from his unpublished journal: Impressions of a Dublin Playgoer*, eds. Robert Hogan and Michael J. O. Neill with a preface by Harry T. Moore (Carbondale and Edwardsville: Southern University Press, 1967), 171.

19. Originally published in Lady Gregory, *Seventy Years; being the autobiography of Lady Gregory, 1852–1922*, edited and with a foreword by Colin Smythe (Gerrards Cross: Colin Smythe, 1974).

20. In Bernard Shaw, *What Shaw Really Wrote about the War*, edited by J.L. Wisenthal and Daniel O'Leary (Gainesville: University Press of Florida, 2006).

21. From Gregory's manuscript *Memoirs*, 7–8 May 1915, Berg.

22. Bernard Shaw, *What Shaw Really Wrote about the War*, edited by J.L. Wisenthal and Daniel O'Leary (Gainesville: University Press of Florida, 2006), 115.

23. The series of three articles, "How to Settle the Irish Question," were published simultaneously in Ireland, Britain, and the United States that November (27–29 November 1917 in the *Daily Express* and in several Irish papers, and in four parts in the *New York American* 23, 30 December 1917 and 6, 13 January 1918. The Talbot Press in Dublin (together with Constable & Company in London) issued them together as a separate pamphlet in December 1917.

24. Æ had written a Swiftian letter "To the Masters of Dublin," printed in *The Irish Times*, of barely restrained outrage assailing the Dublin employers for their behaviour towards the Dublin workers (7 October 1913): "It remained for the twentieth century and the capital city of Ireland to see an oligarchy of four hundred masters deciding openly upon starving one hundred thousand people, and refusing to consider any solution except that fixed by their pride."

25. For an account of the short-lived National Land Bank, which was absorbed into the Irish Land Commission in 1923, see Denis Cogan's account at: http://www.bureauofmilitaryhistory.ie/reels/bmh/BMH.WS1556.pdf

26. These was another possible William O'Brien, James Connolly and James Larkin's associate William X. O'Brien—the three had founded the Irish Labour Party in 1912 as the political wing of the ITGWU.

27. In an article on Robert Gregory for *The Observer*, Yeats wrote three weeks after his death: "Major Gregory told Bernard Shaw, who visited him in France, that the months since he joined the army had been the happiest of his life." In *Uncollected Prose of W.B. Yeats* Vol. 2, eds. John P. Frayne and Colton Johnson (London: Macmillan, 1975; New York: Columbia University Press, 1977), 431, qtd. in Stanley Weintraub's *Shaw's People*, 110. Weintraub also notes a BBC talk by Yeats as late as 1937, where he acknowledges that he learned from GBS that Gregory "was never happy until he began to fight."

28. See, http://landedestates.nuigalway.ie/LandedEstates/jsp/family-show.jsp?id=2811. And, http://www.thepeerage.com/p24615.htm#i246146. The novelist Elizabeth Bowen of Bowen's Court in north Cork was connected to the Dripsey Bowen-Colthursts.

29. See Peter Gahan, *Bernard Shaw and Beatrice Webb on Poverty and Equality in the Modern World, 1905–1914,* (Palgrave Macmillan, 2017). After their 1910 trip to Coole, Shaw had delivered a major lecture on "Irish Destitution" at the Ancient Concert Rooms, Dublin, reconstituted and edited by Nelson O'Ceallaigh Ritschel in *SHAW 33: The Annual of Bernard Shaw Studies* (University Park: Pennsylvania State University Press, 2013).

30. *Shaw Review,* May 1959.

31. See Laurence's notes in *Letters 4,* 86; and Ada Tyrrell's recollections of the young Shaw in "The Shaws of Dublin: A Symposium," in *Shaw: Interviews and Recollections,* ed. A. M. Gibbs (London: Methuen, 1990), 3–9.

32. Lady Gregory, *The Journals Volume 1: Books 1–29: 10 October 1916–24 February 1925,* edited by Daniel J. Murphy (Gerrards Cross: Colin Smythe, 1978).

33. *Shaw Review,* May 1959: 7.

34. As Lord Mayor of Cork, McSwiney had succeeded Tomas McCurtain, who had been shot dead in his family home by an RIC squad on 20 March 1920.

35. As suggested in Meda Ryan *Michael Collins and the Women Who Spied for Ireland* (Cork: Mercier, 2006), 128ff.

36. Plunkett's practically illegible handwriting is responsible for the slightly different readings quoting Plunkett's diary for 19 August 1922 in Margaret Digby, *Horace Plunkett: an Anglo-American Irishman,* 253–4, and Trevor West, *Horace Plunkett: Co-operation and Politics,* 1986. Kate Targett's enormously valuable transcriptions available online at the National Library of Ireland (www.nli.ie) do not always resolve the confusion.

37. *Hazel: A Life of Lady Lavery 1880–1935,* Sinéad McCoole (Dublin: Lilliput Press, 1996), 97.

38. The pamphlets (in Shaw's possession at Ayot St. Lawrence at the time of his death) are now in the Shaw Papers collection in the British Library: Erskine Childers, *Clause by Clause: a comparison between "The Treaty" and Document no. 2.* Dublin: Irish Nation Committee, [1922]. Bernard Shaw's own copy. BL: Shaw 33; Eamon De Valera, *The Alternative to the "Treaty" ("Document no. 2").* Dublin: Irish Nation Committee, [1922]. BL: Shaw 21

39. Thomas Spring Rice, Lord Monteagle, of Mount Trenchard in Limerick, one of the founders of the IAOS, was also present (HP). His daughter was Irish nationalist Mary Spring Rice, who had participated with Molly Childers in the Howth gun-running and had used Mount Trenchard as a safe house for the IRA during the War of Independence.

40. Plunkett had dined with John McCormack ("of the build & type of Collins, but coarser") and his wife the previous evening at the Gogartys's house (HP).

41. See facsimile of Shaw's letter to Hazel Lavery of 7 October 1922 printed in *Hazel: A Life of Lady Lavery 1880–1935,* Sinéad McCoole (Dublin: Lilliput Press, 1996).

42. Sir John Lavery, *The Life of a Painter* (1940), 228.
43. From *Seventy Years Young, Memories of Elizabeth, Countess of Fingall* told to Pamela Hinkson (London: Collins, 1937), 408–9.
44. As a leading establishment figure, Plunkett was determined to attend Collins's funeral although Collins's history as a gunman meant his decision was not taken lightly. A conversation between Plunkett and his cousin Fingall illustrates how the old landowners in the new Irish state had the Bolshevik revolution in Russia on their minds, fearing the class-implications of the new order (Thurs. 24 August): "Fingall came up to discuss whether we should go to the funeral. He says we made ourselves conspicuous at Griffith's funeral, & were criticised by our class. But Collins was a gunman & if he did not (as Carson asserted in the Lords he did) kill people with his own hand, he must have been privy to the assassination of the police and secret service officers in 1919–20. My view is that these things are due to be forgotten now. Collins has been highly praised by H.M. Gov't for the way he behaved in the making of the Treaty. Certainly he is better than the Republican leaders" (HP).
45. Gregory directly negotiated with the local Republicans, commenting in her journal: "I suppose they have found out the authorship of the *Nation* articles; and though I had not spoken of them or claimed any credit I was pleased" (Gregory, *Journals 1*, Book 15, 288).
46. George Moore accused Gregory's strongly evangelical Protestant Persse family of proselytizing during the 1845–50 famine, with the implication of souperism, that is, using soup as a bribe to convert starving people
    .Charlotte Shaw had sold Derry House, Rosscarbery, in 1915 to Sergeant A.M. Sullivan, who had so inadequately defended Roger Casement at his trial in 1916. His father had been editor of *The Nation* associated with the Young Ireland movement in the 1860s. However, during the Anglo-Irish War (Irish War of Independence), as a Crown appointee Sullivan led prosecutions against Irish Nationalists, earning the enmity of Republicans and making "Derry" vulnerable to attack.
47. From copy of 1948 letter in the Plunkett Foundation, Oxford, from Bernard Shaw to Margaret Digby, Plunkett's biographer.

REFERENCES

Childers, Erskine. 1922. *Clause by Clause: A Comparison Between "The Treaty" and Document No. 2.* Dublin: Irish Nation Committee.
Digby, Margaret. 1949. *Horace Plunkett: An Anglo-American Irishman.* Oxford: Blackwell.
Foster, Roy F. 1998. *W. B. Yeats: A Life: The Apprentice Mage (1865–1914).* Oxford: Oxford University Press.

Gahan, Peter. 2012. Bernard Shaw: Dégringolade and Derision in Dublin. In *Shaw and the City, SHAW 32: The Annual of Bernard Shaw Studies*, ed. Desmond Harding. University Park: Pennsylvania State University Press.

Gibbs, A.M., ed. 1990. *Shaw: Interviews and Recollections.* London: Methuen.

Gregory, Augusta. 1974. *Seventy Years; Being the Autobiography of Lady Gregory, 1852–1922* . Ed. and with a Foreword by Colin Smythe. Gerrards Cross: Colin Smythe.

———. 1978. *The Journals Volume 1: Books 1–29: 10 October 1916–24 February 1925.* Ed. Daniel J. Murphy. Gerrards Cross: Colin Smythe.

Holloway, Joseph. 1967 *Joseph Holloway's Abbey Theatre: A Selection from His Unpublished Journal: Impressions of a Dublin Playgoer.* Ed. Robert Hogan and Michael J. O. Neill with a Preface by Harry T. Moore. Carbondale/Edwardsville: Southern University Press.

Laurence, Dan H. 1977. *Shaw: An Exhibit.* Austin: Humanities Research Center, The University of Texas at Austin.

Laurence, Dan H., and Nicholas Grene, eds. 1993. *Shaw, Lady Gregory and the Abbey: A Correspondence and a Record.* Gerrards Cross: Colin Smyth.

Lavery, John. 1940. *The Life of a Painter.* London: Cassell and Company.

McCoole, Sinéad. 1996. *Hazel: A Life of Lady Lavery 1880–1935.* Dublin: Liliput Press.

Peter, Gahan. 2017. *Bernard Shaw and Beatrice Webb on Poverty and Equality in the Modern World, 1905–1914.* London: Palgrave Macmillan.

Plunkett, Horace. 1904. *Ireland in the New Century.* London: John Murray.

Plunkett, Elizabeth. 1937. *Seventy Years Young, Memories of Elizabeth, Countess of Fingall,* Told to Pamela Hinkson. London: Collins.

Russell, George (Æ). 1916. *The National Being.* Dublin: Maunsell.

Ryan, Meda. 2006. *Michael Collins and the Women Who Spied for Ireland.* Cork: Mercier.

Shaw, Bernard. 1985. *Collected Letters: 1911–1925 Vol. 3.* Ed. Dan H. Laurence. London: Max Reinhardt.

———. 2006. *What Shaw Really Wrote About the War.* Ed. J.L. Wisenthal and Daniel O'Leary. Gainesville: University Press of Florida.

———. 2013. "Irish Destitution (1910)" at the Ancient Concert Rooms, Dublin, Reconstituted and Edited by Nelson O'Ceallaigh Ritschel in *SHAW 33: The Annual of Bernard Shaw Studies* University Park: Pennsylvania State University Press.

Valera, De, and Eamon. 1922. *The Alternative to the "Treaty" ("Document No. 2").* Dublin: Irish Nation Committee.

West, Trevor. 1986. *Horace Plunkett, Co-Operation and Politics: An Irish Biography.* Gerrards Cross: Colin Smyth.

CHAPTER 12

Shaw's Ireland (and the Irish Shaw) in the International Press (1914–1925)

Gustavo A. Rodríguez Martín

Bernard Shaw has been widely neglected within the Irish literary tradition and within the Irish cultural heritage at large. Particularly in earlier times, a reductionist fixation with the Gaelic language, and other somewhat chauvinistic ideas, relegated Shaw not simply to the "no-man's-land" of the Anglo-Irish tradition, but practically to English literature. The rationale behind this classification was apparently due to his plays not being "informed by the spirit of the race."[1] This is not to imply that part of this critical neglect is not Shaw's "fault" to some extent, for his kingdom was not, at least, of this country. Take, for instance, the recurrent interest in internationalism in his political writings throughout his ideological evolution.[2] Or the two proselytizing world tours he completed alongside his wife in the twilight of his life and career, mostly for the sake of spreading the Shavian gospel.[3] However, it is worth mentioning that Shaw and Charlotte registered as citizens of the Irish Free State[4]—while retaining British citizenship—after the passing of the Irish Citizenship and Nationality Act of 1935[5]; an event that added to the widespread confusion about his nationality, as he acknowledged in a letter to Sydney Cockerell:

G. A. Rodríguez Martín (✉)
Universidad de Extremadura, Caceres, Spain

© The Author(s) 2020
A. McNamara, N. O'Ceallaigh Ritschel (eds.), *Bernard Shaw and the Making of Modern Ireland*, Bernard Shaw and His Contemporaries, https://doi.org/10.1007/978-3-030-42113-7_12

237

> My nationality is confused by the fact that out of my 88 years, only 20 have
> been lived where I was born. Correctly, I am an Irish Londoner; but I retain
> my Irish citizenship and nature, and am still a foreigner with an objective
> view (invaluable) of England, that "distressful country" in whose public
> service I am a missionary.[6]

Regardless of nationality controversies, it is true that "Shaw's ambitions
never included celebrity as an Irish playwright" as he was more interested
in the wider scene of "international capitalism and aspiring international
socialism."[7] Quite a different matter, of course, is the role Bernard Shaw
played in how Ireland slowly gained a say in international forums and was
incipiently recognized as a free country in its own right. His popularity
and socio-political influence made him the perfect spokesman for Ireland's
political claims and the perfect advocate against Britain's intrusion in Irish
affairs—particularly after he had proved everybody in Britain wrong
during the Great War in matters of international policy. In Shaw's own
words, "Common Sense About the War" turned out to be an "intolerable
document which afterwards turned out to be so exasperatingly right in
every detail."[8]

The purpose of this chapter is to gauge Shaw's international influence
as a supporter of Irish political independence—albeit in his own, paradoxical terms—by analysing what was reported of his political opinions in the
press outside Britain and Ireland, and how much media coverage those
opinions received. In order to do so, the first section of this chapter will
analyse the type of public image Shaw enjoyed—both as a playwright and
as a committed activist—according to the international press of the time.
Later, I will try to use that public image as the basis for a specific analysis
of his role in the growing worldwide concern for the political situation in
Ireland, from the outbreak of the Great War to the mid-1920s, in the
wake of the Irish Civil War. This "foreign" perspective reveals itself as particularly relevant in light of the sad truth: Shaw was the living paradigm of
the Biblical axiom that "no prophet is accepted in his own country"[9]:

> His countrymen did not listen to him very often, but that is the nature of
> things. Outside his country the prophet was not without an audience, and it
> was undoubtedly a larger one than any other Irishman of the day could
> command. For a period of more than sixty years that audience listened to
> what he had to say about virtually every important question in Ireland's
> political and social life.[10]

Although what this chapter tries to assess is the impact Shaw had on that larger audience, some methodological caveats are in order. First, Shaw's views were on occasion initially made public in journalistic texts published in the British Isles, later to achieve wider circulation in the foreign press. Consequently, the conclusions herein will be drawn not only from the literal content of the articles in question, but also from the divergent reception that the same statement may have had at home and abroad. As is often the case with all textual exegeses, much can be inferred from what is absent, downplayed or misquoted.

Additionally, from the point of view of the type of newspapers that will be covered here for the most part, it must be said that a deliberate effort has been made to include references to papers of limited range and/or circulation. It is my contention that much of the significance of Shaw's opinions in the press can be assessed by examining how minor regional publications also sought to include his statements, even when they had already been reported elsewhere and the newspaper in question would normally focus on a limited number of international news items.

Finally, the nationality of the newspapers that will be mentioned here is also worth commenting on. For obvious reasons—ranging from linguistic affinity to political relevance—former British colonies and member countries of the Commonwealth are the most usual propagators of Shaw's views. In addition, it is not uncommon to find Irish journalists and editors who migrated to countries like Australia, New Zealand, Canada, or the United States and founded their own newspapers there.[11] These newspapers usually contain a larger share of Irish news items, Shaw on occasion being their source. This chapter, however, also tries to provide readers with a sample selection of European and South American newspaper articles that will hopefully complement the general picture with opinions from outside the Anglo-Saxon world.

BERNARD SHAW AS AN INTERNATIONAL FIGURE

One of the earliest references to Shaw in the overseas press fittingly focuses on his physical appearance and personal eccentricities:

His particular métier is art-criticism, and at every Press View, a tall figure, pencil in hand, with a fair beard, regular features, and a general appearance of smoothness about him, may be seen making the round of the pictures with his brother critics. His attire, too, is peculiar; it is all-wool, of a light-brownish tinge, neither linen collar nor silk tie being tolerated. This is but one of Mr. Shaw's little feats; their name is legion.[12]

This is not the only example of a clipping that shows the playwright in an aura of mystery and mysticism. Some later press releases speak of Shaw as

a rugged-looking, bearded man, who dresses in a rough suit of "home-spun," and disdains the arts of the toilet. His face is remarkable chiefly for the darkness and brilliance of his eyes, which proclaim him a man of striking originality and force. He is an apt platform speaker, his strong earnestness of utterance being relieved, but not lessened, by a marked vein of caustic humour. He hates shams above all the rest.[13]

These outward characteristics were, and still are, one of the reasons why he enjoys such enduring popularity as an icon of culture. At any rate, we immediately find in the above quotation many of the features that will define Shaw's worldview and, consequently, his view of Irish politics as well. Even if well known to the reader, it is worth reiterating that elements of early self-awareness, socio-political commitment, and anti-conventionalism shape much of what he would go on to express on the "Irish Question."

In strictly professional terms, Bernard Shaw became an internationally acclaimed playwright soon after his first plays premiered in London—or elsewhere.[14] To give readers a general idea of how much press coverage these plays received in Europe alone, it suffices to cite a small sample of the European newspaper articles that mention or review productions of his plays outside the country where the newspaper is published.[15] For example, *La Stampa* describes the Court Theatre's production of *Major Barbara* as a case of "satire going hand in hand with paradox and sophistry."[16] A year before that, *The Sunday Star* (Washington DC) includes a short paragraph on how "Miss Annie Russell [...] gets down to London every fortnight for a conference with Bernard Shaw over" Major Barbara, "which he is writing for her."[17]

In addition to the international attention received by the production of his plays in London, these were later (sometimes earlier) performed in translation all over continental Europe at a rate that much exceeds the scope of this chapter—a quick look at Appendix I of Henderson's *George Bernard Shaw: Man of the Century* gives an immediate idea of how popular his plays became in countries as distant from each other as Egypt, Japan or Argentina.[18] Even these plays in translation were mentioned in press reports in other countries; for example, *Le Temps* reproduces a translated report of the Berlin theatrical scene, where "Bernard Shaw [his plays] is at home after a couple of years" and "*Major Barbara* ran for a few nights."[19]

The above excerpts suggest that Shavian drama was always analysed both from an artistic point of view and from a socio-political perspective. Indeed, in ideological terms, Bernard Shaw soon gained a reputation as a provocative, forward thinker who would "make you open a discussion with yourself and change your points of view."[20] Already during the 1900s, Shaw's witty remarks were quoted to illustrate the most disparate topics— from the alleged national pessimism in France[21] to the anarchism of the German socialists—all the while Shaw accusing them of being conservative members of the bourgeoisie.[22] These examples are only the consequence of his early commitment with the socialist cause at large, and much more specifically with Fabianism. For instance, in 1895 Mary Oswald published a historical account of socialism in England in *La Revue Socialiste*[23]—a text that cites Shaw as one of the leading members of the then-emerging Fabian Society. Later on, the progressive detachment of the Fabian Society from the more radical wings of Marxism earned Shaw a few ironic comments in the international press, arguing that he wanted to found a socialist party "for perfect gentlemen" who "occupy the high ranks of the gentry."[24] However, Shaw retained throughout his entire life a caustic vein that buttressed his zeal for world-betterment. A popular favourite was quoted in a Canadian newspaper when the Purity League movement expressed their outrage at "an Empire Music Hall girl who was earning £30 a week from a life of shame."[25] Shaw (only "a critic" at the time) retorted: "this single utterance is calculated to make more women turn to a life of prostitution in one week that would result from the exhibition of living pictures for ten days."

Finally, the rejection of violence is a major personality trait in Shaw that was also underscored by the foreign press. As Alejandro Plana notes in his review[26] of "Common Sense About the War," "Bernard Shaw abhors violence. Death is odious to him, both in the slaughterhouse and in the battlefield. That is why he is a vegetarian and an anti-militarist." The fundamental nature of this notion poses, as we shall see, central limitations on his showing "any form of patriotism either for the country he left one day or for the country that has bankrupted him."[27]

If Shaw had earned a worldwide reputation thanks to his personal, professional, and political inimitableness, the international resonance of his views on the Independence of Ireland and the ensuing years of turmoil turned out to be second to none. We shall try to look into those resounding echoes as this chapter progresses.

SHAW IN THE AFTERMATH OF THE EASTER RISING

Readers are no doubt familiar with the controversial opinions expressed by Shaw prior and during the Great War, but what remains relevant nonetheless is that "the moral shock they produced" put Shaw in the spotlight forever.[28] From the middle towards the end of this global conflict, the Irish revolutionary period began as a not entirely unrelated side-effect that Shaw was morally obliged to address. First, because he was the "objective foreigner" who knew all too well the weaknesses of the three factions that the Irish Convention was meant to reconcile; in his somewhat cynical pragmatism he was aware that—despite patriotic fervour,

> [a] wise Irishman might well pray that his country may have the happiness to be forgotten when the lions divide their prey: one hardly wants the unfortunate island to be flung like a bone to a half-satisfied dog as Cyprus was at the Berlin conference.[29]

At the same time, he became an (un)willing symbol of Irishness for many outside Ireland. Shaw was, in the eyes of many, "the most fanatical dreamer of the sons of Ireland."[30] And his words were carefully observed because "in Ireland we justly regard him as a much greater man than Shakespeare."[31] On a broader scale—in a notion that parallels what was said above about his literary ascription—Shaw was considered a major member of "the splendid band of progressive thinkers and writers" that had aided and reinforced the British Parliament.[32] This is not to imply that those who listened to Shaw did not know that he was, first and foremost, Irish. Thus, Émile Legouis argues in the *Revue des Deux Mondes* that Shaw's critical attitude was partly due to the fact that he was Irish.[33]

Given the status that he was granted as a sage—as the spokesman of unusual yet useful ideas—Shaw's views after the Easter Rebellion were reproduced all over the world. Specifically, his article in *The New Statesman* ("Neglected Morals of the Irish Rising") was quoted extensively alongside reports of the events.[34] Poor translation and different journalistic agendas account for the different sections of the article that were quoted, sometimes erroneously. *ABC* (Spain), for example, speaks of the "slain Irish men and women," instead of the "Sinn Fein Volunteers" and focuses on the "patriotism of the Irish martyrs"—an assimilation that is to be expected in a Catholic newspaper.[35] *La Vanguardia*, in turn, published a telegraphic report that equally stresses how "the Irish rebels died for their country, just like the soldiers."[36] Part of the Canadian media, however, chose to highlight Shaw's satire in the concluding remarks of his article, when he suggested that "the members of the Sein Finn [*sic.*] should be handed over to General Joffre to be formed into an Irish brigade, and allowed to expiate their offences by fighting for France."[37] A similar focus was placed by *The Sydney Morning Herald* and *The Washington Post*, an indication that form is almost as important as content for an idea to be successful and spread quickly—Shaw no doubt needed visibility for his suggestions.[38] In New Zealand alone, the "Shavian proposal" is quoted dozens of times, including articles in the dailies with the widest circulation in the country.[39]

A few days after the publication of his "Neglected Morals," when Shaw abhorred of the executions following the Easter Rising, his voice was echoed by many of the leading newspapers, especially in America.[40] One can also find reports on his condemning words in the most disparate newspapers in the United States, such as *The Rock Island Argus*, *The Topeka State Journal* or *The Harrisburg Telegraph*.[41] Shaw's reputation was heightened by his response to these events, to the extent that Frank Harris suggested that Asquith should resign and give his job to Bernard Shaw, "the ablest man in England." It is worthy of note that these laudatory opinions were also reproduced in the foreign press, both within the English-speaking world and elsewhere.[42]

The coverage that Shaw's statements received worldwide is even more noteworthy, at least in these early stages of the Irish process for independence, given the British censorship on the question. For example, *El Nacional* (Mexico) is able to report "despite English censorship" that "many Irish rebels are still in arms."[43] Censoring discordant voices like Shaw's was a logical choice for the British government, particularly because during the Great War political criticism was eagerly reported by the press of the German-speaking countries, partly as a means of war propaganda. Understandably, Shaw's letter "Shall Roger Casement hang?" was rejected by *The Times* and was finally published by the *Manchester Guardian*.[44] Immediately, Shaw's support of the cause of Sir Roger Casement was summarized in the *Hamburger Anzeiger*, throwing in relief the fact that "with bitter irony he [Shaw] attacks the British government and proves that Casement should be hanged, not because he is a traitor, but because he is an Irishman."[45] An analogous reading of Shaw's stance was made in a much more detailed article in the *Altonaer Nachrichten* where, together with the ironic argument that Casement was to be hanged on nationalistic grounds, the letter is quoted or paraphrased practically paragraph by paragraph, including Shaw's implicit tipping of the scales in favour of Germany when he presented his personal case as a parallelism for Casement's situation:

> I have been employed by Germany as a playwright for many years, and by the Austrian Emperor in the great theatre in Vienna which is part of his household. I have received thousands of pounds for my services. I was recognized in this way when the English theatres were contemptuously closed to me. I was compelled to produce my last important play [*Pygmalion*] in Berlin in order that it might not be prejudiced by the carefully telegraphed abuse of the English press. Am I to understand that it is therefore my duty to fight for Germany and Austria, and that, in taking advantage of the international reputation which I unquestionably owe to Germany more than to any other country to make the first statement of the case against her which could have convinced anybody outside England, I was biting the hand of the venerable Franz Josef, whose bread I had eaten? I cannot admit it for a moment.[46]

To add fuel to the fire, the article was signed by the British Consul General. Unsurprisingly, it is not at all uncommon at the time to find articles that consider Shaw some sort of "germanophile" who displays "Teutonic buffoonery"—though always outside Germany.[47]

Part of the agenda of the anti-British media in trying to make the most of Casement's trial and execution had to do with exposing how outraged America was at the whole process, thereby damaging the relations between both countries.[48] In fact, the only other newspaper that printed Shaw's letter in full was *The New York American,* a gesture that secured further attention to Shaw's words in the United States.[49] For example, to mention a few of the lesser-known newspapers that publicized and supported Shaw's plea—even before the letter was reprinted in full by *The New York American*—the *Goodwin's Weekly* "earnestly hope that Bernard Shaw's appeal for Sir Roger Casement will be heard by the British Government and granted."[50] Similarly, *The Ogden Standard* reproduces Shaw's argument that Casement should not be executed because "high treason is not a sin, but often is an act of exalted virtue"[51]—a notion that was also reported by the *Richmond Times-Dispatch* in making the case that Sir

Roger should be treated as "a prisoner of war."[52] Even after Casement's death, we find examples of support for his cause based on Shaw's claims. Thus, Luis Araquistáin condemns the execution and reminds readers of *España* that "Britain's prestige would rise among the neutral nations if his life was spared, as Bernard Shaw said on the day before the execution" and wonders "why England would refuse such an easy moral triumph."[53] The effect of Shaw's appeals and their impact on the American press should not be taken too lightly, for they seemed to make an impact on international relations. Take for instance, the open letter that Henry Arthur Jones addressed to Anatole France, published in *Le Journal des Débats Politiques et Littéraires*, in which he cites Shaw as one who "despite bleating most loudly for peace" tried to "create conflict between England and America."[54]

Major media attention was again afforded Shaw after he published his "How to Settle the Irish Question" in November 1917.[55] One of the main tenets of this series of articles was the unclear political status of Ireland— strictly speaking, neither part of the United Kingdom nor a colony of the Commonwealth. In this respect, Shaw attacked "the now hopelessly obsolete institution at Westminster that calls itself an imperial Parliament, and is neither imperial nor national nor English nor Scottish nor Irish, neither flesh nor fowl nor good red herring." Of course, readers in the "colonies" were very interested in the effects these ideas may have; thus, the following cablegram (with minor alterations) was published in several of the leading newspapers in Australia:

> Mr. Bernard Shaw, in an article, propounds as a solution of the Irish question the establishments of National Parliaments in Ireland, Scotland, and England, and also a Federal Parliament for the British Isles, in which Ireland would retain representation; also an Imperial conference, in which Ireland would be represented, and similarly Australia and New Zealand.[56]

Although the Irish component may have been overlooked to a certain extent, it is nonetheless possible that these articles stirred a sense of solidarity among other members of the Commonwealth, especially Australia. At the same time, a much more political reading of Shaw's articles can be found in the American press, as reported by *The Washington Times*.[57] In fact, by then Shaw's interest in politics was well affirmed, and even his alleged pursuit of an MP seat at the 1918 general election was echoed widely in countries like New Zealand, Australia, the United States, or Canada.[58] The truth is that Shaw did not want an MP seat, but he may have been seen as an ideal candidate when—Labour being resolved to become the second party in the United Kingdom—he provided the inspiration for Labour Ministers to abandon the government coalition:

> [Shaw] achieved his one historic moment, at a special Labour conference on 14 November, with the words: "Go back to Lloyd George and say: Nothing doing." Most Labour ministers resigned. The few who remained—including George Barnes in the war cabinet—ceased to be members of the Labour party. Labour fought the election uncomplainingly as an avowed Opposition.[59]

Despite the fact that he was reported as a candidate for East Middlesborough, it is interesting to note how most newspapers chose to put this piece of news alongside news about the Sinn Fein candidates and other articles on Irish politics before the election. The news of his running for Parliament did not attract as much attention outside the English-speaking world, despite his plays and dramatic art being favourably reviewed all around the world.

Once the Great War was over—if it ever was—Shaw's focus turned towards Irish politics without the dangling side-effects of the global armed conflict and what we now call geopolitical strategy. For example, the religious dimension of the Irish conflict was open again to be addressed from an Irish perspective, because during World War I, as Shaw put it, "the church of the Prince of Peace has been turned into a recruiting station.[60]" It is interesting to note that—despite his criticism of "crosstianity" and his controversial opinions on religion at large—his vision of Ireland was largely framed by religious questions, albeit with the usual socioeconomic lining.[61] The following anecdote, recorded by *The Edmonton Bulletin* on occasion of his 61st birthday, suffices to illustrate this point:

> During his address [to a big meeting of Protestant Home Rulers] Shaw argued for the cessation of petty religious strife in Ireland, so that social reforms in the Emerald Isle could proceed. [...] "Both [my parents] were Protestants... A large part of a mother's duties to me were discharged by an Irish nurse. That nurse was a Roman Catholic, and she never put me to bed without sprinkling me with holy water." Referring to the laughter which greeted his remark, Mr. Shaw added: "I cannot imagine anything that is less worthy of laughter, or more touching, than this picture of an Irish Catholic woman sprinkling holy water, and you know what holy water was to her, on a little Protestant child whose parents grossly underpaid her."[62]

At the same time, it is now becoming clear to all the press that Shaw can no longer be called an Anglo-Irish writer, and that his commitment to the Irish cause—even if in his own terms—is unquestionable. This Shavian take on Irish politics fittingly had cultural and literary roots, as reported by *El Paso Herald* after his lecture on "Literature in Ireland" at the Little Theatre. The political interpretation of the lecture seemed to be the most interesting one for the newspaper, for it highlights:

> Most of the poetry connected with the Irish rising was not Irish at all in any particular way, nor was everything represented by the Gaelic League and Sinn Fein Irish literature, he said. An Ireland of the Gaelic League and Sinn Fein was as much a tourish [*sic.*] guide book Ireland as was the Ireland of Charles Lever.[63]

Thus, we can now find evidence to explain why "some have doubted Bernard Shaw's Irishism which seems the queerer as nearly everything he has written has carried a shillelagh concealed between the covers."[64] This misguided notion—one of the key factors that frames this chapter, as stated at the outset—resulted in the occasional joke at the expense of bigoted national stereotypes.[65] For instance, *The Washington Herald* laughs at Shaw when he "recommends that every able-bodied man in England be made to work" because "he didn't mention Ireland." It is in this context that Shaw becomes "an Irishman" who is "always advancing the most preposterous ideas."[66]

Around this time, we find a transition period during the Irish War of Independence and before the Irish Civil War. This period is dominated by a growing tension framed by the need of a strong government in Ireland; a tension that some sought to assuage with initiatives like the Dominion League—both issues discussed by Shaw in articles in the press.[67] Shaw was, like many others, surprised by the events that unfolded—later leading to crueller alternatives. However, even though his involvement and presence in the foreign press was rare outside his literary career, his stature as an icon of culture led the *Gettysburg Times* to describe the Declaration of Irish Independence at the Dail Eireann as "paradoxical proceedings" that "no writer except an Irishman like George Bernard Shaw could do justice to."[68]

During this period, Shaw remained engaged with several other political causes, such as the English miners' strike of 1920, where the Spanish press mention him as being "the leader of the department of propaganda in the

Miners' Confederation."[69] He also maintained at this time his political commitment to international affairs. For example, he was publicized by *The Washington Herald* as one of the Big Six who were called on to share their expert opinions on the Conference on the Limitations of Armaments that was to be held in Washington DC.[70] It is therefore of interest that—outside his playwriting career—Shaw's presence in the media is not limited to Irish issues. To cite just two illustrative examples, soon after the end of the Irish Civil War, the Italian press made reference to his forthcoming visit to Soviet Russia—just a few months before the same newspaper had commented on his words on the occasion of Lenin's death.[71] Furthermore, French newspapers quoted his alleged intentions to run for Parliament in 1922 for the constituency of Edinburgh, whereas several New Zealand papers focused on the more accurate element that he had been "invited by the West Edinburgh Labour leaders to contest the seat at the next election."[72]

This transition period was summarized by Shaw in his article "The Irish Crisis," which was again echoed extensively in the foreign press.[73] Once again, different newspapers or the press from different countries as a whole had varying takes on the contents of the article—hence the passages they quoted. To begin with, it suffices to look at the fact that the version in *The New York American* used a much longer headline that included the phrase "Ireland will have to govern itself," whereas *The Manchester Guardian* chose the shorter, less compromising title of "The Irish Crisis" by which the article is usually known. In general, many reports on Shaw's article decidedly emphasized the common ground of his socialist internationalism. Consequently, one often finds references to independence being "a fine shibboleth for a slave; but the moment he is free he discovers that we are members, one with another, and that independence is an egocentric dream."[74] This idea is not entirely alien to the uprisings in Egypt and India, and not entirely unrelated to the Irish situation either. For example, Shaw was quoted in *The Advocate* (Melbourne) thus:

> "British may declare that they never shall be slaves," says Bernard Shaw, "They should also see to it that they do not make slaves of anyone else." The risings in India and Egypt are but the forerunners of the great struggles that are to come, and which will free the peoples of those lands, for, with each successive rising, the conquered grow more conscious of their powers. As Ibrahim Rashad says in the "Irish Tear Book":—"But, when all is told, we find ourselves faced with one fundamental fact, and that is that 'God helps

those who help themselves.' Ireland learnt that lesson from experience very dearly bought. Egypt, although she learnt it in a much shorter time, knows it well, and has definitely made up her mind to live free or perish on the altar of liberty."[75]

At any rate, the plea for the independence of Ireland, and the fact that "the oath to the King was a mere incident," did not escape the press overseas either.[76]

As a rather curious note, one must point out that by now Bernard Shaw is such a popular figure that his public image is associated on occasion—even tangentially—with whatever point a journalist wants to make. This is, indeed, a question that goes beyond the scope of this chapter, but it is nonetheless striking that the wife of the Sinn Fein Minister of Propaganda (Mabel Fitzgerald) should be referred to as Shaw's former secretary. All along, however, part of the puzzled public still wondered whether Shaw was Irish or English.[77]

Once the Irish Civil War broke out, Shaw's opinions in the press became, if not more prominent, certainly more relevant; and they also helped to define his position on the question within his general ideological disposition towards war. During the war, it was clear for Shaw that the time to die for Ireland was over—it was now "time to live for Ireland." This refrain is informed by his disapproval of the armed conflict and its appalling consequences for all, as he was able to witness first-hand after his 1922 visit to Ireland.[78] His comments, made on the eve of his return to London, were reported by numerous newspapers abroad—particularly within the English-speaking world.[79] Most of the excerpts from his article in the *Irish Times* that were quoted abroad emphasize his repulsion towards recent events. This, in turn, made him express an understandable lack of confidence in De Valera's political genius and in what he could do to avert "another massacre of Irishmen by Irishmen." The whole situation was described by Shaw as Ireland suffering "from an epidemic of homicidal mania under the guise of patriotism."[80] In addition, another of the oft-quoted passages from his article at home highlights the "idiocy of the rebels."[81] Both notions seem to signal a personal, moral exhaustion due to the constant confrontation—an exhaustion that was in all likelihood shared by many of Shaw's countrymen. As he himself put it in the introductory section to his article, "what can anyone say that has not been said already until people are so tired of it that the words have lost all meaning?" Despair and helplessness are unusual feelings in Shaw's writings, but being at a loss for words is even rarer. A corollary to this can be extracted from Shaw's words after Arthur Griffith's death, reproduced in *The New York Times*, stating that "the madness of Ireland is a matter of principle."[82] This sentence was later quoted by the French *Bulletin Périodique de la Presse Américaine*, which takes it to epitomize the sentiment among those who "do not yet know what to say" amidst such a rapid succession of shocking events.[83]

A few weeks before the civil war ended, and after Shaw had been "sounded as to whether I would, if invited, accept service on the Senate of the Irish Free State," he published an article on "How to Restore Order in Ireland" that, once again, earned reprints and commentaries all over the world. Full reprints are to be found in countries as far apart as the United States and New Zealand.[84] Among the excerpts that were picked out from the article, most foreign newspapers chose the following paragraph, carefully scandalous in its wording:

> Every citizen should receive, on registration, not only his card, but a gun (in the general American sense) and a supply of ammunition... it should be impressed on him that if, on receiving an official alarm by whistle, bell, maroon, or what not, or on hearing shots or cries for help or sounds of disturbance in the streets, he did not at once sally from his house, weapon in hand, by night or day, to co-operate with his neighbors in shooting down all rioters and incendiaries, and arresting all persons whose registration cards proved them to be strangers, he would be liable to be shot for cowardice and desertion.[85]

The most important thing, however, is the question of how to "make Ireland a country fit for civilized men to live in."[86] Indeed, Shaw's concern for safety, order, and civilization in his country rubs off onto other political writings of his, even when they are not directly related to Ireland. So, for example, his commentary on the British Parliamentary elections includes "an illustration from Ireland" because "the Irish people have taken to indiscriminate sabotage. They destroy buildings, and they destroy railways, and then they destroy each other. And that will continue unless somebody with no nonsense about democracy takes the situation in hand."[87]

In the aftermath of the civil war, however, Shaw dropped much of his previous irony and caustic paradox and strived to restore a positive image of Ireland. The best way to publicize the gradual return to normalcy was "venturing into the South of Ireland for my summer holiday," an experience he described in a letter to the London *Times*.[88] The letter ends on the superlative claim that Ireland "is therefore at this moment probably the safest country in the world for visitors." Although it is difficult to ascertain how much good this letter did for the tourism industry in the country, at least the international references in the letter must have contributed to the slow recuperation of a normalized image of Ireland, especially among the countries that were on the receiving end of the Irish diaspora, where the news from Ireland was a serious matter.[89]

This attempt at improving Ireland's outward image also had an internal counterbalance in Shaw's writing agenda. He was afraid that the new political system would soon fail if Ireland poured "the fresh water of the Free State into the dirty water of Dublin Castle."[90] His article "On Throwing Out Dirty Water" was reprinted partially or in full in different newspapers from the United States, Australia, and New Zealand, for example.[91]

At this point in time, Shaw reached what may be deemed a plateau in his production in all areas: after he completed *Saint Joan* (1923), he did not finish a new play for five years.[92] In addition, he had just published his political and economic *magnum opus* (*The Intelligent Woman's Guide* in 1928), and had reached the summit of international recognition when he was awarded the Nobel Prize (1925). Either because he did not foresee the twenty-odd years of creative life that were still ahead of him at the time, or simply because he had already said everything he had to say, Shaw would not return to the public arena as often—nor as intensely. Up until the end of the Irish civil war, however, his opinions and press references thereof suggest a series of pervading traits in his views about the political situation in Ireland.

To begin with, Shaw always envisioned an ideal, future Ireland as a country that would override the ethnographic clichés that still persist to this day, unfortunately. This Copernican revolution needed a country that would look outwards rather than inwards—a natural consequence of his advocacy for internationalism. This, in turn, earned him a great deal of criticism because his ideas necessarily implied acceptance and understanding towards the "enemy" in many of the Irish narratives: England; and also because in a period of heightened international tension his discordant, personal voice made him an enemy of all national causes, for he did not blindly support any of them. The line from *O'Flaherty V.C.*, as many others of his, turned out to be prognostic: "You'll never have a quiet world till you knock the patriotism out of the human race." However, it is obvious that an independent Ireland had to begin by acknowledging its interdependence in international forums and cut the apron strings from the nanny metropolis—however cruel and dictatorial she may have been. This whole process had to be accomplished, furthermore, with the smallest amount of bloodshed possible. For Shaw, it was painful to witness "massacres of Irishmen by Irishmen"—much more so when there were many other pressing issues that were the real oppressors of the Irish: poverty, inequality, illiteracy. Needless to say, the Gordian knot of the Irish conundrum lay in the "petty religious strife" that prevented many of the much-needed advancements from materializing. At any rate, regardless of his sardonic choice of words, Shaw remained an optimist—a stance that fleshed out in his self-appointed role as cultural ambassador of Ireland and in his thoughtful warnings about the precarious balance that any emerging political system must try to keep. In the words of José Alsina, "Shaw's strong personality does not exclude, but affirms, his Irish nature."[93]

But for all his ideals and thunderous, insightful opinions Shaw could not have made such an impact if it was not for the media attention he received. This is, first and foremost, a direct consequence of his successful playwriting career—and also a by-product of his carefully crafted persona. But let us discard for a moment the motto of Shaw's beloved London School of Economics (LSE) ("rerum cognoscere causas") and abandon the pursuit of the causes of things. Then, what is left is the realization that Shaw's public image played a major role in heightening the visibility of the political situation in Ireland. He helped to shape what the world knew and thought about Ireland in these years of widespread upheaval. If Shaw had done nothing else, he would still be worth writing about.

NOTES

1. Ernest A. Boyd, *Ireland's Literary Renaissance* (New York: John Lane Company, 1916), 8.
2. See, for example, Bernard Shaw, *Irish Nationalism and Labour Internationalism* (London: The Labour Party, 1920); or "Socialism at Seventy," In *The Socialism of Shaw*, ed. James Fuchs (New York: Vanguard Press, 1926), 153–4.
3. Anthony Matthews Gibbs, *A Bernard Shaw Chronology* (New York: Palgrave, 2001), 288 *et passim*.
4. "G.B.S. Registers as an Irish Citizen." *The Daily Express* (22 July 1936), 3.

5. This Act sought to warrant citizenship rights to those who were not covered by the 1922 Constitution, which only provided for citizenship for people alive on 6 December 1922. The full text of the Act is available online at http://www.irishstatutebook.ie/1935/en/act/pub/0013/print.html

6. Shaw, *Collected Letters 1926–1950*, 725.

7. Martin Meisel, "'Dear Harp of My Country'; or, Shaw and Boucicault," *SHAW: The Annual of Bernard Shaw Studies* 30 (University Park: Penn State University Press, 2010), 43.

8. Bernard Shaw, "The Limitation Conference. After You, Sir." *The Nation & The Athenaeum* (19 November 1921), 302.

9. See Luke 4:24, Matthew 13:57, and Mark 6:4.

10. Dan H. Laurence and David H. Greene, eds. *The Matter with Ireland* (New York: Hill and Wang, 1962), xiv.

11. To cite but one illustrative example, Henry Blundell (born in Dublin in 1813), after working for almost 30 years at the *Dublin Evening Mail*, migrated with his family to Melbourne in 1860, and then to New Zealand in 1863, where he worked for the *Otago Daily Times* and later went on to found *The Evening Post* (Wellington, NZ) in 1865.

12. "Select Socialists." *The Pittsburg Dispatch* (22 September 1889), 18.

13. "Notes and News – British and Foreign." *The Mercury Supplement* (4 March 1893), 2.

14. It is well known that some Shaw plays were not performed in public theatres for years after they had been written—and for different reasons (e.g. *Widowers' Houses, Mrs Warren's Profession*). Therefore, the first major London productions took place in the 1900s, with a comparable lag in media coverage throughout Europe. For specific dates and venues, see, for example, Margery Morgan, *File on Shaw* (London: Methuen, 1989), or Anthony M. Gibbs, *A Bernard Shaw Chronology* (New York: Palgrave, 2001).

15. For the sake of clarity and brevity, all the quotations from the press in Spanish, French, Italian, and German have been translated into English. The reader can read the original text by consulting the relevant bibliographical reference, most of which are available online (sometimes by subscription) on some of the newspaper archives listed at http://en.wikipedia.org/wiki/Wikipedia:List_of_online_newspaper_archives

16. "Notizie D'Arte." *La Stampa* (30 January 1906), 5.

17. "Playhouse Paragraphs." *The Sunday Star* (19 November 1905). The section also lists a notice on the forthcoming dramatization of *Cashel Byron's Profession*.

18. Lucile Kelling, "Appendix I: Shaw Around the World," in *George Bernard Shaw: Man of the Century*, Archibald Henderson (New York: Appleton-Century-Crofts, 1956), 903–944.

19. Frenzel, Karl (trans. by Michel Delines). "Chronique Théatrale." *Le Temps* (8 August 1910), 2–3.
20. Foemina. "Bernard Shaw." *Le Figaro* (3 October 1907), 1.
21. Rafael Altamira. "La Decadencia de Francia." *La Vanguardia* (16 April 1904).
22. "Noticias de Todas Partes." *La Vanguardia* (4 August 1906), 9. This heated argument, echoed by the Spanish press, took place after an interview with Shaw in *Die neue Gesellschaft*. For further details, see Samuel A. Weiss (ed.). *Bernard Shaw's Letters to Siegfried Trebitsch* (Stanford, CA: Stanford University Press, 1986), 108n.
23. Marie Oswald. "Le Socialisme en Angleterre." *La Revue Socialiste*. Tome XXII (Paris: Librairie de *La Revue Socialiste*, 1895), 584.
24. José Juan Cadenas. "La Agonía del Socialismo." *ABC* (31 August 1907), 2.
25. "Cable Letter." *The Daily Colonist* (21 October 1894), 1.
26. Alejandro Plana, "Bernard Shaw: 'El sentido común y la guerra.'" *La Vanguardia* (11 August 1915), 6.
27. Ibid.
28. Bernard Shaw, *What I Really Wrote About the War* (London: Constable, 1930), 1.
29. Bernard Shaw, "Shaw Points Out Folly of Sinn Fein Program." *The Washington Times* (29 December 1917), 5. Similar views had already been quoted by the press in France ("Attitude des Partis." *Bulletin Quotidien de Presse Étrangère* [9 May 1916], 4) and Australia ("An Irishman on Ireland. Bernard Shaw on American 'Patriots'. The Humbug of Home Rule." *The Watchman* [27 July 1916], 2).
30. Siegfried Trebitsch, "Huns Would Adopt Bernard Shaw." *The Evening Record* (16 October 1916), 2. The article reproduces a translation of the original text by Trebitsch—a celebratory birthday paragraph—initially published in *Die Neue Freie Presse* (Vienna).
31. "Irony for Erin" (Letter to the Editor). *Evening Public Ledger* (22 August 1917), Sports Extra.
32. Stevenson, J. A. "Britain's Fight for Democracy." *The Grain Growers' Guide* (1 March 1916), 10.
33. Legouis, Émile. "La Guerre Vue par les Écrivains Anglais." *Revue des Deux Mondes* (1 May 1916), 306.
34. Shaw, Bernard. "Neglected Morals of the Irish Rising." *The New Statesman* (6 May 1916).
35. "Los Disturbios de Irlanda: Un Comentario de Bernard Shaw." *ABC* (18 May 1916), 11.
36. "De Bernard Shaw." *La Vanguardia* (18 May 1916), 12.
37. "Bernard Shaw's Idea." *New Zealand Herald* (12 May 1916), 6. The same "idea" was reported elsewhere in New Zealand—as well as in other

English-speaking countries. See, for example, "Irish Brigade in France." *Otago Daily Times* (12 May 1916), 5.

38. "Novel Proposal." *The Sydney Morning Herald* (12 May 1916), 7. A similar view is reported in "A Bernard Shaw Proposal." *The Western Australian* (12 May 1916), 7. "Underwood Irish Leaders Died Heroes in the Cause of Liberty Says George Bernard Shaw." *The Washington Post* (14 May 1916), 14. The American newspaper quotes several other fragments from Shaw's original article, including the passage denying the accurateness of the word "traitor" to refer to "he who fights for the independence of his country."

39. For a representative sample, see, for example, "Bernard Shaw's Proposal." *Malborough Express* (12 May 1916), 5; "A Shavian Suggestion." *Wanganui Chronicle* (12 May 1916), 5; "Bernard Shaw's Idea." *New Zealand Herald* (12 May 1916), 6; "A Shavian Solution." *Grey River Argus* (12 May 1916), 3; "The Irish Problem Agitates Political Circles." *Wairarapa Age* (12 May 1916), 5; "Ireland." *Hawera & Normanby Star* (12 May 1916), 5.

40. Shaw, Bernard. "The Easter Week Executions." *The Daily News* (10 May 1916). For an example of the reception of this article see, for example, "Dublin Executions Stir Irish Wrath (Shaw Defends Irish Rebels)." *The Evening Star* (10 May 1916), 1.

41. "Famous Writer Pleads for Irish (George Bernard Shaw Decries Executions of Rebels of Ireland Uprising by the British)." *The Rock Island Argus* (10 May 1916), 1; "Stirs His Irish (George Bernard Shaw Resents Execution of Rebels)." *The Topeka State Journal* (10 May 1916), 12; Associated Press. "Bernard Shaw Declares Shot Irishmen Martyrs." *The Harrisburg Telegraph* (10 May 1916), 14.

42. "Irish Critic Calls Asquith College Boy." *New York Tribune* (11 May 1916), 2.

43. "La Represión en la Isla de Irlanda." *El Nacional* (10 May 1916), 5.

44. Shaw, Bernard. "Shall Roger Casement hang?" *Manchester Guardian* (22 July 1916), 4.

45. "Bernard Shaw als Verteidiger Sir Casements." *Hamburger Anzeiger* (27 July 1916), 2.

46. "Bernard Shaw über Casement." *Altonaer Nachrichten* (28 July 1916), 6.

47. "Bernard Shaw germanophile." *Le Siècle* (6 June 1916), 1; "Nos Échos: On dit que..." *L'Intransigeant* (23 February 1916), 2.

48. "Amerikanische Entrüstung über Casements Hinrichtung." *Berliner Börsenzeitung* (6 August 1916), 6.

49. Shaw, Bernard. "Casement's Crime was 'Being an Irishman', Says G. Bernard Shaw." *The New York American* (13 August 1916), 1–2.

50. "The Appeal of Bernard Shaw." *Goodwin's Weekly* (15 July 1916), 2.

51. "Bernard Shaw Makes Protest." *The Ogden Standard* (9 July 1916), 5.

52. "No Real Defense Put Up for Sir Roger Casement." *Richmond Times-Dispatch* (9 July 1916), 5.
53. Araquistáin, Luis. "Casement y Torras." *España* II. 81 (10 August 1916), 1.
54. "Au Jour le Jour. Lettre Ouverte de M. Henry Arthur Jones à M. Anatole France." *Le Journal des Débats Politiques et Littéraires* (5 January 1922), 1. The opinion that Jones professed towards Shaw accounts for some amusing press releases. For example, "Mr. Henry Arthur Jones is engaged on a new book dealing with 'Bernard Shaw as a Thinker'. The title is, presumably, a sarcasm." From "News and Notes." *New Zealand Herald* (31 March 1923), 6.
55. Shaw, Bernard. "How to Settle the Irish Question" (Three-article series). *Daily Express* (27, 28 and 29 November 1917).
56. "Irish Solution: Suggestion by Mr. B. Shaw." *Examiner* (30 November 1917), 5; "The Irish Question: Mr. Bernard Shaw's Solution." *Daily Telegraph* (30 November 1917), 5; "The Irish Problem: Mr. Bernard Shaw's Scheme." *The Register* (30 November 1917), 9; "The Irish Problem: Mr. Bernard Shaw's Solution." *The Age* (30 November 1917), 7; "The Irish Question: Mr. G. B. Shaw's Solution." *The West Australian* (30 November 1917), 6; "The Irish Question." *Western Mail* (7 December 1917), 22; "Perambulator." *Kilmore Free Press* (6 December 1917), 3.
57. Bernard Shaw, "Shaw Points Out Folly of Sinn Fein Program." *The Washington Times* (29 December 1917), 5.
58. "British Politics: The Coming Elections. Nomination Day." *Timaru Herald* (6 December 1918), 5; "Mr. Bernard Shaw as Candidate." *North Otago Times* (6 December 1918), 4; "British General Election: Bernard Shaw a Candidate." *Otago Daily Times* (6 December 1918), 4; "British Elections: Bernard Shaw a Candidate." *The Ballarat Courier* (5 December 1918, 3); "British Elections: Bernard Shaw a Candidate." *The Brisbane Courier* (5 December 1918), 7; "Mr. G. Bernard Shaw a Candidate." *Barrier Miner* (5 December 1918), 1; "Bernard Shaw a Candidate." *Darling Downs Gazette* (7 December 1918), 5; "G. Bernard Shaw Labor Candidate." *The Washington Times* (4 December 1918), 4; "Shaw Becomes Candidate." *Arizona Republican* (4 December 1918), 2; "G. Bernard Shaw is Labor Candidate." *The Ottawa Citizen* (4 December 1918), 3.
59. Taylor, A. J. P. English History, 1914–1945 (Oxford: Oxford University Press, 2001[1965]), 125.
60. Beynon, Francis Marion. "The Country Homemakers." *The Grain Growers' Guide* (13 December 1916), 10.
61. See, for example, Warren Sylvester Smith (ed.), *The Religious Speeches of Bernard Shaw* (University Park: Penn State University Press, 1963).
62. "Little Stories of Big Men." *The Edmonton Bulletin* (26 July 1917), 10.

63. "The Irish as George Bernard Shaw Sees Them." *El Paso Herald* (2 January 1919), 2.
64. Grant M. Overton, *Why Authors Go Wrong and Other Explanations* (New York: Moffat, Yard, and Co., 1919), 193.
65. *The NZ Truth* exploited the "lazy Irish" stereotype a few years later when it quoted Shaw as declaring that "labor for everybody and idleness for nobody is the only policy that can make Ireland sound." "The Critic." (29 December 1923), 1.
66. "He Didn't Mention Ireland." *The Washington Herald* (7 September 1919), 6.
67. "Mr. Shaw Tells Us." *The Irish Statesman* (30 August 1919), 245–246; "Wanted: A Strong Government." *The Irish Statesman* (11 October 1919), 378–380.
68. "Formed Republic of Sinn Feiners." *The Gettysburg Times* (22 January 1919), 2.
69. "La Cuestión Minera." *La Vanguardia* (16 September 1920), 13.
70. "The Big Six." *The Washington Herald* (10 November 1921), 3. The other five were William Allen White, Frank H. Simonds, Mark Sullivan, Ida M. Tarbell, and William Jennings Bryan.
71. "Bernard Shaw in Russia." *L'Unità* (27 August 1924), 4; "Giudizio di B. Shaw su Lenin: 'il più grande statista europeo vissuto.'" *L'Unità* (13 February 1924), 1.
72. "Bernard Shaw candidat au Parlement." *Le Petit Parisien* (18 January 1922), 3; "Invitation to G.B.S." *The Evening Post* (16 January 1922), 8; "British Politics. General Election Prospects." *The Press* (17 January 1922), 10 and "Bernard Shaw a Candidate. A Labour Invitation." *New Zealand Herald* (17 January 1922), 7.
73. "The Dail Debates Are a Storm in a Teacup; Ireland Will Have to Govern Itself in the Future." *The New York American* (25 December 1921). Reprinted as "The Irish Crisis" in *The Manchester Guardian* (27 December 1921), 3–4.
74. See, for example, "Interdependence." *The Watchman and Southron* (7 January 1922), 4.
75. "India and Egypt Rise Against the Oppressor." *The Advocate* (5 January 1922), 21.
76. See, for example, "Oath to King Mere Incident, and Erin is Free, Says Shaw." *The Washington Herald* (25 December 1921), 1.
77. See, for example, "Questions and Answers." *The Arizona Republican* (7 September 1921), 4 or "Questions Answered." *The Evening Public Ledger* (21 October 1921), 17.
78. "G.B.S. on Ireland [statement on the eve of civil war]." *Irish Times* (21 August 1922), 4.

79. "Ireland. Misguided People. Memories of the Past. Idiotic Battle Song." *The Hawera and Normanby Star* (23 August 1922), 8; "Sanctified Idiocy. Time to Live for Ireland. Mr. Bernard Shaw's Comments." *The Evening Post* (23 August 1922), 5; "Irish Rebels' Folly. Mr. Bernard Shaw's View." *The Press* (24 August 1922), 7.

80. "Government or "Self"?" *The Evening Post* (28 August 1922), 6; "Bernard Shaw's Views." *The Kalgoorlie Miner* (26 August 1922), 5; "In Name of Patriotism." *The Tweed Daily* (26 August 1922), 5.

81. "Situation in Ireland. Bernard Shaw's Views. Open Warfare Ended." *The Daily Telegraph* (23 August 1922), 5; "Rebel Idiots. Bernard Shaw on Ireland." *The Register* (23 August 1922), 7; "Ireland. Bernard Shaw's Criticism: Rebel Idiots." *The Bathurst Times* (23 August 1922), 1; "Bernard Shaw's Opinion." *The Southern Cross* (25 August 1922), 9.

82. "The Curse on Ireland." *The New York Times* (22 August 1922).

83. "La situation en Irlande. La mort de M. Arthur Griffith." *Bulletin Périodique de la Presse Américaine* (13–14 September 1922), 14.

84. The article was originally published in three parts in *The New York American* (5–7 Mar. 1923). For further details, see Dan H. Laurence (ed.), *Bernard Shaw: A Bibliography* (Volume II). Oxford: Clarendon Press, 1983: 696; "How to Restore Order in Ireland." *The Maoriland Worker* (2 May 1923), 1.

85. See, for example, "No Armistice." *The Auckland Star* (1 May 1923), 5. "George Bernard Shaw in the 'New Leader', an original contribution toward the solution of the question, 'How to Restore Order in Ireland'." *The Houston Post* (8 April 1923), 21. "Shaw Suggests Irish Peace Plan." *The Ottawa Evening Journal* (16 March 1923), 1.

86. See, for example, "Freedom in Ireland." *The Australian Worker* (16 May 1923), 8.

87. For the international repercussion of this article see, for example, "Democracy." *Newcastle Morning Herald and Miners' Advocate* (5 April 1923), 5.

88. "Holidays in Ireland." *The Times* (31 July 1923), 5.

89. See, for example, "Holiday in Ireland. G. Bernard Shaw's View." *The Cairns Post* (30 October 1923), 6; "Ireland the Safest Country in the World, Says Shaw." *The Advocate* (20 September 1923), 11; "Shaw Finds Cork and Kerry Safe." *The Southern Cross* (5 October 1923), 15; "Items of Interest." *Alexandra Herald and Central Otago Gazette* (17 October 1923), 6.

90. "On Throwing Out Dirty Water." *The Irish Statesman* (15 September 1923), 8–9.

91. "On Throwing Out Dirty Water." *The Living Age* (20 October 1923), 105–108; "Irish Policy and Prospects. Bernard Shaw's Criticism." *The Catholic Press* (8 November 1923), 7; "Bernard Shaw on Ireland." *The Maoriland Worker* (12 December 1923), 13.
92. See, for example, Arthur Ganz, *George Bernard Shaw* (New York: Grove Press, 1983), 202.
93. "La Expresión Nacional." *ABC* (26 July 1924), 8.

References

Boyd, Ernest A. 1916. *Ireland's Literary Renaissance*. New York: John Lane Company.
Fuchs, James, ed. 1926. *The Socialism of Shaw*. New York: Vanguard Press.
Gibbs, Anthony Matthews. 2001. *A Bernard Shaw Chronology*. New York: Palgrave.
Henderson, Archibald. 1956. *George Bernard Shaw: Man of the Century*, 903–944. New York: Appleton-Century-Crofts.
Laurence, Dan H., ed. 1983. *Bernard Shaw: A Bibliography*. Vol. II. Oxford: Clarendon Press.
Laurence, Dan H., and David H. Greene, eds. 1962. *The Matter with Ireland*. New York: Hill and Wang.
Meisel, Martin. 2010. 'Dear Harp of My Country'; or, Shaw and Boucicault. In *SHAW: The Annual of Bernard Shaw Studies*, vol. 30. University Park: Penn State University Press.
Morgan, Margery. 1989. *File on Shaw*. London: Methuen.
Overton, Grant M. 1919. *Why Authors Go Wrong and Other Explanations*. New York: Moffat, Yard, and Co.
Shaw, Bernard. 1920. *Irish Nationalism and Labour Internationalism*. London: The Labour Party.
———. 1930. *What I Really Wrote About the War*. London: Constable.
Smith, Warren Sylvester, ed. 1963. *The Religious Speeches of Bernard Shaw*. University Park: Penn State University Press.
Weiss, Samuel A., ed. 1986. *Bernard Shaw's Letters to Siegfried Trebitsch*. Stanford: Stanford University Press.

Index[1]

[1] Note: Page numbers followed by 'n' refer to notes.

© The Author(s) 2020   261
A. McNamara, N. O'Ceallaigh Ritschel (eds.), *Bernard Shaw and the Making of Modern Ireland*, Bernard Shaw and His Contemporaries, https://doi.org/10.1007/978-3-030-42113-7

Printed by Printforce, the Netherlands